Which is fun)
Debbie

About the Author

Farming and the people in it have been intrinsic parts of the author's life since she left school at sixteen. Cured of her shyness during her transformative years working on farms, the author has remained on the periphery of farming all her life, working with various governmental bodies including the Countryside Agency where she assisted farmers wishing to take advantage of new markets in the Eat the View Campaign, she has lived amongst the friendly country folk of rural Norfolk for more than twenty years.

Lost Sheep: One Woman's Memoir of a Farm Worker's Life

Deborah Best

Lost Sheep: One Woman's Memoir of a Farm Worker's Life

Olympia Publishers
London

www.olympiapublishers.com
OLYMPIA PAPERBACK EDITION

A CIP catalogue record for this title is
available from the British Library.

ISBN: 978-1-80074-383-0

First Published in 2022

Olympia Publishers
Tallis House
2 Tallis Street
London
EC4Y 0AB

Printed in Great Britain

Dedication

For Adam and Shân. Gone before their time.

Acknowledgements

I'd like to thank Nick, for his tireless work in ghost-writing and preparing Lost Sheep for publication without whom, this book would have continued to remain in the author's imagination! I also want to thank Laura and Sophie for their patience and love whilst their mother covered every table in the family home with old photos and letters!

"A life lived in the silent company of animals teaches us a reverence for lives lived moment by moment in dignity and without pretence." Deborah Best, June 2019.

Prologue

So how, you might ask, did a painfully shy girl, brought up in rural Essex and educated at St Mary's Catholic boarding school in Cambridge, wind up working on a farm? It's a question I often asked myself at five a.m. on a dark winter's morning whilst I fumbled for the light switch in a freezing dairy or when I'd just been knocked to the ground by a reluctant ewe in a lambing shed. But farming it was always going to be. For me there was no finishing school in Switzerland as it was for some of my contemporaries. All those years ago, when I left school at sixteen and made my fateful decision to 'get behind a cow rather than a desk' as I so succinctly put it in one of my diaries, the why of it just didn't seem to matter Or perhaps the why simply got lost somewhere in the mists of time. However, it was during the aftermath following the untimely death of my beloved brother Adam from a brain tumour that I took some time for an emotional trip down memory lane. Ostensibly to find some old photographs for a gathering to celebrate Adam's life, I soon came across my old diaries. Written by my younger self during my final two years at St Mary's, in my early years on farms during my pre-college year and at the Welsh Agricultural College (WAC) in Aberystwyth. I searched the densely written pages to remind myself of what it was during those pivotal years of 1974–75 that pushed me towards my decision to become a farm worker, and a female one at that. What was it that separated me from my contemporaries and sent me down an alternative path to become a lost sheep whilst others followed the rest of the flock into comfortable, well-paid jobs? You might think that, being a vet, my brother and I might be kindred spirits working, as we both did, with animals. Adam ministered to sheep and cows on farms, whilst I cared for their daily needs and tended my flock. However, the life of a vet, and even the large animal vet he became when his family moved to Wensleydale, is very different to that of a person actually working on a farm! I was also a woman working in a man's world where female farm workers or farm owners were, and still are, rare. In fact, back in the 1970s and '80s, the female in agriculture was as scarce as hens' teeth, and nothing much has changed even today. Working in an industry with such a significant gender imbalance, one might assume that my story would contain a long list of instances where I encountered sexist behaviour; however, this, with only a few rare exceptions, was never the case. But it mattered. I always felt I needed to prove myself and show that I was as good, if not better than those around me. Perhaps that is what pushed me to excel at what I did, I like to think so at any rate.

"Our destiny is written through the actions of our younger selves." Anon.

Part 1
Boarding

Chapter 1
Memory Lane

Not snowboarding, but boarding, living at school away from your parents and from home comforts, family and friends. The first part might seem enticing, preferable even, but it's the second part I've always had a problem with. My school-age life and that of my older siblings, Sarah in the middle and Adam, the eldest, was spent at boarding school. Forget Harry Potter and think Stalag Luft III, with occasional accompanied outings into town, the odd party and regular 'escapes' or trips home at weekends for Sarah and me or once a term for Adam. [1] Sarah and I attended St Mary's School for Girls in Cambridge as weekly boarders, so we were allowed home at weekends, whilst Adam was sent, at the age of seven, first to Cumnor House Prep School and then Westminster in London and only came home in the school holidays. Given my upbringing, it's always been a mystery to friends and family why I swerved off the path towards the sunny uplands of finishing school, society drinks parties and marriage to a comfortably off somebody or other working for some big something or other somewhere or other, most likely the City of London.

My rather unsatisfactory recollection is that the notion of working on a farm simply emerged as a fully formed idea sometime during my last couple of years at school, but how? Determined to finally answer this vexing question, early in February 2019, I cleared the clutter off the big old wooden chest that's sat on the landing since I moved into a converted schoolhouse in the wilds of rural Norfolk and began to sort through mountains of old photographs and letters. Rather like a detective in one of the pulp fiction crime novels I like to read, I began to unpick the tangles of a young girl's view of the world and find clues that might indicate why I'd gone for the farming life. At St Mary's, I was rather

---

[1] A prisoner of war camp in Nazi Germany made famous in the movie, The Great Escape.

plump (called Plum by friends and family), intensely shy (I was more confident writing to people than speaking to them) and found interacting with people difficult; perhaps animals were easier? Starting with the premise that awkward shyness may have pushed me towards farm animals rather than people, I decided that a visit to St Mary's might trigger some memories.

So, on a breezy, bright day in early March, I emerged from Cambridge Central Station, marched across the swish new Station Plaza and down Station Road; which now resembles 5th Avenue in New York, it's newly-built tall buildings on the left side of the street frowning down on passers-by and casting a long shadow over the thoroughfare, bustling with taxis and cyclists. Instead of turning left and heading over to my place of work in Shaftesbury Road, I went right on to Hills Road, where I could already see the head of Bateman Street beckoning to me. How often I must have half walked, half ran, from the station after a helter-skelter whirlwind of a journey from home in Hainested, driven at breakneck speed by my father, Dougie, to Audley End Station, to just catch the overcrowded seven forty-five a.m. train. Then, sandwiched between eager commuters with my bags filled with books, spare clothes and any illicit snacks I'd managed to pinch from my mother Esme's cupboards before I left, my heart always sagged at the thought of the week ahead. It was rarely a happy trip to school. Walking now, past the piles of students' bicycles attached three deep to the rails of terraced houses lining either side of the street, I finally stood outside the rather urbane and unassuming façade of St Mary's. In our day, reminiscent of a Victorian poorhouse, the windows were fitted with bars to keep us in, or was it to keep 'them', the untutored, unwashed and non-Catholic rabble, out? Happily, the bars have long since been sawn off in a welcome nod to modernity. I'd made an appointment to have a tour around the school, an unlimited privilege awarded to every ex-girl. Arriving at the school's familiar gates, I stood for a while prevaricating. I had suddenly become extremely nervous and my stomach churned just like it did all those years ago; I didn't know if I had the strength to go in

'Ah, Deborah, we've been expecting you!' The friendly secretary bustled out from behind her desk and guided me over to a seating area in the foyer. 'One of our guides will be with you presently.'

Sitting in the reception area, memories come flooding back. St Mary's girls are no longer taught by nuns as we were; there simply aren't enough to go around nowadays! But in my mind's eye, I could still see the nuns walking around the corridors in their flowing black robes. Being unable to see their legs, you got the disturbing impression that they were floating, and because of this, we used to call them Daleks; however, unlike Daleks, they could go up and down stairs! From reception, we passed through a door at the back leading to a covered cloister, on through an area that was used by the nuns and into the refectory. From there, it was up the rather grand staircase to the dormitories. In 1974–75, I was a senior girl in the last couple of years of school, so, as such, we had the privilege of sleeping in a room with just two others; one of which was, and still is, one of my best friends, Lucy, then a strong-willed and rebellious tomboy, who liked to dress for parties as a punk rocker with pink hair and a green streak, she hated school, but mysteriously managed to still get excellent grades.

Surrounded by the 'scene of the crime', so to speak, the pulp fiction detective in my head got to work. Walking into the actual room where I slept was creepy and I was reminded of a June evening of torrential rain in 1974 when Lucy came back from a punting party on Sunday night. The difficult to read entry in my diary written in yellow ink appears in my mind. *'As a joke, Lucy and [my other room-mate] Amanda, suddenly grabbed me, bound my legs and arms and gagged me. I was then tied to a post in the bathroom. And you'll never guess who came along? [Sister] 'Fatty' Thomas. In the panic, Amanda couldn't open the bathroom door, everyone thought it was hilarious!'* Standing there more than forty years later, I could still feel the prickle of a blush beginning to colour my neck. I chuckled to myself, oh happy days! You should see Lucy now, a paragon of efficiently and professionalism in her job as the editor of a well-known magazine, but back then, she was my heroine!

'Is there anywhere else you'd like to see?'

My guide breaks into my reverie, jolting me back to the present and from the time machine of my memories. I ponder her question for a moment and consider briefly my current theory around my shyness.

'Yes, can we go to see the drama hall?'

We headed back down the grand staircase and entered the refectory again, its serried ranks of empty tables eerily silent. As we walked along the corridor past the kitchen serving area, despite the fact that the girls were on their half-term holidays, and school had been empty for a few days, the sulphurous odour of boiled vegetables still hung in the air. In common with institutional cafeterias the world over, boiled cabbage appears to become infused into the very fabric of such buildings, and despite its pretensions, St Mary's is no different. They say that smells can trigger intense memories: wood smoke conjuring up camping holidays or ozone triggering memories of walks along the beach. On this occasion, as the cabbagey molecules entered my nose, they provoked an intense memory of an unpleasant occurrence that, until then, I must have blanked out. I instinctively turned my head to follow my mind's eye once again. A cacophony of girls' chattering voices and chairs screeching on the linoleum floor fills my mindscape. There at the window end of one of the long tables furthest from the corridor towards the back of the hall stands the corpulent form of Sister Thomas, her head bowed as if in supplication. However, she's not praying, but hovering ominously over the diminutive form of a small dark-haired girl with a pudding bowl haircut and florid cheeks, which are intermittently being pushed out by air being sharply expelled from her pursed lips. The source of her distress sits in front of her, the starchy, congealed remains of a meal of cauliflower cheese that was unappealing when it was served up the previous evening, but is truly horrid to behold now.

'Come on Miss Best, I want to see you eat your supper this time. You know that we'll just bring it out again tomorrow. The Lord provides for us and we must be grateful for His blessings. Think of the starving millions who would be very grateful to eat this food. You know that if you don't eat your food, you'll feel the hairbrush on the back of your hand!'

In my imagination, Sister Thomas's high-pitched, sing-song voice continued in a similar vein, but then faded into the background as the little girl's face contorted with distress before finally bursting into tears. The heads of girls sitting at nearby tables turned almost in unison, their faces delivering a mixture of passive stares, through mirth to disdain. Stifled tittering echoed around the otherwise silent hall. I remember clearly, the shame and embarrassment of being forced to eat that horrible meal. It was brought out to me several times and I'd had to survive on food given to me by my friend Lucy or bought using my pocket money from the tuck shop which was run by the dreaded Sister Scholastica. Tears well up in my eyes as the humiliation I felt is as powerful now as it was all those years ago. Just then, the guide appeared beside me with a concerned expression and she gently patted my shoulder.

'For some of the old girls, coming back to St Mary's stirs up deep emotions. The nuns were strict in the old days, we know that now; many of the girls had a hard life here.'

My guide's friendly voice causes my trickle of tears to become a torrent and I begin to sob uncontrollably. Holding me by my shoulders, the guide shepherds me over to a nearby bench and we sit silently together as my sobs reverberate around the echoing refectory hall. We never make it to the drama hall where I enjoyed stunning success playing Antonio in a school production of Shakespeare's Twelfth Night. Acting at school, and subsequently in amateur productions, was an antidote to my overwhelming shyness, but it wasn't the cure; farming achieved that.

Why did our parents send us to this awful place that seemed like it was nothing more than a prison camp for children? It wasn't as if they didn't love us, so what was it? Perhaps it was the prestige of having three children at private boarding schools? Or was it because, with us children at boarding school, they could spend their time socialising at their flat in London where, during the week, my father and mother hosted dinner parties for the likes of Sir Richard Attenborough and Anthony Quayle, part of a sizeable retinue of film industry 'luvvies' who, as a film director, my father needed to, or liked to, court in those days. What was it that caused them to send us all away? The dysfunctional family that our time at boarding school created could have been an important factor conspiring to drive me away from the family home after leaving school. Another driver was my father's cancer and the events surrounding the aftermath of his subsequent death.

Chapter 2
Chimneys

With the evidence starting to fall into place, it was time to reprise my role as my favourite pulp fictional gumshoe, DS Roy Grace, and take a look at another part of the puzzle, Hainested and our family homes there, Chimneys and Quail Cottage. [2] So, when another cold and wet day in March found me in Saffron Walden making arrangements for a family gathering and memorial to my brother Adam, I decided to take the opportunity to make a trip out to nearby Hainested and continue my sleuthing.[3] Leaving the venue for our future memorial, I took the familiar old road from Saffron Walden to Hainested along which, as I've already mentioned, I'd hurtled at breakneck speed many hundreds of times in the back seat of my father's car as he drove me to Audley End Station on Monday mornings. Reminiscences of the terror I'd experienced during these hair-raising journeys were temporarily put on hold as the engine warning light came on, an occurrence that usually heralded the emergence of my car's resident army of precocious gremlins. Sure enough, the speedometer needle slumped unceremoniously to zero miles per hour, the engine bucked like one of Buffalo Bill's broncos, the 'stop' light came on, the engine cut out and the old bus gently cruised to a standstill, damn! The car, a sprawling Peugeot 406, always had a mind of its own, bless her, but since she came to the halfway point towards her second thousand mileage century, the gremlins had been increasingly in control. Not content with turning on erroneous and false warning lights, their mischief could extend to shutting off the heating. But fortunately, in view of an arctic blast associated with the final death throes of Storm Dennis, as I turned the ignition key to restart her, the engine jolted back into life and warm air reassuringly whistled though the ventilators.

Driving along Hainested High Street, the familiar outline of the Rose

---

[2] The famous detective featured in a popular series of murder mystery novels written by Peter James.

[3] That never took place due to the COVID-19 pandemic.

& Crown hove into view. Standing opposite the turn into Church Road leading to Chimneys, this blue distempered edifice, which holds many memories for me, is reputedly haunted by the ghost of one of England's most famous, or infamous sons, the highwayman, Dick Turpin. In Turpin's day, plague-infected drinking water forced everyone, including children, to drink copious quantities of ale. However, in the 1970s, children weren't welcome in pubs. So that this inconvenience wouldn't get in the way of a convivial drink, our parents came up with a cunning solution, we were simply left outside the pub in our family transport, a huge Morris minibus, while Dougie and Esme held forth inside. To keep their fractious brood entertained, Esme would occasionally come out and pass us bags of crisps and bottles of ginger beer through the open windows of the van; oh joy!

As I crept slowly up our lane, the trees in the little copse to my left were buffeted by Dennis's angry gusts. On past the trees, there's the vicarage and the gravel track leading to St Andrew's Church. I pulled off the road and onto a little layby to the left of the path leading into the churchyard. After shutting down the engine, I sat quietly, staring out of the windscreen, watching fine rain drift in the wind whilst I tried to summon the strength to do what I needed to do, namely, to pay my respects to family and two dear friends for whom Hainested will remain their home and final resting place for ever; cold, indeed, are their graves. Walking through the iron gate, past the church and into a crowd of dense trees, I glanced around for a moment and then spied my father's familiar slate flagstone. After I'd scraped away the remnants of last autumn's leaves, I knelt and read the inscription carefully several times as though I were committing it to memory, Douglas Best, and then the dates, 1925 to 1974. The words are to the point and without sentiment, however, the stone itself isn't completely unadorned. A large, Celtic cross fills the space left by the inscriptions, and at its head, a small circular grave marker inscribed with my mother's name had been recently placed beside that of my father's, Esme and Dougie are together again.

Standing for a moment among the rows of gravestones, I'm once again struck by the rather absent way the graves have been crammed into a relatively small, gloomy patch of ground at the back of the churchyard, almost as though it were an afterthought to have them there at all. I recognised many of the names on the gravestones. Some I remember as friends, whilst others I can only recall as stern faces staring down at me when I was a fearful little girl. The great and good (and perhaps not so good) of Hainested arranged in serried ranks, as they had been on pews whilst they sat through endless Sunday morning church services. A whole generation that, like mine, had hopes and fears and had worked hard and played hard, but now their lives were spent and their names destined to live on only as family memories. Fighting off a wave of melancholia, I decided it was time to visit a couple of old friends. Back at an open patch of lawn at the front of the church, I stood in front of another marker, a simple, and rather singular, four-foot-high stone obelisk. Checking off the list of other names inscribed there, I find those of Paul Oar and that of his wife Jill who has also now been recently interred beside her husband. Paul, Jill and their boisterous family, Ben, the eldest, Sam, Kate and Sophie were my second family when I lived in Hainested and steadied the ship whilst our family was rocked, first by my father's death and then by my mother's alcoholism. Not having any flowers to place at their graves, I nodded in farewell and returned to the lane and walked along it.

Chimneys, our family home for many years, is grey, austere and seemingly empty, standing, as it's always done, directly opposite 'Orchard Cottage', the rambling family home of the Oars. Although now a single building, Chimneys is in fact a portmanteau of three cottages knocked together resulting in a lot of odd nooks and crannies and a creepy stairway that led nowhere. Or maybe, like Harry's Platform 9¾ or C. S. Lewis's wardrobe, if you were brave enough to climb those steep treads, you emerged into an alternate reality. However, I never plucked up enough courage to test this notion before the house was sold in 1973 to fund the purchase of a flat in London. Walking past, I spied the pond in the front garden, now clearly visible through the leafless trees and bushes. It was the pond's deceptively solid-looking covering of duckweed that lured me to attempt a dash across it on our first day whilst we were moving in. Nearly drowned and soaking wet, it was, perhaps my cries and the shouts from my parents that brought Jill out of her house and over the road to see what she could do to help, thus starting a lifelong friendship. I stood for a while, looking up at the second floor where I had a bedroom overlooking the large back garden that constituted Dougie's green gym where he spent many hours mowing the lawn in the summer. Chimneys holds memories, but it's Quail Cottage that holds ghosts.

Renamed Quail Cottage when the foul-smelling barn was converted into a residence, it was originally built to house Esme's quail breeding and production enterprise that she started whilst we were living at Chimneys so she could earn some much-needed extra cash. After Chimneys was sold, the barn was converted into a house and it's where we lived during my last two years at St Mary's. It's also where my father died of cancer. Walking on past our neighbour's house I stopped at the head of the long gravel driveway leading to Quail Cottage situated behind Chimneys. The new owners had added a cheery red brick garage; otherwise, the house remains largely unchanged from the time it'd been converted. I stepped forward as if to enter the driveway, but something held me back, not the fear of being caught trespassing, but the dread I associate with the place. Its thin partition walls acted as a sounding board for my father's gasps for breath and heart-wrenching moans of pain during that fateful summer of 1974. I still remember the occasion when, one evening, I finally couldn't bear it any longer and ran out of the front door and into the lane where I walked for hours contemplating thoughts that my father would be better off dead than to go on suffering so cruelly. The image of my father's huge oxygen tank sitting like an uninvited guest in his bedroom seemed too awful to contemplate. I finally wound up on our neighbours', the Oars, doorstep in hysterics. Jill Oar kindly took me in and fed me hot, sweetened tea.

Contemplating Quail Cottage's simple rectangular form in the, now sheeting rain, I recalled a poignant entry in my diary where my younger self had written, '*at least they've found out what's wrong with Daddy, he has cancer of the liver, but it's okay they've found it at the early stages and he's now having radio[therapy] treatment. It doesn't frighten me now that much seeing as I've read Cancer Ward. It makes you really understand it.*' It was clear that I had no idea about the severity of my father's cancer since I was kept pretty much in the dark about it to the extent that it was Jill who informed me of his death during a children's party and sleepover at a neighbour's house. Shivering, or was it a ghost that brushed past me, I turned abruptly on my heel and made my way back towards Orchard Cottage.

With all this talk of quail farms, you might be forgiven for thinking that I'd come across a key piece of evidence for why I took up the farming life; well, you'd be mistaken! Whilst I did help my mother cleaning out the barn and collecting eggs, it was done grudgingly and I hated the awful smell. Seeing the place again, I was now convinced that it was my daily feeding of the ducks on our pond and happy hours watching and looking after the little piglets frolicking in Farmer Beaton's barn (that dear Sarah accidentally set fire to whilst playing with matches) that set me on the road to my agricultural nirvana; that and Stanley! My chance to actually own a pig came when Dougie won one at the Hainested Fete tenpin bowling for a pig competition. Miraculously, my father got the highest score and the pig was ours! We named him Stanley and what better food for a pig owned by a couple of regular pub goers than to feed him on beer slops from the Rose and Crown. Needless to say, after his lunch, Stanley would often get quite inebriated. On one memorable occasion, Stanley made a break for freedom and ran off across our neighbour's garden. With the Bests in hot pursuit, we gathered a posse of pig hunters to track Stanley down. This wasn't difficult since he left a trail of destruction in neighbours' gardens; even breaking the Oars' kitchen window trying to get at a tasty morsel he'd spied there! I absolutely loved Stanley and still have a deep affection for pigs in general.

Chapter 3
Top farm

From my visits to St Mary's and Hainested, a picture of my childhood self was emerging. I was shy with few close friends and a love of animals, especially pigs; and let's not forget my beloved pet goldfish, Ping and Pong, who'd also been won at a local fair! So what about people? How had family and friends influenced my decision to get into farming? I needed to interview some key witnesses, however, this being a 'cold case', some of the protagonists are no longer with us. As we've seen, four of them lie in their graves in St Andrew's graveyard in Hainested and my poor brother Adam's ashes are scattered to the four winds in Wensleydale. So, it was back to the big old wooden chest for another rummage through old photographs and letters. After my father's death, Esme descended into despair. Where drink had once been the lubrication needed to ease my, otherwise quite shy, mother around the film industry social whirl, it now became a refuge and solace to make living through each day more bearable. Adding to her woes was a serious shortage of cash, due largely to the fact that Dougie had invested a substantial amount of the family's private capital into a feature film project, The Hummingbird Tree. Five years of dinner parties, courting investors and cajoling of industry contacts, my father's Welsh charm had finally borne fruit and sufficient funds had been raised for filming to start, but a cruel twist of fate and his untimely death had turned triumph into financial ruin. Without my father's direction his film project floundered and the family lost almost everything. Fortunately, St Mary's hardship fund made it possible for me to complete my education there rather than having to attend a local school. So, where once, returning to St Mary's on Monday morning was to be dreaded, I now welcomed it. At least at school, I didn't have to witness my mother's descent into an alcoholic pit of despair. Whenever I did return home, mountains of empty whisky bottles that lurked in the closet, on shelves, under the bed and behind the sofa, would ambush me unexpectedly during my weekends at Quail Cottage. As one or two glasses became one or two large glasses to several glasses and finally, a bottle a day, Esme's lucid moments became few and far between. Although I worried about my mother's health and her state of mind, at the same time, I was also somewhat detached. The ties to home and family that were loosened during term time had been further stretched as I was shunted around a small army of extended family and friends who'd become my female role models during the school holidays as Esme spent much of her time with my father in London or over at his film studio in Malta. Therefore, it was my maternal grandmother, Lilly Miller-Smith (Granny) who lived in a sprawling manor called Top Farm in Worcestershire, Babs and the Irish cousins and Dorothy, my godmother and family friend in Surrey who became my female role models during my childhood.

Due to my parent's hectic lifestyle, school holidays were often spent with Lilly, Jimmy her husband and her live-in housekeepers, Mr and Mrs Royal. Whilst not as sinister as Mr and Mrs Barrymore, the housekeepers in Conan Doyle's Hound of the Baskervilles, Mr and Mrs Royals' duties and functions within the household were similarly many and various. Living as she did, alone after the death of her husband the Royals and my frequent visits must have been a welcome relief from her splendid isolation in the Clent Hills. Whilst my siblings, Sarah, with various friends and boyfriends, and Adam with his girlfriend, Vanda, enjoyed what seemed to me to be a vibrant social life, I was forming a close bond with my granny! The interior of Top Farm was the epitome of genteel, yet practical country living and had all the accoutrements you might expect. There was a large well-organised kitchen that inevitably housed a rustic table around which we would all sit and bask in the glorious warmth of a large oil-fired Aga during our family visits at Christmas time. Looking back, the homeliness and strong bond I had with Lilly created a template for domestic bliss that has stayed with me for the rest of my life and has been the benchmark for all other places I've lived ever since. For me, Granny's separate food and china pantries were indispensable, as were the organ in the living room that I learnt to play, the drawing room you never went into, the morning room which gave onto an extensive lawn and that other indispensable accoutrement of any aspiring country manor, the croquet lawn. Whilst the Irish originally invented croquet, it's the English, including myself, that have embraced and revelled in the game's delightful eccentricity. In view of the affectionate bond we forged during my long stays, it's not surprising that Granny Miller-Smith became my cherished second mother. This makes it all the more surprising that all record of her sudden death in a road accident in May 1974, the same year as my father's is completely missing from the diary I kept at the time.[4] Perhaps it was too upsetting for me to contemplate.

Whilst, at one time, Top Farm may have been the squire's residence surrounded by the bucolic bliss of a country manor, Lilly wasn't a farmer and there was no farming. So if it wasn't my mother's quails or Granny's farming prowess, then who was in the frame as the female figure that influenced my decision to go into farming? That honour goes to Babs and the Irish cousins. My mother's second cousin, Terence was the managing director of a large retail company in Northern Ireland where he'd bought a smallholding farm in the wilds around Creevy, County Down where Babs, Terence's wife, was able to keep her beloved horses. Now, I've never been a great fan of horses and horse keeping, but Babs had an important redeeming feature, she also kept pigs! In 1973, I was an impressionable thirteen-year-old when my father had the brilliant idea that I should stay with the Irish cousins over the Easter holidays while he and my mother travelled to his film studio in Malta. You might think I'd got a raw deal, a couple of weeks on a farm in cold rainy Northern Ireland compared to sunny Malta, but I couldn't be more excited.

Even at my tender age, I was vaguely aware of the 'Troubles', however, the sight of armed guards at Belfast Airport was still a little unnerving as I searched the arrivals lounge for my cousins. But when Babs stepped purposefully forward and I recognised her bony, angular frame from the few photographs my mother had of her, it immediately felt like I'd arrived home. We hit it off from the start. Babs was outgoing and bubbly, not a native of Northern Ireland, but of Canada, perhaps this added to her air of mystery and charm. Two things stick in my mind from that visit; well, three if you count Babs' handsome youngest son Tim! The first was Babs' favourite pony, Angie, suffered a terrible injury that required the attention of the local vet and the second was one of the sows

---

[4] She was a passenger in a car driven by the local vicar who was also tragically killed.

gave birth to a litter of piglets — manna from heaven for a pig lover! As I recall, I'd been Babs' assistant 'midwife' with the piglets all morning and was just beginning to anticipate when the next piglet would pop out by the tell-tale guttural grunt of the sow, when disaster struck. Tim burst into the farrowing shed to announce that Angie had been injured when she, for some reason best known to herself, had tried to jump over her paddock fence. Although the gash under her girth was stomach churning, it wasn't the sight of the wound that I remember. When we got to her, the pony was thrashing around and clearly in considerable pain, so much so, that no sane person would dare go near. However, Babs somehow managed to approach and calm the animal, and after a few minutes, she was able to stroke its mane and whisper into its wildly twitching ears. Babs' ministrations were so effective that the vet was able to administer stitches without needing to sedate the animal. I was totally in awe of this heroic Amazon of a woman with bare legs sticking out of a pair of muddy green wellies! Thinking back, it was Babs' strong character, no nonsense attitude and confidence in the way she ran her farm that left a deep impression on the shy and impressionable young girl I was then. That and the serious crush I'd developed for Babs' youngest son, Tim!

Chapter 4
Straying from the flock

Fast forward to May 1975, the larks were ascending, the first warm days of summer had finally arrived and the lazy screeching of swifts could be heard as they played in the benevolent blue skies above merry England, but as any schoolgirl will tell you, May and June is exam time, so the sunny days passed unnoticed in a haze of exam time mystery. The gloom was made worse by the sounds of carefree laughter coming from throngs of small, happy girls in the playground of St Mary's Convent Primary School. I've never been an academic, but glancing now at a curriculum vitae carefully typed by my mother in 1989, I'm surprised to see that I passed all my O Levels. Well, all except one; I got a 'D' for religious studies, which I take to be a small token of rebellion from a girl that was educated in a convent! A joyous entry made in my diary on 26th June declares, '*the most exciting thing [has happened] I've finished all my O Levels and that I have left school for ever and ever!*' So, it's clear even at this stage that I had no intention of staying on at school! Wild horses, pigs, cows or sheep for that matter, couldn't keep me from leaving. But what provided the final impetus to go to agriculture college and not only leave school, but to leave home at the tender age of sixteen? If agriculture college was where I was headed, why did I choose one that was so far away from home? My choice of institution, the Welsh Agricultural College, is situated in Aberystwyth, a seaside town at the opposite side of the country to Hainested that can only be reached by mind-numbingly windy roads or a clapped-out single-track railway, a journey that can take all day even now. To answer this question, I needed to return to my research and the family archives to decipher more of my increasingly dense writing in the final pages of my schoolgirl diary.

If my mother's drinking, the death of my father and favourite grandmother had made the prospect of home life unappealing, then at least a boyfriend might have kept me anchored to home and hearth. However, looking at the pool of potential boyfriend material I was considering at the time, I began to see my problem. There was Pete, a lad

I'd met at a neighbour's barbecue who I'd fruitlessly bombarded to no avail with a steady flow of unanswered letters, including a rather ill-chosen gift of toothpaste. Our neighbour's son, Sam had been polite towards my clumsy advances and lavishly decorated birthday cards over the years, but I was clearly not getting anywhere with him. Tim, Babs' son didn't profess undying love. Finally, there was Rick, whose advert for a companion for a youth hostelling tour I'd answered in a fit of desperation. Rick and I exchanged several promising letters, but we actually never met, dammit, but for the girls at St Mary's, there was one last chance to find romance before leaving school. Traditionally, once the exams had finished, the after-parties started. For girls, especially those who'd been cooped up in a boarding school, post exam parties were a happy hunting ground for females on the prowl for a boy. Bizarrely, perhaps in a throwback to the festival of the Feast of Fools, a seasonal debauch licensed by the church in medieval times, the nuns at St Mary's organised an end of exams party at the nearby Leys Boys School. Caution appears to have been thrown to the wind on this occasion, and the nuns, who, in the past had gravely told us to never sit on a boy's knee without the intervening thickness of a telephone directory to protect our modesty, had set up a number of mattresses around the margins of the games hall where the party was held. Perhaps this was some kind of weird Catholic mating ritual! I remember that, as the evening wore on, the lights dimmed and smoochy '70s numbers were played, quite a bit of furtive groping and French kissing happened on the mattresses furthest from the glare of the disco lights. But shyness and the thought of being groped on a damp mattress didn't appeal so I crept quietly away before the fun got started.

If it wasn't romance, there was one last thread that could've kept me tethered to Hainested, Jill and Paul Oar, who'd looked after me through thick and thin and had been a tower of strength after my father's death. However, even this relationship, and a burgeoning friendship with their youngest daughter, Sophie, or Suds as she liked to be known, had been momentarily soured at this point. This temporary severing of my bond with Jill and the Oars, stems from a collision of circumstances. Firstly, the older Oars, Sam and Ben, had moved on and away from Hainested. Then Suds had been sent to an even more posh girls' boarding school further away. However, the last straw came from an unfortunate incident that, even today, makes my blood run cold. Having finished our exams,

I was rather deflated by my schoolmates' lack of enthusiasm for my suggestion to have a final farewell punting trip on the Cam. It was the end of June 1975, the sun was warm, food and drinks had been bought (by me), but I'd been collectively stood up and left fuming. It seemed that everyone had already moved on and I'd been left behind. There was one ray of hope in my misery, the Oars' end of school party!

Sam Oar, then about seventeen, had finished at Uppingham Boys School and had invited a posse of attractive male friends to the family home for a weekend of drunken mayhem; and I'd been invited. Parties at the Oars' house had always been something to look forward to, but shyness still tugged in my stomach as I walked down the lane from Quail Cottage, done up in a new summer dress, patent leather shoes and wearing lipstick that I'd managed to purloin from my mother's dressing table. As I approached the house, I could already hear 'Best of My Love' by the Eagles blasting out of speakers situated outdoors. Pied Piper-like, all eligible sons and daughters of the neighbours had been enticed into the melee en masse; leaving their parents to hunker down indoors, rather like pets kept inside on Guy Fawkes Night until the party maelstrom had passed. Entering Orchard Cottage's gravel drive, as I had done so many times before, my head brushed through the long tendril-like branches of the weeping willow at the gate. Pushing through the willow fronds always made me feel like I was parting a green vale that opened onto a magical land full of possibilities that I could only dream of back at Quail Cottage just a few hundred yards away. Assuming that I'd be swimming in the Oars' pool at some point in the evening, I had my bathing costume and towel pushed into my little shoulder bag along with other female essentials; why did my period always start at the most inconvenient times!

Passing the pool and the cavorting crowd already in or around it, I almost collided with Sam who was accompanied by several of his school friends.

'Freddy, Mark, Ian, meet Plum, one of my neighbours.' Having made his introductions, Sam rushed on up to the back lawn with a crate of beer bottles.

Left on my own in front of three rather attractive young men, the inevitable happened, my cheeks and neck flushed red and nervous perspiration prickled the skin of my back. Seeing I was at a loss for words, it was Freddy that broke the ice, while the others drifted off towards the pool. We swapped stories about school; Uppingham sounded a lot more fun than St Mary's Convent! The evening wore on. Freddy and I remained tethered to each other most of the time, right up until it finally got dark and slow dance numbers started playing. At this point the raucous swimming pool action had died away leaving heads languidly bobbing in the water with bodies quietly doing who knows what out of sight in the depths. At that moment, 'I'm Not in Love' by 10cc came on, and at a loss for what else to do, Freddy pulled me close and we swayed back and forth for a while. Our close bodily proximity meant that I vaguely became aware of something stirring against Freddy's tight-fitting bell-bottom jeans. Somewhat alarmed and totally inexperienced, I felt I should just play along with it, I mean, I'd been wanting to find someone who was interested in me, so it'd be churlish to back off now. After our 'dance' Freddy indicated that we should go for a walk and I naively agreed. At the time, the grounds around the back of Orchard Cottage and away from the back lawn were quite extensive and included a full-sized tennis court; it was here that we finally ended up. Now that we were completely out of sight, Freddy pulled me close and pushed his tongue into my mouth. Unable to resist once he'd started, panic began to rise and I made to pull away, but Freddy had me pinned against the nets. As he pulled down his trouser zip and opened his belt buckle, even I twigged what was going to happen next, and I struggled, but he was stronger and pushed forward so that the tensioning rope of the net bit into the small of my back. Pulling my dress up, Freddy grappled with my panties, but fortunately, men, particularly young hormone drenched adolescents, are rarely able to multitask, so as he grappled with his fly, the concentration it took to do this caused him to relax his grip on me and I dived backwards over the net, picked myself up and made a run for the tennis court gate and back towards the lit portion of the back garden. I felt stupid and humiliated, but in my haste, I bumped into Jill who was having a cigarette by the kitchen door. I made a pretty unintelligible apology and said I needed to go home. Subsequently, I confessed to Jill what had happened, although I felt that I was partly responsible. Jill was shocked to the core and said she'd have a word with Sam and his errant friend; however, it changed the way I felt about Orchard Cottage and I didn't go back there for quite some time after that.

Having now read my school diaries and sifted through mountains of old photographs and letters, I took up my trusty spiral notebook and reviewed the evidence. It was clear that my younger self was painfully shy around people. Finding it difficult to express her love, her caring nature found an outlet through looking after animals. Ties with home loosened by years at boarding school, her father's death and mother's subsequent despair made home life seem unbearable. Feeling isolated as her friends moved on, she was clearly searching for a way out, a new life and a new circle of friends. But what was it that inspired me to set out alone at such a young age? Examining the final pages of my little school diary, I find that they're crammed with a veritable treasure trove of memorabilia including an iconic photo of my father directing on set at Granada Television, a programme from a production of Henry the Fifth at Stratford-upon-Avon, a ticket and a small plastic bag of 'snow' from an Elton John concert at Wembley Stadium and a clipping from a newspaper article — a critique of the movie, Dove, starring Joseph Bottoms. Reading between the lines, it was clear that I'd idolised Bottoms for his performance of the real-life character, Robin Lee Graham, a sixteen-year-old boy who set sail in a twenty-three-foot sloop named 'Dove' to circumnavigate the globe solo. This story clearly made a deep impression at the time and may have provided me with inspiration to make a new life for myself at the tender age of sixteen. In the final pages of the diary, last, but not least, an important piece of physical evidence caught my detective's eye, a newspaper advert for OND and HND courses entitled, 'A career for men and women in agriculture or the food industry' with a handwritten note confirming that I'd applied to at least two colleges.

Thus, at the end of summer 1975, I wanted to leave Hainested permanently, and vowed never to make it my home again! The big wide world of agricultural college beckoned. Although my voyage of discovery didn't quite take me as far as Robin Lee Graham's epic journey, the Welsh Agricultural College in Aberystwyth, or WAC, as we've already noted, is a pretty long way from Hainested and a million miles away from the life I'd lived at St Mary's Convent. 'Aber-yaba-doo!'

Part 2
Heat wave: pre-college year 1976

Chapter 5
Porkers!

All of us with a few years on the life-clock, and old enough in 1976, will remember the heat wave. In fact, if you've ever looked back at those lazy, hazy days of sun and thought, 'yeah, that was a pretty good year', then you'd be in agreement with quite a lot of your contemporaries; and the Daily Mirror newspaper. The Mirror recently published an article on 1976 that concluded it was Britain's best ever year. Whilst the online article leads with the inevitable photograph of a couple of bikini-clad girls sipping white wine on the terrace of a London flat, there is also some substance to the story. Amongst a lot of boring stuff about the retail price index, low inflation and Steve Jobs starting Apple Computers, it's the popular music soundtrack to '76 that I can really remember. The Eagles released 'Hotel California', The Rolling Stones played Knebworth Fair and then there was f-ing and blinding from Sid Vicious and the Sex Pistols on TV; my punk friend Lucy was in awe! But we had to wait until Virgin Records signed the Sex Pistols in June the following year for their defining moment when they upstaged the queen's silver jubilee barge pageant by sailing down the Thames and bashing out 'God Save the Queen and Her Fascist Regime'!

In the fiery crucible of that year, when the temperature topped 28^{0}C for a record twenty-two days in a row, my resolve to go into agriculture was sorely tested. Since I hadn't had any farming experience, agriculture colleges stipulated, that entrants without farming experience must complete a pre-college year. Essentially, this consisted of long periods of hard work interspersed by infrequent and exceedingly small pay packets. My ability to live on very little money and to withstand long hours of physical work had, however, already been tested in a small way in July of the previous year during a bicycle ride with a school chum, Anna. Whilst we didn't have to suffer the gruelling heat that was to be seen in 1976, our two-hundred-mile slog on ill-fitting bicycles from Bath to Little Haven in Pembrokeshire was pretty tough! Fear and trepidation in

Anna's family meant that her mother insisted that she follow us in the car. After much eye rolling from Anna and assurances from me, we came to a compromise, we agreed to be chaperoned until we got over the Severn Bridge and onto the quieter roads beyond. Good as her word, but still with reservations at leaving two young girls to travel the open road, we waved goodbye at Chepstow YHA. That bicycle ride was to be the start of my final break from home. Looking at our few photographs, I see two sixteen-year-old girls revelling in the freedom of the open road as they cycled through the wild beauty of the Brecon Beacons, reminiscent of scenes of the Golden Valley in Herefordshire made famous by Anthony Hopkins in the movie Shadowlands. On one memorable day riding to Capel-y-Ffin YHA we decided to take a minor road onto the Brecon Beacons rather than follow the river [Afon Honddu], which would have been the most obvious route.[5] Flies while we rode, and midges when we stopped, fed on our perspiration and other body fluids as we climbed never-ending slopes onto the top of the Beacons. From there, the views were stunning, and through the heat haze, the patchwork quilt of the Abergavenny fields stretched away below. But more excitement was to come. Around a corner, we spied a yearling lamb with its head wedged in a gap at the bottom of a fence. It's mother's anxious bleating was heart wrenching. Without hesitation, I got off my bike and propped it purposefully on a wall.

'You're not going in there are you? We should find the farmer.' Anna was always rather bossy, but I was determined! Arriving at the fence, I could see the lamb's head and forequarters were well and truly jammed. Looking around for help from Anna, I could see she was standing in the lane with her arms firmly folded, a stern look on her face, and her long pony tail twitching. Clearly no help was going to be forthcoming from her! The lamb's mother's loud bleating was in contrast to the strained breathing from the lamb, which seemed to be half suffocated. I reached under his fleecy stomach and got my arm around his head and pushed it downwards. Suddenly freeing himself, he thrust hard with his little legs and popped out like a cork from a bottle, sending us both tumbling backwards. Whilst I sprawled on the ground, off he ran to his mum; however, I imagined that they both gave me a nod of thanks before haring

---

[5] Sadly now closed.

off back up the field to join the flock. So that, readers, was my first bit of shepherding successfully completed even before starting my pre-college year, I was chuffed to bits!

While I'd covered myself with glory by freeing a wayward lamb on our bicycle trip, at the start of my pre-college year, I actually knew virtually nothing about farming. My total lack of knowledge of just about everything agricultural was highlighted by the, now famous (or should I say infamous) 'potatoes story', a tale that has since gone down in the annals of Oar family history. One balmy evening in September 1975, Jill asked me to nip out and dig up a few spuds for supper. Dutifully jumping to it, I grabbed a spade and set out for the vegetable patch. I'd been fruitlessly digging for about half an hour, when a family friend, Clive, then the focus of an overwhelming crush, was dispatched to find out how I was getting on. Finding I was empty-handed, and claiming that there weren't any potatoes to be had, Clive promptly grabbed the spade, dug manfully down into the soil and unearthed a veritable treasure trove of huge tubers! I was so embarrassed. Shortly after that rather inauspicious start to my career in agriculture, my mother drove me over to Newdigate in Surrey to start my first pre-college placement. At the time, I remember having a rather rosy, chocolate box view of what a farm should look like that was probably largely based on the popular TV comedy show, The Good Life starring Richard Briers and Felicity Kendal as two earthy urbanites who'd essentially converted their suburban home into a smallholding. But wait! The address we'd been given for the farm actually brought us to the door of 'The Gables', not the residence within a grand manor, but a humdrum suburban house in Banstead. In my mind's eye I had a vision of an approach along a winding gravel drive leading to an imposing farmhouse set within the rustic bliss of a large farmyard, however, we simply parked in the street and knocked on the front door. Had the Stern family similarly converted their suburban house into a farm? Surely not! It wasn't even an authentic farm; I felt cheated! To top it all, the farmer's wife, Mrs Stern, had an addiction to chintz of the worst kind! My diary at the time records that the first thing to go was the frilly eiderdown on my bed in the guest room, which my diary records, '*was promptly banished in a cupboard.*' In addition to the initial disappointment at the perceived lack of authenticity, there was another

41

more practical downside: there was a commute to the farm every morning, sometimes with Mr Stern, or with Bob Burnet, the cantankerous old stockman who drove an ancient Ford Cortina. The round trip added at least an hour to an already long, twelve-hour day that started at five a.m.

Banstead is part of a busy conurbation of towns fringing Epsom Downs just a few miles from Hickstead, the former famous for its horse racing and the latter famous for showjumping. As it turned out, it was no coincidence that the Sterns lived so close to this pulsating epicentre of equine achievement; Mrs Stern and her daughter Eleanor were horsey in the extreme, replete with posh accent, large backsides and brusque impatience for anything other than their beloved horses. It quickly became clear that Eleanor was aspiring to compete in horse jumping trials at Hickstead, so when she wasn't down the yard fussing over her pair of rather truculent mares, she was off competing or showing them at some horsey do or other. I think it was during my stint at the Sterns, that my loathing for all things horsey was born. To make things worse, on the first evening, Mrs Stern casually informed me over supper (that nestled on a particularly unnerving swirling rose-patterned tablecloth) that I'd be expected to groom and muck out the horses in my meagre spare time during the weekends! However, whilst receiving this unwelcome news, I caught Mr Stern's rather bashful and apologetic glance in my direction. It was then it clicked; it was the Missus rather than the Mr that wore the riding jodhpurs in the Stern family! Constantia Stern was a Greek-Cypriot with the characteristically fiery temperament of women from that sunny part of the Mediterranean, which meant he was constantly walking on eggshells and anxious to do anything for a quiet life!

With the farm separated from the house, my dependence on lifts from the Sterns or farm staff, little time off and very modest pay of £8 per week, my overwhelming memory of my first taste of farming was one of isolation. I'm sure that most sixteen-year-old girls would have found the strict routine difficult to bear, but my 'training' at boarding school stood me in good stead. Every morning at four thirty a.m., the raucous sound of my faithful alarm clock, Big Ben, wrenched me out of the kind of fitful sleep one gets after a day of physical toil. How often at boarding school I'd looked into my alarm clock's luminescent face unable to believe it was time to get up already! Some things never change! Also, like school, I was provided with full board — breakfast, packed lunch and supper flowed out of Mrs Stern's florally challenged kitchen; however, unlike St Mary's, the food was edible. Bacon and scrambled eggs with toast and cereal was a strong inducement and never failed to draw me out of bed; my body going into autopilot to follow the aroma and sounds of a hearty breakfast being prepared downstairs.

On the second morning, during my first week, Mr Stern peered at me over his copy of the Banstead Herald and said, 'Bob's going to take you in this morning and show you the ropes in the farrowing shed.'

During the rest of the week, I reprised the role of midwife I had on Babs' farm looking after batches of five or six sows lying in separate farrowing pens connected to runs that extended outside. The whole process was handled like a military operation. Sows, in separate cubicles, gave birth to their piglets, which were then grown on to pork weight. The Stern's pig unit was exemplary for the time, applying the latest methods and highest standards of hygiene and husbandry; Roy Stern loved his pigs! His claim that, and I quote, '*you can walk around this farm in your bedroom slippers*' was no idle boast. I've been on many farms since where you're wading knee deep in muck battling to keep your feet as the boars chase the sows around the pen. Compared to that, the Stern's farm was pig nirvana!

After that first week, my main job on the farm was to look after groups of sows that were about to give birth to their litters. Reminiscent of my time on the farm with the Irish cousins, I watched in awe as piglets that'd just shot out the sow's uterus, shook themselves off and promptly attached themselves to one their mother's teats as easy as you like. I needed to ensure that sows, when they were ready to give birth, were properly 'crated' or shut behind the gate inside their stall to ensure they lay down whilst doing their thing. Once the piglets appeared, and for their safety, the gate was opened and piglets enticed away from the cumbersome, and potentially lethal, bulk of their mother by the warmth of an infrared lamp and a hearty bowl of 'creep' feed, a tasty (for a piglet) concoction of milk powder to help wean them quickly. To this day, the sight of little groups of piglets rushing around, over and under their mother always makes me smile. These feisty little creatures all have their own characters; there are bold ones, cheeky ones and bullies. Then there were the runts, little chaps that needed a bit of extra TLC and hand rearing. I loved the way they used to become so tame, sucking at my finger ends and basking in my care and attention.

Later during my stay, I was entrusted with the job of staying overnight in the farrowing caravan. During a midwinter night, I'd be shivering under the blankets in the caravan and Big Ben's clarion call would rouse me for another look around the stalls. Swinging my legs off the caravan bench, fully clothed in my boiler suit, my feet would instinctively find the openings at the top of my welly boots. Finding my torch, I'd stumble down the wobbly steel caravan step and I'd follow the beam across the yard and into the shed. Entering, I'd momentarily exult in the increased temperature before following the sounds of tell-tale grunting and raucous squealing to check whether any of the sows needed crating or un-crating or whether piglets needed to be rescued from certain death under their mother's churning hooves. The subdued light in the shed, the warm glow of the heat lamps and the life going on all around was somehow comforting and provided a strong sense of purpose; probably similar to NHS nurses as they do their nightly ward rounds!

Life on the farm is not always so cute or harmonious. Sows don't get pregnant and produce hordes of piglets by divine intervention, sex is involved, and since the aim of all animal production is to increase breeding success and improve efficiency, this often means getting down and dirty with even the most intimate moments of your animal charges. Like us humans, pigs, unlike cows for example, are ready for sex at any time of the year. Once a sow has given birth to a litter of piglets, she's ready, back on heat and raring to go again just ten days later after weaning. To hasten the process, a sow's fractious brood is tempted away from the sow with creep feed, essentially a candy sweet snack to lure the youngsters away from their mum so she's ready for the boar again. It's rather unsettling to be cast in the role of some dodgy stranger tempting children with sweeties, but the lure of the creep feed seems to be totally irresistible to a piglet. Just the sound of a rustling bag of feed is enough to elicit squeals of delight.

Once the 'kids' are out of the way, the boars are introduced into a separate but adjoining pen running along one end of the sow stalls. The sows are fed individually whilst being kept in contact with, but are not actually able to access, the boars, effectively 'teasing' them to reduce the time between weaning and oestrus. Once the sow start showing interest in the boar, basically, she just stands still and allows the boar to nuzzle her; pigs are quite romantic really! Once she's in oestrus and ready to go, the two of them get straight to it when the sow is introduced to the boar. The older animals are rarely a problem, however, the first timers often need a bit of, 'ahem', assistance if you know what I mean. During my time at the Sterns', I remember one young breeding boar that was well known for being completely clueless when it came to carrying out his breeding duties; Hopeless Henry, we called him.

One freezing cold January morning, I was checking the farrowing pens when the stockman, Bob Burnet, wandered in with his hands in his pockets and a rather bashful look on his face. My first thought was, 'Oh my God! He's going to ask me out or something!'

But instead, he simply said, 'Debbie, could you come over and help me in the sow stalls?' Thoroughly relieved, I finished what I was doing and went over to the shed where the gilts (young unmated sows) and older sows were held in the 'teasing' pens.

By the time I got there, Bob was nonchalantly leaning on one of the sow stalls while a boar was running with the gilts.

'Well, how shall I put it? If you don't know much about sex at the moment, you will after today!' Bob was watching a young boar trying, and failing, to do his duty and mate with a fairly sizeable group of females. 'Now, this here's Hopeless Henry, he's a quality sire, but he's absolutely hopeless when it comes to mating, so we're going to need to give him a hand getting the job done. Now, he's a pretty big bugger, so I'll coax him into position, but you're going to have to help him get it in the right hole, so to speak.'

I could see that Bob was having trouble explaining the ins and outs of mating to a fresh faced seventeen-year-old girl, but by the time he'd explained what I needed to do, my face was flushed with embarrassment and all I could manage was a nod, so, without further ado, we got cracking.

Henry was keen enough to mate, but his aim was terrible, so as he mounted a sow and his hips started up their thrusting action, Bob steadied him while I grabbed the hapless boar's pulsating 'manhood', thrust it into the sow's vagina and hey presto! After the first couple of times, it became a routine and an hour later we'd managed to help Henry serve his morning's harem of sows and had tucked everyone back up in their pens. Henry may have been a quality sire, but his continued poor performance meant, unfortunately for him, to use a business euphemism, he had to be 'let go' and most likely ended up as several pounds of sausages. I remember thinking it was pretty tough on poor Henry, but as you quickly learn in this business, once an animal's not fit for purpose, it gets the chop, or pork chop in Henry's case. That being the case, you might assume that farmers are, by and large, fairly unsentimental when it comes to the fate of their animals, however, you'd be wrong. Not long after arriving at Henfold Farm, Mr Stern asked me to help load a group of pigs into a truck to be taken to the slaughterhouse. It was a fairly dismal day with a steady drizzle being driven by a chilly wind so everyone was keen to get the job done as quickly as possible. The farm reared piglets to pork weight, so at about four to six months old and around 65 kg in weight, the animals could be pretty feisty and difficult to catch. Using large sheets of plywood board like riot police shields, Roy Stern, Bob and myself, cajoled and pushed the protesting porkers towards the ramp of the truck. The rain made everything slippery, and judging by the struggle some of the animals put up, I'm pretty certain that they knew something was up and were, not surprisingly, reluctant to go up the ramp and into the truck. When we'd finally got them all aboard, and Bob and I heaved a collective sigh of relief, I remember looking over at Mr Stern and being surprised to see tears welling up in his eyes as the truck pulled away from the yard. Roy Stern, like many livestock farmers, really was fond of his animals, and during my days in farming, I too often felt a tug of emotion especially when the lambs went to market. However, I always consoled myself that I'd ensured they had the best treatment possible and took a great deal of pride in that.

What, you might ask, were my contemporaries from St Mary's and my siblings doing whilst I was playing the latter-day Florence Nightingale to a bunch of squealing porkers? Well, brother Adam was enjoying married bliss with his new wife, Vanda, and had recently started as a junior partner at a veterinary practice in Saffron Walden, not far from our family home. Their (characteristically for Adam) whirlwind decision to wed, announced just a week before the happy event, had caused a fair amount of panic, with muggins (that's me by the way) offering to bake the wedding cake.[6] All had gone well up until the family dog, Muldoon, who'd been craftily waiting his chance all afternoon by moping around in the front room occasionally making probing attacks into the kitchen before he finally had a clear run when I popped to the loo. On returning, I found the devil hound had scoffed a corner of the bottom tier. After first collapsing in a heap of despair at the kitchen table, I had the cunning plan of simply inserting an enormous chunk of fondant icing into the gaping hole left by Muldoon's ravenous attack. Subsequent communications suggested that neither Adam nor Vanda had noticed anything amiss; thank goodness! Meanwhile, Sarah had settled down with her boyfriend, Steve, and was fretting over the run up to her final exams for her degree in Economics and History at Anglia Polytechnic.[7] My mother had decided to stay in the old family holiday home, The Grange, to visit her sisters Ester and Fleur, who lived near Haverfordwest in Pembrokeshire. This was a rather unwise decision given that both of them were incipient alcoholics and well known locally for their hard drinking and therefore likely to be of little help with my mother's ongoing state of despair. That just leaves my contemporaries…

Having chosen such an outré direction for my future career, I think most of my fellow boarders had dismissed me out of hand, all except Lucy! Despite having gone on to sixth form college at the super posh Francis Holland School situated in Sloane Square, London, dear Lucy's letters were amongst the very few I received whilst I was struggling during those early months of my pre-college year.[8] Reading her letters years later, they provide an amusing and candid snapshot of what was, quite literally, an alternate universe of parties, boyfriends and leisure travel that was as far removed from what I was doing as cigarettes and chocolate milk. For example, a letter from Lucy in September 1975

---

[6] In September 1975.
[7] Now the Anglia Ruskin University
[8] The term, Sloane Ranger, dates from 1975 when writers, Peter York and Ann Barr, coined the term to define a recognisable group of young people living in parts of Chelsea and Kensington. See their enormously entertaining book, the 'Official Sloane Ranger Handbook', which became a bestseller in 1982!

recounts a breathless round of school reunion parties, buying tickets for a Roxy Music concert at Wembley Stadium with her boyfriend Mark and hooking up with a second boyfriend, Jon, at a party at the beginning of the summer holidays. Although I have no record of my corresponding letters to Lucy, I can assume I was either jealous or flabbergasted since I'd spent the previous summer trying, and consummately failing, to snag even one eligible young man, never mind two! In October, Lucy was lamenting my abysmally low wages and in February 1976, she was inviting me on a holiday in Crete with school friends. I'm sure I'd have loved to go to Crete, but since the day I'd started in the previous September, I'd not received a single penny in payment from the Sterns!

There was, however, one physical reminder of the world outside the farm. On the occasional weekend when I wasn't mucking out and grooming the wretched horses, I stayed over with the Oars' cousins, the Marchwells. A Saturday morning trip over to the Marchwell's pristine, and very posh house in Cobham, a hilly fourteen miles by bicycle from my digs in Banstead, was like taking a voyage to a promised land of milk and honey. However, before entering this Garden of Eden, I had to undergo rigorous cleaning, a process that started at the elegant porticoed entrance. Reminiscent of the rigorous decontamination that scientists had to undergo in Michael Crichton's famous 1971 sci-fi movie, Andromeda Strain, the process started with removal of my clothes, a deep-cleaning shower and dressing in a separate fresh set of garments kept by Margaret Marchwell for my visits. On the first of these visits, I remember a lively conversation in which I recounted, in detail, how their Sunday lunch of roast pork had found its way onto their table. With all the exuberance of a recent convert to some strange religious cult, I went through mating, weaning and fattening in a level of detail that my tutor at agriculture college would have been proud of. However, judging by the looks of horror and revulsion on the faces of my fellow diners, I made a mental note to keep details of animal husbandry firmly out the conversation in future visits!

Chapter 6
Dismal dairying

With just one month to go before my six-month stint at Henfold Farm was due to end, I was trying to find a farm for my second six-month placement. I had in my back pocket a muted, but not unenthusiastic, letter of recommendation from Roy Stern confirming that, *'despite having no previous experience, Miss Best was a hard worker who was willing to learn.'* Critical to the core of their being, this was not feint praise coming from a farmer, so I must have done all right! Armed with this relatively glowing reference, I scoured appointments pages of the Farmers Weekly looking for positions vacant for students. A very polite letter I received in response to my application to a mixed dairy and sheep farm in Tunbridge Wells indicated that the job would've been mine for the taking, but I chose instead a sixty-cow dairy called College Farm run by the Faulding family in the village of Butlers Marston, a tiny scrap of a place in the vast undulating patchwork quilt of fields that comprise the Warwickshire countryside. Why I chose one over the other entirely escapes me, but it wasn't the potential for a vibrant social life. Butlers Marston was then, and still is, quite literally, a one-horse town with neither a shop nor a pub. My memories of the place are sketchy, but since a plethora of information is just a mouse click away, I checked Wikipedia to see if there was some information to jog my memory. However, all the folks at Wiki could come up with was *"the village originally lay to the east, beyond the church, but was evacuated after the Black Death in 1349."* And that about sums it up. There probably hasn't been any big news coming out of Butlers Marston since the Black Death!

It was the beginning of March 1976 and the end of an exceptionally mild and dry winter and the start of an exceptionally warm, dry spring that saw me packing my meagre belongings into my kitbag for the three-hour train journey over to Stratford-upon-Avon station where I was to be picked up by the farm's head stockman. Having no description to go on, I wondered how I was going to recognise someone I'd never met before, but I needn't have worried, the station was tiny and there on the platform stood a man of medium height, stocky build, ill-kempt hair, wearing a pair of muck-caked welly boots.

'Hello, Mr Styles? I'm Debbie Best.' We shook hands and I liked him from the start. After he'd unceremoniously plonked my bicycle in the back of the Landrover, Bill Styles took a pleasant meandering route along the River Dene, saying that it wasn't the quickest, but we'd need to drop into the grocery shop at Kineton before it shut so I could pick up some supplies as the caravan where I'd be staying wouldn't be stocked with food. Up to that point, I'd assumed that I'd be getting bed and board since I'd only be getting thirty pence per hour. Sure enough, the accommodation was a caravan parked in the farmyard with windows covered in grime and carpets caked in mud and straw. I'd complained about my previous accommodation lacking 'authenticity' but at that point, I'd have given anything for a bit of chintz now!

I was just emptying a tin of beans into a pan and trying to work out how to get the gas stove going when there was a knock at the door; it was Mr Faulding. He'd just been doing the evening milking and was still wearing his dairyman's green overalls. He explained that I'd be expected to start work at six a.m. in the dairy, followed by helping his dad with the milk round before coming back to scrub down the milking parlour and feeding the calves. I'd also have to work half day on Saturdays and Sundays and do the evening milking. Phew, I feel tired now just thinking about it! Out of my wages, I'd be paying rent for the caravan and for any milk I wanted to use; however, I would get a free pint of cream once a week. I remember thinking, I'm not so bothered about the cream, but it'd be nice to have a free pinta for my breakfast in the morning!

One big advantage of actually living in the same place as you work, in my case, the caravan was literally backed up against the wall of one of the cowsheds, is that you don't need to commute. All you have to do is role out of bed, and straight into your overalls. However, there's something very disorientating waking up in a strange bed in a strange house, I think it's something to do with all the unfamiliar little noises, the squeaks, groans and sighs that issue from the fabric of the building almost like it's breathing. It puts you on high alert, and you can almost feel your ears moving as your senses strain to find something familiar, or warn against something threatening. But waking up in a caravan you've got to also contend with outside noises like the pigeons scuffling on the roof, the bellowing cows, the dawn chorus of Mr Robin Redbreast and Co singing their hearts out at first light. Then there are the smells. The first thing that hits you is the damp, followed by the cow muck caked to the carpet and then the age-old cigarette smoke staining the ceiling and running down in little ochre-coloured rivulets under the impetus of the ever-present condensation. Last, but not least, there's the rancid smell of decaying food and the overflowing waste bin in the closet under the sink that nobody's thought to empty before the next guest takes up his or her tenancy. Since my little stay at College Farm, I've lived in many a caravan, some small, like this one, some large, but all filthy dirty!

Once I'd been settled in my digs and had received my 'orders' from the boss, I assumed I would be left to get on with fending for myself; however, I was pleasantly surprised. On the first morning in my new caravan abode, whilst I was contemplating my full bladder and where I was going to empty it, there was a polite knock at the caravan door. Before answering, I ensured that my woolly dressing gown was presentably covering my convent nightie.

'Hello, good morning! I'm just getting up.'

'It's Bill Styles. My wife, Margaret and I wondered if you'd like to join us for breakfast since it's your first morning here.'

Bill and Margaret Styles lived in a modest, but cosy little red brick tied cottage across the fields and only a stone's throw away from the farmyard. [9] Whilst Bill's wife was welcoming, I detected a slight wariness, something I've become used to over the years, i.e., "*my husband's just brought a young woman into our family home and he will be spending the day with her at work*", kind of look. Looks aside, the bacon, eggs and toast were very welcome and definitely better than the bowl of unsweetened muesli I was planning on having. After breakfast, Bill dropped me off at the dairy where Mr Faulding (David) and Mr Faulding senior (Ted) were togged up in their green cotton dairy jackets,

---

[9] Traditionally, a tied cottage is a house owned by the farmer's family that is provided as part of a farm worker's wages. Nowadays, farms rarely provide this perk as many of the farm workers' cottages have either been sold or privately rented to bring in extra money for the farm. However, it's debatable whether the slightly increased wages fully compensate, especially today when rents are so expensive.

flat caps, sturdy-looking corduroy trousers (baggy at the knees, of course) and indispensable muck-caked welly boots. Added to this garb, they were both wearing waterproof aprons, a much-needed defence against fountains of urine that the cows were wont to throw in your direction, or worse on some occasions. For some cows, being relieved of an udder full of milk is a perfect moment to relieve themselves of all their other body fluids at the same time in a single cathartic release. Sometimes you can be literally up to your neck in milk, urine and poo!

At six a.m., work was already in full swing. Cows to be milked with their full udders swaying painfully against their legs, were being ushered into one end of the shed and onto little concrete plinths about one metre apart. College Farm ran a classic example of an abreast, no, not breasts, abreast, which meant that the cows had to be backed out of their stalls (like parking slots) after milking (see footnote).[10] Fortunately, rather than manual milking, which would have taken ages with sixty pedigree Guernseys, the parlour was equipped with pneumatic milking lines in which milk flowed from individual cows into glass recorder jars before being sent to the dairy's refrigerated reservoir tank. Ted ambled over and set me to work cleaning the cows' teats and udders before milking and washing in iodine solution afterwards before backing the cows out and herding in replacements. The Fauldings had a cow naming system that was similar to the old car number plates with the first letter, the 'A' in April, for instance, denoting the first-born to a given sire, or bull. The rest of the name, the numeric part, referred to where in the country the cow was bought and its discrete dairy ID number. I quickly learnt that each cow had her own character and physical peculiarities. For example, April had a very low-slung udder, which made it the devil's own job to get the milking cups on, especially on a dark morning. Cactus had half a tail and was quite excitable, whist Pansy was a Friesian, and so was the odd 'man' out so to speak.

About halfway through the process, I was sent over to the dairy where I was shown how to use the bottling plant so I could get the pints

[10] For those interested in such things, an abreast parlour allows cows to enter individually and stand side by side (standing abreast) enclosed in sturdy metal railings. An embellishment of the abreast parlour allows cows to leave their cubicles forwards after milking, rather like a Mac D's drive through, otherwise, they're just parked with their noses to the wall and have to be (carefully) backed out after milking.

ready for delivery after we'd finished milking. Although rare now in the age of supermarkets, huge automated dairies and block chain supply systems, back in the day, many large dairy farms had their own bottling facilities so they could deliver direct to their customers' doorsteps. In what was to become one of the few, and rather enjoyable, opportunities to get off the farm and meet some of the local people, I helped old Ted with the milk delivery to the village and surrounds. Still wearing his green dairy jacket with distinctive farm logo, rather like Postman Pat, Ted sat at the wheel of an old Bedford Post Office van; however, unlike Pat's black and white cat, Jess, who sits serenely in the passenger seat while Pat delivers the mail, I was in and out of the van humping heavy crates of bottles up garden paths and returning with the empties. After a few weeks I acquired a small fan club of locals who'd be waiting for me to skip up their garden path to exchange a bit of early morning banter, and sometimes, the odd packet of chocolate digestives or some other small token of appreciation would exchange hands. Of course, being a fresh-faced, prim and proper convent boarding school girl, I was always terribly polite and quickly became a favourite with a large retinue of lonely little old ladies. Once the highlight of the day was over, it was back to the dairy to clean the milking parlour and wash, by hand all the dirty milk bottles; a bit like clearing up the house after a raucous party the night before. Then it was time for a cuppa before feeding the calves their dried milk ration. Looking back at my diary, it was incredible how much milk powder we got though, so clearly, there must have been quite a few calves because it was brought in by the ton. It's amazing how much you can get done before lunchtime when you get an early start! I then, just about, had time after lunch to get a few personal essentials done, a trip by bicycle to the local shops for food for example, before it was back in the parlour for the evening milking.

The dense, impenetrable script of my pre-college year diary records that the daily grind at College Farm proceeded with regimented efficiency. In fact, the Fauldings' set-up was pretty advanced for the time. No hulking bull strutting his stuff at mating time for them, the cows got into calf through AI — artificial insemination, not artificial intelligence. Come to think of it, a certain amount of intelligence was needed from the vet, or cowman, to avoid a stiff kick in the balls, whist inserting the semen straw. Some cows draw the line at having a bloke's arm shoved up their vagina! Besides AI, I learnt a lot about spotting milk fever, a metabolic disease in dairy cows close to calving caused by low blood calcium. Then there was administering antibiotics to counteract mastitis (a bacterial infection of the udder that means a cow needs to be taken out of milk production) and Brucellosis vaccination to control this previously common cause of late pregnancy abortion. Such valuable on the job training and know how was all grist to the mill for any budding agricultural college student.

However, things didn't always run smooth as silk with clockwork efficiency. One afternoon, I decided, for educational purposes, to watch the vet during a routine visit to the farm. I clearly remember standing around the calf pen whilst the vet was taking blood samples for bovine tuberculosis testing and dehorning the calves.[11] On getting to a calf, I knew to be weak from a bout of scouring (cow diarrhoea for want of a better word) the vet began to take a blood sample. Suddenly, the animal started to gasp for breath, flopped down onto the ground and started having a seizure, something that can happen under the stress caused by handling. The vet administered a stimulant to get the calf breathing normally again, but it just lay down and died in front of the assembled audience of the Fauldings, senior and junior, Bill Styles and myself. Like an audience watching an escapologist die during a routine show, we stood in silence and stared bug-eyed at the dead animal resting on a bed of straw while the vet offered an apologetic explanation. I could really feel for the vet and I know my brother Adam would have been mortified if the same thing had happened to him, but these things can and do happen out of the blue when you're looking after farm animals.

After a while, we looked at each other and Mr Faulding confirmed what we'd all been thinking and said bitterly, 'Well that's another one for the knacker yard then.' Then he walked away.

So what happens to the dead and dying on a farm? In the 1970s, the death of farm animals was the domain of the knacker man. In my young woman's fevered imagination, the knacker man conjured up macabre

---

[11] For those who believe that the practice of dehorning calves is cruel, the process is carried out after anaesthetic has been administered. Without dehorning, animals can inflict painful injuries on each other and to farm staff, so it is necessary to prevent accidents.

and frightening images. I only once came face to face with the knacker man when out on an errand on the furthest regions of a farm I was on where I strayed closer than I'd intended to the knacker shed, easily identifiable by the awful stench and the busy hum of flies. As I passed the usually closed and locked shed, I noticed the door was open and the knacker man was busy at his odious task of rendering down a carcass. Back then, we were not so squeamish about using the meat from dead and destroyed animals. Although it didn't go into the human food chain, it did go into pet food, pig offal and to make a range of products including horse oil used to protect shoe leather and Neatsfoot oil used by doctors as a balm to ease their patients' joints!

Whilst I found my flourishing milk round little old lady fan club to be quite sweet, the attentions of the new cowman were rather less welcome. Just before I arrived at the farm, the Fauldings had fired the previous cowman for some fatal misdemeanour or other. His replacement, a youngish lad called Nigel, is described in my diary as being rather drippy, a disapproving term for somebody rather lacking in energy with a few pints less than a full gallon in the intelligence department. I described him further as rather short, wearing blue nylon trousers and a flowery shirt. This last item was seen as a fashion faux pas even in the '70s; which can be only described as one huge fashion faux pas if truth be known. From the first day Bill introduced us, Nigel had spent the entire time talking to my breasts, I took a strong dislike to the poor chap. When he wasn't mucking out or performing some other endless task around the farm, Nigel would follow me around like a puppy. However, whilst most young women tended to make their low opinion of a would-be suitor very clear in words and actions, here my convent etiquette worked against me. Due to shyness, my overly polite responses to Nigel's attempts at conversation were interpreted as a green light to further advances. It seemed to be the story of my life on farms that I always attracted, well, how shall I put it, the Nigels of this world rather than the guys I really did fancy who seemed to be repelled in equal measure by the same shy and overly polite manner that was like catnip to the Nigels!

To cut a long story short, Nigel finally plucked up the courage to ask me out for a drink at the local pub. Once he'd got the notion into his head, he wouldn't let it go and worried it like the proverbial dog with a bone. The worst thing was I couldn't get away from the farm and I had nobody to see or anywhere else I could go. So I started to make up excuses. However, at the time, I didn't have the benefit of gazillions of miles of fibre optic and millions of Pentium processors called the Internet at my disposal to search for, and find, new excuses. Believe it or not, there are now whole websites set up with the sole purpose of cataloguing excuses a woman can use to reject unwanted male interest! In the end, all I could come up with was number seventy-five on the list of the top one hundred excuses, namely, *"I'm washing my hair this evening and it takes ages for it to dry"* and then variants of this, I'm having a bath, I'm trimming my nails, etc, etc. Why, oh why couldn't I have thought of, *"You remind me too much of my cousin/brother/father"* (number six in the global top one hundred) or, *"I'm far too emotional to be with someone"* (number thirteen) or, number one on the list, *"I have this big wedding/funeral to attend to"*. Without the benefit of being able to tap into the Internet's plethora of excuses, I resorted to hiding in my caravan (not easy, but possible) whenever I saw Nigel coming my way. This simple strategy must have worked because I can't find a diary entry recording a night out with him, or maybe I just blanked it out of my memory! Flippancy aside, of all the men I met during my time at Butlers Marston, Bill Styles, with the forbearance of his wife, was always friendly, kind and genuinely helpful to me. Like the solid rock resisting the shifting sands and grating pebbles that makes up the beach of life on any farm, there's always been at least one, solid, dependable bloke which I could lean on to get me out of the various scrapes I used to get myself into.

I know, I know, this part of the book is called Heat wave, and so far, I haven't mentioned anything about heat or waves. Actually, I've been keeping the best to last. Like the final act in the crew of Apollo 13's ordeal when they had to endure the fiery crucible of re-entry into the Earth's atmosphere, I had to endure the stifling heat and sixteen-hour days during haymaking at the height of the 1976 heat wave. But rather than working all those hours for virtually no money, with the help of the Welsh Agricultural College, we turned defeat into a stunning victory. So to quote the immortal words of Mission Controller, Gene Kranz who said in response to the NASA director's assertion that, 'this could be the worst disaster NASA's ever experienced.'

Kranz emotionally replied, 'With all due respect, sir, I believe this is gonna be our finest hour!' But I'm getting ahead of myself, and you'll have to wait to the end of the chapter to find out about my finest hour!

My ordeal began on Wednesday 9th June. The mission involved haymaking in two fields, Jack Dale and Fishway Ground, which together totalled ten acres. A furious, emotional and unsent letter to my friend, Sophie Oar, captures the ire I felt towards the Fauldings. In the 1970s, big bales and big-baling machinery hadn't been invented yet. I remember an advert promoting big balers in the Farmers Weekly, which asked a simple question, "big bales, or big muscles?" Well, we needed big muscles!

The part of the haymaking process that involved sitting on tractors was composed of four steps: mowing, tedding (a tractor-drawn rake used to disperse the hay to facilitate drying), turning with another tractor-drawn machine and baling with a machine with a vicious-looking claw that draws hay into its bowels where it's compressed and bound with baler twine, that ubiquitous orange string to be found all over farms in various situations where things have broken and need a temporary fix. That was the tractor part of the job. My role in haymaking was the bit that needed physical grunt, namely, dragging the 80 lb bales (just over half my body weight at the time) into groups of six so that a tractor-mounted loader could scoop the bales up and place them on a trailer for transporting to the barn where more physical grunt, my job again, was needed to stack the ruddy things in the barn. Oh, and to make things worse, the conveyor belt contraption that could have assisted in getting the bales up to the top of the stack broke down so we had to pitch them up with forks, the cowman went off sick and let's not forget it was more than eighty degrees Fahrenheit, or about thirty degrees Celsius. So that was the state of play. The division of labour was simple, the Fauldings sat on machines and Bill and myself did the bale carting. The icing on the cake was that thunderstorms were expected at the weekend, so we had to get all the bales stacked in the barn pronto, without allowing the hay to dry fully, which made the damn bales heavier.

Out in the searing heat, the sun beat down and sweat flies crowded our faces and tear ducts desperately looking for some moisture to suck on. Our task was to shift the bales into groups of six for the loader. Being about four foot long and heavy, the bales were cumbersome and uncooperative, rather like dragging corpses from the battlefield. At the time, I could swear that the Mr Faulding was purposely dropping the bales as far away from each other as possible to maximise the amount of dragging we had to do. At lunchtime, back in the day, jovial farm girls would have come out to the fields with jugs of cool cider and a hearty ploughman's lunch. Suitably refreshed and rejuvenated, the farm lads would have returned to their task with renewed vigour. That was then, all we got was a half hour break to eat whatever sandwiches we'd brought with us to the field. There wasn't even a water trough available to slake our thirst. On the first day, after walking back to my caravan at ten p.m. after sixteen hours in the field, I collapsed in bed only to be woken by Big Ben's merry chimes to discover I'd slept through to morning without eating supper!

On the second and third days, to try and reduce the physical effort needed, Bill made sure I worked in the barn stacking the bales. I was thankful, but as I already mentioned, the conveyer belt kept jamming, so, in the end, the bales had to be stacked manually. As I got closer and closer to the roof of the barn, the heat from the corrugated iron sheeting cooked my brain and my head throbbed from a mixture of mild heat stroke and dehydration. Surely this would be the point when Mr Faulding Jnr would offer to give us a hand: not a bit of it! He directed operations from the seat of his Massey Ferguson, pointing here and there, indicating a bale needed re-stacking here, or turned around there. For four, sixteen-hour days of backbreaking work, I earned £4.80 per day, a financial injustice that later caused me to write a treatise on farm wages at college that got me top marks! My subsequent agitation for higher wages has more than once earned me the title of Red Deb from farming friends! With the notable exception of the left-leaning father of my dear friend, Shân (who I met at WAC and are sadly both no longer with us) I've never met a farmer who'd agree he should pay his workers higher wages, and that's a fact!

Now for the bit about my finest hour. Stan Blowers, a tutor coordinating students' pre-college placements, visited the farm and was so taken aback by the hours I'd been doing and the measly rate of pay that the college took the Fauldings to court and I got £1,000 out of it; a very handy boost to finances which was extremely helpful in my first year at college. I'm guessing my name has been mud down on College Farm ever since. But I kept in touch with Bill Styles for quite a while after I left; it seems I'd made a positive impression on him at least! So at the end of August and after six months at College Farm I'd only had one weekend off and I now had to prepare to travel to Aberystwyth for my first term at college.

Part 3
W.A.C!

Chapter 7
One of the 'lads'

Aaah, Cymru; the land of sheep, rugby, leeks... and the Welsh Agricultural College. WAC, as it's better known, sits just outside the blustery and windswept town of Aberystwyth, huddled at the centre point of Cardigan Bay, a huge bight out of the west coast of Wales. In that isolated spot where, during term time, gown outnumbered town two to one and winter storms could inundate the hotels on Marine Terrace and push large stones up its pebbly beach, (mostly) farm lads, and a few farm girls enjoyed two years of unfettered drunken partying away from the shackles of life on the family farm. Bizarrely, and somewhat disturbing for those concerned, two miles out of town and away from the main university, WAC shared its campus with the Welsh College of Librarianship. We'll come to why that fact was disturbing later on, but for now, we can just marvel at why the planners thought putting a ravening horde of agriculture students on the same campus as librarians was a good idea. In the mid-1970s the UK was in the grip of a long period of austerity. We'd just had the three-day week and a series of miners' strikes that culminated in a final bitter stand-off when Margaret Thatcher was elected prime minister in 1979. To the chagrin of the French president, Giscard d'Estaing, we had just joined the Economic Union after a referendum in 1975, presumably in the hope that it would breathe life into Britain's ailing economy as it weaned itself off cheap labour and food after the disbandment of its empire during the 1960s. Austerity and low wages aside, evidence gleaned from letters I received at the time suggest that my contemporaries from St Mary's appeared to be shielded from these slings and arrows of misfortune and continued to venture away on holiday to sunny climes and spend an inordinate amount of time at dinner parties or chatting over Beaujolais Nouveau in a growing number of trendy London wine bars. Whilst foment brewed between society's haves and the have-nots, I entered a hermetically sealed world of green fields filled with sheep and bars full of hard-drinking WAC students. My contemporaries and I were of the lucky last few who benefited from a student grant system that provided us with accommodation and three-square meals a day throughout our two years at college. Oh, happy days! With only a handful of women in my OND intake and a few others doing an HND I was suddenly thrown in at the deep end with sixty young men.[12] Up until that point, there'd been a dearth of eligible bachelors available at home, but now there were more men than you could shake a stick at! But casting around the boisterous registrations hall at the beginning of term, I couldn't see any that were fanciable Instead, I saw a lot of loud, and mostly Welsh, young farmer types in check shirts and Barbour jackets whose minds were focused largely on rugby, yards of ale competitions and finding a suitable female to help run the farm. I was disappointed, but what was I expecting? Looking now at the first-year photograph taken outside the then recently completed administrative block at WAC, most wore the stern faces of serious young men who'd come to college to learn how to run their family farm. This was a forbidding prospect for my younger self who was still so shy and unsure of how to be around men.

As I surveyed this impenetrable mass of young lads who all seemed to already know each other, I saw another woman who, like myself, was hanging back and seemed very unsure of herself, so I wondered over and introduced myself, 'Hi! I'm Debbie.'

I remember her looking round as if surprised that somebody had noticed her, she replied with a soft Welsh accent, 'Shân Joyce. I feel a bit of a fraud really, since I've only travelled over from near Hay-on-Wye!' She smiled and had a twinkle of intelligence in her eyes and a prepossessing friendliness; in that moment, a lifelong friendship began. Practical and straightforward, I always knew where I was with Shân; however, she was a bit of a hermit and tended to spend most of her time in her room. However, Shân's reclusive tendencies were more than counterbalanced by the two other women in our year, Mary-Jane, the joker and Jane, the athlete. These women formed a formidable dynamic duo ready to take on the world and were more than a match for a bunch

---

[12] The OND, or Ordinary National Diploma in Agriculture, was aimed at farm workers, whilst the HND, or Higher National Diploma, was for farmer, or, in other words, farm owners, so there was a clear-cut divide built into the system from the start.

of farm lads! Inevitably, since we were a small group of women in a very much male-dominated world at agriculture college, we formed a strong bond that has lasted a lifetime. So did our band of women have the 'right stuff' to survive two years in mixed dormitories? Whilst Jane was playing hockey and football and attracting a large group of male admirers and Mary-Jane was eating herself into a few extra pounds during cake eating competitions, I was left to try and coax Shân and another very shy woman, Ann, out of their rooms. Oh, I should also mention that there were a couple of very religious third year HND men in our block who were so mortified by having to share accommodations with women, that they'd barricaded themselves into their rooms long ago. With such unprepossessing material to work with I wondered how I'd get through the next two years at college since I didn't fancy any of the men and most of the women appeared to be a dead loss! So I dug deep, put on a pair of Doc Martens, slicked my hair with Vicks vapour rub, and like my friend Lucy, I became a punk rocker. After three months of dreary nights in and a few tentative forays to the college bar on my own to watch beer drinking competitions, I decided to burnish my new persona as a punk rocker, and literally, if necessary, drag Shân out of her room. Approaching her door, loud music was playing so it seemed she already had a party on the go. After much gentle tapping and finally banging, her door opened and a strong waft of aniseed flowed out into the corridor. Shân unsteadily let me into her room where, it turned out, she'd been secretly drinking Pernod to summon sufficient Dutch courage to leave her room in the evening. The tipple of choice of aged Frenchmen sitting outside cafés watching boules, Pernod was a rather expensive source of courage; presumably this was why, up until that point, she hadn't been able to consume enough to leave her room!

So, if my band of WAC females was a mixed bag of mostly shy and retiring farming folk, what of the males? During the first year, I built up friendly relations with a small group of men, most notably Steve and his mate Gary. Steve and Gary were something of a Mutt n' Jeff pair. Whilst Steve might be considered quite handsome and self-assured, Gary was gangly and awkward. Steve had a steady girlfriend, so our relationship was friendly and platonic, however, Gary developed a soft spot for me that I successfully resisted for my whole three years at college. Steve and

Gary acted as my guides to the farming male, decoding the bluster and exuberance that often acted as a cover for lack of confidence and anxiety over their role and commitments on the family farm. On one notable occasion towards the end of the first year, Steve, an ardent Liverpool FC fan, invited me to the FA Cup final with Manchester United that was playing at Liverpool's ground at Anfield. I'd never been to a football match before and felt totally out of place in a sea of boisterous males, rather like a foreigner in a distant land. We flowed in through the turnstiles at the 'Kop', or home end of the stadium; apparently, a reference to the ill-fated battle during the Boer War where British forces were routed after trying, unsuccessfully, to defend a hill called Spion Kop. Lord only knows why the home end of a football stadium is named after a hill in South Africa where we lost to the Boers, but that's the topsy-turvy logic of the British for you! Looking down from our position towards the back, or top of the kop hill so to speak, the players were tiny, like the little plastic figures you use in Subbuteo table football. Flummoxed, and not understanding anything about the game or the rules, I immediately asked the obvious question, which team was which, to which Steve quietly replied that Liverpool were in red (their home colours) and Manchester United in white and black. He seemed embarrassed that he'd brought such a newbie along with him! With the game in full swing, I found being in the presence of so much heaving humanity overwhelming and strangely emotional and I think it was then that I fell in love with the experience rather than the game itself. The crowd began to sway, my neighbours' hips nudging me from left and right, nothing sexual, but I was compelled to join in with the sea of bodies and the roar of the crowd as Liverpool scored. Alas, it was a 2:1 defeat for Liverpool, but I was hooked. From then on, I always had a topic of conversation that was sure to get a response even from the most taciturn of the male species, including my brother!

***

Nobody who's spent any time there can fail to notice that Wales is a place synonymous with grazing animals. Given that I was studying agriculture and took a close interest in farm animals, one might expect that I'd grow to love the place whilst I was at college. I'm not going to deny that I did, but it was tough love, the kind you experience in life with highs and lows where I needed to make it through obstacles and challenges. Having learnt to appreciate Wales during my first year — the place, its weather and its people, I also found myself becoming fascinated by its grassland! In Wales, grass is king. The green fields that people see from their cars whilst they're on holiday is made up of grass species and varieties that have been bred to be productive and appealing to farm animals. However, the arcane world of crop science, and specifically grass breeding, is virtually unknown to the general public; however, I was captivated by it, in other words, I became a grass bore! During my first and third years I studied pasture improvement strategies at Trawscoed, a byword for excellence in UK grass breeding and the birthplace of varieties that have become milestones in grassland production. After a couple of terms, names like S23 and S24 effortlessly tripped off my tongue. I could talk about their nutritive value, growth rates, biomass index, use in silage or grazing and resistance to crown rust for hours. Farming in the 1970s and '80s was an era of produce or be damned. Farmers were encouraged to chuck on the nitrogen, rip out unproductive meadow grass so they could plant acres of verdant green: a sight for sore eyes for any ewe aspiring to produce twins or triplets and cows aiming to increase their milk yield. Except for bloat, there was thought to be no downside.[13] This drive for efficacy spread beyond the home fields and up onto the fells above the farm. Bracken fern was rolled to keep it at bay. The natural vegetation growing on high pastures was usurped by highly bred invaders and brought a twinkle to the eye of any aspiring stockperson. For years after leaving college, I couldn't look at the rolling hills of northern England and Cumberland and just take in the view, I felt an urge to improve it, make it more productive to allow an increase in stocking rate; the only heresy was an unproductive pasture! It was only years later that I've been forced to grapple with the environmental impact of this clarion call for productivity in the form of environmental degradation, nitrate pollution and the collapse of insect populations including the pollinators we rely on to fertilise our crops.

---

[13] Basically trapped wind caused by overindulgence in all this green "candy"!

Chapter 8
All work and no play

After having had a rather shaky start, by the end of the first year, I'd assumed the grungy persona of a young woman with a bit of attitude who'd gathered around her a small retinue of male friends. However, just at the point where I'd found some confidence, we were packed off to various parts of Wales for our sandwich year placements. Interestingly, the concept of working on a farm that wasn't run by their family was a more troubling and alien concept to the large percentage of people with farm-owning backgrounds. For me, it was just another placement on a farm; however, it turned out to be one of the longest and hardest years I've ever done. My 'short straw' in the draw for a sandwich year placement was Llover Gyfall, a seventy-five-acre smallholding on the uplands above the village of Plowden near the Welsh border in Montgomeryshire near Welshpool. Llover Gyfall was to be my accommodation for a year from July 1977 to the following August. A tenuous umbilicus with the college was to be maintained through occasional visits by my trusty course tutor, Stan Blowers, and quarterly reports. Reading those dry documents years later, quaintly written with a pen and black ink, conveys little impression of the difficulties I faced when I was there. Why I chose a fountain pen to write my reports escapes me, but it was certainly fitting, even back in the '70s I felt like I was going back to a Dickensian era, Bleak House, perhaps? Memories of being there on my own still have the power to move me to tears of misery.

I clearly remember my first train journey to Welshpool. Before privatisation, one of the advantages of travelling by train with a bicycle was you got an opportunity to see behind the scenes in the guard's van. There would be mail and other interesting packages for pubs and restaurants piled high in the caged area of the van where you'd prop your bike. If you were lucky, and I was on this occasion, the guard even plied you with tea made on his little stove and the odd biscuit! The journey had been a much-needed tonic after a rather miserable stay with my mother at Quail Cottage as she was in both mind and spirit at a halfway house during a move near to Haverfordwest in Pembrokeshire to be with her alcoholic sisters, Fleur and Ester. One afternoon, soon after arriving home, I was helping her pack up some boxes for storage. I'd been given the task of sorting through my father's business suits that were still hanging in the wardrobe of the master bedroom. Even though he'd died over three years ago, I fancied I could still smell his distinctive eau de cologne battling its way through the naphtha coming from mothballs in the pockets. Unpleasant memories had begun to surface, causing me to involuntarily back away from the closet and into my mother who'd been standing watching me in the doorway like a pale ghost, slowly swaying from her early-morning fortification. Apparently unperturbed by our collision, she aimlessly drifted back into the sitting room leaving her own scent of eau de Whyte & Mackay lingering in the air. I'd left the next day. Shaking off these troubling memories, I pushed my bike into the station building at Welshpool to get out of the drizzle blowing on a surprisingly cool breeze while I rearranged my belongings and re-packed my trusty tartan panniers.

As I distractedly turned the map upside down to trace my route to Plowden, the stationmaster stepped over to offer assistance.

'Where are you heading to?'

Prodding the map, I replied, 'I'm going to Plowden.'

A sharp intake of breath from the stationmaster was followed by, 'Well there isn't much up there to speak of. Where are you staying?' I paused, anticipating the inevitable struggle with pronunciation of Welsh place names, but I gave it a try. The kindly chap's features looked puzzled, so I pointed to the map. 'Ah, it's pronounced "letty gumba". Yes, I know it actually. It's the Williams' farm. It's a pretty stiff climb up onto the top from here though.'

After the stationmaster had explained the route, I manfully, or was it womanfully, started out. The five miles, or so, from Plowden took almost an hour. Avoiding the main road as I'd been advised, I crossed the Severn River, and set off up a steadily increasing incline. A final steeper climb out of Plowden, saw me at the entrance to the farm. Stepping across the cattle grid at the gate, two sheep dogs dashed out of the farm buildings, followed by Mr Williams himself. I was hot and rather bothered, but Mr

Williams had a kindly way about him and we walked together to the farm buildings where he introduced me to his son, Bill, from whom I received a limp handshake and a brief nod. Not a rolling out of the red carpet, but friendly so far. That was before I met Mrs Williams. She was standing with her arms akimbo on her doorstep staring at the three of us, her hard face clearly showing resentment for this intrusion.

'You're late! If you're expecting tea, we've already had ours and I've cleared up already. You'll need to find something for yourself.' Seeing that this was the only welcome I was going to get, Mr Williams rather apologetically guided me over my accommodation; which turned out to be another caravan. However, this specimen was somewhat newer and larger than the one I'd had at Butlers Marston and it was parked up in a small paddock at the back of the farm buildings, so at least I'd get a bit of privacy. The downside, as always, was that I'd have to rely on using the farm bathroom and laundry facilities. Only recently going into dairy, the farm was originally reliant on beef, pig and sheep production. The caravan was quite well looked after as it had been used for family holidays. Mr Williams explained that accommodation came with the job, but I'd have to pay for the gas I used and the milk. I'd also have to make my own meals using the caravan's stovetop and small gas oven. That first evening, I sat looking out over the hills munching on a pack of digestive biscuits, the only food I had with me. My first priority tomorrow would be to cycle back down to Welshpool and pick up some food at the local Spar; so much for the warm welcome! As I had done many times during my 'career' in farming so far, I wondered what I'd let myself in for.

Over the next few weeks, I helped in the farrowing shed giving creep feed to the latest group of piglets and helping in the dairy, washing teats, bringing in the cows, scrubbing down the parlour. So far, so familiar. Up until that point, I'd not had much to do with sheep. Since I'd arrived in the summer, some of the early lambs were ready to go to market in Welshpool. Bill used his collie dogs, Lad and Jet, to break out a small group of the fat lambs and bring them down the field for loading and to also get a few white-faced ewes with bad teeth that would also go to slaughter. I remember watching intently while Bill, using just hand signals, guided the dogs to split the sheep and bring the right animals to him. Using his right, he indicated to Jet that he wanted him to go right and then come around behind the sheep. Lad was sent to the left. The dogs met in the middle behind the sheep and they drove them down towards the shed. I loved the way the dogs sprinted up the field, turning their heads occasionally to watch what Bill was doing. The party trick came when Jet approached a reluctant and toothless old ewe. Stalking her like a wolf, the dog held the ewe's gaze, almost as though he was mesmerising her. Slowly he moved forward, keeping her still long enough for Bill to catch her with his crook. Up until that point, I'd not seen the sheepdog's 'eye' in action, but I was well impressed!

After this brief introduction to sheep, I had little to do with them until lambing time the following spring as they spent their time up on the common grazing. However, on the bright days at the end of summer, I'd look up from my labours to the fells and see the white dots of sheep nosing around the stands of bracken in search of the odd tender morsel of grass and wish I could be up there with them rather than spraying creeping thistles with a knapsack sprayer of herbicide! But before the spring, there's autumn and winter, the annual tussle with the elements, and the bane of every farm worker, long nights and cold mornings. But additionally in my case, there was self-doubt. I always think that November's the worst. Winter's not even really started, but you're already beginning to get the short days and the weather is raw with cold rain. I remember a particularly ugly day after the afternoon milking. I was trudging back up to the caravan for supper; I felt lonelier than I'd ever been and my heart was in my boots. The remnants of daylight mingled with the harsh illumination from yard lights on the cowshed that had just come on automatically; it was only four p.m. I had groaned in despair at the thought of the nights, drawing in. Moving past the yard and out towards the fields, I could see long, ragged strips of fleece hanging on a barbed-wire fence running from the dry-stone wall behind where my caravan stood, like a caravan park, but I was the only camper. The strips of wool fluttered in the drizzle-flecked wind like Himalayan prayer flags. But what would I pray for? The strength to get through this winter and to progress through my OND? But what would it get me? A life of solitude and hard work on an isolated farm like this? Until my lines show, like the crow's feet at the corners of that harridan of a farmer's wife, Megan Williams' hard eyes, all bitter and twisted like a dog without a bone. Was it to be my lot to marry a man from the hills? A farmer with his sights firmly set on the seasons, the farm, the toil? I had tried to push away these morbid thoughts whilst I wrestled open the caravan door and stepped inside. The wind quieted, but then I was enveloped in the caravan's cold embrace. Juggling with damp matches, cursing that I'd not closed the box and put them in a drawer, I coaxed the Supersur gas heater into life. I'd always wondered about the wisdom of using these contraptions in confined places like caravans. You've got rubber tubing carrying gas next to a source of flame, not safe surely? There's also the danger of carbon monoxide, maybe one of these days I'd wake up dead, at least it'd be quick and pain free. I remember taking a long moment to reflect on what it would be like to just end it all. But what was I thinking about! Surely things couldn't have been that bad?

Almost two years into my nascent farming career, if you discount my first year at college, my experience of farm work so far was one of long hours and drudgery. On top of that, there'd been little respect or encouragement shown to me by the farming folk I'd worked for, just cross words if I'd made a mistake or had taken too long to do something. If Agriculture PLC was looking to nurture the next generation of willing young workers to take up the challenge of a rewarding career in farming, my experience so far suggested it was going about it the wrong way! Reflecting on my time at WAC, one might assume that there must have been a high point to record from my pre-college and sandwich years. Surely there's one heart-warming tale of camaraderie or of a denizen of the soil gratefully and generously passing his (or her) lifetime's experience on to the younger generation? Well, actually there is one example, but it's tiny and it needed much looking for and long hours searching my memory banks to find. But here it is.

Just before Christmas Mr and Mrs Williams had taken a rare weekend off and had left the responsibility of running the farm for a few days with their son, Bill. Up until that point, Bill had treated me with the offhand demeanour he might have reserved for an inconvenient sister if he'd had one. However, on the second evening after the Williams senior had left the farm in our capable hands, Bill came and knocked on my caravan door. Since my bottom half was clothed in only a towel after a trip to the shower in the house, I opened the top half of the door and leaned on its top. In front of me was a young man struggling with conflicting emotions that might have been, (1) embarrassment, (2) irritation and (3) resignation, in that order. The embarrassment probably came from the fact that he was doing some asking rather than telling, the irritation was down to the possibility that his father had asked him to come and speak to me and the resignation was that he was now standing outside my caravan.

'My dad suggested that I should ask whether you'd like to come to the Young Farmers pre-Christmas bash down in Berwen.'

There, you see, I was right. There was no need to check my diary; I hadn't anything arranged on that evening. I'd just been to the shower, so I couldn't use that as an excuse not to go; I was trapped, so I said, 'Yes, that'll be great, thank you!'

When it comes to pubs, Berwen is a village of two factions. The posh lot that frequented the Lion Hotel and the rest, who crossed the stone bridge across the Severn and drank at the Talbot. As it had a large back room for functions and was less averse to rowdy youth spilling beer and making a lot of boisterous noise, the do had been organised at the Talbot. Once we arrived at the pub and I'd been set up with a glass of ale, Bill rapidly abandoned me to my fate; which was to be chatted up by an earnest young man in a checked shirt and nylon tie. The upside of this turn of events was I was plied with copious quantities of Double Dragon ale. Brewed by Felinfoel, pronounced affectionately in Wales as 'feeling foul', Double Dragon is fairly powerful stuff for a slight young woman like myself to be drinking, so after just four pints (to avoid feeling foul in the morning, geddit!), my beer intake was high enough at the end of the evening so as to be unconcerned while I watched Bill attempt, and fail several times, to successfully get his key into the lock to open the Land Rover door. Whilst drunk driving was an offence in the 1970s, it hadn't acquired the stigma it has now, but the ride back along high-banked single-track roads was pretty scary. Returning to my caravan after arriving back in the yard in one piece, I snapped on the lights and immediately noticed the icicles hanging from the ceiling like embryonic stalactites, mmmh, how cosy! Setting Big Ben for five a.m., I crawled under my bed covers fully clothed. The next morning was bright and mind-numbingly cold. As I walked around to the dairy, I could see the cows were waiting expectantly, but the lights were off and no one was home. This was bad news! Bill should have at least started the preliminaries, so I went in search of him. After ten minutes of fruitlessly searching the yard, I decided he was still in the house. However, the house was still and quiet as I approached, no cheery BBC Radio 2 music to be heard and no response to my banging on the front door. My heart sank. I really didn't feel confident to do the whole milking operation myself, and in any case, it would have taken ages and Mr and Mrs Williams would have returned before I'd finished, a heinous crime punishable by death! Okay, maybe not death, but lots of shouting. I therefore weighed which was the lesser of two evils. So, picking up some gravel from the drive, I started throwing it at Bill's bedroom window. Still getting no response, I found a stool and a yard broom, and precariously balanced on the former I used the broom to tap on the window.

After several minutes of this, a terrified face appeared at the window; which quickly disappeared and was followed by a wailing sound, 'Oh God, they're due back this morning and they'll have my guts for garters if the milking's not been done.' All the while, Bill was doing a very good impression of Edvard Munch's painting The Scream!

For once, we worked shoulder-to-shoulder as a team. I ushered cows into stalls and cleaned their teats while Bill got the milking parlour up and running. We soon had a good rhythm going, so when the Williams seniors' Peugeot crunched into the drive, all was looking spick and span and squared away.

Whilst I was walking back to my caravan for breakfast, Bill approached me with a very contrite look on his face and said, 'Debbie, I can't thank you enough! You really saved my bacon; you're a mate, that's what you are!' And that, ladies and gentlemen, is an example of one of the rarest things in farming, a thanks and some genuine respect. Okay, perhaps not as rare as a wages' increase, but still pretty rare!

So what of my contemporaries? How were they faring during the sandwich year? Communication with my college friends was intermittent, and due to workload and lack of weekends off, it was reliant on letters. One has to remember that in the '70s, communications were not much different from the situation in the '50s and '60s. Computers were still monstrous leviathans occupying a whole floor of an office building and the first personal computers, which would be introduced in the early '80s, were clunky, eye-wateringly expensive and would have to wait until 1992 to be connected to the internet. Mobile phones would be introduced in the mid '80s but an affordable handset that weighed less than 30 lbs. in weight was years away. So we had phone boxes, those little red cubicles with overly strong door hinges that have now been culled in their thousands since mobile phones really took off so that more of them now occupy museums and pub beer gardens than stand on city streets. However, back in the day, whilst you could find a phone box fairly easily in, say, London, out in the countryside they were few and far between, placed by the GPO at a central point equidistant from all dwellings in a village so everyone would be equally inconvenienced. If a village was really spread out, as they often are in Wales, this resulted in some fairly strange placings. Sometimes you'd be cycling along a country lane, miles from anywhere and bump into one loitering on the roadside as though it'd just landed there like Dr Who's Tardis.

Without ready access to a phone, we really relied on letters and the cheery postie was one of the few links we had with the outside world. Receiving a letter became something akin to winning the lottery. It was intensely exciting to see the postie's red van arrive at the farm and I'd be over the moon if one of the Williams family brought me a letter. The joy of mail I experienced must have been similar to that of prisoners of war in WWII receiving a food parcel from the Red Cross; and I did feel like a prisoner at times. Reading through the letters I've saved from college friends suggest wildly different fates for the writers. For instance, Steve, my friend from Liverpool, who was based near Rothin in Clwyd, writing in November after eleven weeks at his sandwich posting had been home twice and appeared to be indulging in a vibrant social life with his mates in young farmers having just returned from a coach trip to Blackpool. On the downside, he'd been stopped and breathalysed by the police whilst driving his MG, casually commenting that he was looking to buy a decent car. At the time, I'd have given my right arm to have any kind of car! On the other hand, I have two letters from the amorous Gary based near Porthirnaun in Dyfed indicating he was having a pretty miserable time of it. In one of them he moans that, *"Mr Griffiths [the farmer] does not like me*", and "*the family are extremely Welsh and I don't feel welcome at all*". A letter from Charlie based in Warminster in Wiltshire informed me he'd been so exhausted by constant work he was unable to find the energy to go to the pub nor the money to afford a beer or organise a party for his twenty-first birthday. To make matters worse, he'd been kicked by a cow into a pile of muck he'd been scraping out. So a pretty mixed bag of fortunes all round!

Chapter 9
A taste of freedom

If you're thinking that my life was all work and no play (making Jill a dull girl) from the moment I signed up for an OND in agriculture, you'd not be too far off the mark, but I did have some time off, it was just interspersed with very long periods of loneliness and continuous work! The only positive was that at least I'd been able to save some money. I finished my year's stint at Llover Gyfall at the beginning of July 1978. On my final Saturday, I'd skipped out of my caravan to the sound of the early-morning larks, hitched my panniers to my trusty bike and sailed down to the train station at Welshpool after a parting that I can honestly say was completely free of any regrets. Since then, I never found myself missing that place and I've never been back since. On the day I left, I had the light-headed euphoria of a person that was headed to the sunny shores of holiday land, a place where the sun always shines and the possibilities are endless. My itinerary for the next month or so, before term started in September, consisted of a three week stay with family friends, Margaret and Karl Orensson, at their villa near Arezzo in Tuscany. As if that wasn't wonderful enough, from there, I'd arranged to meet sister Sarah in Greece for a beach holiday. So, Thursday 6th July saw me boarding a plane to Pisa Airport for the start of my festival of fun in Tuscany.

How should I describe Margaret Orensson? An Englishwoman from Birmingham that divided her time between homes in Rhode Island and Tuscany, married to Karl, a quiet, unassuming Norwegian who worked as a high-ranking official at the United Nations in Rome, Margaret was the yin to Karl's yang, a partnership of opposites that can, and does, often work. Whilst Karl worked in Rome, Margaret escaped the scurry and strife of the city and enjoyed long stays at their villa at Antechia near the ancient town of Arezzo, located in south-eastern Tuscany, on a hilltop at the crossroads of four valleys — the Val Tiberina, Casentino, Valdarno, and Valdichiana. Tanned, relaxed and exuberant as always, Margaret met me at the airport with a huge hug that went on for several minutes attracting the stares of fellow travellers and even the Italians who are famously into a good hug and a kiss! Once the gridlock and honking motorists of Pisa were left behind, Margaret's driving, which had been erratic in the city, got steadily more leisurely, and somewhat dangerous, as the dry rolling hillsides spooled past. Waving an arm here and glancing there, she acted like an enthusiastic tour guide, her little Fiat weaving around on the road as it followed her flamboyant gestures. Forking left at the town of Ginestra Fiorentina, we took the scenic route via Siena, where the Tuscan countryside is stunning and sparsely populated with just an occasional craggy hilltop crowned with cypress trees obscuring the odd terracotta-tiled villa here and there on their shadowed promontories.

At one point, accompanied with a little gasp of pleasure, Margaret pulled into a roadside produce stall.

'Come along my dear and help me choose some fresh fruit and vegetables for this evening's meal!' On seeing us, the ancient woman minding the stall smiled and Margaret fluently broke into the regional patois. She didn't need my help, but it was fascinating to watch her in action! At one point, Margaret turned to me, 'Do you know how you can tell whether a fig is ripe?' I was agog to know, so she immediately answered her own question. 'It has the texture and softness of a man's testicles!' In answer to my embarrassed and puzzled expression, and breaking into the American vernacular, she offered, 'You do know what a man's balls feel like, don't you?'

'No, I've no idea I'm afraid.' Because, you see, at that point, I'd never seen a man's genitals let alone got to grips with them.

Whilst my face burned with embarrassment, Margaret was chuckling to herself and must have said something to the old woman, because she came over to me, a kindly, but very wrinkled smile playing on her tanned features.

'Per te, mia cara, per la tua educazione![14] She handed me a couple of the largest figs I'd ever seen. Unable to help myself, I caressed them in the palm of my hands whilst the two women laughed and nudged each other knowingly; it was a lovely moment.

I could fill a chapter recounting the hazy days of my time in the

---

[14] Roughly translates as, 'for your education.'

Orenssons' villa; breakfast on the terrace overlooking the vineyards and the chirping crickets in the evening as we enjoyed a glass of the local Chianti. It was such a contrast to my life on the farm I sometimes had to pinch myself to check whether I was dreaming. But this is a book about a woman's life in agriculture! However, since it's about a woman, and at this moment of my life, a woman coming of age, I should mention another memorable occasion from my time in Antechia. Shortly after my arrival, maybe the second or third morning, someone moving around the creaky old floorboards awakened me. Feeling hungry, the smell of coffee drew me from my overheated bed and I wandered downstairs and headed for the kitchen. Being a little hard of hearing, Margaret didn't notice my approach. I was about to wish her good morning, when she suddenly stepped out from behind a kitchen cabinet and I saw that she was completely naked. Surprised, but also intrigued, I stayed out of sight and watched as she stepped outside and crossed the patio to a little wooden table where she placed her coffee cup down. Sighing contentedly, she took in the view and completely unselfconsciously enjoyed her nakedness and the feeling of the morning air on her skin. For me, a young woman of nineteen who'd been educated in a convent, I was, at the time, grappling with intense feelings of body shame. I worried about the appearance of my breasts, my genitals, my perceived chubbiness. I was, therefore, in awe of Margaret's acceptance of her body as it was, stretch marks, wrinkles and all! It is only now as I enter my sixties that I am, at last, becoming less self-conscious and more at ease with my own body. I should have followed Margaret's example at an earlier age, I would have avoided a lot of angst along the way!

My stay with Margaret had been a wonderful tonic after what had seemed like a prison sentence at Llover Gyfall. During our two weeks together at Antechia, she'd become like a second mother. I felt guilty about it at the time, but my own mother just wasn't there for me when I felt I needed her most, struggling as I was with my decision to go into agriculture, with the loss of my father and the feeling of being left behind by my siblings. Speaking of which, Sarah, who'd now completed a masters in language and speech therapy, had decided to take a break before starting her training as a speech therapist, and as it turned out, from her boyfriend Steve.

Planning a holiday and now needing a companion, Sarah had arranged a call with me one evening a few weeks previously.

'Plum, I'm taking a break from Steve; men are all shits anyway. Let's get away together when you've finished in Wales at that place you're working, oh I can't pronounce it! We've hardly seen each other since you went to ag. college. I've seen a cheap package holiday to Greece, let's do it Sis!'

The cheap package turned out to be in northern Greece. Having spent a year doing virtually nothing social in the wilds of Wales, I'd managed to amass sufficient overtime to pay to afford both trips to run consecutively. I've always prided myself in running my life on a small budget — a useful skill if you're a farm worker! That prudence had granted me a little taste of paradise. So I met Sarah in Antechia and we travelled together from Brindisi by boat to Corfu to do a bit of island hopping before turning our attention to the mainland and Thessaloniki, which sits at the head, or should I say, the hand of a huge peninsula that is almost cut off from mainland Greece. The hand or should I say, the Halkidiki Peninsula, has three fingers that stretch into the aquamarine blue of the Aegean. Those parched, sun-drenched fingers of land are like a trio of sisters, Kassandra, Sithonia and Athos, who beckon like tempting sirens of the sea. It's a place where you could get lost and remain hidden from the outside world for years. We'd booked a couple of nights at a little B&B at the tiny fishing village of Agios Nikolaos on the tip of Kassandra, the first of the three 'sisters' but other than that, the world was, quite literally, our oyster.

Nowadays, Agios Nikolaus bustles with tourists who jostle for attention in its crowded bars and restaurants, however, back in the 1970s it was a sleepy little fishing village at the end of a dusty track off the main perimeter road around the peninsula, its rustic shibboleth still to be deciphered by the world of mass tourism. It was early evening when our brightly painted local bus finally bumped along the rutted lane to Agios Nikolaos after a two-hour journey from Thessaloniki. Emerging from air-conditioned comfort, the early-evening air that met us at the door of the bus was like a tangible wall of heat that we almost needed to swim into. Sweat sprang from my skin immediately, and the layers of clothing we were wearing on the bus were stripped off. As we stood in our crumpled summer dresses, Sarah asked the bus driver for directions to our guest house, the Villa Pefnos. Patiently standing by the bus, heat plumed from the engine exhaust and fine, white dust particles settled on me from the cloud that had accompanied us on our journey down the dusty lane, adding grime to a stain on my dress I'd already acquired from a run-in with a small glass of Cab. Sav. during our long journey. Discussions with the driver were seriously impeded by his lack of English and Sarah's lack of Greek. Undeterred, and rather like the language equivalent of a set of skeleton keys, Sarah tried Italian, in which she's fluent and pigeon French. Neither of these 'keys' unlocked the information we needed from the driver. Trying to prevent further grime settling on my dress, I edged away from the bus, just as Sarah had been forced to resort to speaking English very loudly, clearly and slowly like the queen during her Christmas speeches. Away from the hubbub of the bus and Sarah's strident voice, I was enveloped by the calmness of the place. Noticing a splash of colour nearby, I absently walked away from the bus-stand towards a group of riotously flowering plants resembling Lupinus that had found a home next to the wall of the bus-stand.[15] Chirruping crickets and the rushing sound of cicadas mingled with the mournful cries of seabirds.

Captivated by the scene around me, I didn't notice Sarah approach. 'Come on Plum', she said. 'I've found where we're going, thank God!' Following Sarah as she hurried off towards the nearby harbour, we were greeted by a stunning tableau. Groups of men were hurrying on and off colourful high-prow fishing boats unloading boxes of squid and octopus like their lives depended on it whilst others violently thrashed the poor creatures to death on the quayside steps. An idyll of paradise was thus juxtaposed with feverish activity and a violent end. I'd been looking forward to a bowl of fried calamari that evening, but now I wasn't so sure I wanted to add to the poor cephalopods' misery!

After spending two days at our B&B, Mrs Kratides had treated us like royalty, so we agreed to stay on rather than finding somewhere else to stay. We also decided to take a trip around the huge bay separating Kassandra from Sithonia, the Kolpos Kassandras, on the Kratides' boat. Mrs Kratides' husband Georgios, had been an inshore fisherman all his life, and from what we could gather, knew the peninsula and its wildlife

---

[15] Most likely, they were Bear's Breech or Acanthus mollis, the National flower of Greece

like the back of his hand. As a further inducement, he even had an English version of the Pocket Guide to the Birds of Greece for us to borrow. Since the sea is about tides, and skippers of small boats in particular need to pay attention to them, we were woken by Mrs Kratides at the ungodly hour of six a.m. Such an early rise was bread and milk to a budding farmhand such as myself; however, it was a bleary-eyed Sarah that joined me at the breakfast table. Hurriedly downing coffee from our bowls and grabbing a doggie bag for the boat, we rushed out of the door; time and tide wait for no man (or woman)! Seated amongst the lobster creels and general nautical and fishing paraphernalia in the back of Georgios' battered truck, we'd been told we would be picking up three other tourists on the way to the harbour. These, a Dutch couple and a single man, we found standing at the side of the road next to a sign for a campsite a few miles up the coast at Haniotis. After a nod and some pleasantries, the Dutch couple got back to what they were doing previously, which was staring lovingly into each other's eyes. The single man, on the other hand introduced himself. By the time we arrived back at the harbour, we'd discovered his name was Fred, he was a Californian and he'd been travelling around the Halkidiki Peninsula for the last month on a battered old bicycle he'd bought from one of the locals. Mostly sleeping on the beach, he'd checked in at the campsite for a couple of nights to grab a shower. Fred was an archetypal Californian with all the expected accoutrements including sun-bleached fair hair, fine tanned features, relaxed persona, self-assured manner and outgoing personality. Although he spoke to both of us, I could see from the start that Fred gravitated towards me; which I found both flattering and unnerving.

During a moment whilst everyone assembled on the quay, Sarah nudged me and girlishly giggled, 'I think he fancies you Plum! Watch yourself with these Americans, they're all teeth and trousers!'

I supposed since Sarah was still, more or less, fixed up with Steve and the Dutch couple were fixed up with themselves, I had a clear field. So, while Fred and I spent the boat trip talking to each other, Sarah chatted to Georgios about nautical matters (she's always been keen on boats) and the Dutch couple indulged in some French kissing. Something for everyone then! I don't remember much about the tour of the bay, except that I do remember seeing a pod of dolphins.

Back at the quay, Sarah simply gave me a knowing smile and said,

'See you back at the B&B Sis, I'm going to check out the covered market,' and wondered off into the village centre.

With Sarah now out of the way, Fred took his cue and said he knew a great place for swimming. Walking together on warm sand in bare feet is one of the sensuous pleasures of beaches in the Aegean, another is skinny-dipping in private little coves; we found the perfect spot up near Neapolis. Skinny-dipping at this point in my life required caveats, which in my case that meant I swam in my bra and panties, whilst Fred peeled off his clothes and dived straight in. However, there was no risk of having to put my clothes back on top of wet underwear, the sun was more than warm enough to dry them after a few minutes of lying on a flat rock situated in a shady part of our cove where Fred came to join me. The effect of the heat, the sand and our conversation had made me quite light-headed, and at some point during a discussion of the pros and cons of surf spots near Santa Monica, or was it the talents of the famous guitar-playing Rastafarian on skates that cruised Venice Beach, Fred had begun holding my hand and staring intently into my eyes. Unsure of what to do next, and with very little experience, a part of me below the waist made a decision on behalf of the prevaricating part of my body sitting on my shoulders and I went with the flow. The flow involved removal of what remained of my clothing and a reprise of what the Dutch couple had been doing during the boat trip, except, this time, it was happening to me. I do remember that at various points during the process that started with handholding, then kissing, progressing to kissing parts of the body accessible with clothes on to parts accessible wearing a swimsuit, and finally, to parts only accessible when you're naked, there was an unspoken permission requested and then granted at each stage. That is, until we'd got to the part where Fred's hips became lodged firmly between my thighs. At that point further progress required some verbal communication. 'Is this your first time?' And 'are you on birth control?' Armed with a 'yes' to first question and 'no' to the second, Fred produced a condom from his satchel with a flourish. I'd read somewhere that American GIs never went into battle without military-issue condoms, and luckily Fred was no exception; but at that point I don't think I could have stopped myself even if he hadn't been so well prepared! I can report that my first time went well, but sand got everywhere, and I mean, everywhere!

Chapter 10
The last lap

Waking with a start, I struck my head painfully on the window. Easing back in my seat, I absently watched the scene passing outside the train carriage like a filmstrip. Hills, small farmsteads, dairy paddocks and sheep on the hillsides combined together within the somnolent countryside of West Wales. A smell of freshly cut grass wafted through the open ventilation window above me. It was September, we'd had some good weather, but the fields were verdant and lush after a rainy August. But how would I know? I'd been in foreign climes. My thoughts drifted back to my holiday. Greece, the beach, Italy and the smiling faces of Fred and Margaret were like images from an alternate universe. I'd boarded the train, one of those dinky-toy single-carriage DMU jobs, at Haverfordwest at around ten thirty a.m. after a visit with my mother, who, at this point, had moved to the nearby Pembrokeshire seaside village of Little Haven semi-permanently. [16] Which brings me to an incredible fact. It takes over six hours by train to make a journey that would take only an hour and half by road. How is this possible? By making a huge detour inland to Shrewsbury and then catching the achingly slow stopping train to Aberystwyth! Thank you so much Lord Beeching for buggering up the West Wales rail network! After an unconscionably long journey, the soporific sound of wheels passing over rail joints on the last long stretch of single-track railway after Machynlleth always had me fast asleep before I reached Aberystwyth! [17] However, if my first year had been a little dull and the train journey back to Aberystwyth had sent me to sleep, my final year at WAC was to be

---

[16] DMUs, or diesel multiple units are basically a single carriage with the engine combined in a single unit. There's a driver and usually a guard, a bit like a bus that goes on rails. If you're catching a train and a DMU appears, it usually means you're going on a little single-track branch line with 'passing places' so that trains can travel in the other direction, or has short platforms that can't accommodate a multiple carriage train.

[17] Machynlleth is famous for the Centre for Alternative Technology that, when I was at WAC, had just been founded in 1973 in an old slate quarry — it's well worth a visit!

momentous in many ways, filled with some wild parties, thrills and spills and a couple of lasting mementos of my college life. Oh, and I did also do some studying of course!

Although returning to WAC for my third and final year was a momentous moment for me, arrival at Aberystwyth station was rather an anti-climax. I'd arrived a week before the start of term, as spending time with my mother in Pembrokeshire had become very difficult, so the throng of students that would arrive the weekend before Freshers' Week, were yet to invade. At seven p.m. on Sunday 24th September, exactly a week before the start of term, the streets were empty and the town seemed to be collectively holding its breath in anticipation of its annual invasion. The swelling ranks of the student population was, and still is, regarded by the dour and staunchly Welsh townsfolk as both an economic imperative and deeply vexatious in equal measure. Deciding, like the Welsh, to cherish this brief moment of calm before the storm, I turned left out of the station and sauntered down to the beach and along Marine Terrace. The sun was setting and I idly watched the daily light show over Cardigan Bay as its orange orb touched the sea and turned it into molten gold. Aberystwyth's motto should be, 'Sunsets 'R' Us'!

Having now got as far as Victoria Terrace, I could clearly see the Cliff Railway in the gathering gloom and chuckled to myself as I recalled a conversation with the wag of a barman who used to always chat us up in Downies Vaults. On one occasion, he heard us conclude that Aberystwyth was one place in the world where nothing ever happened. Slightly outraged, the friendly barman suddenly broke into our convivial chatter.

'Did you know that Aberystwyth Cliff Railway was the scene of the only known incidence of an elephant causing an accident on a funicular railway?'

There were gasps of astonishment all around and we all cried, 'Please go on!' Seeing he had our full attention, the barman gleefully told us that back in 1911, just a week or two before King George V was due to lay the foundation stone of the new National Library of Wales, one of the elephants from Bostock and Wombell's Menagerie, who was entertaining the town at the time, broke away from its keeper and ran onto the funicular railway just as it was descending, causing death and mayhem. Astonished, we all agreed it was an extraordinary tale and that Aber, should henceforth be known as a place where *hardly* anything ever happens!

At this point, I feel I should recount a humorous tale of my own that also had rather disastrous consequences. All had gone swimmingly well during the autumn term as I reconnected with my little circle of female friends that had recently been widened by the arrival of Pat, a strikingly tall first year OND student, who, like myself, was a complete newbie to farming, so we'd immediately got on like a house on fire. So it was, one afternoon during the run-up to Christmas and a week before the Student Review, I was studying my lines for a part as Juliet in a humorous skit on Shakespeare's famous tale of star-struck lovers when Pat, Mary-Jane and Shân lured me away from my studies to join them downstairs for the cleaners' party. As I've previously mentioned, as a student in the 1970s, and in common with prisoners detained 'at Her Majesty's pleasure', HM Government provided us with three square meals a day and free accommodation. However, unlike lags serving their time, we also received that now, almost unheard-of accoutrement of student life, spending money in the form of a student grant. Now, if all that wasn't enough, in addition, we had a friendly army of cleaners to keep our halls of residence and dormitory kitchens spotlessly clean. In annual thanks for what they did for us, we used to all pitch in and buy gifts for our cleaners, which included a party in the afternoon before they went off shift. The cleaners' party had, over the years, become yet another chance for drunken shenanigans with an added benefit that it happened during the day when we should have been studying. By the time our cleaners said their thanks and bid us a cheery farewell, we were all pretty stoked up and there were still plenty of bottles of various alcoholic beverages to be consumed. At some point, I must've crashed out in my room for a snooze because I remember being woken from my slumbers by Shân banging on my door and reminding me that I needed to go to rehearsal. Staggering out of my room, I shakily headed for the stairs, and much to everyone's alarm, promptly fell head over heels down them straight onto my face! Fortunately, the booze both anaesthetised and enveloped me in the drunk's protective stupefaction; however, it couldn't prevent me smashing my front teeth as they met the unyielding concrete at the bottom of the stairs.

Rather aptly, in the circumstances, my erstwhile Romeo whisked me to A&E at Bronglais General Hospital, but when I presented my swollen, bloodied face and fragments of my two broken front teeth to matron in the forlorn hope that they might be able to fix them, she simply said, 'She's drunk! Take her home, there's nothing we can do for her!'

Despite this setback, and in honoured thespian tradition, the show did go on! In fact, since it was a skit on Romeo and Juliet, during the poignant balcony scene where Romeo describes Juliet's beauty, the parody of opposites worked perfectly! Whilst achieved at great cost, my hilarious performance in the review earned me considerable respect from my fellow students; I was no longer a boring female, I had a bit of spirit! However, as I write this account of that fateful day, my tongue instinctively fiddles with the steel brace holding my denture in place. Almost forty years later to the day since my angelic self, had quite literally fallen from grace, and after much desperate capping and fruitless treatment for gum recession, I finally had to admit defeat and have what remained of my front teeth removed. For quite a while afterwards, staring into the bathroom mirror whilst struggling to get my wretched denture plate into the hideous gap left in my front teeth, I've often felt that I resemble another of Shakespeare's famous characters, one of the three witches in Macbeth! One sometimes pays dearly for the foolishness of youth!

I might've previously mentioned that WAC students in the 1970s had a reputation for working and playing hard. With many having slipped the leash tethering them to the family farm, three years of unfettered freedom lay ahead. Speaking of leashes, for a lot of our male counterparts in particular, it often seemed like a descendant of Julius Caesar's avenging spirit had entered them, and spurred by the mischievous Atë the Greek goddess of ruin and folly, they frequently appeared hell-bent on squeezing in as much of a lifetime's worth of excess as was possible to achieve in three years. Perhaps because everyone sensed that student life would soon come to an end, during the final year at WAC things became particularly crazy! Two events in the summer term of 1979 stick out as being instances when the boundary between work and play was strained to the limit and mayhem was definitely the result. In common with schools, one of the privileges enjoyed by students at college and university, is that not only do they observe all UK public holidays, they also take long holidays in the summer. However, there is one event that's not in primary and secondary school calendars, Rag Week. Ostensibly, Rag Week is an opportunity for students to give something back to the local community that's had to put up with noisy parties and shenanigans in the pubs and clubs all year by organising events to raise money for charity. In other words, it's a chance to demonstrate that students can be a positive force for good and aren't all just drunken hooligans sponging (at that time) off the state. That's the intention, but the reality is often very different! Without doubt, the centrepiece of Rag Week for us was the annual battle of wits and skill between Aber's two great educational institutions. The Hooray Henrys at Oxford and Cambridge have the boat race, a posh annual event played out in the blaze of public and media attention along the banks of the Thames in London; however, our version was somewhat less highbrow, but much more fun! The raft race between WAC and the university was always much anticipated, and whilst tongue was always firmly in cheek all the way, it was, nonetheless, very competitive. The Aberystwyth raft race took place on the River Ystwyth (Welsh: Afon Ystwyth). A happy, or perhaps for the competitors, unhappy convergence of Rag Week events meant that the WAC eating and drinking competition always occurred on the evening preceding the raft race. I shall explain why this was important. The eating and drinking competition held during Rag Week was not an isolated instance of competitive excess during the year, but it was certainly the most extreme. Eating and drinking to orgiastic excess, the inevitable outcome, or should I say, output evokes another mainstay of ancient Roman mythology, the vomitorium, where revellers are popularly believed to purge their stomachs of excess food and drink in specially constructed rooms, or vomitoria, before continuing with the feast on a newly empty stomach. Whereas vomitoria turn out to be a linguistic slip up that's led to an abiding urban myth, the eating and drinking competition really did involve vomiting up excess food and drink so as competitors could return to the fray. However, even within the myth of the Roman vomitorium there's no parallel with what was eaten in the 1979 competition, which included, in order of excess, sponge cake, boiled eggs, yards of ale, partly-cooked pigeons and a dead pheasant (uncooked).[18] If that wasn't bad enough, in the final stages of the competition, the outputs of excess were recycled and vomit and urine were added to the menu. These same outputs were also saved in plastic bags and used by supporters to pelt the opposing teams during the raft race! Whilst not making the cut for either the WAC 'A' or 'B' teams competing in the raft race, I was involved in construction of the rafts from old silage containers and I will admit to dumping bags of cow manure over the university rafters from the bridge on Penparcau Road in the centre of the town. A very belated 'sorry' if you were one of those rafters in 1979!

Another highlight of my final term at WAC actually has to do with agriculture! An obligatory part of my OND course included a field trip to the Republic of Ireland to further our understanding of different farming systems. In common with farming in the UK, the 1970s was a period of change for the better for Irish farmers after the republic entered the EU. Our trip to Ireland in May 1979 came at the end of what has since become known as a golden era of dairy farming. Prior to EU entry in 1973, farmers in the republic supplied the internal Irish market and their biggest trading partner was the UK; entry into the EU had changed all that. The 1970s witnessed a large-scale modernisation of Irish farming and a huge investment via the Farm Modernisation Scheme introduced in 1975. Ireland had always been an important dairy producer, but the EU marketplace provided a huge boost to market diversity, and in some cases, prices increased by two hundred percent during the decade following entry into the Common Market. Our visit in May 1979, therefore, came at the end of almost a decade of change and modernisation in Ireland, and a renaissance I never saw on the dairy farms I worked for on the mainland. I think one reason for this was the fact that Irish farmers embraced the EU and its market opportunities in a way that British farmers never have. Where Ireland's farmers saw

---

[18] Whilst ancient Romans did love their food and drink, even the wealthiest didn't have special rooms for purging. To Romans, vomitoria were the entrances/exits in stadiums or theatres, so dubbed by a fifth-century writer because of the way they'd spew crowds out into the streets. At some point in the late 19th or early 20th century, people got the wrong idea about vomitoria. It seems likely that it was a single linguistic error: "vomitorium" sounds like a place where people would vomit — sorry to disappoint everyone with facts!

business opportunities and the chance to invest in the production of new products, British farmers only saw competition from producers on the continent whilst they simply pocketed millions of pounds in subsidies and farm area payments. The corollary of British Agriculture's decades long resistance to the EU and its regulatory framework has brought it to the cliff-edge of Brexit; but that's another story!

So it was, on a Friday morning in early May, fifteen or so excited students gathered in front of the main administrative building. Having joined Mary-Jane, Shân and Jane in the car park, we watched the lads arriving. We knew this was going to be a boozy trip, but I think we were all amazed by the sheer quantity of plastic bags full of beer tins that was assembling before us. Our tutor, Stan Blowers, had told us to keep our personal gear to a minimum, as storage would be limited in the minibus. The male contingent had responded to this challenge by leaving their personal stuff behind and exchanging sensible items like a change of clothes, wash kit and so on with two or more plastic bags of booze! By the time Stan arrived with the minibus at ten a.m., some of the lads were already on their second or third tin of Export, and we hadn't even started our journey! Taking the scenic route to Holyhead via Machynlleth and the Snowdonia National Park, we caught the lunchtime ferry to Dublin. Unfortunately, the grey clouds and rain we'd picked up in the Snowdonia hills followed us to Holyhead.

By the time we boarded the Irish Ferries 'Isle of Inishmore' grey seas and surging tides awaited us off Holyhead Point.

'I think we should avoid the bar and the stern rails. Rough seas and large quantities of Guinness don't mix!' We all nodded in agreement to Mary-Jane's wise words and let the guys disappear off towards the bar while we trooped up onto the observation deck to watch Holyhead slip into the distance.

Moving inside out of the rain, we stopped to talk to Stan Blowers who was sitting at a small table by himself nursing a cup of coffee whilst intently watching a group of five WAC lads at the bar.

'I hope we get them all to the hostel in Dublin okay! An Óige (Irish Youth Hostels Association) won't know what's hit it with this lot on the way!' Stan looked worried, as well he might! As we met the swell in the Irish Sea, Stan's coffee cup sailed across his table and was brought to a stop by the little wooden buffers at the edge. Half-empty beer glasses and cans rolled off other tables and crashed to the floor. As we watched, a couple of our WAC party at the bar staggered off and headed outside, no doubt heading for the stern rails, whilst others stoically leant on the bar, consumed their pie and chips and looked on contemptuously as their fellows retreated outside. The last man left standing at was Di Williams, a physically sizeable character from North Wales. Di stood at the bar throughout it all like a giant ship of the sea; even when the brown beer dregs flowing around the bar were joined by, I daren't even think what, flowing out of the gents' toilet next door!

If you ask a bunch of Irish farming experts which part of the Emerald Isle is the best place to farm, you get as many answers as there are people in the room.

One might say, 'It has to be Cork'.

But another might point out that, 'Kilkenny has the highest average single farm payment, that makes it the best.'

To which another might answer, 'But that's just because they've got a lot of mixed beef and tillage farming — it doesn't make them the best.'

And so on...

That's the view of the experts, but how Stan and the tutors at WAC decided the itinerary for the 1979 field trip I don't know, but one thing was for certain, we left a trail of destruction behind us through counties Dublin, Kilkenny, Kildare and Kerry! Our Irish hosts, a couple of tutors and a group of students from Clonakilty Ag College in County Cork, met us at the hostel in Dublin like long lost family. Picture the Irish change in the scene in Braveheart depicting the battle of Falkirk! If our tutor, Stan Blowers, had hopes of controlling excessive drinking in the evenings, the arrival of the Irish contingent was the equivalent of throwing petrol onto a fire! Our hosts knew the most convivial local pubs with the best craic and the finest ale that were frequented by locals with the silkiest singing voices and the best fiddlers. Poor Stan didn't stand a chance! To cap it all, we'd arrived during a strike by switchboard operators fighting a desperate battle to turn the tide of automatic switching technology; a bit Canute-like, but you could sympathise with them for wanting to retain such a valuable source of employment in the branch exchanges. The striking telephonists effectively cut Stan Blowers off from the WAC 'mother ship', which was probably a good thing since he didn't have to receive the complaints made by angry youth hostel managers coping with devastation in the male dorms we were leaving in our wake. On the downside, the wrath and fury were saved up for his return to Aberystwyth and a quiet chat with the Dean; so you could understand his apprehension. On one memorable evening, I think it was at the youth hostel at Kilkenny, two of our party, who will remain nameless, crossed the line from excessive but convivial drinking into grotesque and outright dangerous. A student from Abergavenny fell out of the second-floor window of the male dorm but was saved from serious injury by the flower beds below, and the other, unfortunately for the chap in the lower bunk, wet the bed in his top bunk. Stan's firm talking to the next morning over breakfast did something to rein in drinking during the following couple of evenings, but WAC still got banned by An Óige from using their hostels in future; a ban that likely stayed in place until WAC was merged with the university in 1995!

What, you might you ask, did we did learn during our field trip? An abiding memory for me is the little stone cottages strewn about the countryside that seemingly popped up unexpectedly like mushrooms emerging from the vivid green sward of the Irish countryside. The manufacturers of distemper wall paint must've had a field day selling all the shades of the rainbow to farming families keen to try and outdo each other for the title of the most garishly painted cottage. Farming is still crucial to the Irish economy with most production taking place on more than two hundred thousand family farms making up eighteen percent of Ireland's gross domestic product. Since joining the EU, the urge to modernise and invest has been strong in the Irish provinces where the fifty billion euros that Irish agriculture has received since joining the EU has been put to good use. Back then, some of the farms we visited were similar to the crofts you might see in the Hebrides of Scotland where the whole family pitched in to help and farm incomes were subsidised by wages from second jobs like painting and decorating, building or working for the council. But many more farms had a new barn, or new milking parlour or newly concreted yard. The farmers themselves were welcoming and happy to show us how new investment was making their farms more profitable and easier to run. I saw none of the complacency and dogged adherence to the old ways and hierarchies I saw on farms I worked on in the UK. Here was a farming community that, perhaps, remembered the devastation of the potato famine in the 1840s and was determined never to go there again. In the 1970s, complacency appeared to have no place in the vocabulary of the Irish farmer! So, filled with Irish zeal and enthusiasm and minus quite a few brain cells due to alcohol poisoning, our little party made its way back to WAC and a roasting by the Dean!

**

Nearing the end of my third year, there was one final hurdle I had to cross before I could graduate., and lest I should ever forget, in the closing weeks of the final term, I also received a second parting gift that would, like my broken front teeth, provide me with a lasting memento of my sojourn at WAC. First, the obstacle. Machines and machinery turned out to be my nemeses. The farm machinery module of my OND had to be passed otherwise I would fail to get my diploma, so everything was riding on my ability to remember the minutiae of engine parts and drive shafts. During that time, I often stared, almost in tears, at the kind of exploded diagrams you see in Haynes' manuals for home car maintenance. For years afterwards, just seeing a Haynes manual on the shelves in a Halfords auto parts store would make me shudder! In contrast, most of my fellow students appeared familiar with machinery, especially big machinery, and would like nothing better than a long chat about the pros and cons of the latest Massey Ferguson or David Brown tractor. For me it was a closed book and the names of engine parts could be written in Latin for all the meaning I could extract from them. To make matters worse, Shân, Mary-Jane and Jane could all hold their own with the lads and talk glibly about camshafts, tappets and big ends as if they were budding mechanics. I remember a few occasions when, in desperation, I'd turn up on the doorstep of Shân's dorm room in tears, unable to complete a mechanics assignment. She did her best, and her kindly Welsh voice was reassuring, but after a couple of hours of patient, and finally, exasperated tuition, I still couldn't tell a camshaft from a rocker arm! In the end, it was my mechanics tutor, Mr Bradshaw, who got me through. With a lot of private tuition, often in his own spare time, Mr Bradshaw would draw engines and engine parts on a flip chart and we'd go through each component step by step, a bit like the song Dem Bones.[19] However, instead of learning that the toe bones connected to the foot bone, the foot bones connected to the heel bone and so on, it was the rocker shafts connected to the rocker arm, the rocker arms connected to the push rod, the push rods connected to the camshaft. In the end, my focus topic for the exam was the combine harvester. For some reason, the arcane and rather Heath Robinson inner workings of the combine with its myriad of rubber belts and little pulley wheels seemed to fit better with the way my mind works and I passed the exam with flying colours.[20] Unfortunately, I was never able to put my exhaustive knowledge of the combine to good use since I spent most of my time after college working on livestock farms. Oh well, such is life!

Now, I guess, you all want to know what that parting gift was? Although Fred and I had practiced safe sex during our encounter on the beach, I'd actually started taking the contraceptive pill when I was away on my sandwich year holiday. So, back at WAC, and fresh from my introduction to the pleasures of the flesh, I was keen to try out this new-found freedom. My opportunity came during a college disco. A lad I'd had my eye on for some time, Greg, finally showed some interest in my newly burnished persona as Debbie, confident woman of the world. Physically handsome, and resembling Tom Cruise as he was in the '80s movie, Top Gun (was and still is a favourite of mine!) I thought Greg would be like Fred, slow, deliberate and gentle. Unfortunately, like Cruise's character Maverick, Greg felt the need for speed. So, as soon as we'd sneaked back to his dorm room and quietly closed the door, it was off with the clothes and wham, bam, thank you man! Getting between my legs after a foreplay that consisted of commenting on and briefly kneading my breasts, Greg thrust his penis into me, and after a few frenetic thrusts, his copious, and as it turned out, infected semen was

---

[19] "Dem Bones" (also called "Dry Bones" and "Dem Dry Bones") is a spiritual song. The melody was composed by author and songwriter James Weldon Johnson (1871–1938) and his brother, J. Rosamond Johnson And first recorded by The Famous Myers Jubilee Singers in 1928.
[20] William Heath Robinson was an English cartoonist, illustrator and artist, best known for drawings of fantastically elaborate machines to achieve simple tasks.

making its way into my unsuspecting vagina. My new-found confidence in men was shattered and I never let him near me again. A few weeks later, I was standing in front of the full-length mirror in my room, when I noticed that a group of little pink spots had appeared around my vaginal opening. Thinking (or hoping) it was razor rash, the infection progressed to genital warts, which had to be removed by a very stern nurse at the Aberystwyth Sexual Health Clinic.

I've never been a great fan of hospital or doctors, but up until that point, I'd only ever needed to go to the school nurse for minor cuts or the odd vaccination. On these occasions, the nurse would say something like, 'Okay, it's just a going to feel like a tiny scratch.'

But this occasion, as the nurse dipped the end of her application rod into her little flask of liquid nitrogen, she said, 'I'm afraid this is going to hurt!' I remember thinking of all the young pigs I'd castrated at Henfold Farm and how they must have felt when I made reassuring noises and then got on with the job. The nurse was not wrong: bloody hell, it hurt and I was fuming!

Part 4
The company of cows

Chapter 11
Joining the 'grad set'

Most students after graduating have their eyes set on stellar careers in business, finance, science, etc. However, in agriculture, if you're graduating with an OND rather than a HND and don't have a family farm to go back to, you'd effectively graduate to the bottom of the pile. In my case, the bottom of the pile was a job as a night milker in a three-times-a-day dairy in Wyddial Bury Farm near Buntingford in Hertfordshire. My prospects at this point seemed very bleak. Although I'd shown some aptitude and proved I was a hard worker on the farms in my pre-college and sandwich years, in the agriculture industry you were (and still are) only as good as your actions rather than your words. Book learning meant little compared to practical experience and respect had to be earned. On top of all this, I was a single young woman. As I'd already seen, perceptions were harsh and there were more questions than answers in the minds of would-be employers. Was I physically up to the job? Was someone without a farming background ever going to know his or her trade? Is a young woman on the farm going to district the other workers? Or take my husband into her bed? That last one was a pretty big consideration for farmers' wives! In August 1979 as I travelled to start my first 'proper' job, acceptance as a professional seemed a very long way off indeed.

The company of cows is a very apt title for this part of my story. Even now, years later, and long after the time when farm animals were my charges, I like to have their images around me as I work in my kitchen. The doe-eyed passivity of the Friesian cow staring at me from my Aga pads, the reproduction close-up painting of a pair of sheep's faces in winter and an idealised painted scene of 'Daisy' the cow in her field reproduced on a tea towel. You might be forgiven for thinking I've gone daft or senile in my old age, but even now I find their images comforting and familiar like a circle of friends, or at the very least, acquaintances. Pondering that my need for, and connection to, farm

99

animals was borne from a deep sense of responsibility and love for the animals I looked after, tears well up and my chin caves in… I slump down on a stool that sits under the kitchen table and sob quietly to myself. Even after nearly forty years, the memories of my first job on a farm as a professional still have the power to move me to tears. As the months rolled by after starting at Wyddial Bury (I lasted twelve in total), the lack of meaningful human contact I experienced and the possibility that this might be my lot in life really got to me. It seemed like I wasn't a lost sheep that might be found, but more like an exile. The letters I'd received from college friends during my sandwich year dried up and I began to wonder whether they still remembered me. My siblings were making their own lives. In my huge wooden box of memories, I can find no letters from them either. Had my mother, Sarah and Adam as well as even the Oars, forgotten me? The dearth of correspondence from this period is like a long, deafening silence. Was it because I was suffering in a predicament of my own making that was too embarrassing to be discussed in the polite circles my family moved in? In my imagination I can almost hear my mother saying in answer to a guest's enquiry about me at a dinner party, 'Oh, yes, my youngest daughter, is, well, how should I put it? A farm labourer.' To which the answer might be, 'Oh, how interesting; she's bought a farm?' In answer to which there would be another embarrassed silence from my mother, followed by, 'Well, no, not exactly.' And the conversation would then move quickly on to someone's holiday in the Caribbean or an account of a riveting visit to the site in Mexico where Our Lady of Guadalupe mysteriously appeared.

The abundance of images of cows around my present home notwithstanding, on leaving college, I'd been keen to find a job with pigs or sheep to extend my knowledge; however, the job as a night milker at Wyddial Bury Farm caught my eye. I was propped up on a couch one evening munching a digestive biscuit and sipping a cup of hot chocolate during a stay with Adam to reprise my role as Aunty Plum with their latest arrival, Daisy, when I noticed the advert for a night milker and showed it to Adam who said, 'Wyddial Bury, that's near Buntingford, so only a few miles from here. Night milking, mmmh, that'll be tough going, I've never understood the point of three-times-a-day milking, it can impact the cows' wellbeing without much additional financial gain.

Ovarian transfer technology used in breeding our pedigree Friesians", well, that's cutting-edge stuff Plum, all good for your CV.'

As always, at least in my mind, Adam's was the definitive analysis, but there were other positive features. Buntingford is indeed only a relatively short journey by road from Radwinter where Adam had recently settled with Vanda and their new baby, Alice, so he could start as a vet with Mercer & Hughes in Saffron Walden. Buntingford was also close to our old family home in Hainested and the Oars. So it'd be like moving back into the vicinity of family and friends. Then there was professional interest. The advanced procedure of ovarian transfer was a technique that had only recently been developed in the late 1970s which, as Adam said, was all good CV fodder. So, there and then, I'd written my application and included a copy of the swish new curriculum vitae that my mother had painstakingly typed for me. About a week later, I was still at Radwinter when I got a positive reply and an invitation to an interview. So, mounting the yellow Honda 125cc motorbike I'd recently bought from Sam Oar, I headed over to Buntingford with a devil-may-care kind of attitude, 'I'll either get it, or I won't.'

Puttering along the familiar winding lanes, the wind had an autumnal feel to it, like the weather gods were in conference on when autumn should get her chance. For a change, finding the farm was easy, there was a glossy sign at the entrance of a long drive up to the yard confidently proclaiming Wyddial Bury Farm as the home of "one of England's finest herds of pedigree Friesians". For the interview, I'd been asked to come to the Manor House, so I continued on along the lane and pulled up at a substantial Georgian-style house with obligatory portico complete with antique boot scrapers. I rather nervously pulled on the doorbell chain and waited.

Expecting that a butler or maid might open the solid wooden door with a flourish, Mr Hodge surprised me from behind, having emerged, not from the front door, but from the farm office next to the house.

'Miss Best?' I must've visibly jumped, because he apologised. 'The interview's over here in the farm office, I've got the farm manager, Mr Guest, with me. He'd be your boss if you get the job.'

Mr Hodge's posh home counties accent was in contrast to the farm manager's lilting rural Essex version, when he spoke at all in the presence of his master. During the interview, it was made clear that the night milker was pretty much a dogsbody and general factotum. When he finally got his turn to speak, Mr Guest outlined a punishing three-shift milking rota, five to nine a.m., three to six p.m. and eight to eleven p.m. with two nights off per week. In addition to milking, I'd be helping the herdsman, Mr Wright, with the calf rearing. No mention of high-tech procedures involving embryo transfer, just a lot of early mornings, graft, mud and cow manure, but what did I expect? I accepted the job without hesitation when it was unexpectedly offered to me on the spot. During my journey back to Radwinter through the winding lanes and open parklands of Hertfordshire, I processed what I'd just agreed to. For my mergre hourly wage I was going to work ten-hour days with little or no time off. But it was a start, and at the time, I was contented.

Arriving back at the house, I almost bumped into Adam on his way out the back door.

'Hello Plum! Look, Daisy's asleep and Vanda has settled down for a nap. I heard you returning, so I thought, let's sneak out to the tavern for a pint before supper?'

As we entered the public bar, a traditional handover was taking place as the old geezers who'd been nursing their half pints all afternoon in desultory conversations about the state of the economy, the wisdom of having a woman prime minister and the lengthening dole queues, were being replaced by a better heeled set of people fresh off the train from their office jobs in London popping in for 'a swift one' before surrendering themselves to the inevitable routine of family life in one of the poshed-up barn conversions that were springing up everywhere. So, just as the daytime mainstay of warm ale was being replaced with orders for vodka Martini and large glasses of chilled Pinot Grigio, Adam bought us the first of several pints of Abbot.

'Well Plum, how did it go?'

'I got the job; they offered it to me there and then!'

'Well, they knew the right candidate when they saw her, cheers!' As our glasses clinked, I stole a glance at my brother. He was relaxed, engaged in our conversation and in a jovial mood; a condition that was rare then and became increasingly so as the years wore on and the strain of being on call as a vet took its toll.

Perhaps keen to find out more about a potential customer, Adam said, 'So, did you find out anything more about the embryo transfer system they have up there? It's still a pretty new technique, but it's already having an impact on breeding.'

Then, for a brief moment, Adam veered into a world where breeding success could be enormously improved by increasing the production of high value animals by bringing together their ova and semen *in vitro* and transferring them into the uteruses of surrogates. When he finally looked back in my direction, I think it suddenly clicked.

Pausing for a moment he said, 'Well, I'm sure you'll get a chance to find out more about it once you've learnt the ropes.'

I think, for a moment, Adam had briefly mistaken me for a fellow student at vet school discussing the latest advances in reproductive science because our conversation changed course after that. At a time when his sisters idolised their big brother, I felt like I'd disappointed him in some way. We both worked with animals, but there is a million miles of social and economic distance between the status held by a newly qualified vet and that of a newly qualified farm worker. It's a bit like talking about a familiar subject using different dialects of the same language, one glitzy and fascinating like American English and the other stoic and practical like the one used by the old boys who'd just shuffled out of the pub as we arrived. Stumbling outside hours later, we managed to navigate our way back to Adam's house. I must've collapsed on the couch because the next I knew, Adam rushed past me on his way to work and I turned over and tried to make believe it wasn't morning; the Abbot's benediction was having its predictable effect!

Chapter 12
Reality hits home

I'd been waiting for the luminescent hands of Big Ben to crawl around to four thirty a.m. for the last two and a half hours, but his raucous ringing still made me jump out of my skin. Milking must start promptly at five a.m. Pedigree cows have an uncanny knack of knowing the time, so I knew they'd be standing by the gate for me to take them into the parlour; a bit like royalty, they can't be kept waiting. Dairy staff live for their cows! Pitch black and freezing on a Sunday morning. I wiped a rime of ice that had formed out of condensation from my breath off the inside of the window and propped myself up on one elbow before progressing to stage two, legs over the side of the planks of wood and thin foam mattress that constituted my bed in my latest of caravan residences. The thinness of the foam and the hardness of the boards had conspired to force me out of sleep at the appropriate moment, which is a blessing in disguise; if I was sleeping in a comfortable bed, I'd never have found the willpower to leave it! Despite being freezing cold, a strong scent of sweat and body odour wafted up from the depths of my bedclothes; I made a mental note to take a bath at some point during the day. But why bother? I'm not going anywhere.

I'd just turned twenty-one and I hadn't even been able to celebrate in the way most people would have done for such an auspicious birthday. If I needed further evidence that I'd been forgotten about it was the lack of birthday cards sitting on my little bedside shelf that served as my credenza. I say none, but what I mean is one, from Adam, he always remembered, but he never seemed to have any idea what to write in birthday cards, or any cards really. This one carried a photograph of a sheep wading through snow, with a typically arcane inscription, "*I know the snow hasn't arrived yet, but once your birthday's been and gone, I always know that it's not far around the corner. Happy birthday Plum!*" I say arcane, but I actually knew what he was alluding to. Basically, since my birthday is so close to Christmas, I, like many others in the same boat, suffered the disappointment of 'birthday-cum-Christmas present syndrome', which always used to infuriate me. It meant that I'd get a token present at Christmas whilst everyone else was ooh-ing and aah-ing as large, substantial-looking gifts were distributed from under the Christmas tree. My ignominy was further intensified when we went over to the Oars for Boxing Day drinks to find Sam showing off his portable cassette player or Sophie playing with her Cher doll with real 'growing' hair. However, one year the Oars/Bests got what can only be described as a pejorative Christmas present. In the '70s, when mobile phones that you could physically lift never mind carry in your pocket were still years away, Adam and Ben came up with an ingenious way of communicating between households, a WWII British surplus field telephone complete with an old-style handset and a little handle to turn and make the call receiver's phone ring. If you've ever watched Alistair Maclean's movie, Where Eagles Dare it's like the radio used by Richard Burton's character to call headquarters with his eponymous call sign, "*Broadsword calling Danny-boy!*" We girls were allowed to use it for a short while before the handsets disappeared up to the boys' rooms and were never seen again.

Drifting back to the present, I noticed there was no card from Sarah, although I was sure I'd get a belated and apologetic one at some point, and nothing from my mother. I thought to myself, 'Stop it! Deborah, you're beginning to sound like a spoilt brat.' But recollections of past birthdays and Christmases all added to my feelings of injustice and general malaise. Then my body jolted in unison with the sudden realisation that my boss, dear old Mr Wright, would be returning from his fortnightly weekend off, which of course meant that I'd worked the whole weekend on my own. Not that it made much difference, I'd actually been volunteering for additional work at weekends to fill the time. No, it was the 'official' handing over ceremony I'd have to go through when Mr Wright inspected what I'd been doing and checked that everything had been done to his satisfaction. It was a bit like kit inspection in the army where the drill sergeant goes around the men's living quarters checking for dust with his white gloves, or worse, like a room inspection by the nuns back at convent school. Wright will always find something wrong; it was almost like a proverb. There was always tut tutting and a long, humiliating lecture to go through.

A mid-December morning awaited just beyond the flimsy portal of my caravan, and despite two cups of very strong tea, I stumbled down the rickety steps and almost fell headlong onto the frozen ground. Torch in hand I followed its uncertain beam towards the cowsheds and dairy. Low mooing, grunts and the sort of shuffling sounds made by large, expectant animals could be heard in the complete silence. Down at the field gate, the old matriarch Genevieve, number 56, was the first in line. As usual, she was backed by her staunch followers, numbers 52 and 67, Gemma and Jemima. Their warm breath with added slimy drool briefly warmed my hand as I unlatched the gate and let the cows walk along the walled entrance lane towards the parlour. Getting ahead, I got the lights on and the cows headed towards their customary stalls; they really are creatures of habit. As I washed their teats and attached the cups of the humming milk pump to the cows' udders, muscle memory kicked in and I engaged autopilot. But unlike many other milking staff, I never shut off completely. Instead, I keep my senses alert and ready to react to a swollen, overly sensitive or overheated teat that could indicate the start of mastitis; number 44 had the tell-tale signs. I switched the little lever in the milk line so her milk went to a receiving bottle rather than into the tank. 'No milk from you today old girl!' And I made a mental note to ensure that she went on the list to receive a dose of antibiotics. With my first batch of 'customers' hooked up to the milking machine, for some reason a strange euphoria compelled me to dance wildly around the parlour with an imaginary partner. The cows looked up from munching on their concentrates, their eyes following me, as I waltzed around the parlour, like appreciative bystanders watching from their tables. By the time I'd milked the herd, cleaned down and tidied up, I emerged into a slate-grey morning complete with chilling wind and scudding dark clouds; I could sense the bite of snow in the air. I'd kept the gas heater in the caravan on whilst I was out, so I had a warm fug to return to for breakfast. I cooked some pancakes from some mix I'd stored in the fridge and had them with syrup. For the umpteenth time I studied the label on Tate & Lyle's Golden Syrup tin and read the inscription under the illustration, "*a dead lion with a swarm of bees.*" I'd always wondered why T&L had used such a strange scene until someone told me its biblical origins from the story of Samson in the Old Testament, "*Out of the strong came forth sweetness.*" I should have known that coming from a convent school; mind you, I did fail Religious Studies.

Whilst I was girding my loins and preparing for a freezing fifteen-minute motorbike ride over to Buntingford village stores to pick up supplies before they shut at noon, there was a 'knock, knocking', the sound of an unsubstantial caravan door being lightly struck by tentative knuckles. Such a door needn't demand that a visitor should wait for the occupant to answer, if you live in a caravan, you're the bottom of the heap; a visitor of higher status simply needs to knock and enter. But my visitor knocked and waited, so I knew such a visitor must believe they were of lower status than even me.

Opening the door carefully outwards, I found Christine standing a little distance away having left a little Tupperware box on the step. I opened the lid and said, 'Oh how lovely, fairy cakes! That is so, so kind of you. Thank you!'

'I made them for the kids' school packed lunch boxes and I had a few left over.'

Christine turned to go, but I stopped her.

'Please, don't rush off, come on in for a cuppa, I'm just having another before I go out.' She hesitated, looking round to check for watching eyes, then made a decision and quickly entered. At first, I busied myself with the stove, mugs and teabags, but when I finally joined Christine at my little foldout table, I could see that her raven black fringe and long straggly hair were covering a new crop of bruises. Wordlessly, I reached over and touched her hand and she clasped mine like she was drowning and needed some help to stay afloat. Christine's story was one that I became familiar with over my years in farming, namely, the one about the beaten and abused wife. In Christine's case, she was married to Andrew Geddes, a tractor driver and a Scot from Renfrew. I frequently talked to and worked with Geddes as he scraped out the parlour and the cowshed; his expert use of the big rubber scraper blade regularly saved me many additional hours of scrubbing. We had the bond of workaday friendship that often develops between people in a similar position in the pecking order: Geddes and I occupied the bottom of the heap at Wyddial Bury. After he'd scraped out the shed, or if we met in the yard during a break, we'd chat together. He was affable and friendly, but I could always sense the demon rage in him lurking just under the surface just waiting to be evoked by a wrong word or misplaced comment.

Looking back over at Christine, I could hear a crunching sound and I feared that the toast I'd made for her was a little bit too hard.

'Sorry, that's my fault; I've left it in the toaster too long. I've got some crumpets if you'd prefer?'

I always loved listening to Christine's Scottish brogue, but on this occasion, she dropped her eyes as though ashamed.

'It's my jaw, it's been broke a few times you see and it's not mended up properly...' Her words hung in the air for a moment, waiting for a response.

'I'm so sorry... I should have realised...' It's then that I noticed that the sound of sobbing had joined the quietness and gentle rushing of wind outside. Christine had taken my hand again and we sat opposite each other crying for a few moments. Considering the hard life she had, her humanity was, and still is, an inspiration to me.

Returning from the village store a couple of hours later, I picked up my towel and wash bag from the caravan and headed over for my bath in the farm manager's house. On the way, I checked in on the calves to see if they had enough concentrates and bumped into Geddes as he came into the shed to do some scraping out. He said, 'it looks like the weather's turning. We could get some snow before Christmas at this rate. Mind you, it'll be mushy English snow that'll no doubt be gone b'teatime.' He chuckled to himself and cocked an eye at my wash bag. 'You off to Guesties' house to do your ablutions? I'd rather not wash at all than have to put up with the snooty Mrs all high and mighty manager's wife.' The last few words were spat out. 'Take care of yourself.' Then, as Geddes turned and headed off towards the little tractor that was hitched permanently to the scraper blade, I wondered if he'd seen his wife walking to or coming from my caravan, and if he had, he'd no doubt ask her about what we talked about. Oh God! I fervently hoped I hadn't put her in danger of getting another beating. These melancholy thoughts chased me towards the Guests' front door. It was then my turn to tentatively knock on the door of the manager's more substantial portico. 'Come, come!' Mr Guest's words, uttered in a tired and resigned way, met my ears from behind the closed door shortly before it was swiftly opened.

'Is it okay for me to take a bath Mr Guest?'

'Yes, yes, we agreed, every Sunday afternoon, didn't we?' He was talking to me as though I was a complete moron. I passed him, entered the hall and trudged up the stairs turning right onto the landing and left into the small visitors' bathroom. I latched the door closed and quickly started taking my clothes off while I ran the bath. Steam filled the room and I imagined it must be a bit like a steam room at one of those fancy spas Sarah used to talk about. As I carefully eased myself into the bath, I felt a searing pain in my thighs. Jumping back up, I looked down and examined the rash of large, angry swellings on my thighs and buttocks. I've always had fleshy thighs, but my weight had diminished significantly recently in response to the exhausting onslaught of three times a day milking so I felt a bit aggrieved that the fates had chosen this particular moment to send me a fresh crop of chilblains. I ran cold water into the bath and had to make do with a short lukewarm soak rather than the long hot one I was looking forward to. I quickly dried my body, and whilst doing so, noticed that the chilblains were pulsating, or were they winking at me?

Fully dressed, with towel over my shoulder, I swooshed open the door and a cloud of steam followed me out. There, at the head of the stairs stood Mrs Guest.

'Well, I hope you've dried up the tiles in there. You left quite a mess last week!' Mrs Guest's look of disdain was so perfect that I wondered if she'd practiced it in front of a mirror in order to impart to the beholder the maximum amount of shame. Not finding any words to say in reply, I crept back down the stairs and quietly shut the front door. I was angry with myself that I'd not thought of a sufficiently cutting reply. Checking my little wristwatch, I noticed it was three thirty p.m. Time to rev up the milking parlour and for the little weekend handing over ceremony with Mr Wright. At the entrance to the parlour, I was met by his florid face framed by long salt 'n' pepper sideburns. His forehead was already creased into an expression of weariness in readiness for my report on all the misdemeanours and wrongdoings I'd made during his weekend off.

So, without further ado, I started my report.

'I think the most important thing is that number 44 looks like she might have mastitis in one of her quarters, so she'll need a shot of antibiotics.'

At this, he stopped me short with the outstretched palm of his hand.

'You don't need to tell me what to do to treat mastitis. More importantly, did you ensure that her milk didn't go into the tank?'

I simply replied, 'Yes.'

'Is that a yes, I let it go into the tank, or a yes, I threw the milk away?'

'Yes, I threw it away.' And so it went on for five or ten minutes, but it felt like half an hour and I was drained afterwards when I walked over to the parlour for the afternoon milking.

Much, much later after the night milking, I was suffering a lower than usual mood as I skirted around the slurry lagoon where all the dairy runoff found its way from the sheds after Geddes' diligent scraping. As I passed by, the moonlight danced on the calm surface of the lagoon and for a moment, it looked almost inviting, like one of those hotel swimming pools you saw in magazines advertising package holidays to Costa this, or Costa that. Only it wasn't and I was looking into a stinking cesspit after having worked my fifth week in a row without a break. If this was my life, how was I going to be able to bear it! My family didn't seem to care. I felt so alone. In the midst of this reverie, my feet had somehow carried me to the edge of the pit. A false slip at night down the steep, slick sides, it would be impossible to climb back up and there would be nobody to hear my shouts for help. I'd literally drown in cow shit. A shiver went up my spine at the thought of such an end. I stepped back from the abyss and walked back to my caravan.

***

"*Learning to do, doing to learn, earning to live, living to serve. The Future Farmers of America provide opportunities for young men and women for further training and to gain valuable new experience in the most important industry on earth, agriculture.*" The quotation and impressive yellow and blue badge of the FFA Organisation caught my eye in the Guardian Weekend Supplement where a piece had been written extolling the virtues of this international organisation. At the bottom of the advertisement there was a form you could cut out, fill in and send off to receive more details. The FFA was offering a twelve-month exchange programme for OND and HND level college graduates wanting to take the opportunity of further practical training and academic study to enhance their careers. I stared at the FFA's insignia and the photograph of young, smiling graduates, their teeth gleaming from happy smiling faces. That could be me. I needed a new opportunity, I needed a change, and this looked like an escape route. I filled in the form and posted it the next morning.

Part 5
A future farmer in America

Chapter 13
Armada

I love the way that town signs in the US always give you some vital statistics so at least you know what you're getting into before entering. In the case of Armada, Michigan, then with a population of one thousand two hundred, it was *"The small village with a big heart"*. And in 1980, that was about all I could find out about my would-be home for the next eight months, but as a stateside newbie, I needn't have worried about a lack of information about America. The dearth of letters and communication that had depressed me so much during my time at Wyddial Bury turned into a deluge once everyone found out I was going to America. Then as now, and you're a Brit, if you say *"I'm-a going to America"* to friends, family and just about anyone you meet on buses or trains and just happen to say you're going to the US, they will bombard you with a million useless facts and figures they've picked up from the news, the TV, the radio or simply overheard in the pub. America is the biggest, the wealthiest, the most vulgar, the most trigger-happy... the list goes on and on, but always with the words, 'the most' as the prefix to what follows. America is, quite literally, the author of its own cliché and a place where you can experience déjà vu around just about every street corner. The reason for this? Hollywood. You're walking in downtown San Francisco and you think to yourself, these steep crossway streets look familiar, the reason? They've been bumped over during so many bad guy/good guy car chases from Steve McQueen in Bullitt through Clint Eastwood's Dirty Harry and beyond, that people have lost count. It's America's self-styled clichés that are the reasons why everyone wants to bombard you with stuff they know about it. On top of useless facts, I'm part of a family that has quite a few friends in the US, so I was also provided with a huge, long list of people I ought to go and see from Cape Cod to the Bahamas; which, by the way, has never been part of the US, but it was, until 1973, part of colonial UK, but is still part of the Commonwealth. Phew!

This tumult of activity and breathless communication was all triggered when an airmail letter from America addressed to me plopped through the letterbox of my mother's new base in Pembrokeshire, The Grange, in Little Haven. The itinerant lifestyle I was leading at the time is starkly highlighted by the fact that she had to re-address said letter and forward it to my brother's home, Church View Cottages, in Radwinter. Interestingly, both Esme and Adam were, at that time, renovating ramshackle properties. In Adam's case, he was doing it himself, bought it for a song and subsequently made a fortune when he sold it, whilst my mother was struggling to afford renovations and sold it at a huge loss.[21] So, the winners and losers of Margaret Thatcher's property-owning democracy were, therefore, neatly encompassed within a single family. In fact, I still have the fateful letter and envelope that I received from Ohio State University on July 23rd 1980 — I hold my hands up, I'm an inveterate hoarder! So, as I write this, I notice that, by chance or by design, the postage stamps used on the envelope hint at another juxtaposition, this time of American political history and values. First in the line are two 6^c stamps carrying the image of the warlord President Ike Eisenhower followed by two 25^c stamps carrying the head and shoulders of the great social reformer and abolitionist, Frederick Douglass. The stamps with Eisenhower's image are cheap and won't get you far, whilst Douglass' are more valuable and will get you further, mmmh, is my fevered political brain over thinking this? Anyway, it was the contents that were important! Briefly put, I'd been accepted onto The Ohio State University Agricultural Intern programme. Hooray! There would be an eight-month placement on a farm and three months at Ohio State University. But there was a catch, well, two catches. The first was I'd be an intern, so, apart from some pocket money, I wouldn't get paid and the second, I'd been assigned to a dairy farm in Armada, Michigan. I was disappointed, as I'd expressly hoped to be placed on a beef or sheep farm, but as the programme coordinator pointed out in the letter, the farmer, Roy Jacob and family, "[were] *very impressed with your experience in dairy farming and hope that you will be interested in their offer*." You could see their point though, my CV at that time shouted

---

[21] Albeit with a hefty 75% grant from the local council as the house was deemed to be of "conservation value"!

cows, cows, cows!

***

Mamma Mia! One too many pints of sultry Abbot Ale with Adam in The Radwinter Tavern the night before was not the right way to prepare for an early-morning 'redeye' flight to Detroit, Michigan, but that was how it was. Using the flying analogy, my dear brother, so often our sensible bulwark against flights of fancy that might end in disaster or economic ruin, suffered a rare flight of fancy himself and malfunctioned as a sober guide to his younger sister. When he should have been preparing her for a four a.m. wakeup call and himself for the two-hour dash around London (no M25 in those days to 'speed' you around the city) to Heathrow Terminal 3 and my eight a.m. flight, neither of us was capable of this feat of timing in the morning, so Vanda stepped nobly into the breach and got me there instead. Never the most confident of drivers, Vanda seemed quite up for the task having been up all night with baby Daisy who, as was her habit at the time, had cried solidly all night. Vanda seemed quite excited by the prospect of fighting her way through rush-hour traffic, or was it that she was suffering from a psychosis through lack of sleep? By the time we were passing through the dingy concrete valley leading to Terminal 3, I'd managed to face-slap myself into some kind of consciousness and felt ready to lug my army issue kitbag out of the car and into departures. After a fond farewell to Vanda, who was immediately swept away by the scrum of hackney cab drivers, I headed off towards the swarm of people.

For the princely sum of £160, which I'd saved from my measly pay-packets and hours of overtime, Pan Am provided me with a cramped window seat at the back of a Boeing 747 near the toilets, which I was glad of, up until the point that a very rotund businessman arrived, nodded in my direction, plonked himself beside me and promptly went to sleep with his hulking shoulders pinioning me against the fuselage! I spent the entire flight slowly absorbing sweat from my neighbour's shoulder. Having spent several hours in the squalid conditions of super-economy class, it's always something of an eye-opener to pass by the posher seats towards the front and observe how the legroom, menus and service gets incrementally better as you move forward. Finally, as I neared the exit and passed through the detritus of first class and the piles of empty Babycham bottles strewn on the floor, I managed to catch a glimpse of the 'stairway to heaven', or the carpeted, spiral steps leading up to the sky bar. My nostrils filled with a heady waft of perfumed air mixed with the faint tang of gin, presumably coming from the cocktail lounge. Not that I'm in the least bit jealous you understand. It's just that it always amazes me how much luxury airlines manage to pack into such a short time and a small space. Mercifully, the connecting flight to Detroit from Chicago was fairly empty and I could stretch out onto an empty seat next to mine. Arriving at Detroit Metropolitan in the mid-afternoon, the first thing to hit me, quite literally, was the heat and humidity. The second thing that hit me was, oh my God, I'm going to have to do hard physical work in this heat! Checking my diary and the notes I'd made on the journey, I knew I needed to catch a bus to a place called Gratiot. From there, I'd be met by one of the Jacob family for the drive over to Armada and the farm out on Ridge Road. It proved remarkably easy to find the right bus, a number 34 D-DOT (Detroit Department of Transport) bound for Gratiot swished open its mid-section doors, I threw my kitbag into the luggage rack and walked down the aisle to find a seat. Situated not far from the Great Lakes, I imagined that Armada might be at least quite close to huge forests and the wild frontier, so I was expecting some spectacular scenery, maybe even a glimpse of a bloke looking something like Davy Crockett riding by wearing a raccoon on his head.

I found a seat beside a woman travelling with her young daughter. When we started passing a lake, I asked whether it was Lake Huron. 'No darlin' Huron's about a two or three hour drive from here honey!' And then I had my first of hundreds of conversations in the US that started with, 'Are you from England?' When I replied that I was, the woman was awestruck and asked whether Diana and Charles were going to get married in a way that suggested I might have an inside track on the upcoming nuptials. I disappointed her there, but was able to confirm that I had, at least, seen the queen even though I wasn't personally acquainted. I suppose if you live in a nation of two hundred and eighty, or so, million people, the UK must seem rather colloquial by comparison, so surely everyone must know everyone else! However, by the time the urban sprawl of Detroit had finally dissipated and we got into the countryside proper, I'd begun to accept that Davy Crockett and his ilk had left years ago and in place of the wild frontier, somebody had planted endless fields of corn that went on to the horizon and when it wasn't corn, it was ripening wheat or soybeans; I was obviously visiting Michigan one hundred and fifty years too late!

As we arrived at a row of long bus-stands at Gratiot bus terminal in Ithaca, I spotted a silver-haired lady standing next to a large light blue and white Ford utility wagon opposite the Detroit stand watching passengers getting off the bus. I reckoned she fitted the description of an American farmer's wife I'd conjured in my imagination, so I walked over to her and said, 'Mrs Jacob?'

The lady smiled, 'You must be Debbie! Welcome to Michigan!' She took my bag and deftly swung into the load bed of the ute like it was a hay bale. 'You must be exhausted. I won't be offended it you get some sleep, it's a one-hour drive over to Armada.'

But I was too excited to sleep. We left Ithaca fairly quickly, and rode out of town on a gun barrel straight highway, passing huge corn fields interspersed with wheat and what must have been alfalfa and soybean. As it was now mid-August, tracts of land outside the radius of the circular irrigation pivots were parched and devoid of colour. A few beef cattle were visible outside and clusters of huge grain elevators and long, low barns suggested that most, if not all, livestock was kept indoors due to the heat. Much of the time, the only sign that farmsteads existed at all was the occasional post box, either on its own or clustered together in a little group like they'd sprouted there on their own.

The early evening sun cast a golden light on the white and grey clapperboard buildings as we coasted down the quiet main street of Armada, passing a bar and a restaurant or two, but literally, that was it. 'Yep, there ain't much to Armada, but it's got mostly what we need. There's a couple of bars and some nice little homey places to eat like Papa's and Chaps on East Main Street and the Tivoli there does a decent Pizza to dine-in or takeaway. Then there's the Kozy Corner Saloon on West Main Street, so between East and West Main Streets, you can make quite a night of it!' She chuckled at her own joke: I liked her already.

Eating breakfast one morning in a cosy nook in a corner of the kitchen a few days after arriving at the Jacobs' farmstead, I had one of my first stateside déjà vu moments! Not the Hollywood thing (they don't do big budget movies about Michigan) no, I mean the whole farming family hierarchy thing. To use the American vernacular, farms, like corner hardware stores in the US, are mostly a mom-and-pop outfit. Mr Roy Jacob was at the apex, he's the farmer. Then there's Mrs Genevieve Jacob, or Mrs J, she's the farm wife. Then there's the son, Jack, he's third in line until he takes over when Pop dies. Then there's the farm workers and finally the migrant workers; that was me plus a Polish guy called Dimitri and two young German women called Krystal and Annetta. Don't ask me how or why there should be so many German women with an urge to work on a farm in upstate America, but it seemed to be not unusual at the time. The people that don't figure in this line-up are the Jacobs' three daughters, Helen, who lived with her husband, Dane, on the shores of Lake Huron, Patty, who lived with her partner in Detroit and Angela, the youngest, who was studying economics at Ohio State University. I never met Patty, but I got the impression that she was a bit of a black sheep. Being the lost sheep in my family, I'm sure we'd have had a lot in common if we ever did meet! Whilst I was pondering the fact that the farming status quo had successfully made it across the Atlantic with the first white settlers pretty much fully intact, my eye fell upon a neat stack of back issues of the Farm Wife News that crowded the kitchen counter-top next to the stove where I guessed Mrs J spent a lot of her time. Intrigued, I opened an issue sitting on top of the pile and skimmed through an article extolling the virtues of peeling fruit for canning and another on what farm wives can do to 'handbag' the US President (when I arrived, it was still the peanut-farming Jimmy Carter) on various issues relating to farming, like damaging regulations curtailing the use of certain useful pesticides and opposing irrigation limitation. A lot of these issues sounded like the sort of thing a farmer, i.e., her husband, would be saying in any case if they could be bothered to take the time to lobby their senator. From this, I deduced that a farm wife's role in life is, like Dolly Parton extols in her famous song, [to] "Stand by Your Man", which is, no doubt, still a firm favourite on both sides of the Atlantic!

So, if the farming hierarchy turned out to be the same as the UK, and I was at the bottom of it, what were my duties? The Jacobs' operation was, in essence, a giant zero-grazing unit. This means that the cows stay in sheds all year round and have their food and water brought to them and their effluent cleared away. Why, you might ask, in the hard-nosed world of agribusiness, do we offer such a pampering service to cows? Do we even offer to bring them their slippers and help them on with their overcoats? Well, overcoats for the cows aren't a bad idea given the severity of the weather. Michigan, in common with other neighbouring states, Ohio, Indiana and Illinois, has an annual temperature differential summer versus winter, that's a staggering sixty degrees Celsius. This isn't quite as severe a differential as you might experience on, say, Mars (-125 ^{0}C versus 20 ^{0}C) but it still has a potentially significant effect on the physical condition and productivity of livestock, and people for that matter! It's for this reason that, on average, dairy cows in the Midwest spend at least half of their time indoors. In the case of the Jacobs' farm, they'd opted for a fully housed approach for their one hundred and fifty cow Holstein dairy herd, which meant that the three hundred acres of land they farmed was mostly used to produce the fodder (corn and alfalfa silage) needed to get the cows through the year. Their operation ran with very few farmhands. Whilst Mr Jacob spent most of his time tractor driving, cultivating, harvesting and managing the fodder crops, my time was allocated exclusively to milking in the morning and afternoon, interspersed with cleaning and other maintenance tasks in between. Dimitri helped Roy with cultivations in the field and also did the scraping out and other machine-based work around the dairy. The Jacobs' young son looked after the calf rearing, Mrs J kept the books and did a part-time job in Armada, whilst Annetta and Krystal did various odd jobs around the farm, including helping me in the dairy.

With mechanised feeding via an auger-based system, a walk-through herringbone milking parlour (it's a bit like a cow version of a drive-through McDonald's) and little or no need to go out on the field and get the cows in for milking, you might think this was a breeze, but you'd be wrong! The reason? The fully automated feeding system was on its last legs and kept on breaking down. This meant that I quite often needed to manually shovel the feed out of the storage tank and onto a trailer and then shovel it back out again and into the troughs for the cows to eat. Other issues with a fully indoor system often made me worry about animal welfare. Apart from the fact that you were keeping animals indoors and away from the pleasures of the sun and the open air, the cows' feet would often get painful infections that led to lameness, so I'd constantly have a hoof-cleaning tool handy to check for foul-smelling foot rot. Leg infections associated with injuries were another problem for large animals living so close to each other. With so many infections around, the animals frequently required a dose of antibiotics. Therefore, since federal law prohibits milk from antibiotic-treated cows from entering the food chain, I had to keep my wits about me to ensure their milk didn't go in the tank. And woe betide any farmhand who suggested that we might get a vet in to look at this or that leg wound or bout of mastitis. Vets in the US were, and probably still are, on the same pay grade as brain surgeons in the UK! Adam should have moved to the US, he'd have been, quite literally, living in clover. So, with these, and so many other animal health issues to deal with (I won't go into problems with bovine respiratory disease in zero-grazing units) I often used to enter the barn on a stifling hot afternoon and hear the buzzing emitted from swarms of flies and smell the rank odour of foot rot and think to myself, this is not a humane way to keep animals. It was actually a bit like a prison and I was the prison guard. Just like prison, I had to ensure that the cows had some time outside in a small, enclosed exercise yard; however, coaxing some of the lame animals out for a walk was pretty challenging, and that was in the summer. In winter, the cows would just look at me and I could almost hear them thinking, 'not a chance! You're making us go out there for a walk in these conditions? You must be kidding!' On occasions like that, there was no way on earth that a sixty-kilogram woman was going to coerce a five-hundred-kilogram cow out into the yard if she didn't want to go!

Like the status quo, another similarity between farm work in the UK and the US related to time off: there wasn't any. In what little free time we did have, interns were requested not to travel away from the farm unless we had a member of the family with us. Thinking back, this was probably due to stipulations laid down by the US Department of Immigration who didn't like the idea of migrant workers sneaking off and potentially staying in America illegally. When we did go out, we had to have a member of the family with us, or we needed to make a special request to Ohio State University authorities if we wanted to leave the farm, even if it was to visit friends or family. So, trips out for interns were very rare and it sometimes felt that we, like the cows, were imprisoned on the farm.

Like an army, a farm runs on its collective stomach. Hard work requires calorie intake, and plenty of them. A forestry worker is said to have one the highest calorie intakes of any manual labourer. I would suggest that a woman shovelling tons of maize silage in and out of trailers all day can't be far behind! But I was in America, a country synonymous the world over with the excessive overconsumption of food. Surely in a place like that, you'd never go hungry? Wrong! It just happened that Mrs J was on a never-ending diet. This fact meant that portion sizes were drastically reduced, not just for Mrs J, but for everyone. On the first night, I came down after settling into the attic room that the Jacobs had kindly prepared for me, to a small plate on which had been placed two beef burgers, some lettuce and a couple of slices of bread. A similar plate had been provided to her husband and son, so it wasn't an assumption that a woman might have a smaller appetite. Mr J told me that they'd just slaughtered one of the cows, so the freezer was full of beef patties; why couldn't more of them have found their way onto my plate! From the get-go, I noticed that, after supper, Roy and Scott both went into the kitchen and got themselves a huge bowl of ice cream from a massive five litre tub. This was combined with an equally large bag of sweetened popcorn. In fact, I soon learned that this combination of ice cream and popcorn was Roy's top up ration and it was available twenty-four seven should I need a pick-me-up. Most times I just couldn't face it, but out of sheer starvation, I did occasionally join Mr J in a large bowl of popcorn, or three. If supper tended to be meagre, breakfast, at least, was good. We're told that breakfast is the most important meal of the day. For farm workers with four hours of solid work under their belts before nine a.m., it was a big deal. Thankfully, Mrs J saw the importance of a decent meal at breakfast time, so while she nibbled on a small bowl of Special K cereal, us migrant workers sat down for a diet-busting meal of cereal, pancakes with fried eggs and bacon, or pancakes with breakfast sausage, which was basically a cylinder of ground pork that'd been sliced into patties and fried on the griddle. Thoroughly stuffed, we'd waddle back to work. Lunch, also prepared by Mrs J, consisted of a couple of sandwiches that Weight Watchers would have been proud of — I basically starved all afternoon. So, when my dear sister Sarah quipped that I must be piling on the pounds under the onslaught of huge portion sizes and calorie-rich food, I surprised her immensely when I said I'd lost weight — I sent her a photograph to prove it!

Besides the availability of copious quantities of ice cream and popcorn, there was another culinary lifesaver, Polish sausage. Our Polish, slurry-scraping tractor driver, Dimitri, had a largish retinue of fellow countrymen as friends and they used to bring him a bewildering array of sausage on a regular basis. Visits to Dimitri's trailer for an after-supper feast of delectable sausages became a firm favourite with myself and the other two women. The great thing about cooked sausage is that you can just cram it straight in your mouth; however, after accidentally eating an uncooked sausage or two, I quickly learnt to recognise the Polish 'brutalny' (uncooked) and 'gotowany' (cooked). I also learnt several other sausage-related Polish words during these little midnight feasts; foreign languages are often learnt via osmosis on a need-to-know basis!

If rations at the farm were small, then surely, I could simply go into Armada and have a slap-up meal? Unfortunately, the Immigration Department lockdown thing made that difficult. However, I did get an early chance to check out the local food. As I'd arrived in summer, there were still a few agricultural shows and events being held in and around Armada. Shows, the world over, like our own cereals events that were organised by the British Home Grown Cereals Authority, are places where farmers (and farm wives) can meet, admire big machinery, see the latest tech and eat at the expense of the exhibitors. In a rare day out Krystal, Annetta and I were allowed off-farm to go to a tractor-pulling event. Since, under the guidelines of our internship, we weren't allowed to drive or leave the farm on our own, the Jacobs' seventeen-year-old son, Scott, acted as our chaperone and driver. Although Scott was a nice enough lad, I was rather glad that Annetta bore the brunt of his attentions so I was able to join Krystal in the back of the double cab ute, which meant I would have a chance to rubberneck out the window and have a natter. What I'd forgotten was that Krystal was a chain smoker, so by the time we arrived at the event, I was thoroughly kippered and smelt like an old ashtray. Intrigued to find out what tractor pulling involved, we used the combined force of our relatively diminutive female forms to push through the scrum of large beefy farmers lining the tractor-pulling track. We were in luck! Just at the moment we emerged from the crowd, a huge, black tractor called the 'Black Devil' was squaring up to the competition, an equally huge red tractor called 'Popeye'. On first appearances, the Black Devil looked like a drag racing car, but after a second glance, I could just about make out the form of what looked like a John Deere tractor with what might have been an F-111 jet engine sticking out of the back. We'd arrived during the end of the morning's event at the 'drag off', where competitors dragged heavily loaded sleds along a one hundred metre track. If all the competitors pulled the sled the whole way (called a full-pull) more weight was added to the sled until a winner emerged. I nudged Krystal and nodded over at Scott. He appeared to be mesmerised and it looked like his arm was inching its way around Annetta's shoulder, so we decided to leave them to it and hit the food stalls. Like escaped convicts (or convent schoolgirls) we were both starving through lack of sustenance due to Mrs J's Weight Watchers regime. The first thing that caught our eyes were 'elephant ears', huge sugar-coated elephant ear-shaped pastries. At just thirty cents each, even we could afford them. The smiling woman selling them gave us a paper bagful each for a dollar; we must've looked like we needed the calories! God, they were manna from heaven! Made from bread dough, fried and coated with cinnamon sugar, they had a delectable crunchiness and super sweetness, a bit like a large flat doughnut. The hit of sugar from five of those things gave us quite a high and we floated around the crowds for hours afterwards before Scott and Annetta, who seemed to have hit it off romantically, finally rounded us up. On that particular day, I'd have taken the chance of food over romance anytime!

***

Houses popping up everywhere like mushrooms! I thought it was the Netherlands that was supposed to be one of the most densely populated countries in the world! In what passes for open countryside, we drive past a patch of woods where there's a quaint little white clapperboard house, opposite that there's a rather grand-looking entrance sporting white gates with a picture of two mean-looking Doberman Pinschers and the word, 'private' underneath in large, red letters. Slightly further on, there's what appears to be a little suburban close with four smart new villas arranged around a small tarmac circle, and so on and on and on! The US is always touted as being over-endowed with wide open space with the few people living in its rural areas heroically battling the elements and wild animals to survive; however, this vision of virgin wilderness seems unfounded! In merrie England like a good story, villages and towns, especially in the country, have a beginning, middle and an end; they don't drag on for miles and merge into the next town or village. UK city, town and parish council planning committees may not be perfect and a few dreadful carbuncles make it through our planning system (T Dan Smith the corrupt Newcastle Council leader, to name one prominent example) but the regulations usually work so that we mostly have clear spaces between settlements.[22] Regulatory inertia in state planning departments from a time when space was plentiful and land was cheap seems to have blighted the US. As dear old Margaret Orensson pointed out in a letter to me in August 1980, *"[the] automobile has ruined America, doing away with tighter, smaller villages and towns [and has encouraged the construction of] dreadful shopping arrangements that spread like a disease all over America."* Margaret's little diatribe on US planning laws had been accompanied by a very welcome cheque for fifty dollars to *"help with expenses and to get yourself some decent food!"* My plan was to use the money to visit Margaret and Karl at their home in Wakefield, Rhode Island over Christmas, just a mere twelve-hour hop, skip and a jump from Armada by Greyhound bus.

I'm pondering the lamentable state of US civic planning whilst riding in the back of the Jacobs' huge double cab ute with Krystal. Annetta has stayed back at the ranch with Scott to hold the fort whilst

---

[22] During his time as leader of the, then Labour-controlled, Newcastle City Council in the 1960s, Thomas Daniel Smith, known as 'Mr Newcastle', set about the highly laudable task clearing the city's slums, replacing them with rather grand edifices, including the Eldon Square Shopping Centre and the Newcastle Civic Centre, that became Marmite icons, you either loved them or hated them! But Mr Newcastle was a flawed hero. After a much-publicised trial, he was sentenced to six years in jail for taking bribes from developers.

we're all enjoying a very rare trip out. I'm guessing there's more to Annetta's decision to volunteer to do my shift in the dairy than meets the eye. I'm in no doubt that sultry looks will be exchanged between her and Scott in the fetid confines of the cowshed. They're welcome to a romantic day shovelling cow manure; I'm on my first proper road trip!

Planning malfunctions and endless suburbs aside, as we enter Richmond (I'm starting to get used to encountering familiar English place names in weird settings) Mrs J remarks, 'Oh, there's Dane's old dental practice, Dental Care of Michigan.' To no one in particular she explained that, 'Ever since our daughter, Helen, married a dentist I keep seeing them everywhere! I do believe, I know more about the pros and cons of various dental plans than is rightly healthy!' She titters at this, but Mr J keeps his eyes on the road and appears to be in a rather uncharacteristically sullen bad humour.

On both sides of the Atlantic, my experience of farmers so far indicates that they absolutely hate being, (1) out of their comfort zone (which ends at the farm gates) and (2) dragged away from anxiously fretting over what needs to be done, what hasn't been done and what should be done if they could remember what it is. Basically, farmers will become anxious if they can't think of anything to be anxious about. Helen, the Jacobs' eldest daughter, was married to Dane Zemont, a senior partner in a dental practice in Port Huron. All I knew thus far was that they were recently married, had no kids, they'd just moved into a beachside villa near Lakeside State Park and they owned a speedboat. This all sounded rather thrilling and much more aligned with what I was expecting to see in America.

As we were travelling through the centre of Port Huron, Mrs J acted as our travel guide.

'Now, over on the right is one of the city's oldest buildings, Fort Gratiot and the lighthouse; built in the 1800s. It's still the base for the local coastguard.'

At the mouth of the St. Clair River, we finally got our first clear view of Lake Huron. Expecting something like Windermere in the English Lake District, the shimmering arc of Huron's waters stretched to the horizon looking more like an ocean than a lake; a fringing beach of golden sand completed the maritime illusion.

'It looks like the sea!' This rather banal observation was forced out of me by the sheer wonder of it.

'Yeah, it has tides and sometimes big hurricanes that can sweep away all this lakeside property in the twinkling of an eye!' Mr J said this with a certain relish in his voice.

The threat of tropical-style typhoons hadn't got in the way of the property developers making money though. Place names were all 'beachside' this and 'lakeside' that. I guessed that a moniker of 'behind the beachside' just didn't have the same appeal. So if you could get the merest smidgen of a view of the lake, even if it was reflected off your neighbour's front window, that was good enough to be lakeside. Upmarket houses sat on the actual lakeside at the end of long, relatively narrow lots to give the impression of a substantial drive through 'boundless' acres, whilst at the antithesis, crowds of lakeside condos or trailers huddled together in rows, each jockeying for a position that afforded the coveted lake view. Just before arriving in a little town called Lexington, we pulled onto a dirt track heading out towards the lake and through a stand of maple trees that were showing just a hint of the riotous colour they'd be showing off in the autumn. Ahead was a huge property partly hidden by trees with its own private beach. I thought, wow, dentists really do get paid well; however, before getting to its white gate posts, we turned left into the drive of a smaller property, still big with a view of the lake, but not palatial like its neighbour.

A smiling couple stood in the drive near their front door, and as we approached, he, Dane I supposed, waved us into a slot next to a large Chrysler sedan that looked superficially like a Rolls Royce.

'Great teeth'; more commentary from Mr J. One of the advantages of marrying a dentist, is the wife gets to have great teeth. I guess if she'd married a plastic surgeon, she'd have got...'

His wife, with a withering look and a wag of the head, cut Roy off short. As I got out, a large oval swimming pool glinted in the sun. I'd been advised to bring a bikini and now I was glad I did. The pool was slightly larger than the Oars' pool in Hainested, but having seen it being dug by calloused hand and sweat of brow by Paul and Jill with help from my father, I could appreciate how Irish navvies felt when they were given picks and shovels and told to start digging the London Underground! The help generously given to the Oars earned us Bests a free pass to use the pool whenever we liked, so in the end, as with most things, it was us children that reaped the benefit of our parents' hard work!

Helen stepped over to meet us as we got out of the car.

'You must be Debbie and Krystal! Come along in, we've got some cold drinks waiting for you. Mom says you're from England Debbie. We visited there, last fall; London was just the best! We're planning another trip in summer next year, so we'll be picking your brains on the best places to visit.'

In the corner of my eye, I could see Krystal was a bit put out by all the attention I was getting and no doubt thinking, 'well hi, I'm from Düsseldorf in Germany, nice to meet you too!' Still, neither of us could complain, we were both going to get a dip in the pool. Walking across the expensive-looking brick weave patio and through lavish sliding doors, we entered a chilled environment that harboured a strong scent of fresh leather and furniture polish.

I noticed that Dane had disappeared from view, and rather than join the chatter, he was mixing some drinks and letting his wife do the talking, so it was a bit of a surprise when he appeared suddenly in an armchair opposite where I was sitting alongside Krystal.

'How long are you guys gonna be with the Jacobs? Helen tells me it's pretty hard physical work, you guys must be pretty damn fit by now!' He chuckled at his own joke and we got the benefit of his gleaming molars. I thought to myself, God! I should move to the States and get a dental plan! I'm sure he could sort out my broken front teeth. In comparison, Brits' teeth look so yellow, like rats' teeth. I'm told it's down to all the tea and unfiltered woodbines we consume.

Despite my shyness, Krystal's mute silence compelled me to kick-start the conversation.

'You have a lovely view of the lake Mr Zemont! It reminds me of holidays on Lakes Windermere and Coniston in the English Lake District.'

Dane responded immediately as though I'd given him a cue to start a new topic of conversation.

'Well, by coincidence, a house around the lake just outside Lexington used to be the holiday home of a famous Brit author, Len

Deighton, when he lived in New York. I'm a bit of a fan of spy novels and I've got all his Harry Palmer books. I prefer Deighton's straight-talking, working-class Palmer to Fleming's swashbuckling James Bond any day!'

At that moment, I thought I'd unleash a secret weapon that I'd been told by Margaret always gets an American's undivided attention; fame.

'Well, funny you should mention Deighton, but my father was a film director with Granada Television. Although he didn't direct any of Deighton's films, he did do some work on a TV series of his spy novels, Game, Set & Match.'

I was getting through, Dane was listening intently!

'That is so cool! I'd love to meet your dad.'

'I'm afraid he died while I was still at school.'

Dane gave a sympathetic nod, 'Sorry to hear that.'

So as not to end on a low, I lobbed in my second secret weapon.

'The lake reminds me of the time that Dad filmed Donald Campbell's attempt at the water speed record on Lake Coniston.' Dane was mesmerised! 'He was filming on the day he died in that terrible crash. Dad was devastated, they were quite good friends.'

'That's incredible! Helen, did you hear what Debbie was saying about her dad? He filmed that famous speedboat crash in the English Lakes!' Mrs Zemont bustled over with a dish on which sat, what could only be described as, a large green confection topped with cream and glacé cherries.

At the sight of food, Krystal and I turned our heads like starving supplicants who were about to receive communion bread.

'I thought I'd make you a real American speciality, lime jello salad!'

Seeing our ravenous eyes locking onto the huge crystal bowl that'd been put on the table, Dane dropped his own surprise,

'Since your family has already been around speedboats, your gonna love what we've got lined up for you this afternoon! Waterskiing!'

Hardly paying attention to polite conversation, I'm sure neither of us heard what he said; however, I gathered that we were going to immerse ourselves in water, so, after stuffing ourselves with jello salad, basically a sickly-sweet concoction of jelly, cream cheese and whipped cream, we went upstairs to change. Rather disconcertingly, as soon as we'd been shown upstairs into a large bedroom to change, Krystal stripped completely naked and changed into her bathing costume rather than using the adjoining en suite bathroom. She then smiled politely, sat on the bed and waited while I did the same thing. Embarrassed, but not wanting to offend her by going into the bathroom, I tried doing the 'changing the bra under the blouse' thing, but gave up halfway through and I just turned away from her and changed as quickly as I could. I'd forgotten that the Continentals don't have our hang-ups about nudity. Suitably attired in our swimsuits and the towelling gowns that Mrs Zemont had provided, we emerged onto the patio and the blazing sun.

The two families were seated at a table under a large parasol where Mr J was holding forth, no doubt regaling everyone of some tale of farming daring do. By chance, we'd emerged just when he'd reached his punchline.

'If you can fall in love with a girl while you're looking inside her mouth, she's definitely a keeper! Another way of looking at it is, don't look a gift horse in the mouth... he did, and look what happened!'

Helen rolled her eyes.

'Oh Dad, let up already!'

For the second time that day, Mrs J looked scornfully over at her husband.

'Roy, you're such a tease, let up, you're embarrassing Debbie and Krystal!' Dane was laughing, but I could see he'd heard it all before a thousand times. His mouth was smiling, but his eyes fixed Roy with a disdainful stare; for a 'professional' like himself, the old farmer was clearly far too colloquial to be good company for him.

Our moment had come. We crowded into our respective cars and drove past the faux English manor house that sat in front of the Zemonts' villa. As if in answer to my unasked question, Dane nodded in the direction of the big house.

'Old money gone bad in the Great Depression and the family had to sell plots of land to make ends meet.'

With that cautionary tale of the often-bitter end, to overweening fortune seeking, we arrived at what I hoped wouldn't be our bitter end. A flash red and white speedboat with two large outboard motors attached to the back was moored to a little orange buoy bobbing a few yards offshore.

'Debbie, Krystal, we're gonna just watch you guys; neither of us are much good on water.' Roy and I'll take a walk around the lake. Enjoy yourselves!' With that, the Jacobs left us to our fate!

To get the show started I said, 'Well, who's first?'

Krystal shrugged and said, 'I've done a bit of water-skiing when I visited Greece. I'll have a go first if you like.' Then, seeing my reluctance, Krystal turned to me and said, 'It's a bit like skiing on snow, just bend ze knees and stay loose.'

'I've never skied on snow let alone water!'

We both turned towards a shout from the boat.

'Come on Debbie, Krystal, it'll be fun!' Dane was in his element, he'd got three young women in his boat and the sun was shining. As an added sweetener, two of the women had discoloured teeth, so they might even be potential customers, things couldn't be better.

After taking us for an exhilarating run around the little bay, we stopped and Dane explained to us what was going to happen.

'Once you've gotten the skis on, just drop over the side, sit in the water with your skis pointing straight up and allow the line to play out as I move forward. Once you're up, we'll open it up to 25 mph. It's a flat, calm day, so we could go up to 30 mph if you'd like to go faster!' Krystal and Helen skied singly and as a pair; they made it look really easy. We were doing about 30 mph with the women out back when Dane turned to me and shouted, 'Really, the hardest part is getting up, once you're going you'll be fine.'

After her turn, Krystal flopped down beside me in the boat panting hard. She removed a pair of little rubber overshoes and handed them to me with a smile.

'Bend ze knees!' And then she giggled.

Flopping over the side, having inserted my feet into the skis, I sat in the water letting the life vest buoy me up; so far so good! The line played out and I rose out of the water; the nuns at St. Cathy's would have been jealous, I'm finally going to be able to walk on water! Excitedly, I made a thumbs up sign, but Dane interpreted this as 'go faster!' Speed increasing; I tried to move to one side and away from the outboard wake. That was a bad mistake; I immediately pitched over and felt like the water was pulling my arms off. Rather terrified and feeling like I was drowning, I finally remembered to let go of the line. As Dane curled around, I checked myself over. Peering into the crystal clear, and surprisingly warm water, I noticed that my bikini bottoms had disappeared!

The sting of embarrassment had already reached my cheeks by the time that Dane drew alongside me.

'You all right honey, you pitched over pretty hard!

As Helen helped me into the boat, she noticed I'd lost my bottoms.

'Oopha! I'll get a towel. Don't look around Dane! I said, don't look around!' Helen playfully thumped her husband's shoulder with her fist. I then unclipped my life vest, and to my further embarrassment, my naked breasts flopped out along with my skimpy bikini top.

'Well, that's a first, losing both your bottoms and top! You Brits don't do things by halves!' Chuckling, and unabashed, Helen surveyed my breasts before they were enveloped in the towel. 'Well, *you* don't need the services of a plastic surgeon darl'n. I feel quite jealous! I've been wanting to go up a couple of cup sizes for a while, but Dane just says, more than a handful is a waste!'

Not to be left out of all the frivolity, both Helen and Krystal pulled down the top of their swimsuits, jiggled their breasts and burst into hysterical giggling just as Dane turned round and made like he was cupping Helen's breasts.

I couldn't believe how Helen and Krystal reacted to Dane's comments, seemingly without a care in the world. It was quite refreshing. In the UK, it's usually just the men talking about breasts but apparently, in the US, women get in on the act as well!

Chapter 14
Christmas in Rhode Island

Riding on a Greyhound bus speeding across America on a twenty-four-hour journey through the snowy planes of Ohio, Pennsylvania and Connecticut to Rhode Island, I was so excited to see my godmother, Margaret, and the Orenssons again. Margaret's generous gift of fifty dollars had meant that I had enough money to pay for the trip. "We're so eager to see you", she'd written in a letter I received from her with a birthday gift and a cheque. However, when I'd bidden farewell to Mrs J at the Gratiot bus station in the middle of a snowstorm, I never thought it'd be possible for the bus to leave Ithaca let alone cross nearly eight hundred miles of snowfields that would have made even a polar explorer like Captain Scott think twice. However, as if by magic, an armada of four-wheel drive utes had appeared out of nowhere with small snowploughs fixed to the front. Like a swarm of little black bees, they'd worked feverishly and surprisingly effectively all morning as we travelled east, clearing the county highways leading to the interstate. It was still touch and go though. Only once we'd got onto the Interstate 80 out of Cleveland, had I allowed myself to believe I was going to make it. The second week of the Christmas vacation, like the first, was as hallowed a time for the Orenssons as Christmas itself. A staunchly nuclear family, the Orenssons lived within a few miles of each other in Providence, Rhode Island. There was Margaret & Karl, then Sally who was married to Margaret's eldest son Steven, an academic who worked at Woods Hole Oceanographic Institution and finally, Margaret's younger son Peter, an up-and-coming lawyer (who sister Sarah thought was 'rather dishy'), married to Clara.

The Orenssons were a dynasty with Margaret at its head like a benevolent Don Corleone who called her family to her for Christmas. On more than one occasion she'd had to drag Steven off his scientific survey ship and away from his beloved oceanic studies in order to make the circle complete. Steven and Sally had a six-acre smallholding, where they kept chickens, pigs and vines. Although Steven spent much of his time at his studies that often took him out to sea, Sally was essentially a housewife and a new mother with aspirations for her family to be fully self-sufficient. Around the time of my arrival, the big talk was about getting a house cow and which breed would be suitable for the purpose. Sitting down after my first full day after arriving at the huge wooden kitchen table that sat at the epicentre of Sally's domestic world, I think I finally solved the mystery of why I went into farming! It was a dream based on self-sufficiency. I'd bought John Seymour's classic book as a present to myself whilst I was at WAC and had devoured it whole from cover to cover. This was at a time when Felicity Kendal and Richard Briers were entertaining the nation as the eponymous couple the Goods who'd turned their suburban house with three acres into a self-sufficiency heaven. Here at last in their home built by Steven and Peters' own hands, I knew that this was what I'd always dreamed about. As I sat at the table, I made a visual tour of the homely kitchen where I admired the wood fired range and stove, an impressive looking pantry and baby Sven sleeping peacefully in his cot.

I was just wondering how Steven and the 'dishy' Peter had manhandled the huge oak beams holding up the roof into position, when I became aware of six pairs of eyes staring intently at me.

'Well Debbie, we want to tap into your knowledge of cows and dairying.' Sally smiled and continued, 'Our burning question is not whether we should get a house cow, we're all agreed upon it, but what breed would you advise?'

If this'd been a question in the specialist subject round of the TV quiz show, Mastermind, it would have been a gift! That's because I'd only recently reread the section on purchasing a house cow in Seymour's book! I said, 'well... whilst the Friesian is a higher milk yielder, the smaller and docile Jersey produces higher milk solids fat content than a Friesian and is better-suited to once-a-day milking.' I could almost hear Magnus Magnusson's clipped reply, 'Correct!'

Sally was impressed

'Well, funny you should mention Jerseys, we were thinking the very same thing, and they're so cute!' Once the burning house cow question was out of the way, as if it was a reward, Sally produced a huge tureen of soup.

'Ta-dah! Since we've got a special guest, I thought you couldn't go back to England without trying a local Rhode Island speciality, clam chowder! And there's seven fishes pie to follow!'

My salivary glands leapt into action with such force, they almost hurt.

'This looks delicious Sally. You'll never guess what I got for Christmas dinner at the Jacobs', hotdogs!' There was a collective gasp at this piece of information.

Margaret wagged her head

'Well, I'm always saying that America's gone to the dogs, and this proves it!' Everyone laughed at Margaret's intentional or unintentional double entendre. 'You see my dear, America is totally enslaved to convenience. It's all convenience store living with no thought about the environment and sustainability.' Nods all around. 'It's like the three-legged stool, the US has one of the biggest economies on earth, that leg is strong, but the other two are weak. America has a huge population of poor people with little access to healthcare and a total disregard to the environment, especially when it comes to farming.' More nods. 'I'm guessing that the Jacobs in Michigan, who keep their cows in a barn all year long, pour fertiliser and pesticides on their land to keep up production.' Margaret turns and looks at me.

As the only professional farm worker in the room, I'm in a bit of a quandary on how to answer this. All my training so far demanded that efficiency was king, but it conflicted with my dreams of self-sufficiency. Finally, after much humming and hawing, I had to agree with them and hand Margaret the triumph of having the last word on the subject!

As Sally finally settled herself at the head of the table, she smiled at me. 'C'mon Debbie, we're all dying to know your family news.'

As the last Orensson to visit England, Steven took his cue.

'The last time I saw your mom and dad was when I was doing some post doc research at Southampton Oceanography Centre and stayed with them at their flat in London for a few days. I recall that I also met your brother and sister.' I suddenly felt a pang of jealousy. Why wasn't I there? Most likely I'd been left with the Oars or Granny so everyone could go gallivanting around London. I was the lost sheep then, and was the lost sheep still; would it ever change. 'I was so, so sorry to learn of your dad's untimely death.' The emotional tone in Steven's voice brought me out of my self-righteous indignation and back to the present. 'When I knew him, he was full of energy and charm; quite literally, the life and soul of any party. He had such hopes and dreams for a new career in feature filmmaking, and his Hummingbird Tree movie project. When such a vigorous and energetic person passes, it seems all the more tragic.'

Steven's emotions briefly got the better of him and I intervened.

'My mother was devastated by Dougie's death, but the family finances were in a terrible state. My mother sold the London flat and moved back to Quail Cottage. None of us wanted to admit it, but she'd become an alcoholic and finally moved to a new house in Little Haven.'

I could see Margaret nodding sadly next to me as she gave my shoulder a gently supportive squeeze and broke in

'Yes, and those sisters of hers in Little Haven wouldn't have been much help! But tell us about the new man in her life, John? Typical of your mum, she's been keeping her romance under wraps. C'mon, I think you've some news for us!'

I looked into Margaret's benevolent face. For her, love and romance had the power to heal all ills; her optimism was always inspiring.

'Yes, well, she actually sent me a letter in October saying she'd received an offer of marriage from a man she'd met at her bridge club; that was literally the first I'd heard of it. Next thing I knew, he'd proposed and my mother was deeply torn about whether to accept. I mean, on the one hand, it'd solve her financial problems, but on the other, he was a pretty quiet sort of man, quite unlike my dad! Anyway, I sent her a telegram from Armada and told her to say yes! And she did! The wedding happened so fast; Sarah and Adam almost missed it. Almost missing weddings seems to be habit in our family. We almost missed my brother's!' Everyone laughed; the sombre moment had passed. 'Did I tell you? Adam and Vanda are thinking about volunteering in Bolivia. It's veterinary project in a place called Charagua. Apparently, it's near the border with Paraguay.'

Steven whistled

'If Charagua is near to the Paraguay border it must be really out in the middle of nowhere! They've got two young kids, right? Wow, that'd be quite a challenge!'

Sally just nodded.

'They should just do it. It's a chance of a lifetime to really make a difference. If everyone could just do one thing in their life to help communities in developing countries, it would transform our world. I love that they're considering doing it. I'm gonna write them and tell them to go for it. The biggest regrets in life are the opportunities you never took.' Nods all around. Sally is so wise. 'Just do it', maybe that should be my motto from now on!

Chapter 15
Polar milking

'I'm just going outside and I may be some time.' Captain Oates' famous last words were ringing in my ears as I looked at the ugly-looking snowstorm brewing outside. A dense crowd of fine snowflakes was drifting past my bedroom window. Straining to see further, I could just make out a single bright light down in the yard with snow swirling around it that reminded me of an illustration I used to love of the lamp post next to Mr Tumnus' house that marked the start of Narnia. Unfortunately, in this case, the lamp post marked the start of four hours of freezing milking before breakfast; my heart sank to my boots. Shadows danced around the kitchen in the light of the wood-burning stove as I made a morning cuppa. Sitting in the snug warmth at the big old kitchen table, the local country and western station in Port Huron played quietly on the Jacobs' radio as I sipped my cup of tea; I'd brought English teabags with me, the American alternative was deplorable!

My ears pricked up as the cheery radio announcer read out the weather forecast.

'Well folks, I'd advise you to wrap up warm today, there's a doozy of a storm head'n our way with heavy snow and temperatures falling to minus thirteen Fahrenheit. Brrrr!' The announcer went on, 'Unless you didn't know, yesterday was February 2nd, and that means Groundhog Day. Yep, and to make matters worse, Ohio's very own official woodchuck, Buckeye Chuck, saw his own shadow and disappeared back into his burrow. Well, you-all know what that means don't ya? Six more weeks of winter. Oooeee! Sorry if that's spoiled y'day!'

I'd been told about the weird story around Groundhog Day. I was frankly amazed that the combined scientific capabilities of the US Meteorology Department, NASA and weather satellites of a so-called advanced nation like the US could be so easily subverted by a huge rodent! As the invigorating effects of my strong mug of tea kicked in, I struggled into my bulky insulated boiler suit, put on my thick ski gloves and wrapped a muffler around my neck. The performance took several minutes and was a bit like the preparations an astronaut must have to perform before going out onto the lunar surface. However, as if to confirm the radio announcer's words, as I opened the back door, a large drift of powdery snow fell backwards onto the doormat. It was then I realised I'd left my snow boots outside, 'damn!' I eventually found them under a burial mound of snow just far enough away from the doorstep to force me to have to go out in my stocking feet; the ice crystals sticking to my socks immediately melted on returning indoors, freezing my feet before I'd even gone outside. My snow boots were frozen solid and it took me ten painful minutes to thaw them out in the oven before I could put them on, at which point my fingers were frozen as well.

I was just removing them from the stove when Mrs J entered the kitchen.

'Left your boots outside huh? I can lend you a pair of Scott's if you like.'

'Thanks Jenny, it's my own fault. I think I've managed to thaw them enough to get them on!'

'Up in North Dakota, it used to get so cold inside my momma's house, we used to sleep with our boots on in the winter!'

I left Mrs J to have her cup of strong coffee by herself as she always did before taking one up to her husband. As I waded through snowdrifts towards the cow-barn under the yard light's harsh illumination, it felt like I was inside a snowstorm in a jar when it'd just been shaken up. Despite the lights, I could barely see where I was going, maybe I was walking into the wilderness and I'd never find the barn! My thoughts returned to the mysterious fate of poor Captain Oates and I shuddered. I'd been to the Scott Polar Museum when I attended St Mary's and had been thoroughly fascinated about polar travel, but polar milking was a first for me! As always, I was concerned about the welfare of the cows in such low temperatures. Whilst Holsteins originated in the Netherlands two thousand years ago, even on the chilly coasts of the North Sea, they'd be unlikely to experience minus twenty-five degrees Celsius! Whilst I was working in the milking parlour, at least I benefited from the cows' collective body heat, like the polar explorers did when they huddled together for heat, or even shared double sleeping bags, but the cows have only themselves to rely on. I'd been gleefully told by Scott that North American Indians used to get inside their just-expired horse to survive a night in the open in freezing temperatures; not that I'm suggesting I'd do the same with one of the cows, of course, but if one did happen to keel over... At least the intense cold had chased away the flies and reduced the incidences of foot rot; unfortunately, the flies had been replaced by rats scrounging the cows' tasty corn silage from the troughs and biting at their ankles causing suppurating wounds that needed frequent treatment. My stomach turned whenever I saw one or heard their frantic squeaking.

At last, I'm able to just make out the dairy building. Nobody's about yet, so no lights are on. As I quicken my pace, the snow squeaks under my feet like polystyrene. Polystyrene! They used industrial quantities of the stuff in Star Trek. I have to admit I'm a bit of a Trekkie. Fake snow featured in several Star Trek episodes, but I particularly like the one where Spock and McCoy jump through a time portal into a polar world.[23] Spock gets the girl that they mysteriously find there; which makes a change, since it's usually the obsequious Captain Kirk that gets to tangle with the female 'interest'. My God, the '60s were sexist, oh, and so were the '70s, and I have to admit, so were the '80s. Oh well, so much for progress! Talking of romance, Scott's been pining for Annetta. She had to go back to Germany last week as her work visa had expired; migrant labour is kept on a pretty short leash by the Immigration Department and if she'd delayed, they wouldn't let her back into the US if she'd wanted to return. I wish I could say that Scott was compensating for his loss by throwing himself into his work, but the calves are in a terrible state and I've had to start keeping more of an eye on them to make sure they're being properly looked after. So, before I start in the dairy, I take a quick look in the calf shed. At the moment, I'm mothering an early-born calf. As far as we could tell, the mum wasn't served by the bull or given AI, so it might be an immaculate conception! The nuns at St Mary's would've loved it. Even though it's not human, it'd be a 'sign'! If you'd spend your whole life devoted to God, I guess it'd be nice to get a confirmation every now and then. Why assume that He would return as a human being anyway, especially after what we did to Him last time! As I wrapped the calf in a spare padded jacket, he looked just like the baby

---

[23] For those who aren't Star Trek fans, this one's called 'All Our Yesterdays.'

Jesus. I was going bonkers. I'd seen the second coming in a calf! I'm sure he winked at me! Then I knew I was going bonkers, it must have been hypothermia kicking in, or possibly hypoglycaemia; it was hypo something at any rate. Working for hours in the early morning before breakfast was a real trial in sub-zero temperatures, it's enough to push anyone over the edge. Shackleton and Scott wouldn't have been impressed. If I was part of Scott's Antarctic sledge party, I'd have had my breakfast pemmican (a concoction of ground meat mixed with fat) before I'd even ventured outside; however, I'm pretty sure that Mrs J's slimming diet doesn't include pemmican!

Reassured that the calves at least had some rations and that the drinking troughs weren't frozen over, I needed to go back outside to walk around the calf shed and into the main shed so I could herd the cows into the adjoining dairy for milking. As I slid open the door, I was immediately slapped in the face by the stunning cold, and after even the meagre warmth of the calf shed, my nose began to run like a tap. A rime of ice immediately formed on my muffler and stung the already raw, chapped skin between my nostrils. As a distraction against the freezing cold, I'd recently become a bit of a stargazer during my early-morning perambulations. Looking up, stars twinkled in the huge vault of the moonless night sky. Without light pollution that you get in the cities, stars were the one thing that weren't in short supply out in rural Michigan. The Big Dipper was just about the only constellation I could easily recognise before coming to Armada; however, Dimitri had turned out to be quite a buff and we'd often share a cup of strong espresso coffee from his thermos flask while he guided me around the night sky. It was Dimitri who also told me about the fabled green flash you could sometimes see on a clear morning just as the sun's rim appears over the horizon. I was yet to see it; maybe this would be my lucky morning!

But it wasn't to be my lucky morning. Throwing a switch on the feeder control panel, the overhead conveyer started up, so far so good. But the low grating sound I got when I started up the feed auger wasn't good and invariably meant that a jam was about to happen; which would likely cause the machine to cut out and fail to restart. When the inevitable happened, I struck the control panel hard with my fist. It didn't help, and instead of restarting, the red warning light started to flash, but at least hitting the machine made me feel better! People that practice meditation in their daily lives say you come to love red stop lights during your commute to work by changing your perspective so that waiting in a traffic queue provides an opportunity for you to pause and be grateful for a peaceful moment to contemplate. But no matter how hard I tried, I couldn't learn to love the flashing auger jam light!

Just as I was about to do a good impression of Mr Magoo jumping petulantly up and down after Bugs Bunny had yet again foiled his plans, Dimitri appeared at the door of the shed.

'Problems Debbie?'

'Yes! The feeding auger has jammed solid.' I always admired Dimitri's stoic attitude of acceptance on these occasions and this was no exception.

Rather than fruitlessly switching the auger button on and off in the hope the truculent machine would miraculously spring into life, he picked up a couple of shovels and we trudged outside together to try and clear the jam.

In the end, we had to resort to filling a trailer so we could feed the cows manually.

'At least the work will keep us warm!' I looked over at Dimitri's smiling face while we shovelled. 'Have you seen your first green flash yet? I think we might get lucky this morning, the sky is so clear. My father and I used to sit for hours waiting for it if I'd woken in the early morning and couldn't get back to sleep when I was a little boy. He used to say the sky was different in the US compared to where he'd grown up in Warsaw before the war.' Dimitri then looked conspiratorially to his left and right. 'Did I tell you that my father met my mother in Treblinka? It was a concentration camp in Nazi-occupied Poland not far from where they'd been rounded up and sent on a train from Warsaw. During the winter, he told me they'd stolen clothes from the corpses of fellow prisoners to try and keep warm. He also told me that one time, he was taking a pair of gloves from a married woman who'd died the night before. Her husband who'd been sleeping next to her when she expired, was crying and didn't see what he was doing, or had ignored it. As he removed the gloves, he'd noticed that she still had a wedding ring on her finger and it had a large diamond set into it. My father confessed to me that he'd taken the ring and had used it to bribe a sonderkommando into giving him and my mother lighter work.[24] For years, he'd been ashamed to tell me, but when he learned that he was dying of cancer, he said he'd needed to confess to someone. He told me that he'd tried to find the man after that war so that he could ask for his forgiveness, but he never found him. He said the hardships of the camp removed all decency and humanity. After hearing my father's stories of the war, I could never understand why Americans were so afraid of a bit of hard physical work and need so much luxury.' Tears welled up in his eyes. Dimitri suddenly stopped talking and looked around. Krystal walked towards us with a shovel in her hands. Seeing her approach, he immediately changed the subject so she'd not think we'd been talking about her. 'Debbie, I think your Mrs Margaret Thatcher is causing some hardships in Britain. I've read about a winter of discontent and long queues for welfare payments. I thought Britain was a rich country!' I caught on and I remember that I'd made a joke about how Thatcher, and the new American President, Ronald Reagan, had struck up quite a friendship according to Shân, who'd recently sent me a long letter where she'd ranted at length against the Conservatives. She'd also mentioned she'd found a rather nice bloke that she'd 'felt comfortable with' and that they'd gone to bed 'to sleep' after a long night chatting to each other. Shân was always full of surprises!

Dimitri's emotional story left a deep impression on me. Clearly the war still casts a long shadow on relations between Poles and Germans. Many Poles and Jews fled to America both during the war to escape the Nazis and afterwards to escape grinding poverty and Soviet rule. Despite what could be seen as the West's betrayal of people in Poland and Czechoslovakia after having fought alongside us, Dimitri said he was very fond of the British and their spirit and kindness.

---

[24] Sonderkommandos were prisoners, usually Jews, who, in fear of their own death, were forced help the Nazi guards in concentration camps.

Chapter 16
Groundhog Day

That feisty old groundhog, Buckeye Chuck, had been pretty accurate in his prediction back at the beginning of February. We did indeed have at least six more weeks of freezing temperatures and snow to look forward to before we saw the first green shoots of spring towards the end of March. Well, okay, maybe it wasn't exactly warm, but wasn't the -25 ^{0}C we'd been having up until then. As the weather began to show tentative signs of turning into early spring during my last month at the Jacobs' farm, like the sap rising in the hearts of the forest pines, young farmhands' minds began to turn to love and the prospect of being able to venture out to find a mate. One morning, after breakfast, Mrs J sidled up to me as I sat ravenously shoving a folded pancake coated with maple syrup into my mouth. At that moment, my mind was fully engaged in eating as many pancakes as possible before heading back out to help Krystal clean down the cowshed.

Focussed though I was on food intake, I was still able to see that she had something on her mind.

'One of the Bryson boys, Jeb, over at the Michaels' place the other side of Armada would really like to meet with you and take you for a trip out into town. It'd be a real good chance for a look-see around the place before you leave for college. Says he's mighty keen to meet someone from England. Jeb's a good boy; smart and pretty handsome I'd say. No pressure though!'

I thought to myself, 'aah, so that's how matchmaking's done in rural America, upfront and no messing about!' How could a girl who'd been trapped on a freezing farm for weeks on end refuse? I'd been longing for a bit of downtime in what had been a long hard slog. Beware what you wish for! I think Jeb'd been told there was an "available" single woman working for the Jacobs and that she was from Engl, and a fact that had sweetened the deal considerably. So, on Friday evening around six p.m., presumably after he'd finished his chores, there was a jangling ring at the

Jacobs' front door. I could hear Mrs J answering followed by her light footsteps (the diet was obviously working!) and a heavier, more ponderous tread following behind her. I briefly had visions of Quasimodo loping in her wake, but I was pleasantly surprised.

My date for the evening was indeed handsome in a puppyish kind of way, and though hulking in size, he appeared suitably shy and chastened in Mrs J's presence at least.

'Debbie, this is Jeb Bryson. Jeb, Debbie Best.'

Jeb stepped forward and rather formally shook my hand like it was a delicate piece of china

'Great to meet you, Debbie!' As we shook, Jeb's eyes inclined upwards somewhat and his youthful brow knotted into the epitome of someone thinking. 'Mmh, Best, that's an Irish name. Awesome!' Jeb's face lit up like he'd won the jackpot on a Vagas slot machine. Ireland had, no doubt, provided America with many a fine, solid, childbearing woman, so I guess he thought this was his big chance.

As if to deflect Jeb's fevered imagination away from the usual preoccupations of young men when they're around young women, Mrs J broke into our burgeoning conversation and threw in what could have been intended as an admonishment.

'Debbie was brought up in a Catholic boarding school in Cambridge y'know.'

Whatever its intention, this piece of information appeared to excite young Jeb even more! Without further ado, he bid farewell to Mrs J and held open the door for me while I passed through it and started walking towards the biggest Ford pickup I'd seen so far — my carriage awaited! Standing in the Jacobs' yard was what I believed the folks in Michigan referred to as a cowboy car. Clearly Jeb was very proud of his vehicle and must've spent quite a lot of his spare time polishing it, the hubcaps gleamed in the glare from the Jacobs' porch light. The wheels and tyres looked like they should be on one of the oversized beasts I'd seen at the tractor-pulling event. This meant that the suspension had needed to be jacked up to an impossible height. So much so it was a struggle to get my foot onto the running board, never mind hitching myself into the passenger seat. I was just wondering whether I was going to need a rope and some climbing gear to get up there when Jeb's meaty hand appeared from the driver's side to come to my assistance. I thought, 'so that's why cowboy trucks are so high, it provided an opportunity for cowboys to graciously give their little women a hand.' On the downside, it also prevented a woman from making a hasty retreat from their beau's over-ardent advances!

Finally, aboard, the huge wheels crunched on the gravel and we cruised off into the night and to who knows what.

'I've bin think'n of asking you out for a while, ever since my mom mentioned there was an English girl working up at the Jacobs' place. Mrs Jacob says you don't get away from the farm much, so I thought I'd show you the sights in Armada! First, we're gonna check out the Kozy Corner Saloon for a couple of beers before head'n over to Tivoli's for a pizza; I booked us a table for eight p.m.'

Obviously, Jeb had been planning this extravaganza for a while! Up until then, I'd not actually ever been in a saloon, but they always conjured up an image of unshaven, silent and furtive men sitting hunched over a bottle of redeye, their opening gambit on arriving at the bar having been, "*whiskey, leave the bottle!*" So, as we crunched, or should I say, slushed to a stop next to the thawing mass of an ageing winter snowdrift, I was in some trepidation of what we'd find through the battered flap doors. As Jeb pushed through and held a door open for me to follow, the impression was of a light, high-ceilinged room with a long bar on the right and several small, round wooden tables scattered around the remaining floor space. At the far end, I could see the gent's toilet, but no sign for the ladies' was apparent. Near the entrance to the gent's, was a huge shuffleboard table that was crowded around by a large group of young guys in their late teens or early twenties.

Whilst the young lads paid us no heed, the oldies at the bar stopped talking and stared over at us. After a few long moments, their curiosity satisfied, the closest of them cordially nodded in our direction, his gnarled oak face looked as hard as nails. I thought Sergio Leone would've definitely wanted to have some of these guys as seconds in one of his spaghetti westerns! The weight of their stony gaze made me suddenly glad to have Jeb's strapping presence sitting next to me since, when he curtly nodded in their direction, they finally turned their gaze away from us. The next obstacle was the decision about what to drink, but since I wasn't spoilt for choice, it was quite easy. All they had on tap was Coors Lite and Miller Lite, Budweiser, Bud Lite or full-strength. Being an ardent fan of real ale and a stalwart member of the Campaign for Real Ale, it was always going to be Hobson's choice on which beer to choose. It was either going to be watery, bland or tasteless, or a combination of all three. In the end, I went for Budweiser full-strength; however, the first sip confirmed that it too fell in the watery category.

'So Debbie, what're your thoughts about us folks here in the Midwest?' Jeb beamed. 'We don't get many city folks out here and we definitely don't get many visitors from England!' Overhearing the word England brought the intense gaze of our neighbours back over in our direction, but this time the crusty old-timers broke into, in some cases, a toothless smile and there were more nods and a couple of them doffed their Stetsons or raised half-empty glasses in our direction. It seemed like I'd scored a hit!

Having been introduced to the locals, Jeb and I walked our drinks over towards the shuffleboard table. Expecting the young guys to be sullen and moody as they would have been in the UK, I was surprised when they courteously made a 'hole' in their group to let us get to the table.

The oldest of the group spoke up.

'So, you're from England? Do you know the rules of shuffleboard?' In the corner of my eye, I could see that Jeb was looking rather deflated by losing the initiative, so I pulled him in. As a kind of compromise, everyone took turns in explaining the game to me. Surprisingly, I managed to gauge the weight of the steel and plastic pucks quite quickly, and to the astonishment of everyone, I won a couple of games. The judgement needed was a bit similar to bar billiards, and I'd had plenty of time to become a professional at that during my misspent evenings at the WAC Union bar!

I managed to prevail upon Jeb and we walked the few hundred yards over to the Tivoli Pizzeria rather than drove. On the way, when we passed a gun shop called the Gun Barn, I couldn't resist doing some 'window shopping'. From what I could see past a display of hunting rifles, the place looked like an arsenal that a small, private army would've been proud of. Amongst the aforementioned array of hunting rifles that you'd

148

probably see in a UK hunt'n', shoot'n' and fish'n' shop, there were machine guns and what looked like a bazooka, but I'm sure I was mistaken! There was a huge banner hanging behind the till with the word 'FREEDOM' written in big capital letters.

Jeb nudged me and said, 'We can come back tomorrow during opening hours so's you can have a proper look around if you like.'

The sight of all that potential death and destruction on open display was giving me the heebie geebies.

'No, that's very kind of you to offer Jeb, but I don't think British Airways'd let me on the plane with a machine gun!'

'Yeah, you guys have some crazily strict gun laws in England. It's one of the reasons why I wouldn't live there.' I thought, 'and that, my friend, is exactly why I'd prefer living in England rather than the States!'

As we approached the Tivoli's frontage with its garish pictures of huge pizzas oozing mountains of cheese, I reflected on why, when people are entertaining visitors from overseas, do they often choose restaurants that they could've gone to in their own country (or, in this case, continent) rather than a place where they served local food, which would, perhaps, have been more of a novelty. Now, from what I could see from its frontage as we passed Papa's and Chaps, it looked like a good old mom and pop outfit offering local home cooking that would've been a treat compared to Mrs Js tinned and processed offerings. From my limited experience so far, what you tend to get in the US is a radically altered version of the original with added sugar, and in the Tivoli's case, cheese. Think Taco Bell (Mexican) and Norske Nook (Norwegian). However, I resigned myself to the fact that the much-bastardised pizza on offer around the world is generally so far removed from the original simple crispy baked dough with polenta topped with tomatoes, mozzarella and basil that represent the colours of the Italian flag that the US version couldn't do any more harm. But I was wrong! Entering through the takeaway operation, we were shown to a table in the back restaurant that had its walls festooned with the expected tourist posters of Rome and the Colosseum, however, there were also some framed photographs of Tivoli itself, a small village situated in the hills around Rome. The young woman serving us, who introduced herself as Francesca, was actually Italian as was the old guy working the pizza oven who was probably her dad. I kept it simple and ordered a Margherita. To my surprise, what came was the traditional thin crusted offering that you might get in Italy, but in a nod to its new environment, this pizza had been put on steroids and had grown in size to something that barely fitted on the table!

When Jeb's Four Seasons arrived, Francesca had to jostle our plates around to get them to fit on our small table for two.

'So, you said you'd been to Italy? Is this like what you'd get over there?'

I nodded

'Yes, this definitely looks like what you'd get there, but it's just three times the size!'

'Don't worry, you can get a take-out bag for what you don't eat now.' Jeb then did his scrunched forehead thinking thing again and said, 'Y'see it's the languages thing that puts me off going to Europe. It's incredible that over about the same area as the US, there's so many languages spoken. It confused the hell out of Reagan when he did his recent tour out there!' As my mouth was full, I simply nodded. The fact is, the average American, including Reagan before he was elected president, doesn't even own a passport, so no wonder Europe seems rather confusing!

Back in Jeb's truck with our doggie bags and suitably stuffed with pizza, we cruised home along the pitch-black streets of Armada and out onto Ridge Road. After a few minutes of silence, I looked over at Jeb and noticed that the tell-tale signs of his thinking processes had gone into overdrive. Unexpectedly, Jeb pulled over into the entrance to a track at a place I knew to be not far from the Jacobs' farm. Thinking that the truck had broken down or something, I turned to Jeb to ask if there was a problem and promptly met Jeb's puckered lips heading in my direction. Startled, I managed to turn my cheek just in time to avoid a direct hit, receiving instead, a kind of moist glancing blow on the side of my head. Following this only partially successful opening gambit, and while I was searching for something appropriate to say, I felt a hand being placed on my inner thigh. Working fast, Jeb's fingers started fumbling with the zipper of my jeans. I went rigid with shock. Part of me thought if I just sit there and not cooperate, he'd get the message and stop, but he appeared to be interpreting inaction as acquiescence.

By the time I managed to find my voice, Jeb had slid his hand under my panties, I said, 'no! Jeb, please stop this. Take me home!' I started crying.

Jeb recoiled in the face of my tears and stolid rebuff and placed his hands back on the steering wheel. I heard him murmur, 'Frigid English bitch' before he restarted the engine.

The rest of the, mercifully short, journey was completed in stony silence. I literally threw myself out of the truck when we pulled up in front of the Jacobs' porch whereupon; I slammed the door as hard as was possible considering its huge weight and its distance from the ground. Not for the first time, I felt humiliated and thought I'd somehow brought this on myself by being too friendly or naïve. I guess Jeb'd thought that since I'd be leaving soon, he'd get his end away without any danger of further consequences. I was angry and sad that a memory of Jeb's cack-handed advances would now taint what had been, up until then, a pleasant, and rare, evening out.

Chapter 17
O.S.U.

Ohio State University (OSU) sits in the leafy outskirts of Columbus like a huge, enclosed citadel. In common with the winter palace of the Dalai Lamas, the Potala fortress in Lhasa, OSU holds itself aloof from the scurry and strife that exists outside its borders. However, unlike the Potala Palace, you can buy a pass to enter its walls if you can afford the, then, seven thousand dollars per year tuition fees; which, in common with the Forbidden City in which the Potala Palace sits, that puts it off limits to most mere mortals. In fact, the reason why I didn't receive a wage for my hundreds of hours spent working for the Jacobs was that my three-month study tour at OSU had effectively gobbled up all my money. Not always a high and mighty university, OSU started out as an agricultural and engineering college in the mid-1800s but was elevated to university status when the Ohio State Governor, Rutherford Hayes, was himself elevated to President of the United States.

Even after I'd arrived in the US, I'd still not decided which of the hundreds of courses on offer I was going to take. My cash had bought the right to choose four courses to study. The university prospectus resembled the size and thickness of the London phone book and I could choose from the whole academic portfolio, including Mixology; which sounded like fun![25] Fortunately, Margaret and the Orenssons had again come to the rescue. After my stay with them over Christmas, I'd settled on Agricultural Policy (the study of land and labour management in a nod to Sally and Stevens' 'three-legged stool'), Grassland (I'd fallen in love with grass while I was at WAC), Sheep Production (a must for any aspiring lost sheep) and Agricultural Marketing (learnings from my time at OSU were to form the basis of an HNC at Harper Adams in England years later).[26] So, at the end of March 1981, I hefted a slightly heavier

---

[25] Yes folks, Mixology, the not so ancient art of mixing cocktails, takes a whole three years and thousands of dollars in tuition fees to perfect.
[26] Grass, the green stuff cows and sheep eat, not the psychedelic stuff rock stars smoke!

kitbag onto my shoulder, bid a tearful farewell to Mr and Mrs J at the now familiar Gratiot bus station and enjoyed a relatively short, four hour journey to Columbus via the rather forbidding-looking urban sprawl of Detroit.

My first impressions of OSU on getting out of a cab from the bus station, was one of huge size and crowds of fresh young faces. The press of boisterous students and squealing gaggles of overexcited young women was almost overwhelming after my isolation in the wilds of Michigan. Interestingly, for this vast temple of learning, it wasn't the old halls or the central library that dominated the campus, but the OSU football stadium; its hulking mass dwarfed the Liverpool FC's grounds at Anfield that I'd stood in just a couple of years previously. The pre-eminent importance of football at OSU meant that, if you were male, beefy and athletic, good at kicking an oval ball and looked great mincing around in Kevlar body armour, you could get a football scholarship, which was literally a free pass to study at the university so long as you didn't bugger up your knees or get benched, or relegated, or whatever the proper term for being dropped from the team was. Since my early stumble at St Mary's on the ladder leading to academic excellence, success in getting my OND at WAC had given me confidence. I studied hard, responded well to the freewheeling style of the OSU tutors and turned in some pretty high marks from my assignments. Also, my 'status' as the go-to person for any questions about Charles and Dis' upcoming nuptials in July meant that I quite quickly gathered a small, enthusiastic retinue of fellow students around me. Like the ragtag bunch I hung out with at WAC, my OSU gang was a 'big tent' that encompassed males as well as females and a broad spectrum of people from both sides of the economic divide. There was a kind and welcoming black woman called Grace from Detroit doing Business Studies on a scholarship programme. Then there was Jeanette, who, when she wasn't cheerleading up at the football stadium, she did actually study Mixology and several of the hunky football players. Last, but not least, there was Findlay, the son of a banking magnate in New York, who, rather bizarrely I thought, decided to buy an open-topped Cadillac one day when he was out shopping in town.

In contrast to WAC, I was spoilt for choice when it came to nights

153

out and who to spend them with. The only constraint was lack of cash, so I had to be innovative to ensure I made the most of being at OSU. An early introduction to the social whirl came in the form of an invitation by Jeanette to come along to a bash at one of the university bars where she and fellow Mixology students practiced their craft. I know what you're thinking: these students had aced it by integrating drinking into their study programme! But think of it like this, people studying hairdressing have to cut hair in a kind of practice salon and part of any qualification in the hotel trade means you have to stay at hotels. The Mixology training ground was, well, a cocktail bar situated in the campus village.

Jeanette and a couple of her girlfriends picked me up around eight p.m. on one of the first warm evenings of the spring. As we walked over to the venue, she pulled me aside and explained the plan. We were going to watch a couple of her friends do their thing, and hopefully, get a couple, or three, free cocktails that had been 'messed up' and couldn't go for retail. Then, around ten p.m., we'd check out a party being organised by one of the football teams. When we arrived, the evening was just beginning to get going as we took a seat at a table near the bar. Jeanette waved at a couple behind the bar, Jaz and Jamie, who were the students doing cocktails that evening. Jeanette moseyed over to the bar and ordered her cocktail whilst I stood back, watched the show and racked my brains for cocktail inspiration.

Jaz, whose hair was slicked into several spiky-looking points, reminded me of Lucy in her punk phase at school. She explained a bit about what she was doing and gave me some encouragement.

'C'mon, Debbie, is it?' I nodded. 'Throw me a curveball. None of your English G&Ts, I wanna have a go at something complicated.'

No pressure then! I scanned the four-page cocktail booklet.

'What about a Tequila Sunrise?'

Jaz shook her head

'Too easy.'

'Okay. What about a Blue Lagoon?' Jaz again shook her head and gave a punky scowl.

It was then that I had an epiphany.

'Right, what about a Bloody Mary? My dad reckoned that making a great Bloody Mary from scratch was quite a feat, and being a Catholic, he should know!'

Jaz nodded and said, 'Good choice,' and got to work.

'What're you have'n Debbie?' Jeanette was holding a huge mixer glass garnished with a cherry, an orange slice and the obligatory corny little paper umbrella.

'A Bloody Mary.'

Jeanette giggled, 'Great choice for a Catholic!' She then held her fingertips to her mouth 'Oh gosh, I hope I haven't offended; you're not a practicing Catholic, are you?'

It was my turn to laugh.

'Oh God, no! I hated going to Mass when I was at school. I'd be happy if I never went to church again!'

'Phew! That's a relief 'cos we're plan'n on going to the Football Team A party later on!' She giggled again.

The Football Team-A party didn't get started until ten p.m., the members of my little gang, including me, and especially Jeanette, were pretty drunk by the time we got to the venue up in the social area of the football stadium complex. Two burly footballer types were standing at the entrance to the party suite, but Jeanette just nodded and smiled at them and we sailed through. More drinks and much loud music and plenty of bopping around handbags later, I'd lost touch with Jeanette. Since the other girls were planning to leave, I said I'd have a look for her. The crowd seemed to have swelled considerably since the evening had gone on and I had difficulty moving let alone making an effective search. At least Jeanette was pretty recognisable being relatively tall with hugely bouffant bleach blond hair. I finally decided to have a look out the back of the main suite and exited a door that led onto a corridor linking to several syndicate rooms. As the music receded behind me, I could hear Jeanette's trademark giggle echoing in the corridor coming from a room just opposite where I was standing. So, thinking she was in the ladies' room, I opened the door and stepped in. Jeanette was in there all right, but I could see she was with a couple of naked guys. Totally nonplussed, I momentarily couldn't believe what I was seeing. I made a move to back out quietly and rejoin the others.

Seeing I was about to leave, Jeanette said, 'D'ya all want to give me a hand with these guys, there's plenty to go around!' Unsure of how to reply, I backed out and promptly shut the door.

I was shocked but part of me thought I should try and ensure she was okay. But whilst I dithered outside the door not knowing what to do, I heard Jeanette saying, 'Sorry guys, I got a bit distracted there', followed by more giggling. It was then I decided she was firmly in control of the situation and left her to it!

***

Lunch! I'd just come from a gruelling ninety-minute lecture on the role of multinational corporations in world politics and I was desperately in need of some sustenance. Having come in at semester two, I was being thrown in at the deep end where I was wrestling with a rather indigestible chunk of world politics as part of the Agricultural Policy course. Our instructor, Tony McGrew, had just been giving us a surprisingly leftist view of the way in which large corporations seek to influence government policy that I'm sure would've been given a nod of approval by Sally and Steven Orensson!

I was just passing a sign at the refectory counter saying, 'Proud to serve Starbucks coffee' that seemed to suggest that OSU was itself probably being influenced by big business when I noticed that Grace was waving at me.

'C'mon Debbie, come over and sit with us!' Grace was with a group of her course mates, a small gaggle of black women, at a nearby table. 'How's it going girl? You looked like you were a zombie up there, has one of your professors bin fry'n your brain?' She chuckled, her face full of good humour.

I said, 'You're pretty near the mark there, Grace. I've got until the end of the week to hand in a paper for the module world politics so it looks like I'm gonna be stuck in the library for the rest of the week!'

'Well, let me be your guardian angel and grant you a wish. How 'bout you come on up to Detroit with me at the weekend? An old girlfriend from my church group at St John's is having a get-together to celebrate her ordainment as a deacon and we've all bin asked to bring friends along. It's a pretty big deal, she's gonna be one of the first female deacons in Michigan. The church is real old and near the city centre, but we're gonna have a prayer meeting and then a social at a community hall nearby. D'you wanna come? Now, I know you're Catholic Debbie, but we won't be do'n communion or anything like that, but if you'd prefer to take a rain check on the prayer meeting, it's not a problem.'

I felt a little embarrassed. I'd said to Grace I'd been to Catholic school, so I guess she assumed I was practicing, however, I was curious about the prayer meeting. So, in for a penny, in for a pound, I accepted Grace's kind offer and said I'd come along for the whole thing. We rode up to Detroit on a Greyhound bus early on Saturday morning together with a couple of Grace's college friends. It turned out that the church and the community hall were within walking distance of the bus station down near the banks of the Detroit River. In fact, we followed part of the river walk before turning left and along a dark avenue of tall office buildings towards the city. I was actually surprised how pleasant our journey along the river was. Tour boats chugged along its sparkling waters and families walked in a little riverside park. There didn't appear to be any demented drug gangs to be seen!

St John's resembled the kind of church you'd see in the City of London. Sandwiched between towering glass and concrete buildings on one side, overlooking a freeway with a baseball stadium opposite, the ancient edifice looked rather out of place. However, we walked past the church and continued for a few blocks, stopping at the steps of the Sterling Heights Community Center. Mingling with the milling throng of people in the foyer, I suddenly realised that I was the only white face in a sea of mostly black women. I also felt rather underdressed. Most people seemed to be in their Sunday best. Fortunately, I'd had the sense to wear a reasonably clean and relatively uncreased summer dress. Grace introduced me to a few of the people there and waved to the new deaconess, Willamina Blaine, who was crowded around by an excited group of women all trying to get a photograph.

Finally taking the podium and standing on a small dais, Willamina started her address by calling everyone to prayer. I can never keep my eyes closed during prayers, and this was no exception. Since most people's heads were bowed, I took a look around the hall and noticed that a table on which had been placed several photographs of a young black man, had been placed on the dais next to the deaconess.

After the blessing, Willamina briefly swept her eyes over her flock before she began her address.

'Now, I think you're all expecting me to talk about my inauguration and how proud I am to join the small band of deaconesses in this city. Don't get me wrong; I am both proud and so very humbled by the trust our church has placed in me. But I want to talk about a young man, this young man.' Here the deaconess indicated the photographs on the table. 'He was a loving son, a hard-working scholar and a member of this church. Many of you will know Daniel and so will have heard that he was tragically taken from us in a police shooting incident during a church service not far from where we are sitting. Daniel was yet another victim of a system that all too readily associates the black community with crime.' There were nods all round at this last comment.

I glanced up, half expecting everyone to be looking at me, the only white person sitting in the room. But there were no stares, no blame, just sadness. It seemed incredible that police would enter and shoot a suspect in church. However, since arriving in the US I'd needed to rapidly modify my assumptions around what was possible. The rest of her address was more upbeat, but the deaconess's words seemed to hang in the air and cast a shadow over subsequent proceedings.

***

The culmination of my short, but intense, stay at OSU, was the award of a little certificate confirming that I'd successfully completed Ohio State University Agricultural internship program by my tutor, Michael Chilman. I had actually done it, little old me, on my own. It was one of those rare moments in life that fills you with pride and the sort of joy you only get when you've achieved something unequivocal; I'd achieved my goal against all the odds — I was thrilled!

Standing in his office in the School of Agriculture & Home Economics, that, like many offices and buildings on the campus, overlooked the football stadium, the old tutor peered over his glasses and asked a question, which, until that moment, I hadn't yet grappled with.

'So, Debbie, where now? What will you do when you return to England?'

158

'Actually, I'm not going back right away. I'm going to visit a friend in San Francisco.'

Saying it out loud, it sounded rather flash having a friend in San Francisco! Before even considering applying for an internship with Future Farmers of America, I'd been keeping in touch with Fred ever since we'd met in Greece and day-dreamed, when I was at my lowest ebb, about what it would be like to be with him permanently. Unlike many of my correspondents over the years, Fred had replied affectionately to my letters and cards, so I was hopeful that we could rekindle the spark we had in Greece. I even had thoughts of staying in the US indefinitely, applying for immigration status, the whole nine yards. Not that I'd said anything to Fred, I didn't want to scare him off!

By the time I finally burst through the doors at San Francisco Airport arrivals, I'd relived the moment of our reunion so many times it felt like déjà vu when it finally happened. I spotted Fred's sandy locks and his trademark mirror sunglasses perched on the top of his head (solar panels, he called them) in the thronging crowd almost as soon as I'd got through the doors from the customs area. He smiled as he pushed himself away from the pillar where he'd been leaning and did that nonchalant walk that all Californians seem to have, not rushed, but purposeful with a slight swagger. How handsome he looked.

We hugged and kissed. So far so good!

'Plum, I've got us a plan for this evening.' We'd taken our seats on the BART train from the airport and cozied up together to watch the lights of the city float by. 'I wanna show you as many of the sights of the city as possible in the time you've got, so I thought since we're on the BART anyway, we'd do something in downtown before head'n back over to my place on Balboa. What'd ya think?'

I just nodded; I was in romantic heaven!

'I've got my heavy bag though. Is there anywhere we could store it?'

'You British are always so practical! There's a left luggage at Civic Centre, you can leave it there; you'll need to remember to pick it up on the way back though!' At that moment I was floating on air, so I wasn't sure if I'd remember. Not that there was anything valuable in my stuff anyway, so I didn't really care. 'Civic's a good place to get off actually, 'cos we're headed over to the Black Cat, a really cool little jazz club that does great cocktails and has a live band on Wednesdays.' I'd mentioned to Fred that I loved Jazz and went to the Brecon Jazz Festival whenever I could — he'd seemed intrigued when I'd told him there was jazz playing in the street. I hugged him and we kissed, but I felt his heart wasn't in it, or was it my paranoia? On the journey to the club, I started to feel that Fred was taking a role as a friendly tour guide, rather than boyfriend material; however, at the time I thought nothing of it and just enjoyed the moment.

The Black Cat was busy when we arrived, but the greeter managed to find us a table over by the window where we'd just about have a view of the little stage where the band was playing. We'd arrived during a short intermission. Fred ordered drinks and a burger and fries for us both so I made some small talk and said, 'How's your business plans going? You said you're taking on a coffee shop franchise?'

'Yeah, Ritual Coffee Roasters. It's with my friend Peter. We've got the franchise now okay; it's been tough these past few months. Winter and early spring is never a good time to take on a business like that, but things are picking up now. We can head over there tomorrow and you can meet Peter, he's a great guy, I'm sure you'll like him.' Before we could say anything more, the band came on so we just sat cuddled together in a warm haze.

After spending the night on Fred's couch rather than in his bed, I was beginning to have my doubts. Admittedly, we were pretty drunk by the time we got back to Balboa, but a romantic morning in bed would've been nice, however Fred made some spurious excuse about changing the bed sheets. Given what I'd have liked to have done to him, sleeping in unwashed bed sheets wouldn't have mattered!

Answering the inevitable early morning call of nature, we were both a bit jaded when we bumped into each other on the way to the bathroom. 'Ladies first!' Fred bowed courteously and I went first. While I was in there, Fred shouted through the closed door. 'I thought we'd head over to Castro and check in on Peter. We'll be able to get a coffee and some pancakes before heading into town. I thought we could check out the Ferry building Marketplace. You'll love it; it's basically a huge farmers' market in the old Ferry building. After that we can maybe take a walk on Golden Gate Beach. It's gonna be warm and sunny today, so I'd take your bikini.' Now you're talking, I thought. Some more 'action' on the beach sounded like a great idea!

Before arriving in the US, I'd never heard of San Francisco's Castro District, but on that sunny morning in early July, I got the picture pretty quickly. My first inkling came when we got off the bus near Fred's coffee franchise. Two men passed us holding hands, nothing too amazing at first sight, but when they'd passed, I noticed that they were cupping each-other's bare buttocks through holes they'd cut in their jeans for the purpose. Then there were the multi-coloured flags and a lesbian couple French kissing on a street corner. If there was any doubt left in my mind that this was San Fran's gay district, we passed a drug shop selling colonic irrigation fluid; a huge stack of cans of the stuff with a helpful little logo depicting your colonic tract, were piled up on the pavement outside. Okay, so Fred's coffee franchise is in a gay area of the city, not a problem in itself I thought.

Taking a seat in Ritual Coffee Roasters, I could see that Fred was checking on the number of clientele.

'Not bad for a Thursday morning, things could be looking up.'

'Why hello there! So this must be your friend from England. So pleased to meet you my lovely!' A tanned chap with a buzz cut and wearing round, rose-tinted glasses had sashayed up to us.

Fred made the introductions.

'Debbie, this is Peter. Peter, Debbie. Well, actually, she's called Plum by her friends!'

Peter seemed nonplussed by this, so I offered, 'It's a pet name my family gave me; it's a body shape thing.'

Peter smiled broadly and winked.

'Well darling, you look perfectly gorgeous now.' With that, he disappeared off to get us a coffee.

Then the penny dropped.

'Fred, is this a subtle way of telling me that you're gay? Why didn't you say? You know how I feel for you? This feels so cruel!'

Fred took my hand, the first tenderness he'd shown me since I'd arrived, and tears started to roll down my cheeks.

'I just couldn't find the words. I'm so, so sorry Plum. I've been having issues around my sexuality for some time. I've tried to just accept it. I've been to counselling. I thought, perhaps I'm just bisexual; in fact, I had a couple of encounters with men while I was in Greece. It just felt right. We can continue to be friends, just not, boy and girlfriends. Please don't be angry with me, I'm very fond of you.'

I like to think of myself as a pragmatic person. I'd had a fair few disappointments, and I'd always found that the best way to cope was to just crack on regardless. We were destined to be friends, just not lovers. In the end, once I'd reconciled myself to it, I got the best tour of San Fran anyone could ask for. One afternoon, Peter lent us his car and we drove over the Bay Bridge to Oakland, cruised back over the Richmond-San Rafael, passed San Quentin Jail (that's the one where they execute people) and Sausalito, returning to San Fran via the Golden Gate Bridge when it was all lit up and looking amazing. Other highlights of my backpacker's whistle-stop tour included a night's camping in the Redwood Hills State Reserve and an introduction to the delights of a hot tub. On the penultimate evening of my stay, Fred suggested we go to "a great club" in Castro. Of course, it turned out to be gay, the clientele being pretty much all men. I think it was an excuse for Fred to do some accompanied cruising for talent. So I babysat him while he got chatted up by a couple of butch-looking blokes.

I really did lose my heart in San Fransisco, just not in the way I was looking for; it was a time I'd never forget. Once I returned to England and the hurly burly of farming, I eventually lost touch with Fred. I just hope he stayed safe. When I was at OSU, 1981 was the year that saw the beginning of an AIDS epidemic that had caused the deaths of more than three thousand six hundred men and women in the US just three years later. A tragic and sobering thought.

Part 6
Adrift

Chapter 18
Back with a bump

The truth was, I'd left school at sixteen. Even though I'd gone to college, I'd left WAC with an OND, which was basically an A-level equivalent qualification. To top it all, my hard-earned certificate of merit from Ohio State wasn't a recognised qualification in the UK. My career path choices were, therefore, rather limited. If I'd briefly experienced the dream I'd always nurtured of self-sufficiency at Sally and Stevens' farmstead in Rhode Island, my own reality was very different. I'd arrived back in the UK with a bump in August 1981 and circumstances forced me to return to the couch-surfing life of an itinerant agricultural worker. Whilst the hobo life appeared to still hold a fascination and had generated a rich lore and vocabulary in the US, people were rather less generous in the UK; without an address you don't really exist. In a circular repeat of my journey out to Michigan, I had, like a boomerang, returned to Heathrow Terminal 3 and the passenger seat of Vanda's car.

Since I had nowhere else to go, I'd been invited to stay in the converted loft of Adam and Vandas' home in Radwinter. However, I arrived back into a maelstrom of activity. A&V had finally decided to take the plunge and sign up for the United Nations volunteer programme, UNIS and spend the next five years working for a veterinary aid programme in the Bolivian back of beyond. They were due to fly out in October, so the house was being emptied of stuff so it could be put up for rent whilst they were away. It was serendipity that I'd arrived back just when my Aunty Plum skills were sorely needed to keep the girls, Alice and Daisy, now five and eighteen months respectively, out from under their parents' feet whilst they packed. In fact, I was helping Daisy to feed one of her ravenous family of dolls with 'porridge' (actually dry dock seeds that'd been jolly difficult to find due to the extreme tidiness of my brother's garden) when Adam dropped a copy of the Walden Local newspaper in front of me on his way past.

'There you go Plum!' Adam had circled a little ad in the jobs' pages for, "harvest help." However, what with the pressing need to feed Daisy's dolls with dock seeds and helping Vanda pack down a wardrobe, I didn't take much notice of the advert until later that evening. Then, as I sat in my gloomy garret in a converted attic full of the burgeoning detritus of by brother's married life the late August sun filtered through a small window that had been cut in the roof and I got to thinking gloomy thoughts. It felt like I was walking down an avenue of shattered dreams that was full of hundreds of blind alleys and false starts; how was I ever going to find a way through? In an attempt to divert myself from despair, I crammed myself behind a child's writing desk and began a letter to Fred. I told him about the one hundred- and sixteen-pound bill for repairs to the clapped-out car Vanda was leaving for me. Then I ranted on about the sixty pounds I'd just paid to have my bicycle repaired. I'd carefully converted pounds to dollars so he'd understand how cripplingly expensive it all was. Maybe I was looking for some sympathy? I thought to myself how futile it was, and how sad. A man seven thousand miles away who I thought had "feelings" for me had turned out to be gay. I felt as though I was grieving for what might have been. In the end, I didn't get much further than an angst-ridden sentence about poor French workmanship in reference to my Peugeot bicycle. Finally giving up on the letter in frustration, I slowly began to crumple the single page, but I stopped short of disposing of it; I wasn't quite ready yet to let go of hope. And yet, my stay in the US had brought me to another conclusion. Even if my interest in farming started out as a dream of self-sufficiency I'd seen on TV and read in a book, I wanted to show everyone (and myself) that I could do it and be accepted as a professional in my own right. I just couldn't give up hope now after coming so far. I needed to get some work, any work, and bide my time; surely something would come up. "*Have faith Deborah*" as Sister Thomas would have said. It was then that I picked up the Walden Local that Adam had given me earlier in the day. What the hell? Why not get some local harvest work? I noticed that the Northridges' farm was located near Hainested, so I could just about cycle there from Radwinter saving on petrol and further repair bills.

***

166

If Adam and Vandas' house had been a maelstrom of activity, the Northridges' farm was a hurricane. The harvest machine was in full swing and a woman was marshalling the troops. Like Boudicca clashing her shield with her heavy broadsword to encourage her men and cause the enemy to quake in their boots, Mrs Northridge spurred her mechanised army of tractors and combine harvesters forward to the next field. When I arrived, there were five thousand acres of winter wheat and spring barley left to harvest.

Somewhat bewildered by the flurry of activity in the yard on my first day, the lady herself swooped over in her shining new Range Rover to give me my orders.

'We've already bagged the winter barley and oilseeds during a dry spell a couple of weeks ago, so it's full steam ahead on the wheat! Now, I'm sure you've tangled with a John Deere 1640 before; it's a piece of cake to drive. All you need to do is keep up with Ian on the combine and make sure the trailers under the auger, when he's emptying the tank. Just keep an eye on your mirrors and on Ian's signals and you'll be fine!' And off she went to give more orders. Although she was terribly, terribly Home Counties posh, I loved her can do attitude and the way the men snapped their heels and obeyed her command. On Northridges' farm, the boot was firmly on the other foot!

For the next couple of weeks, the rain held off and the dew didn't fall until after nine p.m., so we kept going until after dark. Harvest fever can drive farmers wild with anxiety, and Northridge Farm was no exception. One burning question gave way to another. Will we get the crops in before the weather finally breaks? Will we be able to sow the autumn crops into a decent seed bed? Will it rain once it's planted? For a whole week, we didn't finish until ten at night. It was the height of summer, but I had to buy a battery light for my bike so I could find my way home in the dark! Keeping the trailer lined up with the combine's auger was quite a challenge in the evening gloom with clouds of dust flying about, but I managed it without a major mishap. Then, each day when I returned to the farm in the early morning, clouds of smoke from stubble burning would hang in the air as the sun rose red over the fields like a scene from Francis Ford Coppola's film, Apocalypse Now. To misquote and abuse Robert Duvall's famous lines, "*I love the smell of [stubble-burning]in the morning... it smell[s] like... victory!"* Despite the destruction and pollution caused by burning, the sight of more and more scorched fields did seem like victory! Each time I emptied a trailer, the mountain of wheat in the grain store grew higher whilst the fields were emptied. I loved the strong sense of purpose and Mrs Northridge's leadership. I reckoned she'd have made a fantastic general, or, perhaps more fittingly, a field marshal!

Chapter 19
Be careful what you wish for

By the end of October and the end of my stint of harvest work, I felt buoyed up and more optimistic. Although Adam and Vanda had jetted off to Bolivia, Sarah was working in Italy and Esme was settling into life with her new husband at his home in Little Haven, inertia from my time with Mrs Northridge's harvesting machine carried me forward and into a monthly tenancy in Radwinter's quaint little Old Post Office and a job as a temporary assistant trials officer with Ciba-Geigy.[27] Entering the reception at their flash new building at Duxford near Cambridge, I felt like I'd suddenly gone up in the world! My job was to help Brian, a trials officer on the herbicides team, with sowing the autumn cereal trials. Perks of the job included transport to the fields in Brian's sporty Ford Sierra, free breakfast with Ciba-Geigy's Little Chef corporate account card and a free pub lunch. I was in heaven! And the salary wasn't too bad either. Brian was quite good company, but he was a bit of a rev-head and I often 'enjoyed' the thrill of travelling at breakneck speed down the A14 on the way to a trials site. A typical day in the field was totally different to what I was used to on livestock farms. We started work at the relatively civilised hour of eight a.m. and began the day at one of several local Little Chefs with a titanic food mountain called the 'Olympian' breakfast that was basically everything off the grill menu on one plate topped off with fried bread. This was followed by some hair-raising rally driving to a trials site that was usually on a very posh arable farm. It being a time when the price of wheat was being kept artificially high through EU subsidies, the Cambridgeshire grain barons were making a fortune. In place of milking and mucking out, there was measuring fields and plot lengths with a tape measure and theodolite or checking seedling emergence counts. Then it was back to base and knocking off at five p.m., all very civilised.

---

[27] Ciba-Geigy: now part of Novartis.

At the end of my three months' temporary stint, part of me was hoping I could stay on. But in the end, I didn't get offered a permanent contract. The pay was good, the work was relatively easy, but it just wasn't my karma and I missed the work with livestock. However, I didn't leave Ciba-Geigy straight away, and yet, in a funny sort of a way, I still, briefly, found the herd camaraderie I was looking for, in a job packing vaccines! Desperate for money to keep me going until Christmas and to pay my three-month tenancy at the Old Post Office, Brian mentioned that there might be some work in the Duxford veterinary vaccine packing plant. The conveyor belts at the packing plant were manned, or should I say womanned, by an army of workers whose job it was to ensure that the right vaccine doses were packed correctly into boxes for surgeries across the UK and overseas. A very mundane factory job was, however, transformed by the friendly banter of the women that worked there. Still rather shy and much younger than most of the other women, Pat, who in another life, would have definitely been the matriarch in a herd of dairy cows, took me under her wing, or should I say, hoof, from the very start. The huge maze of conveyor belts and automated packing machines worked pretty much as expected most of the time, however problems did occasionally occur, and if you weren't careful, valuable drugs could be piling up on the floor. Since most of the women were married or otherwise hooked up with a partner, it became part of Pat's mission in life to find me a likely lad from the large pool of delivery drivers.

On top of the 'threat' of having to fend off droves of dilettante drivers whilst I was at the packing plant, I suffered another huge dose of self-doubt. The frigid weather over Christmas and New Year had brought everything to a standstill on the jobs front and I'd taken refuge back at the Oars when my tenancy at the Old Post Office had ended. Whilst Jill did everything she could to help me join in with the family celebrations, I felt like I was a spare part intruding into some else's life. Luckily, in the New Year I finally got a break. I received a positive reply to an application for an assistant stock-person job on a beef farm near Swaffham in Norfolk. For me, the job had all the bells and whistles. I'd be working with beef cattle so I'd increase my knowledge as a stock-person, tick! I didn't have to get up at some ungodly hour in the morning to milk cows, tick! I could continue learning more about arable work and the on-farm production of feed, tick! But the cherry on top of the cake had to be that a house came with the job! This was the golden ticket I was looking for. No more having to knock on someone's door and ask whether I could take a shower or use the bathroom.

**

Ebb's farm was near the village of Holme Hale in a little oasis of small dairy fields planted in amongst acres of wheat and barley. So, with high hopes for a new start, one Sunday afternoon, a couple of weeks after New Year 1982, Jill drove me over to the farm and dropped me off in front of the main house, a large, functional red brick edifice with high ceilings and draughty sash windows. Softening the edges of what looked to be a rather austere building, were large rose beds that had been tastefully arranged in a formal style at the front of the house; definitely a farm wife's touch. However, the beds were copiously filled with mountains of cow muck, definitely a farmer's touch. The farm owner, Mr Trick, met me in the front garden and I waved to Jill as she carefully drove her new convertible back down the rutted farm track. The defining feature of Bill Trick was his copious salt 'n' pepper sideburns that framed his lean, florid cheeks. Thinking I was going into the house, a natural assumption since it was freezing cold outside, I continued towards Mr Trick who was advancing from the front door. Over his shoulder, I could vaguely make out an older, rather mousy woman fussing at the door behind the framer's resolute advance. We met in the middle, and rather than inviting me into the house to meet his wife, he gently but firmly took me by the elbow and guided me towards a track that led away from the main house and over to a small row of cottages behind the cowsheds.

'This way, Debbie, is it? No need to go round to the house when you can dump your gear and make yourself comfortable at the cottage. I've lit the fire and we've had the night storage heating on overnight, so it should already be quite warm.' I was quite taken aback. Up until that moment, I'd never had a farmer offer to do something for me right from the get-go. I felt that I must be rather jaded, but I was quite taken aback. 'I understand from your letter that you've been looking for, and have an interest in, beef production. Well, you've come to the right place. We

171

keep Limousin crossbreds here as feed can be scarce in the summer and they're pretty efficient. We do mainly straights and we have our own crimping machine to produce our own kibbled grains to try and keep feed costs down. An important part of the assistant stock-person's job is preparing the rations.'

Mr Trick had been talking since I'd arrived and he was wearing me out! I'd never known a farmer talk so much to a lowly member of staff. As we approached the line of cottages, Trick indicated that we were heading to the furthest left of the three conjoined buildings, the only one with lap fencing in the back yard, which we entered. We briefly stood in what effectively was the back garden.

'Yep, it's quite a little sun trap in the summer. My previous stock assistant used to do a bit of sunbathing out here!' Chuckling to himself, he opened the backyard door and I stepped into a useful-sized kitchen with a hob, oven and fridge-freezer that looked quite new; the kitchen itself had plenty of storage units. I immediately started thinking about the house-warming party I could have when I'd moved in. Trick then took me into the front room, the guest bedroom and the master bedroom where we paused. There was a large double bed from John Lewis, no less, sitting between a matching pair of rather swish bedside tables with integral lights. It was one of the only items of furniture in the house. 'Yes, well, naturally you'll need to get some furniture. We used to store some bits and pieces in the sheds, but my daughter's taken most of what we had spare when she set up her own house.'

'Oh, not a problem Mr Trick, I have a couple of friends that might be able to help me out with some furniture, and there's always the sale rooms.'

Trick nodded and trudged heavily downstairs where he put his boots back on to go outside.

'Well, I'll leave you to get yourself sorted out. We start at seven a.m., so I'll see you in the morning.'

Emerging from the back door once again, I walked back over to the yard to collect the boxes of food and other supplies Jill and I had picked up at the supermarket on the way over. I still couldn't believe my luck. For once, it felt like I'd really fallen on my feet this time.

***

The next morning, I met Mr Trick in the yard and he explained his operation and what my duties would be.

'I know you've done quite a bit of dairy, but beef production is rather different and has a much greater focus on calves and calf rearing. As I said in the advert, this is a suckler beef operation. We've got about one hundred and fifty Saler-Limousin cross cows and heifers and we keep about twenty-five of the heifers as replacements each year. We run best of the bunch with a neighbour's Saler bull and the rest with our Limousin stock bulls. We've got just over three thousand acres of crops and pasture and run sheep on some of it to keep the grass under control through the year. I know you've done some calf rearing, so I want you to start there.'

As we walked around the calf shed, the shed with the cows in-calf and the cull cowshed, I began to notice how tactile my amiable host was being. A nudge here, an arm brush there and the occasional push in the small of the back, like he was testing the water. At the end of my 'penny tour' around the operation, I'd begun to get the distinct impression that Trick might suffer from the dreaded wandering hand syndrome, so I made a mental note to keep him at arm's length at all times. In fact, the precaution of keeping a heifer, crush barrier or other solid object between me and Mr Trick when he was around paid dividends since I wasn't exposed to any more of his prodding and poking over the ensuing couple of weeks.

On the down side, Vanda's old car was on the blink. Fortunately, the old girl allowed me to do a couple of trips to pick up a few items of furniture from the parents of my friend Pat from WAC who lived not far away at Wells-next-the-Sea. In fact, it was one Sunday evening after I'd made a trip over to Wells to pick up some stuff that I met my neighbour.

I was wrestling an old armchair off the roof when she came to my rescue.

'Let me give you a hand!' Rushing forward, she just managed to catch one of the legs of the armchair before it toppled onto the ground.

'Thanks very much! I wasn't sure how I was going to get it off the roof! I'm Debbie by the way.'

'I'm Pam Stibbins, nice to meet you, Debbie. It looked like you needed a hand! So, you've just started with the Tricks?'

'Yes, a couple of weeks ago, I'm their new assistant stock-person.'

Since we'd started the sort of get to know you, question and answer conversation, I was expecting an immediate response from Pam, so when none came, I looked over at her and was about to offer another nugget of information, when I noticed she was hesitating and weighing up what she should say next. Taking a deep breath, she finally said, 'I thought I should mention something to you… it's about Bill Trick. Well, how should I put it? He has a bit of a reputation with his female staff, if you know what I mean? The last girl who lived in the cottage where you are now, left in a bit of a hurry after being here for about six months. She was a slip of a lass, younger than you I'd say and very quiet. Well, I noticed him,' Pam pointed with her chin over in the direction of the Manor House, 'let'n himself out of the backyard gate a couple of times late at night. He looked right furtive if you ask me. If you want my advice, you keep your doors locked at night. I wouldn't trust him as far as I could throw him!'

Having said her piece, and perhaps thinking she might've said too much, Pam walked off back towards her own front door and disappeared inside. Her words had given me a serious attack of the creeps, so I took her advice and latched the front door and left the key in the back. I also put the chain on for good measure. A couple more weeks passed without incident, however, one morning, I'd just had a shower and had come down into the kitchen to get the kettle on before going back up to change, when there was a knock at the back door. I cracked it open and there on the step was Bill Trick illuminated in the yard light.

Stepping immediately in, he almost pushed past me into the kitchen and sat down at my little fold-down breakfast table.

'Ah, you have the kettle on then? Mine's a coffee, white with two sugars.' Trick chuckled and made himself comfortable.

I suddenly became very aware that I was only wearing a small towel and my thighs and tops of my breasts were showing.

'I'll just pop upstairs to change if you don't mind.'

More chuckling.

'You look fine the way you are my dear, don't mind me.' As he spoke, Trick rose and placed himself next to the kitchen door so I'd have to brush past him to go out into the hall and upstairs.

I hesitated. I'd started to feel quite angry at his unwarranted intrusion.

'Why exactly are you here Mr Trick? Is there something you need to tell me?

His face grew red and I could see his anger beginning to boil as he said, 'Only that I think you've been avoiding me. Why's that? You must realise that free accommodation isn't usually a perk for junior staff like yourself.' With that, he smiled, like a cat that'd got the cream. 'I'm going to be expecting some 'natural payment' in lieu of rent, if you know what I mean.'

I was now becoming quite frightened.

'You can't just come in here!'

'Oh yes, I can! I can come in here any time I damn well please; I own the place remember?'

At that, I pushed past him and ran upstairs. Half thinking he'd come up after me, I was terrified and thought of screaming or banging on the bedroom wall to alert my neighbour. To my relief, I just heard the back door close with a loud slam. I was shaking. Since the car had finally died, I got straight on my bicycle and rode into the village to find a call box. In tears, I phoned Jill Oar and told her what'd happened. She came to pick me up later on that morning.

As we drove away from the farm, Jill put on her legal hat (she'd been a local magistrate for several years) and assumed her stern voice.

'You know you could press charges. He came into your private space uninvited, and from what you've told me, he was quite aggressive.'

I just shook my head.

'It'd just be his word against mine and he's probably got influential friends. I just want to forget all about it.'

Pat's parents arranged to have the furniture removed without me having to go back there and I subsequently arranged for a chap from the local garage to tow Vanda's stricken car off to the scrapyard.

***

So what had looked like a great opportunity turned out to be made of lead not gold. It was a total disaster and I landed back at the Oars' homeless,

175

carless and jobless once again. I was desperate, had no money, and felt very, very low indeed. I even began thinking I'd brought it on myself and I'd thrown away a chance to settle down. Sitting in Ben Oar's silent old bedroom in an attic, I sat at the desk where he'd probably done his homework or crammed for his exams at Uppingham Boys' School and I cried long and hard, my tears dropping like warm rain onto the ink-stained French polish of Ben's old desk. It was then I spotted the old ex-army field telephone stuck in a corner where it'd been abandoned after Ben and Adam had moved out of their respective homes, Ben to start a career as a writer and Adam as a vet. Seeing it again made me even more miserable. It was a reminder that everyone that mattered to me had moved away and was getting on with their lives and here I was back just a hundred yards away from where I started without anything to show for it. My bitter tears had left me exhausted, but resolved. I had to do something; I couldn't just wallow in a well of self-pity. 'C'mon Deborah', I said to myself, 'Have faith!' Pulling myself together, I once again resolved to put an advert into the Farmers Weekly.

Since it was now February 1982, my mind turned to lambing. I knew that lambing was a time when many family farms were hard-pushed and short-handed, but up until that point, my only experience, apart from helping a little during my sandwich year, was during my third year at WAC on a two-week stint over the Easter holidays at Shân's family farm, the Grûg, a hill farm that overlooked the majestic Black Mountains near Hay-on-Wye.[28] Looking back, I've often wondered where my love of sheep really came from. Knowledge of lambing didn't sprout unbidden from my consciousness one day; it had to be based in hands-on experience. Farmers wouldn't entrust their flock to a complete novice, I would have needed to demonstrate that I had some kind of grounding. During that Easter break at the Grûg, where Shân had failed in teaching me about the innards of a tractor engine or a PTO shaft assembly, she succeeded in imparting some of her deep knowledge of sheep husbandry and lambing, in particular, how to manage problem ewes. I'll never forget one occasion where she deftly looped a length of baler twine around the back of the head of a lamb that had become stuck in the ewe's birth canal. Shân was always imperturbable when it came to sheep. She

---

[28] Rather quaintly and also apt for a hill farm, the Grûg is Welsh for 'heather'.

said at the time, 'You should never be afraid to have a go. When you're as far as we are from the nearest vet, you've got to learn some do it yourself tricks of the trade otherwise you'll have a lot of dead lambs on your hands!'

I'd certainly enjoyed the work. Striding across the fells with Shân's sheepdog, Dot, at our heels bringing the ewes down to the shed for lambing. For me, working with sheep seemed to have a perfect combination of outdoor and indoor work. Then there were the lambs, those amiable scraps of life that seemed to reach into my very being to tug at my heartstrings and bring out the tender, nurturing side of my female character. On top of all that, there were also hot cuppas by the Joyces' open range in the evening where we had long political conversations with Shân's dad, Mr Joyce, the only farmer I've ever met that had socialist views. He loathed Margaret Thatcher and what she was doing to the welfare state and the Welsh miners! Crucially, Mr Joyce wrote me a kindly reference in which he said, "*[I] had shown an aptitude for handling sheep and a high level of dedication to the care of ewes during lambing that would be an asset to any stock operation.*" Mr Joyce was a well-known and much respected figure in farming circles. Like anywhere else, in farming it's often who you know as well as what you know that opens doors.

Over the next couple of weeks my desperate plea for work, like a message in a bottle, floated out into the farming community and netted me three months of lambing work, on three separate farms in Yorkshire, Hertfordshire and in Wales at Glantnor Park, just a stone's throw away from Llover Gyfall where I worked during my sandwich year. This offer of a triumvirate of hard but gainful employment buoyed me up, so, with modest expectations, I boarded a train and travelled up to Harrogate.

Chapter 20
Lambing at last!

Dubb End farm near the Scargill Reservoir turned out to be tenanted by a friendly young couple, Ben and Gilly West with help from their five-year-old daughter, Hetty, who loved her plastic tractor and was clearly a farmer in the making! Enterprisingly, to make ends meet (then as now, there was no burgeoning or vibrant market for wool in the UK and New Zealand lamb was keeping the home market on its toes) the Wests had got a grant from the EU to convert a small outbuilding into a campsite toilet block and Gilly was doing B&B. When I arrived, the Wests were running six hundred ewes on their lowland farm and were up to their necks in lambs! Right from the start, it was clear that Ben and Gilly ran their farm as an equal partnership. On the first evening, they excitedly talked about their plans to expand their tourist operation and were thinking of going into free-range egg production in a big way. Their kindness and enthusiasm were infectious. They were welcoming; a refreshing change from my previous experience up to that point. They also gave me credit for the experience I had and treated me with consideration and respect. All this acted like a gentle balm on my nerves that'd been severely jangled by my experience with the devious Mr Trick. Since it was a lowland farm, the Wests were running Suffolk ewes. In contrast with hardy hill sheep breeds like Beulah, the Suffolks needed some pampering, especially as they were lambing in chilly conditions in February. Where a Beulah ewe could rally it out on the fells and pretty much get on with lambing on her own, these soft lowlanders needed to be housed during and immediately after lambing, so the 'maternity' ward could become a little hectic and overcrowded at times! Additional much appreciated perks included Gilly's home cooking and a warm comfortable bed in their guest room, so I felt rather pampered too!

I'd arrived at a point when lambing was really starting to get busy and I could see that Ben was somewhat overwhelmed, so I got stuck in straight away. On my second evening, after a hearty supper of toad-in-the-hole with bubble and squeak, I took my first night shift. Although it looked rather tumbledown from the outside, the thick walls of the old stone barn that acted as the maternity ward, or lambing shed, was fit for purpose and filled with a comforting bed of straw. The barn's low drystone walls belied the true height of the roof once you were inside. The earth floor had been dug out and large quantities of soft barley straw filled the lambing stalls and the races [free-standing steel hurdles that could be moved around] where the pregnant ewes were kept before they gave birth. The whole scene was bathed in the kind of orange glow you get from ancient strip lights attached high up on the rafters of an old barn. The deep straw and hollowed-out appearance of the earth floor gave it the appearance of a giant nest. Nodding in approval I inhaled the mixed scent of straw blended with the pungent odour of sheep muck and lanolin and quietly walked around the pens listening for the tell-tale guttural bleating that signalled that a ewe might be delivering her lamb. At a midpoint between the rows of lambing pens, I checked on the 'nursery' where the orphan lambs were being kept. I'd brought an old feed sack with some bottles of milk for the lambs made up from a special dried concentrate. Just like you'd do for a human baby, I'd warmed the milk so it was about blood temperature. As I got in the pen with the bottles and sat down on the straw, the lambs instinctively crowded around me like they would with their mother. They pushed their dark, fleecy little heads under my arms and nuzzled my legs. Tears stung my eyes. I was captivated by their trust in me and they seemed to trigger my womanly nurturing instincts. The experience was moving and somewhat unsettling at the same time. Opening my bag, I drew out a single bottle with a 'C' marked on it indicating it contained colostrum replacer for an orphan lamb that'd had just been rejected by his mum. The lamb needing the colostrum was a very small specimen. He carried the dewy sheen of his mother's amniotic fluid on his fleece and the drying umbilical cord was still firmly attached to his belly. I carefully scooped up the little chap and cradled him gently while his lips fumbled with the rubber teat on the bottle. After a few attempts, he soon got the hang of it. The rest of the lambs were a bit older and were getting about one hundred and forty millilitres of milk replacer every four hours.

About halfway through feeding the lambs, I started to get stomach cramps. Thinking this was due to my recent heavy meal, I tried to ignore it and carry on with my rounds, but instead of letting up as I walked around the barn, the pain got rapidly worse. Eventually I gave up on my round and was forced back to the house.

I lay on my bed for a while but it was no use, I needed help, so I knocked gently on Gilly and Bens' bedroom door and Gilly appeared almost immediately probably thinking it was Hetty.

'Debbie, are you all right? You look terribly pale!'

'It's my stomach: I've got severe cramps. I haven't been able to finish checking the lambing shed. I'm so sorry, but I think I need to go and lie down for a spell.'

Gilly looked concerned and said, 'I'll get Ben up, he'll take a look around the barn, so don't worry!' I staggered off to bed and again lay down on the counterpane fully clothed expecting my discomfort to pass. After a while, it could have been an hour, the pain was unbearable. In despair, I let out a loud moan that brought Gilly back into my room. 'Debbie, what's wrong?'

Almost unable to speak, I said, 'Sorry, but the pain is really bad, please could you get a doctor?'

Gilly's head immediately disappeared. I could then hear snatches of her loudly whispering to Ben, 'It could be an ectopic pregnancy... NCT... mum had it... needed emergency... ambulance.'[29] I thought, 'I can't be pregnant! But I do need an ambulance!' Gilly came back into the room.

'We've called an ambulance.' She then crossed to my bed and gently pushed the hair away from my brow and checked my temperature. She held my hand and gently stroked my head. 'They'll be here soon, hang on in there my lovely. It only takes twenty minutes to get to the district hospital in Harrogate.' Gilly's kindly expression calmed me slightly, but the pain kept coming in waves. Then, from where I lay, I heard the loud rush of a diesel engine and the squeal of brakes. Blue light washed by bedroom wall. Heavy feet on the stairs was followed by the appearance of two ambulance staff at the foot of my bed.

An ambulance-woman's chiselled features appeared over me.

---

[29] NCT: National Childbirth Trust, a fantastic, grassroots, self-help organisation organised by, and for, new mothers.

'Where does it hurt m'love? Are you pregnant?' Almost unable to speak with pain at this point, I just shook my head. 'We're taking you to hospital right now.'

The tight bend in the steep cottage stairs prevented them using a stretcher, so the woman's male crew member half carried me down and loaded me on a gurney. I couldn't lay flat, so I tried curling into a foetal position in a desperate attempt to relieve the pain. The ambulance sped off at a crazy speed whilst the ambulance-woman stayed with me squeezing my hand.

'Stay with us Debbie. I can't give you any medication, but I'm gonna give you a little bit of gas and air to help the pain.' As soon as the mask was on my face, a gentle whistling sound of gas was followed by a wave of immediate relief, but even so, the pain remained severe. As light from city streets flashed past, the two-tone sound of the ambulance siren started up. Even in my stupefied state, a chill of dread went up my spine. Crashing through doors, I was swept along a corridor, strip lights flashing by above my head. We swung left and right and finally came to rest in what was probably an emergency room.

Other faces appeared above me and a calm male voice began asking questions.

'I've got to ask, are you pregnant?'

'No! Please do something!' Was all I could reply. I was scared and struggling to breathe through the pain.

I think I must've passed out, because the next thing I became aware of was a repetitive beeping sound. Harsh light filtered through my closed eyelids, but everything was still and quiet. I became aware of shifting sounds and the gentle breathing of another person quietly sitting next to me, so I turned my head in the direction of the sound and opened my eyes. A nurse appeared over me.

'How are you feeling Debbie? How is the pain?'

The pain? It was gone, I felt exhausted and drained, but otherwise okay. I breathed a sigh of relief and lay back.

'I feel much better! What was wrong with me?'

The nurse gently patted my arm.

'The doctor will be along shortly to see you. In the meantime, just get some rest. But first, try and drink some water.' The nurse helped me into an upright position and I noticed the pulse monitor on my finger. As she passed me a glass of water, the nurse peered into my face, checked the watch pinned to her chest and made some notes on a clipboard attached to the end of my bed.

As I sat up in bed, shafts of orange early morning light streamed through the window next to me; it felt like a reprieve. To nobody in particular, I whispered, 'Thank you.'

I subsequently spent a whole week in hospital, but no cause could be found for the pain that had poleaxed me that night. Much later, in a card I received from my brother in Charagua, Adam, characteristically prosaic as always, said, 'Well Plum, if you'd been seen by a vet, they'd have definitely got to the bottom of it! I bet it was a volvulus [twisted gut] rare in adult humans, but not uncommon in babies and Alsatian dogs. I'd have sorted you out in no time!' I thought, 'Dear old Adam! Light on sympathy, but always there with a solution to any problem!

***

By the time I'd got out of Harrogate District Hospital, there was just a week left of my temporary stint with the Wests before I had to love them and leave them so I could move on to my next lambing. I felt pretty guilty because I left on the very day when there'd been a group of ewes that'd produced triplets and the whole skein had become impossibly tangled as lambs from one ewe had got mixed up with those from another. Nevertheless, Gilly seemed pretty happy though! When it became clear that a miscreant sperm hadn't maliciously fertilised an egg in one of my fallopian tubes, I think she'd been worried that she might have poisoned me with her cooking! Oh well, as they say in American footballing circles, "no harm no foul."

The location of my next lambing job was at Watersplace, an estate occupying five thousand acres of low-lying land along the banks of the River Ash near Ware in Hertfordshire. Since my lambing jobs ran back-to-back, on the Sunday morning I left the Wests I boarded a train at Harrogate and arrived at Ware that afternoon. Although it was only the beginning of March, it was unusually warm and I sweated profusely as I strained on the pedals of my bicycle up Widbury Hill. From there, I rode past Watersplace Farm's stately red brick pile where the squire of the manor, Henry Buxton, resided and on towards the little village of Wareside and Easneye's Farm, the Buxtons' dairy operation where I was going to be staying for the next month. Pushing my heavily laden bike along the lane towards the largish red brick house of Henry Buxton's dairy manager, Tim Ford, I didn't quite know what to expect. Whilst Tim had seemed amiable enough when I'd spoken to him on the phone, I knew I'd be staying at his house and that Tim was a single chap living on his own. Having recently tangled with a married man and his carnal intentions, I was understandably wary of sharing a house with a possibly unmarried version of the same ilk.

Therefore, it was with some trepidation that I tapped the big brass doorknocker. Almost immediately, Chris's tall frame appeared at the door like he'd been waiting in the hall for me to arrive. He smiled broadly and said, 'C'mon in Debbie!' After enthusiastically shaking my hand, he ushered me along the hall and in the direction of what smelt like his Sunday evening meal. 'You're in luck; I've just finished cooking something for supper. On Sundays, I like to have a bit of a treat.' He winked at me as we entered the kitchen. 'Now, leave your bag in the hall, sit yourself down and have something to eat, we don't want it getting cold.' Crossing to a '50s style gas cooker, Tim drained boiling water from a large pan that'd been sitting on the stovetop. He then removed what appeared to be plastic-covered slices from a gammon joint and set them on a serving plate with a flourish. 'Boil-in-the-bag's so much quicker than a roast! You can even multitask, and boil your veg in the same water as the joint, easy-peasy!' As he liberated the meat from the confines of its plastic wrapping and set about serving up, I allowed my gaze to wander around the kitchen. There was a pantry full of tins and on the kitchen floor, a pair of big muddy boots filled with newspaper sat next to the oven. Straw liberally coated the mustard-coloured hall carpet and just inside the kitchen door, there was a small closet that housed a washing machine with a full laundry basket sitting on top. To complete this rustic tableau, several muck-covered overalls hung behind the kitchen door on a couple of large coat hooks. I smiled to myself, Chris's abode positively shouted bachelor, bachelor! After supper, Tim showed me upstairs and into a guest bedroom. On entering, I was met by a musty waft of mould.

A single bed with an ancient patchwork quilt covering it sat next to a small sash window. Grubby lace curtains hung there, and as I pushed them back along their springy rails to crack open the window and air the room, I noticed the window ledge had become a veritable flies' graveyard. Literally hundreds of them had perished there after exhausting themselves in a futile attempt to get out of the window that must've been closed for years. It took all my strength to force open the sash, and in the process, the sleeves of my woolly jumper picked up droves of fossilised fly bodies. Although slightly damp and infused with the heady aroma of cow muck, my living quarters were comfortable and Tim was a genial and friendly host.

Since Chris's main duties were with the large dairy operation, on my first morning, I was introduced to Dave Rowe who ran the estate's flock of twelve hundred Suffolk ewes with help from his son, Peter. Whist he explained my duties, I got the distinct impression that Rowe was thinking to himself that he'd been landed with a slip of a girl to do a man's job. From my perspective, he was just another grouchy old man who resented the intrusion of an inexperienced outsider. Therefore, during the first couple of days, Rowe directed a chilly and cantankerous demeanour in my direction. However, at the end of my first week there I got my chance to shine. On the day in question, an early evening chill and an unexpected flurry of snow accompanied me on my walk over to the lambing shed to do my rounds. Since it was my shift so to speak, I was expecting to find the place empty, but as I entered, I could see Rowe and his son kneeling beside a ewe, that was obviously in some distress.

Joining them in the pen, I was ignored by the old man, but Peter piped up and said, 'The lambs got itself stuck good and proper. He's got his head and one of his legs out, but he's jammed solid and we can't budge him in or out.'

At this, Rowe huffed loudly and finally deigned to speak to me.

'His head's swelled and neither of us can get a hand past it.' As if to illustrate his point, he held out his huge ham-like hands in an exasperated gesture.

'Why not let me have a go? I have very small hands and thin wrists.' Rowe nodded, he did have to admit that they were indeed, small. 'Just tell me what to do Mr Rowe, let me be your hands so to speak.'

'All right then, we need to push 'is head back in so we can get 'is forelegs out in front of 'im and then pull 'im out. She's exhausted and lost the fight in 'er, so we're likely gonna have to pull 'im out.'

Lubricating my right hand, I thought back to what Shân had taught me when I'd helped with lambing at the Grûg when I was at WAC. Then, as now, a lamb had got stuck and Shân had rolled her sleeves up and showed me what to do. I remembered her saying, 'Now Debbie, you often have to go back before you can go forward. You need to push him back in so you can sort his legs out. But if you're going inside her, take it slow and feel your way around. Try and create an image of what's going on inside from what you can feel with your fingertips.' Weighing this sound advice, I carefully slid my flattened hand into the ewe's birth canal and managed to slip it past the lamb's swollen head and then push him back up inside her against the ewe's contractions.

After a nod of approval Rowe said, 'Right, now tie this baler twine on your forefinger. What I want you to do is put your hand in and get the string around the back of 'is head. Then, once you've done that, I want you to slip a loop of string over 'is hooves.'

Rowe tied a crafty little slip knot around my finger and I slid my hand back up and felt my way around the back of the lamb's head. The ewe still had some fight in her and she bucked hard with the discomfort from my intrusion, but the men managed to hold her down. After a couple of attempts, I worked the string around what I hoped was the back of the lamb's head and brought it back out. After that, slipping a loop over each hoof was relatively easy.

'Now girlie, leave the pull'n to us!' Rowe muscled in and he and his son pulled on the twine. Slowly, slowly, the lamb's nose and feet appeared and once his head was clear, the ewe managed to push him all the way out and the lamb flopped in a steaming heap onto the straw. Peter cleared the mucus from the animal's face and mouth, but it wasn't breathing. Rowe slowly shook his head, 'Damn, it must've suffocated! It was a forlorn hope. But you did well gett'n 'im out. You might 'ave the makings of shepherdess after all! Any road, we managed to save the ewe!'

So, after ten days of grumpy indifference, I'd made my mark. After the incident with the ewe, Rowe gave me some measure of grudging appreciation in the weeks that followed. I felt I'd shown what I could do and had gained some confidence from it. If I could convince a crusty old shepherd like Rowe I was up to the job, then I couldn't be too bad!

Although I'd literally only been at Watersplace for four weeks, the makings of a friendship that was to last a lifetime had sprung up between Tim and me. Taking on some of the cooking duties definitely had something to do with this. A proper pork roast with all the trimmings can have a transformative effect on any relationship, even a platonic one like ours! Reading between the lines, I got the impression that most of the staff at the farm were expecting Tim and me to announce our engagement after a whirlwind romance over a boil-in-the-bag dinner or two! But it wasn't to be. I did, however, come to appreciate Chris's sense of humour that could get quite eccentric at times. One incident that stands out occurred when I popped over to the dairy one evening to find out how he was getting on. I'd got some food prepared for supper and the evening was pleasant, so it was an excellent excuse for a walk.

I found Tim chatting with his stockman outside one of the sheds.

'Well Debbie, have you come for a tour around the dairy? Are you missing the cows?'

I smiled.

'Not a bit of it, I'm actually getting into this shepherding lark!'

'Well, since you're now into sheep, you'll be able to appreciate one of my famous party pieces!' With that, Tim lay on one of the large drifts of straw in the barn and began making the familiar guttural bleating sound of a ewe giving birth. At first, I was quite alarmed and thought Tim was suffering from some kind of seizure, but when it dawned on me what he was doing, I couldn't stop laughing. Tim Ford had turned out to be one farmer that certainly didn't take himself too seriously!

***

The last of my trio of lambing jobs found me back in Wales. Glantnor Park nestles in the butter tub floodplains along the River Severn, the preserve of the gentry class of landowners in Montgomeryshire. If a harder living could be wrested from the thinner soils of the fells around the likes of Llover Gyfall where I'd spent my sandwich year, Glantnor sheep were pampered on rich fields where twins and triplets flowered in their bellies and the cows on their sumptuous meadows produced more of the richer milk. The stately fifteenth century pile of Glantnor itself is the ancestral home of the Wynn-Jones family, its present incumbent, William and his wife Kate, were friends of Prince Charles and were on nodding terms with the queen. I'd needed a family of colleagues with a common purpose and I unexpectedly found them at Glantnor. In the short time I spent there during my first lambing, I felt I'd come home at last. The solitude and despair of my time adrift were to be replaced by a modicum of camaraderie with the estate workers and their families. Since I'd arrived in April, the hedgerows were adorned by early-arrived yellowhammers and the willows along the Severn echoed to the emotive voice of the first cuckoos whilst swifts skimmed over the verdant pastures. Like the Jews' search for their promised land, my journey to Glantnor Park had been fraught, full of self-doubt and difficulty. However, cycling the five or so miles from Welshpool station whilst the sun warmed my back, I felt buoyed up and happy. As I rode along, the words from the first few lines of a medieval English canon I'd learnt at school popped into my head, *"Sumer is icumen in lhude sing cuccu. Groweb sed and bloweb med and springb be wde nu sing cuccu."*[30] Ah, the advantages of a classical private education! Just as I turned into a broad estate road leading up to the farm, I caught site of the big house and thought to myself that things probably hadn't changed much since the Cuckoo Song was written. The lord was still in his manor, the workers still toiled in the fields and I was coming to join them!

Unexpectedly, the first time I met the lord of the manor was during my very first minutes of arriving at Glantnor. I'd been told to come straight over to the farm and the lambing sheds where someone'd meet me. As I approached the sheds a cacophony of bleating filled the air. Getting closer, above the din, I could just make out the harsh sounds of a man shouting. Thinking something was amiss, I quickly propped my bike against a wall and went in the direction of the shouting. Around the back of the sheds and across a farm track, there was a walled paddock

---

[30] Here's the modern English translation! Summer has arrived, loudly sing, cuckoo! The seed is growing and the meadow is blooming, and the wood is coming into leaf now. Sing, cuckoo!

and an orchard. In the orchard was a tallish man in his fifties with a stylish quiff of curly hair wearing a smart-looking Barbour jacket accompanied by a young woman with red hair in her twenties wearing overalls. They were both rushing around apparently chasing something that was out of view behind the wall. It looked such a comical scene that I couldn't help but laugh.

At the sound of my amusement, the man stopped what he was doing and stood with his arms akimbo.

'Debbie Best, is it?'

I nodded

'Yes I am.'

'Well, don't just stand there having a laugh, why don't you come in here and give us a hand!' Trotting over, I pushed open a gate into the paddock and it was then that I saw what they were chasing. No doubt tempted by the sumptuous grass in the neighbouring orchard, a bunch of miscreant ewes had jumped over the wall and were having a fine old time at his lordship's expense. It soon became clear that William hadn't a clue how to round up sheep, neither of them had a crook and there wasn't a dog in sight.

I didn't know much about handling sheep, but I did know something, so I said, 'Mr Wynn-Jones.'

William stopped and held up his hand.

'Please, just call me William.'

'Well,' I said, 'I really think we should get a dog or a couple of crooks at least. We'll never round them up like this!'

William nodded.

'Quite right, quite right. Gwen, could you pop over to Roy's and ask him to come over with his dogs.'

The young woman nodded and walked towards me on the way out of the paddock, but before she passed me, she stopped.

'Gwen Hughs.' We shook hands. 'Good to meet you, Debbie! I think we'll be boarding together at Mrs Jones' in Berwen.' She winked at me and smiled. She had a friendly oval face with freckles and her Welsh accent was soft, like Shân's.

After about ten minutes, a sturdy man with short sandy hair strode purposefully towards us. At his heels were two collie dogs. He carried a long shepherd's crook and he looked like he meant business. William appeared to be somewhat embarrassed.

'I'm sorry Roy, but the pregnant ewes have got out into the orchard again.'

Roy wagged his head.

'We'll need to fix that gate and put some wire on the top of the wall or they'll just be do'n it again!'

Without waiting for an answer, Roy swept his harms forward and his dogs shot off past us towards the back of the orchard, one going left and the other right of the errant sheep. Roy's piercing whistles were accompanied by the occasional command

'Come by! Come by!' The dogs quickly pushed the ewes towards the gate and back into the paddock. Once the gate was closed, Roy came over to introduce himself. 'I'm Roy Jones, you must be Debbie. Don't look so surprised, you'll soon learn that everyone knows everyone else's business around here!' Roy laughed heartily at this. 'I help the estate with the sheep, but look you, I've got my own flock of six hundred hill ewes to look after, so I've got my hands full as well at the moment! But if you need some advice or you think something needs the vet, come and see me, or Tony Croft and we'll sort you out, see.' With that, he waved at William and strode off back up the lane with his collies obediently following in his wake.

I looked a question over to William, who said, 'Ah yes, Tony Croft, he works on the estate, but he and a couple of the other chaps, Simon and Di, also lend a hand fetching and carrying when we're busy.

With the ewes back in the paddock where they should be, William showed us around the lambing operation. It turned out that Gwen, like me, had only just started as temporary lambing assistant. Whilst William mostly knew where everything was, his knowledge seemed largely theoretical when it came to details.

'At the moment we have one thousand two hundred Beulahs and Welsh half-breed ewes. They're kept mostly on the lowlands, so they're mostly pretty easy to handle.'

Gwen turned to me and winked, then she whispered, 'Except when they lead us a merry dance around the orchard!'

After giving his little tour, William said he had to go up to the house for the rest of the afternoon, but before he left, he said, 'Now, there's a person you haven't met yet, Rhys Thomas. Rhys is in Welshpool getting some feed, but he should be back later this afternoon, so if you have any further questions, he should be able to help, but as he's only really just started with us himself, Roy, who advises us on the sheep, can take care of anything else and also either he or Tony have the authority to call out the vet if needs be.'

It was mid-afternoon when we returned to the lambing shed, but as the fates would have it, ten ewes looked like they were lambing at once, so Gwen and I suddenly had our hands full. After an hour, or so, it looked like everything was going okay with most of them, but one ewe looked like she might be having a problem delivery.

I was getting a little concerned when I heard someone opening the gate into the shed. I assumed it was Rhys Thomas returning from Welshpool, but Gwen tapped my arm and said, 'It's Tony. I'll go and get him to come and have a look.'

She returned with a rather suave-looking dark-haired man with a moustache and deep crows-feet lines around a pair of eyes that looked like their owner had done his fair share of laughing and smiling.

'Hello Debbie, I'm Tony. I'm sorry I wasn't around when you arrived; Roy said you'd be coming today. So, what 'ave we got here?' Tony felt the ewe's belly, 'Mmmh, yes, it looks like his head's twisted back and stuck. He'll need his head turning right enough. The trouble is, my hands are generally way too big for this kind of thing.' Looking over at me as I held the ewe steady, he nodded and said, 'Now Debbie, you look to me like you've got a pair of lambing hands.'

So, within a few hours of arriving at a new lambing job, I already had my hand stuck inside a ewe's innards! With a bit of luck, I managed to turn the little chap's head fairly easily. And since the ewe was still going strong, she managed to pop him out and a second one followed. Both were alive and intact. I was over the moon!

Tony looked impressed.

'Well done, Debbie. It looks like you've got a knack there!' Another bit of luck was in store; Gwen had a battered old minivan so I'd have a lift back to Berwen.

As we put my bike and bags into the back of her van Gwen said,

'Now Debbie, it's past four o'clock, so we'd better get back to Mrs Jones so as you can get yourself settled in. She's a stickler at mealtimes, and she likes to have her guests around the table for their evening meal at five on the dot.'

Mrs Jones had a little terraced house in a cobbled lane in the centre of Berwen. She was in her seventies, but seemed as sprightly as someone much younger. She was a classical traditional landlady type who wore a starched white apron and blouse. She was very efficient in a bustling, landlady sort of a way, but she turned out to have a heart of gold and looked after Gwen and me like we were family. Whilst she didn't run a B&B or guest house per se, Mrs Jones was a widow who needed to eke out the pension left by her husband who'd been a gamekeeper up at Glantnor. So every now and then, she did bed and full board for some of the seasonal workers that came to work at the estate.

On my first evening, promptly at five, Gwen and I took our places around a large round table in Mrs Jones' dining room.

'Now, I'm thinking you girls will need something to keep you going this evening up at the lambing sheds, so I've done some dumplings to go with the stew and potatoes.' The old lady then brought in a large tureen of stew with a bowl of vegetables, and lastly, the dumplings.

Gwen just smiled and said, 'I've been here two days and I've not been going hungry!' We both laughed.

***

Glantnor Park was turning out to be one of the best places I'd worked so far, however, there was just one fly in the ointment, and his name was Rhys Thomas. Thomas had started at Glantnor not long before I'd arrived for temporary lambing. Whilst he bragged about his credentials with sheep, he spent more time driving around in his comical little Reliant Robin three-wheeler than actually taking a turn helping with lambing. Gwen reckoned he saw himself more as an advisor on the sheep than a worker; I could certainly agree with that, he was a right know-it-all! When there was work to do like humping straw bales, unloading feed bags or taking a night shift in the lambing shed, Rhys was nowhere to be seen. For the first couple of weeks, Rhys's laissez-faire approach worked fine for me as I didn't have to listen to his barbed comments about women's shortcomings when it came to just about anything to do with farming. But my unspoken resolution to agree to disagree and try to avoid a confrontation with him couldn't last.

Whilst many lambings, especially the difficult ones, tended to happen during the night, I found a ewe in trouble during one of my frequent monitoring rounds of the lambing pens during the afternoon. When the vet had done an ultrasound check (usually at about forty- and ninety-days' gestation) she'd been tagged as likely to have twins. Towards the end of their pregnancy, all twin and triplet ewes were given concentrated feed supplements, so I'd had an eye on her since I started at Glantnor. The ewe was lying on her side in the pen panting and obviously in severe pain. I got into the pen beside her and tried to soothe her with my voice.

'C'mon girl, let's see what's the matter with you.' The animal's eyes were wide and she was frightened. I got around to the business end and had a look. I could see a lamb's tail hanging from her uterus. 'Oh, that's not good', I thought. 'She's definitely got a breech delivery with one of her lambs.' Even with my limited knowledge at that point, I knew she needed a caesarean and I had to get the vet. I ran outside, found Gwen and she stayed with the ewe so I could go and find Tony or Roy to ask them to get the vet out. However, I was just leaving the shed when Rhys showed up.

He was the last person I wanted to see, so I tried to ignore him when he said, 'Oh, I see, it's off for a tea break is it? Can't stand the pace?'

I was stressed and couldn't let his comment pass, so I replied, 'Actually I'm off to get Tony to have a look at a ewe. I think she's got a breech and needs the vet.'

In my short experience of the man, 'Tony' and 'vet', seemed to be trigger words for Rhys, and sure enough, he finished climbing out of his three-wheeler and marched towards me.

'Oh, I see! Well, we ain't get'n the vet and pay'n out for some pricey city guy to come in here and tell us what to do! I've got plenty experience with breech, I'll likely have it sorted out easy like, before you've had time to even phone the vet.' Rhys pushed past me into the shed and marched over to where Gwen was sitting with the ewe. 'Right, out the way lassie, I'll take a look.' Rhys rolled his sleeves up, found some lubricant gel and forced his hand in past the lamb's hindquarters. The ewe bleated in pain and it took all our strength to keep her still while Rhys fished around inside her.

After a few minutes of this, I couldn't stand it any longer.

'Mr Thomas! Rhys! Please, you don't need to do this! She's in terrible pain and the more we delay getting the vet, the more chance we'll lose her and the lambs!'

Rhys just grunted and continued his agonising ministrations and said, 'I just need to turn 'im and he'll come out easy.' I knelt down for a closer look and I could now see the ewe was bleeding profusely, a bad sign that indicated that her uterus had been badly damaged and probably haemorrhaging. Even Rhys could see there was some danger. He wasn't interested in the ewe though, and definitely didn't want to lose face in front of two women.

'I'm gonna cut 'im out, at least then the others'll be able to come out.'

That was it for me, so I said, 'I'm getting Tony. Just please stop what you're doing.' Since it was about teatime, I ran off in the direction of the shed where Tony, Simon and the others usually had their elevenses. But they were nowhere to be seen, and then I remembered they'd gone off to Welshpool for supplies. I was distracted and crying by the time I returned to the shed. But it was all too late, the ewe had died; it was complete carnage.

I found Gwen there on her own. She said, 'Rhys has gone off somewhere and left us to it, and to take blame most likely.' I couldn't find anything to say in reply, I just wept bitter tears of anger and frustration.

That evening, I was so shaken up by what happened with the ewe that even Mrs Jones' delectable apple crumble couldn't assuage my anguish and upset. Whilst Gwen and I were eating, I sat brooding on the incident. The silence sat so heavily in the room that you could hear the metronome ticking of Mrs Jones' grandmother clock in the hallway. Gwen tried to snap me out of it by talking about the collie pup she was training back at her family farm, a pleasant-sounding little smallholding over near Ross-on-Wye, but I was having none of it. Then she hit on a plan.

'Look Debbie, let's nip down the Talbot for a pint after we've checked the lambing shed this evening. It'll take your mind off things.' I smiled at her. It was difficult to be melancholy in the face of her big-hearted exuberance!

As I mentioned previously, I'd briefly visited the Talbot Hotel on a young farmers get-together during my sandwich year at WAC. Then, as now, Berwen is a village of two pubs; the Crown Inn, situated near the centre, was where the posh and the up-and-coming posh went, whilst everyone else crossed the ancient stone bridge over the Afon Rhiw and drank at the Talbot Hotel. Being a Friday evening and fairly warm, it was pretty busy and a melee of Barbour jacketed young farmer types had spilled out into the car park overlooking the river by the time we arrived. As Gwen and I approached the gaggle of florid-cheeked young men, there was a distinct lull in their conversation as we passed through the door into the public bar as few of them paused midway through swigging their pints of ale to watch us enter. A few comments and loud guffaws followed us through the door; obviously we were seen as "fresh meat".

As we pushed through the throng around the bar, Gwen tugged my arm

'There's Simon and Di over there; they work with Tony on the estate.' I looked over and saw two rather dishevelled young men, one (who turned out to be Di) wore a tweed flat cap pulled down to his ears and the other had a crop of unruly hair that looked like he regularly pushed it up between his fingers like Stan Laurel. I remember thinking he also seemed to have Laurel's mirthful comic demeanour and that together they might have done a passible impression of the famous comic duo Laurel and Hardy! Since they'd already spotted Gwen, we decided to join them. I hoped that Tony might also be there so I could talk to him about Rhys, but they were by themselves.

As we approached, Simon smiled broadly and said, 'Ooh, who are these lovely ladies come to check out the male talent no doubt! Which one are you have'n' Di?!'

Ignoring Simon's comment, we sat down opposite them so as to keep the solid and immovable wooden table between them and us as a barrier against inevitable wandering hands. Gwen smiled a devious smile and

194

said, 'Well lads, aren't you going to get us a pint? Mine's a Double Dragon, and Debbie's is...'

I took my cue

'Same for me please!'

Di doffed his cap in comic deference and said, 'My wish is your command!' With that, he headed off to the bar.

Simon then took up where he left off.

'Why so glum ladies? You're in the company of prime Berwen male talent here y'know!' So I spent a few minutes telling him all about what'd happened with the ewe. Simon nodded sagely all the way through my sorry tale and said, 'Yeah, Rhys can be a right miserable bugger! He's got a temper on 'im too, so I'd steer clear of 'im. It's definitely his fault so you'd better talk to Tony about it if you don't want his nibs, William, blaming you for it!' We all agreed it was a plan. Encouraged that he had our attention, he continued in his jovial vein. 'Well, now that's settled, are you two go'n to be staying on and do'n some proper work after this temporary lambing lark? We could do with something more attractive around the place than Tony and Roys' miserable old faces!' Simon then nudged Di as he arrived back with our drinks, promptly spilling a fair bit on the table in the process. As he sat down, Simon cocked a wink at Di, and said, 'I'm just chatt'n these girls up and I think I'm having some success!'

Gwen looked exasperated and said, 'Put a sock in it Simon! We just came out for a quiet pint.' She then gave him a hard stare that cowed Simon into silence.

After that, Gwen and I more or less chatted together for the rest of the evening whilst the boys went to watch an impromptu yard of ale competition. After a few more beers, I think Gwen could see I'd had rather too much to drink, so she suggested we should get going as we had another early start the next day. As we walked back to Mrs Jones', Gwen nudged me and tittered. She then pointed at a clapped-out old Ford pickup with a couple of bales of straw in the back.

'That's Simon's car. He still lives with his mam and he's driving around with bales of straw in the back! He calls his car his 'fanny magnet!' We both laughed hysterically at the thought of tooling around in it on a date with Simon! It was then my drink-addled brain came up with a fiendish plan to get Simon back for all his earlier teasing. So, when Gwen had gone up to her room, I sneaked down to the pantry and grabbed a large jar of marmalade and headed back to Simon's car. I checked the door, and sure enough, it wasn't locked. I then set about coating the driver's seat liberally with the marmalade, using the whole jar in the process. I then quickly closed the door and made my escape back to Mrs Jones'. Later, lying in bed, I smiled to myself at the thought of the fun next morning.

In the sobriety that comes with a new day, I sat at breakfast eating a large portion of scrambled eggs and bacon and rather regretted the trick I'd played on Simon, but I didn't let on to Gwen what I'd done. I had to wait until elevenses, or bait time as everyone called it, before finding out what effect my prank had had on Simon. Gwen and I had already eaten the sandwiches that Mrs Jones had made us and were enjoying our flasks of tea and chatting to Tony and Roy, when Simon arrived. For added effect, he stopped and stood stock still in front of us with his eyes wide.

'Well,' he said, 'you'll never guess what happened last night!' We were all agog, and I tried to keep a straight face. 'Well,' he continued, 'I had a few drinks last night with Di down the Talbot. I was have'n' a bit of luck chatting to these two lovely ladies.' At this, he nodded at Gwen and me. 'Well, I got in my car to drive home. But when I got out at me mam's I felt like I was covered in some't sticky and horrible. I thought I'd shat m'self! Well, you'll never guess! It turned out to be marmalade! Now how on earth do you think that happened!' We were all in stitches at that point so nobody could give a coherent answer. A very long time afterwards, Simon found out that it was me that had played the trick on him. Simon was mad with me for a day or so, but he did, eventually, see the funny side and forgave me!

***

By the time my three stints of lambing had finished I'd contracted glandular fever, probably as a result of physical exhaustion. At that time, my mother had moved in with her new husband John, and was living at his cottage in Little Haven, so I spent a few weeks convalescing there. My stay provided an ideal opportunity to reconnect with Esme and acquaint myself with John, a quiet man and a tower of strength that had almost certainly saved my mother back from stumbling over the precipice of alcoholism. However, before I'd left, William said if I wanted to stay, he was sure he could find something for me to do. So I kept in touch with him and planned to return to Glantnor in June the same year.

Part 7
Glantnor

Chapter 21
Return to Glantnor

How do you summarise and capture the essence of what turned out to be four wonderful years at a place where I finally felt I'd graduated as a professional shepherdess? During my month of lambing work, I'd already formed a bond friendship with Tony and some of the other estate workers. I had even developed a fool-proof method of dealing with Simon's teasing that didn't involve marmalade! The huge and ancient substance of a place like Glantnor Park Estate meant that there always seemed to be a surplus of just about anything and everything. There were even spare accommodations! William had mentioned in a letter formally inviting me back to Glantnor that he'd be able to provide me with a house to live in. I was really excited by this, but nothing prepared me for what, "oh it's just a little place" as William had described it, turned out to be.

Garden Cottage nestled in one corner of a huge walled garden that had been built in the eighteenth century to supply fruit and vegetables for the master's house. The cottage had been the gardener's residence, and it was idyllic. Walking through the house for the first time on a beautiful day in the height of summer, I pushed open the kitchen door and stepped out onto a rustic stone patio that led on to the garden beyond. The walls were doing their job and they concentrated the heat of an already warm afternoon. Espalier fruit trees adorned the aged red bricks of the walls and plots with long rows of lettuces, carrots and potatoes stretched out towards an orchard. The finishing touch was also there, the gardener himself, toiling to clear a bed of its weeds using a long hoe. It was perfect... except for the acrid smell of damp all over the house! In fact, mould liberally coated the chimney breast in the living room. You could actually feel a dewy coating of damp on the walls, and this was in summer. I thought to myself, I'm going to have my work cut out here! But I needn't have worried too much, I had a few willing helpers amongst Tony, Simon and the other estate workers and their families.

There was, however, a downside in this domestic nirvana. William had promoted Rhys Thomas into a position of responsibility for the sheep operation, and so I'd essentially be working under him. But for the moment, I had my honeymoon period at the cottage to enjoy and so I rolled up my sleeves and got cracking. For a short time, I was in nest-building heaven! When I'd mentioned to Mrs Jones that William had offered me Garden Cottage, which, of course meant that I'd be leaving my snug quarters in her little cottage, she was a little sad. Then when I mentioned how damp it was, she suggested that Duncan, a self-employed painter and decorator based near Berwen, would be a good person to talk to for advice on what to do to get rid of the damp. She said she'd have a word with him the next time she bumped into him.

A week or so later, I was at the cottage one evening removing huge cobwebs from the ceiling, when there was a knock at the front door. I was about to have my first guest! I hurried downstairs and opened the door to not one, but two visitors. Standing on the doorstep was a slim, attractive, dark-haired woman in her mid-thirties with expressive mobile features. At her side was a friendly-looking chap with a shy smile and a good-natured twinkle in his eyes who said, 'Hello! Debbie, isn't it? I'm Duncan, and this is my wife, Marilyn.' We all enthusiastically shook hands and I got the kettle on.

Once they'd both settled on the rather mouldy couch in the living room, Duncan said, 'Mrs Jones happened to say that you needed help with the damp up 'ere at the cottage.'

Marilyn nodded in agreement and pulled a face.

'Oh, goodness, she was certainly right, the place has terrible damp! Y'know, it'll play havoc with your health in the winter Debbie!'

At this point, I felt I'd better warn them that I had no money for decorators, so I said, 'I know, water's literally running out of the walls! But I just can't afford a professional job.'

Duncan smiled.

'Oh, I know that Debbie, Mrs Jones just asked me if I could come over and give you some advice. Look, why don't I take a look around while you two have a natter.'

I immediately liked them both from the start, but it was Marilyn who did all the talking! Whilst Duncan made a slow, deliberate appraisal of my slimy green and black walls, she gave me a potted autobiography.

Front and centre in this, was the fact that they'd been trying for children for several years. They'd been to the doctor and had had fertility treatment, but to no avail. She confessed that she was getting desperate. Just talking about it caused Marilyn to dissolve into tears; I instinctively hugged her.

'Thanks Debbie, sorry to be such a misery, but it's the only thing I can think about at the moment.'

Although I couldn't afford Duncan's professional services, Marilyn offered to do what she could to help. Good as her word, one Saturday evening, a few days after I'd moved in, she knocked on my door and came in carrying a huge bag of what turned out to be lime.

'There're two more bags in the car that are too big for me to lift!' We grabbed an end each and brought two more 50kg sacks into the living room. Along with the lime, she'd also brought a couple of buckets and two huge brushes. I thanked her profusely and offered to pay, but she'd have none of it. In fact, she nipped out to her car and returned with a set of overalls for us both. 'Hang on darl'n I'll get these on and I'll show you what to do.' What followed was a couple of happy hours mixing lime and slapping it on the walls. We started in the living room and had completed the chimney breast and two walls when we flopped down onto two old wooden chairs, knackered and covered in lime wash from head to toe! I went into the kitchen and made us a cuppa.

While we sipped our tea and nibbled on digestive biscuits, Marilyn fixed me with her expressive brown eyes.

'I've not said this to anyone.' Her voice sounded serious and confessional. 'You know I said we can't have kids, well; actually, it's Duncan who can't have kids. He's quite a bit older than me and it turns out he's got low sperm count.' She ate another digestive and considered what she was going to say next. She then took a deep breath and said, 'So, I've sort of have been doing some of my own fertility treatment with another bloke. He's actually a family friend, a mate of my uncle. He's quite a bit older too, but… well, he's managed to do the business! I missed my period last month. I've always been a bit irregular, but since I'd been having unprotected sex with this other bloke, I thought I'd better go to the doctor. She did the test and said I'm definitely pregnant.'

Rather taken aback, I wasn't quite sure how to reply to this, so I said,

'You're happy aren't you?'

Marilyn nodded.

'Yes, totally, but I'm not sure how to break it to Duncan. What if he suspects? Physically, the father's not much like him; he has blue eyes and fair hair! I'm just hoping he'll think we got lucky. Since I found out I'm pregnant, I've been coaxing him into having sex every night for the last couple of weeks so it'll look like he got me pregnant. He's been enjoying himself, but I think I'm wearing him out!' We both laughed heartily and I gave her a huge, great big hug.

Chapter 22
Shearing time

As luck, or you could say misfortune, would have it, I'd arrived back at Glantnor at the start of shearing time, one of the most intensive periods of hard work in the shepherd's calendar. I'd heard stories about shearing and shearers at college that made it sound at once both romantic and exciting at the same time. Why so, you may ask. On the face of it, the work is labour-intensive, repetitive and exhausting, however, shearing time brought in an influx of fit, young, and not-so-young, men to the farm from all over the UK and even from as far as the Antipodes. For example, in June 1982, we had a tanned Adonis from New Zealand. I imagine that, back in the day, the presence of fresh young males in a village wouldn't have gone unnoticed by the female population. If one were to use animal husbandry terminology, I suspect that a fair amount of out-breeding occurred between the local farm girls and those outsiders that would likely have given a much-needed boost to genetic diversity in the region! For the local menfolk it may have been threatening. I say may have been, but like so many things in farming, little has changed and so I'm pretty certain that husbands and boyfriends no doubt kept their womenfolk close at hand whilst the shearers were about!

My first morning in the shearing shed started early; in fact, literally at the crack of dawn since I'd yet to put curtains up at my bedroom window, which meant that the first rays of the sun woke me every morning at five a.m. To assuage the nauseating effect of the fetid, damp air that had built up in my room overnight, I threw my window open and enjoyed the already warm air on my bare arms, as I leaned out and took in the buzzing, chirruping and bleating sounds carried up to me from a world that had already been going full steam ahead since four a.m. Then I thought, 'damn! I've got to make my own breakfast.' Since moving out of Mrs Jones', I was no longer enjoying hearty breakfasts and lashings of hot tea in her snug little dining room. I was also missing Gwen, who, after finishing her lambing stint at Glantnor, had moved on to her usual job working with horses as the showing and eventing season was now in full swing. Gwen's really was an itinerant's life, moving from stud to stud, pampering and grooming, primping beasts that could sell for more than the price of a Ferrari. Needless to say, in common with all things agricultural, the wages paid to the grooms and stable hands in no way reflected the responsibility they had for these pricey animals.

As if to offset the downside of having to fend for myself, William had recently handed me the keys to a Honda 125cc motorcycle to convey me around the estate and up the hillsides to minister the flock. As I puttered to a stop outside the shearing shed, it looked like most of Glantnor's flock was milling around the fields around the farm. As I arrived, Roy, Tony and some of the shearers were already setting up their equipment in the shed and erecting the pens and races to create a conveyor belt-like funnel to bring the sheep as efficiently as possible to the voracious clippers of the shearers. Shearing is piecework, that is, each shearer is paid a certain amount for each shorn sheep, so it was in their interests to shear as many as possible in a day.[31] [32] Earnings could be high for an experienced shearer who might shear four hundred ewes per day and earn as much as £300, or ten times the daily wage of the farm workers helping them! That said, whilst the pressure was on them to process as many animals as possible, the onus was on the 'feeders' (which was my job) to get each sheep positioned and ready as quickly as possible for the shearer to do their stuff. Each man, and they were all men, was getting his shearing pitch prepared, so I busied myself helping Tony and Simon get the races ready. Roy was working his dogs and pushing the sheep into a mustering area in the field opposite the shed.

The number of sheep was truly overwhelming and I was deafened by the sound of bleating so I didn't hear Tony approach until he tapped me on the shoulder.

'You all right Debbie? You look a bit dazed!'

'Oh, I am sorry! I was just looking at what has to be done. You

---

[31] In 1982, shearers were getting about 50 pence a sheep, or about £1.20, or thereabouts at today's prices.

[32] An experienced shearer can shear four hundred sheep per day earning them £300, a tidy sum back in the 1980s when an average farm worker would be earning just £13 per day. However, to start getting the big money, a shearer would need several years of experience.

reckon we'll get through that lot his week?'

'Yeah, easy like. These guys are professionals. You won't believe how quick they work. Now Debbie, try 'n' get the sheep as near to the shearer as possible so he don't have to move off his pitch or put his shears down to get hold of 'er. If you do that, he'll give you some sharp language!' Tony laughed, and then gave me a reassuring pat on the back. 'You'll be fine, just watch what I'm do'n 'cos I'll be working next to you today.' I gave him a thumbs up. 'Right!' he said. 'Let's get started.'

Tony shouted to Billy, one of Roy's sons (this was truly a community activity!) to start getting the sheep up the races to the shearers. I hurried over and positioned myself in the pen with my shearer and we quickly introduced ourselves.

'Hi, I'm Debbie.'

The young bleach-blond chap in front of me stopped fiddling with his clippers and held out his hand.

'The name's Jack, pleased to meet you, Debbie.' I'd won the jackpot: he was the New Zealander! I was just admiring Jack's powerful-looking arm muscles flexing as he set up his clippers, when he spoke again. 'So, Debbie, have you done the feeding job much before?'

I felt a little embarrassed

'Well, actually no, I'm sorry, I'm a complete greenie I'm afraid.'

To my relief, he was unfazed by the news he'd pulled the short straw!

'Okay Debbie, no worries. Just get her on her back close to my legs with her head towards me so I can get started on her belly fleece. When you see I'm coming to the end and sheering up her back, get another one ready for me, then wrap the fleece and Bob's yer uncle!'

Jack smiled; the combination of his tanned, open features and white teeth was irresistible! I firmly admonished myself, 'just concentrate on the task in hand and not on his fit body!' My first few ewes must've had training from the escapologist, Harry Houdini, because they all managed to squirm free and out of my grip whilst I was trying to get them on their backs. Jack was patient, but I could see he was getting anxious to make progress. Eventually, I learnt how to get the animal onto its flank by pulling her head gently back and to the side so I could then roll her on her back and pinion her with my knee until the shearer was ready to take her. Added finessing was needed to estimate where I needed to start flipping her so she was close enough to the shearer.

After a few hours I'd got the technique perfected, but I was beginning to flag. Each ewe weighed between one hundred and fifteen to one hundred and twenty pounds. Given that I only weighed about one hundred and thirty pounds, flipping her over was pretty tough going! Since it was a bit like wrestling an opponent to the ground in a judo bout, I learnt to use the animal's weight and momentum going forward to help flip her onto her side; even so she was a dead weight when I tried to flip her on her back. I was just wondering when we were planning on stopping for lunch when I looked up and noticed a little group of young girls and older women approaching with lunch and cold drinks. We all descended on them like a ravening horde! As I was cramming a large, white hoagie into my mouth, I noticed some of the women that'd brought the food were now chatting to a couple of the shearers. In fact, Jack had an enthusiastic little huddle gathered around him asking where he'd come from and how long he was staying. I thought to myself, 'yep, that's how it works. You bring them food and then try and wheedle your way into their affections. As they always say, the surest way to a man's heart is through his stomach!' Then it was my turn.

Micky, a young Irish shearer from County Antrim, came over and sat next to me.

'Hiya, Debbie Best, is it?' I nodded; my mouth was too full to say anything. 'Is that the County Clare Bests Debbie?'

I shook my head.

'No, my mum's from County Down, but most of the family's scattered around in England now in Essex and in Wales; my mum lives in Pembrokeshire. But we still have cousins, the Robinsons, who have a smallholding in Creevy.'

A light went on behind Micky's eyes.

'That wouldn't be Terry Robinson's family by any chance?'

I smiled.

'Yes, actually! Do you know them?'

Micky shook his head.

'I know of 'em, in the news and that.'

Then I heard Tony's voice.

'All right, let's get back to it, lady and gents!' I chuckled to myself;

Tony was in his element leading the troops!

Much, much later, around seven in the evening, everyone knocked off but there was a move to go to the Talbot for a pint or two. Micky stuck with me and we crammed into an estate Land Rover so that Tony could drive us into Berwen. I was positioned so close to the gearstick I had to change gear for him each time he nodded. Then a thought struck me and I said, 'Er, Tony, shouldn't we change first before going to the pub, we kind of stink!'

He wagged his head.

'What? And miss valuable drinking time!'

Nobody batted an eye when we all took our places at the bar in a filthy, heaving mass. Trish the barmaid just set about pulling the pints and getting chatted up by the men. Micky and I stuck together for most of the evening. I could see he was getting keen. Although he'd definitely kissed the Blarney Stone, I couldn't shake off a mental image of Jack's rippling abs when he'd taken his tee shirt off earlier in the day. So, when his female entourage finally left, I grabbed my chance to chat to him later in the evening. If truth were known, the thought of getting with Jack even for a brief encounter was rather distracting. Clearly, in common with the local women who'd joined us down the pub, I wasn't immune to the shearer's charms either!

Chapter 23
Dipping time

With the spring firmly and fully sprung and the urgency of lambing and shearing behind her, a shepherdess's daily care for her flock resonated to the thrum of summer's warmer days, and unfortunately, to the hum of blowflies looking to lay their eggs on a ewe's unsuspecting rump. The lure of a muck-covered and overly long tail brings flies a-plenty and the insidious spread of foot rot can, if not kept on top of, spread quickly. The unholy trinity of scab (irritating mites living in the fleece), fly-strike (resulting in maggots feeding on a ewe's flesh) and foot rot (and scald) inevitably sends happy, grass-gorged sheep into a world of mystery as they acquire the stumbling, shambling gait reminiscent of casualties returning from the front in the Great War. To prevent this happening, a shepherd must take up arms against a myriad of tiny foes. Amongst her armoury of "weapons" is sheep dip, the hoof knife and tail trimmers. To an outsider, these might also seem like instruments of torture, but a moment's timely treatment is way better than the alternative of being consumed piecemeal by legions of maggots or the pain from sores spreading from a rotten foot. For the tiny foes living in the fleece, in the early 1980s we used organophosphate (OP) or synthetic pyrethroid-based sheep dips to control a nasty trio of parasites, ticks, lice and blowflies.[33]

I well remember my first sheep dipping because I got the chance to work with one of Roy's Border Collie bitches, Gem. Gem was one of Roy's most affable working dogs so she was happy to take commands from other people that she knew. A few weeks before we'd planned to do the dipping, I'd been up to Roy's cottage to spend time with Gem so that Roy could teach me a few simple commands, 'here' (come here to me), 'lie down' (stop dead), 'away' (move to the right of the flock), 'come by' (move to the left of the flock) and 'walk on' (go towards the sheep). Roy

---

[33] Sheep dip has now been banned due to the negative health impacts of both chemicals on farm workers and the environment.

was very precise about how I should say these commands, enunciating the first letter and syllable of each command so the dog would immediately be able to differentiate the commands at distance. When their dogs are further away, shepherds use whistle commands, but my whistling has always been hopeless, so I needed to learn the basic hand-signal commands. Before my first session with Gem, I practiced hard in front of a mirror or outside in the garden. It probably looked like I was directing imaginary traffic. If I'd had neighbours, they'd have thought I'd gone completely bonkers!

My try-outs with Gem were, for me, a pure delight, even though Gem would occasionally slow to a halt and look puzzled when she couldn't understand what her rookie mistress was asking her to do. After a week, or so, I was able to direct Gem to round up a small group of ewes in Roy's home field and get them into a makeshift pen; I was chuffed to bits.

Judy, Roy's wife (and Tony's sister) brought out a couple of generous slices of sponge cake in celebration! She said, 'Old Phil Drabble will be inviting you to do a bit on "One Man and His Dog" at this rate Debbie!'[34] The three of us laughed as we sat on a little wooden bench at the back of the house sipping tea. I was so happy, I forgot myself and gave Gem a small piece of my cake. Roy sent a scowl in my direction, but Gem was my best mate from then on!

On the day we'd planned to start dipping, for once, the sun shone out of a cloudless sky. Walking out of the little wicket gate leading to the path across a small paddock behind Garden Cottage to meet Roy at the sheds, I felt rather nervous. I looked up to Roy and rather idolised him even though he could be a hard taskmaster at times. Tony helped me get the races set up around the business end of the dipping trough, to check the water level and to add the dipping chemical. Roy arrived with Gem and his favourite old dog, Jack who was a bit over the hill for handling sheep, but he had a steadying influence on Gem and would hold the line without me having to ask him to, whist I worked with Gem to get the ewes corralled around the dipping bath.

---

[34] One Man and His Dog was a very popular BBC TV series featuring a sheepdog handling competition that started in 1976 and continues today as a special annual edition on 'Countryfile'.

'Debbie, have a go at splitting off a group and getting them down to the race.' Roy nodded encouragingly as I stepped up and shouted 'come by' nice and clearly. Gem shot off to the left and instinctively got around behind and broke off a small group of ewes.

'Here!' I shouted and Gem, with Jack as a backstop, pushed the sheep down towards us. I was thrilled.

After half an hour of this, I suddenly realised I'd been grinning so much, I was getting cramp in my face muscles. Roy had noticed and said, 'You'll break that face of yours if you don't stop your smiling Debbie!' With the sheep now in position, we got togged up in our rubber aprons. It was then we realised we hadn't brought dipping poles. Rather than going back to the farm, Roy expertly made one from a hazel stick. Following his example, I cut myself a stout hazel bough from the luxuriant hedgerow around the field and fashioned a pole that had a fork at one end I could use to 'persuade' reluctant ewes to take their baptism. Even for a hardy hill ewe, a long trench filled with oily liquid pungent with a strong chemical odour was hardly enticing. In fact, it reminded me of boarding school nuns scrubbing our hair with a solution of witch hazel after the walk of shame to our communal bathroom after coming up positive during a louse check! I could, therefore, really feel for the poor animals, but as I said, the alternative was much worse.

'C'mon Debbie, push 'em down so the dip gets to the top of their heads! Y'can't miss anything, or we'll have to do 'em again. Be merciless for once!' Always the perfectionist, I just bowed to Roy's superior knowledge on all things to do with sheep and pushed the floundering ewes under for a few moments. I'm sure they were all giving me evil eye before they ran off as fast as possible down the field!

In the weeks after dipping the flock, I started to notice that quite a few ewes had started limping. We'd had a period of rain, and what with the warm weather, it was perfect conditions for foot problems. Returning to the field armed with a pair of foot rot shears, a hoof knife, a large bucket of seven percent iodine solution and plastic spray gun, I set the paraphernalia down and pondered how I was going to catch my first 'patient'. Without a dog, I knew it was going to be pretty difficult to get near even lame sheep, but I was determined not to ask the odious Rhys Thomas for help. Fortunately, I'd already managed to develop a knack of hooking sheep with my crook so I could pull her back and down onto the ground where firm pressure from my knee was needed to keep her steady. As the day wore on, a pattern emerged. Some fought tooth and nail, but others, probably the worst affected, and in the greatest pain, were resigned and I like to think they understood I was trying to help them rather than eviscerating them for a tasty snack. I worked all afternoon until evening crept up on me and long shadows began to form under the hedgerow oaks.

'Hello Debbie!' I spun my head round and saw Roy with a big smile on his face coming up the field with Gem and Jake at his heels. 'I noticed you up here this morning. You've been busy! You should've come up to the house and borrowed Gem. It can't've been easy catch'n them without a dog. It'd have been easier to push them into the yard and put them through the footbath there.' Here, he chuckled and said, 'I'm think'n you didn't want to ask Rhys for help, right?' I nodded. 'Y'know Debbie, I think you have the natural instincts of a great shepherd. A lot of farmers, the bad ones mind you, don't give a toss about a bit of mild foot rot, but I've seen you keeping on top of it and I have to say that the flock's benefited no end; they're in prime condition. I can see that we'll have to find you a decent Collie to make it easier for you to keep up the good work!' Roy glanced around the field, winked to himself, nodded his approval and then headed on up the field towards his farm. Needless to say, I was glowing with pride.

Chapter 24
Tupping time

During the autumn months, the shepherdess needs her wits about her as she navigates her way through a tricky balancing act. For the ewes, there's flushing, a term used for the pre-mating pampering that they get to ensure they're in prime condition. Upland ewes like those at Glantnor need to be on condition score three.[35] Thin ewes, scoring two or less, are put onto better grazing and those above four are put on a weightwatcher's diet! The tups can't be ignored either; they need to be in good condition for mating. Most tups will have been lounging around doing nothing all year, so they'll have picked up a bit of excess weight, which lowers their libido and puts them at a physical disadvantage when they're trying to mate with a frisky ewe! However, as the days shorten, the flock's body clock kicks in with unerring accuracy, and no matter what an individual's condition score might be, their thoughts turn to "love". And it's not just the sheep! Tupping time always seemed to be a cause for great excitement, especially amongst the younger single males on the estate farm. One morning, Tony, Simon and I were standing outside the tupping shed where we'd put the rams into the races with the ewes. Up until that point, I'd never seen what happened when the rams were put with the ewes.

We were leaning on the rails watching the excited rams mounting the ewes when I noticed a cylindrical object dangling down from one of the rams. I said to Tony, 'is that his... well you know?'

Tony turned and looked like he was trying to stifle a laugh.

'Well, you really don't know much about sheep Debbie!'

Feeling a little embarrassed, I replied, 'I've done quite a bit of the lambing end, but not at this end!'

---

[35] Condition scoring needs the trained eye of an experienced shepherd[ess]. Essentially *ewes* that have a *body condition score* of 1.0 are underfed and skinny, while those with a *score* of 5.0 are overfed and fat. The ideal range for positive fertility and health is between 3.0 and 3.5 — no matter what time of year it is.

Tony nodded.

'Oh, I see! Well, that there is a raddling stick. It should be attached to the harness up on his brisket, but it looks like it's slipped off in all the excitement! We put the raddling harness on the tups so when he mounts the ewe, he makes a mark on their backs. We separate out the marked ewes so he doesn't waste his time shagging ewes that've already been shagged. Sorry Debbie, I don't know quite how else to put it!' It was Tony's turn to look embarrassed.

Not to be left out, Simon, who'd been watching a particularly exuberant tup, piped up.

'Ooh! Look at 'im, the lucky bugger! I'm dying to have a shag right now!' To illustrate his point, Simon held a raddle stick between his legs and did a couple of suggestive pelvic thrusts!

Tony promptly gave him one of his hard stares and Simon turned pale. Tony then turned to me and lowered his voice.

'Simon don't know what he's saying sometimes. Simple Simon, we call him, but he's harmless. Now, if he gets up to anything he shouldn't, just let me know and I'll sort him out.' Tony winked at me and walked off towards the estate Land Rover and drove away.

After he'd gone, Simon wandered back eyes wide and knees still shaking.

'Ooh! Did you see that? Tony gave me the evil eye. Tony's evil eye is enough to get you quaking in your boots!'

With that, Simon made himself scarce and strode off up to the farm with his hands in his pockets like a puppy with his tail between his legs! However, just to be on the safe side, and to make sure Simon wouldn't be further tempted, I let the tups and ewes out of the race and into the field so that could do their thing in peace and quiet with a modest level of privacy!

***

After a week or so, I was getting the hang of the tupping process and felt confident enough to get on with the job on my own. On one particular morning, I'd got a suitable-sized group of ewes in the race and I'd just let the rams in there with them when I noticed Rhys Thomas puttering up

215

the lane in his Reliant Robin. Part of me thought he looked ridiculous driving that thing, but nevertheless, he was a nasty piece of work and my heart sank when he stopped and got out. Ignoring me, he strode over to the shed.

After checking what was going on, he turned towards me with a scowl on his face.

'Now, I told you not to put that ram with the ewes, and now you have!

I walked over to see what he meant.

'Well Roy reckoned he had a good pedigree…'

Before I could say anything further, Rhys turned on me; he was white with fury.

'Since when is Roy in charge? I'm the one that makes the decisions about the sheep, not him!' At this point, Rhys appeared to have lost it completely and was literally foaming at the mouth. 'That ram is in poor condition and shouldn't have been let anywhere near the ewes!' He then marched back over and stood almost toe to toe with me. I was shaking. 'Now look 'ere Miss all high and mighty. I know what you're up to. It's all "please and thank you" to our faces, but I bet you're looking down your nose behind our backs! Well, you're not much good at this job, but you might as well be good for something. See that there tup, he's having a fine old time! At least you're useful for something!' Rhys then bent and picked up a raddle stick. 'Now you hold still like one of them ewes and we'll see what you're good for, Miss high and mighty convent girl. I'll have you now!' At this point, Rhys made a grab for me from behind, but before he could do anything further, I pushed him out of the way and ran off as fast as I could with Rhys wheezing behind me. Fortunately for me, too many Woodbines were seriously holding him back, so I was able get onto my motorbike that I'd left behind the shed and make my escape. I was seriously shaken up.

Passing a shed on the main estate track leading back to my cottage, I noticed Tony and Di in there unloading some feed sacks. I stopped and ran over to them; I was crying.

'Oh Tony, you won't believe what's just happened. That bastard, Rhys, threatened to use the raddling stick on me! I've had enough of him, he's always down on me and never gives me any credit for anything!'

Tony held me gently by the shoulders and tried to calm me down.

'Well, Debbie, he's gone too far this time. C'mon Di, we're going to have word.'

We all got into the estate Land Rover and it wasn't long before we found Rhys having a cigarette over near the sheep sheds. 'Oi You, Rhys. I want to have a word with you boyo!'

Seeing what was coming, Di hung back near the Land Rover with me while Tony marched over to Rhys and pushed him hard on his right shoulder so he stumbled back against the shed and dropped his cigarette. 'Debbie says you were threatening to use the raddle on her just now. Now, I'm warning you, if I hear about any more trouble from you, we'll fix you good and proper see!' Tony balled his fists and towered menacingly over Rhys who backed away.

I turned to look at Di who'd gone white as a sheet.

'Do you think he's going to hit him?'

'Well, Debbie, part of me wishes he would! Tony's pretty terrifying when he gets mad! No, he's just going to scare 'im see, so he don't do it again.'

By the time we looked back over towards the shed, Tony was stalking back up the bank towards us.

'That's scared 'im. 'He won't be do'n that again, but if he does, just let me know and I'll sort 'im out good and proper!'

We were all pretty shaken up by the whole incident, so I invited Tony and Di over to Garden Cottage for a cuppa and some of the Dundee cake I'd made at the weekend. We chatted and laughed and nothing more was said about the incident. It was like a cloud has passed from Tony's demeanour, but I wouldn't ever want to get on the wrong side of him, he was terrifying!

***

Not long after the tupping incident, and brush with Tony, to my profound relief, Rhys unexpectedly left Glantnor. I say unexpectedly, because William had quite a high regard for him and he could sweet talk his way around him quite easily. In the end, I think fear of Tony's wrath finally got too much of him and he scarpered like the cowardly bully he was.

Chapter 25
Beating for the shoot

The 'glorious' first, or should that be the inglorious first of October heralds the beginning of the pheasant shooting season on any farm or estate with elitist pretensions, and Glantnor Park was no exception. Essential to the smooth running and success of the day, is a large army of people. As in most country sports, there's a defined pecking order. The top dogs are of course the guns, they're the people who have shelled out up to £300, or more, for a day's shooting. Then there's the gamekeeper, usually a permanent employee of the estate, who's responsible for raising and releasing the unfortunate birds that'll be the targets for the day. Then it's the loaders. Loaders are basically the equivalent to what caddies are to golfers. They are the quintessential gofers, loading the client's gun, collecting the ejected cartridges and cleaning and maintaining the guns at the end of the day. His Lordship pays gamekeepers and loaders and the guns at the end of the shoot often tip both heavily. Then there are the beaters who twirl football rattles and wave feedbags attached to sticks in order to scare the condemned birds up and into the path of the guns. Finally, there's the pickers-up, the people who handle the gun dogs, usually spaniels, pointers or terriers that retrieve the downed birds. The beaters and pickers-up at Glantnor were a mixture of volunteers recruited from the estate workforce, that often included members of the estate workers' families. It was a social affair and there was an outside chance that one of the guns might actually tip the folks further down the pecking order, so we always lived in hope! My first invitation to beat for a shoot came not from William, but from Tony who'd been asked by Nigel, the gamekeeper, to round up some bodies for a shoot to be held a few days later Flushed with gratitude for Tony's heroic intervention with Rhys after the incident with the raddling stick, I couldn't refuse when Tony sidled up to me as I was working with Roy on deciding which of the spring lambs to separate out for market and which were the keepers to overwinter.

'D'you fancy getting out and about for a bit of fresh air next Sunday Debbie?'

Tony's offer sounded appealing and conjured up visions of a trip to the beach at Borth or Aberystwyth, so I naturally answered, 'Yeah, why not!' at that moment, out of the corner of my eye, I caught Roy averting his eyes and wagging his head.

'Got ya!' Tony smiled like Lewis Carroll's Cheshire Cat. 'Right! Have you ever done any beating?'

My face dropped; I knew what was coming next, so I tried to worm my way out of it, but rather than using lame excuses like, 'I'll be washing my hair', or 'I'll be varnishing my nails then', I came up with an entirely plausible one.

'Actually, I'll likely be busy separating the lambs for the Monday market on Sunday.'

'Nice try Debbie, but William's short of beaters and everyone's trying to make themselves scarce.' It was then that Tony dangled a carrot, 'The shooters sometimes tip pretty well.' That was the clincher; I've always been a sucker for the promise of a bit of extra cash! So, on Sunday morning, I followed the long line of pricey cars including Porches, Mercs and Jags, parked at the side of the main estate road, to find Nigel chatting to a group of shooters. These guys really were kitted out in style. Harris Tweed and Cavalry Twill abounded as it covered the rotund forms of three brace of coiffured gents standing in a huddle in what looked like an ex-army mess tent that'd been erected to provide refreshments. The said refreshments comprised what looked like orange spritzer and caviar. I say, what looked like, because Nigel was making sure that none of the riff-raff, us, in other words, were able to get anywhere near these delectable titbits. The word on the grapevine was that it was a party of bankers out on a corporate jolly paid for by Lloyds of London. I saw this as somewhat of a bad omen on the tipping front since my personal experience of the bankers that my father had entertained on the off chance that they might want to invest in one of his film projects was that they're some of the meanest people on earth! Back then, when I could've been seen as part of the establishment, it might've been me rubbing shoulders with the moneyed set, but I'd crossed that socio-economic line long ago and now felt fully aligned with the farm and estate workers standing around stamping their feet with their hands thrust in their pockets trying to keep them warm whilst the toffs socialised over drinks and beluga.

The shoot began with a line of six of us beaters pacing uphill towards the guns sheltering out of the wind in a small copse. I'd found myself a football rattle and started out enthusiastically emulating a Liverpool supporter attending a grudge match at Anfield. As the morning wore on, and my arm began to ache, I exchanged my rattle for a feed sack flag being waved, by a delighted young chap called Rob. Shortly after our exchange, we were crossing a stretch of boggy ground, when a gunshot from a shooter passed so close to our heads that I could hear the whine of the pellets. Both Rob and I instinctively ducked; which would've been futile if the shot had been just a foot either way.

Immediately, one of the other beaters ran over to us.

'Are you two all right? Have you been hit?' We were a bit shaken up, but we both answered 'No'.

The beater, I think he was a lad from Berwen, persisted and said, 'You'd best check, 'cos sometimes you don't know until after that you've been hit.' Sure enough, when Rob'd touched his earlobe, his fingers were bloodied.

'C'mon, lad, I'll take you over so's you can show that to Nigel.' So, the shooting stopped and we sat for a while whilst a confab took place between Nigel and one of the tweed-coated bankers. Eventually, there were nods all around and Rob returned with a huge smile on his face. One of the very contrite bankers had given him £100 so he'd say no more about his ear.

Whilst we all crowded around Rob to see what'd happened, some wag in our group piped up and said, 'Well lad, it'll save yer pay'n if you ever think about getting an ear piercing!' Everyone thought this was wildly funny, but all I could think of was he'd been bloody lucky it wasn't one of his eyes.

Chapter 26
Harvest-time party

'I've got a great idea for a harvest supper,' I exclaimed one evening over a pint down at the Talbot. We all know that some of the best, or most hare-brained, schemes are hatched in the pub, but I'd got some incredulous looks from Tony, Simon and Di when I first explained my idea to have a harvest supper in one of the cowsheds up at the farm.

That'd been a few weeks earlier, but as we worked the huge yard brooms around the floor of one of Glantnor's huge cowsheds, Simon, who'd been working his broom next to me, said, 'Ow on earth did you manage to talk us into this I'll never know!' Breaking off from his sweeping Simon pitched his broom on the floor and went to sit in the corner to sulk.

It was then I decided that everyone needed reminding why we'd all agreed to my plan.

'Look, it's simple, the reason why we're doing it is it's going to be a great social occasion!' I could see this wasn't enough for Simon, so I continued with a list of reasons. ', and there's gonna be free beer supplied by William, a barbecue and cakes baked by yours truly and I've got a friend coming.'

Whilst free beer and food were tangible inducements, it was the last item that piqued Simon's interest and forced him back onto his feet to find out more.

'Oh, really! Who is this mystery friend and how old is she?'

I rolled my eyes and said, 'She's called Liz and she's a veterinary nurse at my brother's practice in Radwinter.

The word 'nurse' was like veritable catnip to Simon who replied with a guttural-sounding, 'Cor blimey, whoa!'

I made a mental note to keep Liz well away from Simon's fevered clutches at all costs! After we'd scrubbed the floor and finally got rid of the cow muck, the pièce de résistance (Tony's idea) was using raddle paint to colour the strip lights to give the shed a 'sultry' atmosphere after sunset. This was not an easy thing, but Tony managed to wangle the use of the telescopic loader we used for stacking silage and straw big-bales. Using a pallet as a platform, I was hoisted up into the ceiling rafters with a bucket of raddle paint; our friendly neighbourhood Health and Safety Inspector would've been mortified!

The Friday night before the party saw the arrival of Liz. I'd met Liz when I'd stayed with my brother in Radwinter and we'd immediately formed a bond. Fair-haired, slim, attractive and bubbly, Liz appeared 'normal' (whatever that is) on the outside, but I got the impression that a devil-may-care approach to life lurked beneath her calm exterior.

Jumping out of her little Mini wearing one of her trademark striped tee shirts, Liz appeared to be wired already and the party wasn't due to start until Saturday evening.

'Wow Debbie, you've really landed on your feet this time! This place is amazing! I can't wait to see the garden at the back tomorrow. Y'know, I'm trying to buy a place in Radwinter, but prices are going sky high now it's been noticed by the nobs commuting to London.'

Trying to manage expectations before she realised how damp her bedroom was, I said, 'Yes, well, it's a tied cottage and it needs a lot of work doing, but it's the first time I've actually had a place I could call my own.'

The following day, Liz got on with party preparations while I did my rounds of the flock and fixed up a gaping hole in a fence on the top field. By the time I got back, Simon was sitting on the settee in my front room talking to Liz over a cuppa. 'Damn!' I thought, 'She's fallen prey already!'

For some unaccountable reason, Simon had managed to enter into a kind of alternate persona where he was having a sensible conversation about what Liz got up to as a veterinary nurse at Mercer & Hughes.

'I was just telling Simon about the turmoil that's been caused by Adam's departure to South America. Apparently, he's just confirmed that they're staying out there for at least another two years. It's kind of put the cat amongst the pigeons with the partners!'

I'd had a letter from Charagua in which Adam had talked about extending his stay, but this was confirmation. I'd harboured some thoughts of wangling some unpaid leave to go out there and visit them, but it was going to take me ages to save the money; however this changed things. Maybe I'd get out there after all.

Whilst I was contemplating my travel plans, Simon got up to leave.

'Well, I'll leave you ladies to your girlie natter. I'm off up to the farm to help Tony with the barbecues. See you later.' Simon winked at Liz and took his leave.

'Simon seems to be a really friendly guy. Considerate too, looking after his mum at home.

I thought, 'So that's how he's getting round her, the devious bugger!' Oh well, stage two of my plan would surely work; I intended to stick with Liz like glue during the party!

I'd invited about fifty people. Since farming folks rarely got out to socialise, I'd decided to invite friends from various stages of my farming life. There was Shân and Ni, her mysterious boyfriend, Tim from Watersplace, Ian and his partner Robbie who I'd met whist staying with Tim and then there was the Glantnor crowd including Sue, Tony's wife, Judy, Judy's neighbour Nell and of course, Marilyn and Duncan. Marilyn was looking radiant and heavily pregnant. She was still with Duncan, so I assumed he'd either not twigged or he'd decided to play along with Marilyn's 'fertility treatment' plan. Di had put together his disco setup at the back of the barn on some straw bales. Besides his trademark flat cap, we were wearing the cheesiest floral shirt I'd ever seen. Judging by the number of empty bottles of beer up there with him, it looked like he'd already started, and I wondered whether he'd be able to find the records never mind play them by the time it was eight o' clock!

In short, the party was an incredible success. I was on a high all night, and of course, I lost sight of Liz in a haze of strong ale and loud music. The morning after the night before is always a tricky time for partygoers, but I was still on a high and cooking some pancakes when there were the familiar squeaks and thud, thudding of someone coming down the stairs.

This was followed by sounds of the toilet flush being pulled repeatedly in vain followed by some gasps of exasperation, so I shouted out, 'I know! I need to ask William to send someone to fix that toilet flush, it's a nightmare!'

I'd just started plating out some pancakes when I looked up to see

Simon framed in the kitchen door.

'Good morning, Debbie! I bet you weren't expecting to see me at this time in the morning!' My eyes must've been out on storks because Simon continued with an explanation. 'Well! You'll never guess what I got up to last night!' Simon smiled ecstatically and I inwardly shuddered. 'I've been have'n' it off with Liz! Ooh, it was absolutely fantastic! Cor, I'm bloody starving, are those pancakes for Liz? I'll make a start on 'em. She's just upstairs doing her ablutions.'

This was too much information for me and I wasn't sure what else to say, so I just kept putting things out on the breakfast table when a second thump thumping heralded Liz's entry into the kitchen. Her face was a picture of embarrassment. Her hair was a frizzy mess at the back of her head and her cheeks glowed red. She didn't know where to look. So Simon gave her some help

'C'mon Liz, you need to feed yourself up after what we've been up to! Y'know, keep your strength up for the second round!'

However, all Liz could manage was, 'I'll just grab some tea and nip outside for a ciggie if you don't mind.' I followed her out onto the patio.

'Are you okay Liz? Nothing untoward's happened, has it?'

Liz just shook her head.

'No, no, nothing like that. Simon and me just got talking and one thing led to another. In for a penny, in for a pound that's me. I haven't had a shag for a while, so I thought, y'know, why not?'

This explanation just confirmed to me that you can never know what people are really like. Liz seemed totally unperturbed as she recounted how she'd finally given in to Simon's charm offensive. Her casual attitude to the whole thing reminded me of the indefatigable Jeanette at Ohio State! In the affairs of love, or in this case, lust, I still had a lot to learn. In fact, Liz was to turn out to be veritable puzzle wrapped up in an enigma that I'd never get to the bottom of.

Chapter 27
Tosh

Coming from the English heartlands, I sometimes forgot that Wales is a 'foreign' land. Not only do the people there speak a language that will always remain unfathomable to me, but also, I'd noticed that even the birds sang in a local dialect all their own. For example, compared with their English cousins, the Cymric chiffchaff seemed to add an extra little phrase that's perhaps Welsh for chiff and Jenny Wren skipped a note before getting on with her exuberant trilling. In common with the wild creatures, Welsh sheepdogs also 'spoke' a different language. The whistles and commands used by the Welsh shepherd were often subtly different to those I'd heard (rather rarely I must confess) in the sheep fields in Yorkshire and elsewhere. So, when Roy kept the promise he'd made the previous summer, to keep a pup for me when Gem had her litter, I worried that I might need to learn some Welsh; I'm useless at languages! But I needn't have worried, around Berwen, most people spoke only English, Roy and his collies included.

My love affair with a faithful sheepdog began when Roy knocked on my door one snowy evening at the end of November 1982 while I was cooking supper.

'Hello Roy, come on in, it's bitter out there!'

Roy tapped his snow-covered boots on the scraper and entered the hallway.

'Gosh Debbie, it's not much warmer in 'er' than it is outside! Haven't you got a fire going?'

I gave an exasperated sigh and said, 'I know, tell me about it! The fire's slow to get going 'cos the chimney breast is so damp it takes ages to warm up.'

Roy shed his woolly hat and took off his boots using the bootjack in the hall.

'I hope y'don't mind, Debbie, but I think I'll keep my coat on!'

I laughed.

'C'mon into the kitchen, it's warmer in there and I've just made a pot of tea. I also have some fruit flapjacks I think you'll appreciate!' Roy followed me into the kitchen, pulled out a chair and sat at the little folding table I'd recently found at a second-hand furniture shop in Welshpool.

I could see Roy wanted to tell me something.

'I've got a surprise for you Debbie. Gem's had 'er pups and one of 'em, a bitch we've named Tosh, is go'n be perfect for you. She's a friendly little thing. Sometimes you get a sense about a puppy; I think she's go'n to be a good'n.'

I was thrilled.

'Oh Roy, thank you so, so much! It's my birthday soon and this is the best present anyone could ever have!' I was quite overcome and tears formed in the corner of my eyes.

'Oh, now hold yer horses! She's not fully weaned, so she needs to stay with 'er mum for a while yet, but you can drop in whenever you like to see 'er.'

It was not long after Roy's visit, I got my chance to meet Tosh for the first time at a little pre-Christmas gathering at Roy and Judys' just before Christmas. As usual, I'd arrived rather early, so Roy said, 'C'mon Debbie, let me quickly introduce you to Tosh.' I followed Roy into a little boot-room at the back of the cottage. There, snuggled in a large pile of hessian grain sacks, was Gem and her five little furry bundles of delight. We walked slowly up to her and Roy gently picked up the smallest one and said, 'This little'n is the one we've named Tosh.' Roy passed her to me and she squirmed around in my grasp trying to push her nose under my arms. Giggling, I moved her into a position where I could see her face; it was love at first sight!

***

After Christmas, and a month or so before lambing was due to start, Roy suggested it was time I came to pick up Tosh and introduce her to her new home. I was excited and apprehensive in equal measure. I'd prepared a place for Tosh in the hallway outside the kitchen at Garden Cottage so she'd be in the warmth of the kitchen and near to me. However, Roy gave me very clear instructions on how to look after her.

'Now Debbie,' he'd said, 'Tosh isn't a pet or lapdog; she's a working dog. She needs to know who's boss. Don't go let'n 'er onto your bed or even in the living room all the time and no pampering er with titbits from the kitchen table. It'll make 'er soft and she won't take 'er training properly.'

On the day we'd agreed I could come and collect Tosh, I arrived at the back door of Roy's cottage on a raw, drizzly evening in late February. Rather than stepping into the house, Roy shrugged on a coat and took me round to a snug little straw-filled barn where he'd been looking after Gem and the weaned pups.

'She's that one there Debbie, the little'n' with her back to you. She's still got that white patch on 'er nose that looks like an exclamation mark. Go on, pick 'er up and introduce yourself to 'er.'

Following Roy's instructions, I gently picked Tosh up and she pushed up from my arms and licked my face. Still holding her, I sat with my back against a wall stroking her soft fur and letting her lick my hand so she'd know my smell. Roy had also said that I should talk to her and let her know my voice. I suddenly felt a sense of place and history, like I was following in the footsteps of the earliest shepherds. I was starting a bonding process that stretched back to the domestication of sheep and the early drovers.

My attention was so intently focussed on Tosh that I didn't notice that Roy had disappeared, but when he came back, he'd brought me a mug of tea and a piece of Judy's fruit cake; it was a huge slice.

'Oh, thank you Roy! I didn't notice you'd gone back in. That's rather a large slice of cake!'

Roy smiled.

'You were so wrapped up with Tosh that I thought I'd let you two get acquainted. That's an un-iced version of one of the cakes Judy made for Christmas; we haven't managed to get through it all yet, so dig in!'

After our much-needed cuppa, Roy, Tosh and I rode back to Garden Cottage in Roy's truck. As I jumped down from the cab with Tosh in my arms, Roy called after me.

'Now remember, Debbie, Tosh is a working dog, not a pet. Look after her accordingly and she'll work 'er socks off for you! She's a good'n, so I wouldn't want you spoil'n' 'er!'

I could see Roy was a little anxious, so I said, 'Please don't worry Roy, I understand.'

***

However, one of the first things I noticed in the midst of my rather lonely existence, was how much I appreciated Tosh's company and the love and attention we exchanged with each other, which made it all the more difficult to avoid mixing 'business' with 'pleasure' so to speak. In common with all collies, Tosh was rather a precocious youngster. At three months old, she was into everything and it took ages to house-train her, so I had quite a few wet puddles and the odd unpleasant offering in the corner to attend to in the morning or if I'd left her for a bit to check on lambing. Eventually the number of accidents decreased and Tosh became an intrinsic part of the fabric of my life at Glantnor.

Unlike dogs kept as pets, there was a whole additional dimension to my relationship with Tosh because I needed to train her how to do her job and I needed to learn how to guide her actions. At first, I found the thought of this to be quite daunting, but I needn't have worried, Roy was a tireless mentor giving freely of his time to train me how to control Tosh. I often felt a little guilty that he was spending so much time with me on his evenings off when he could've been with Judy. In the end, I think it became a mission in life for Roy, and during the process, we formed a deep bond of friendship. As I'd already experienced with Gem herself, even with the basics, it can be difficult for the handler to learn to give clear and precise commands, however, now I needed to train Tosh to understand what I wanted her to do. I spent hours in a little paddock near Roy's back yard patiently teaching Tosh to sit, lie down, go away and come by. Eventually we were able to introduce a small group of very patient ewes into the equation. Like all collies, Tosh's natural instincts were to herd sheep, but the first step was to get her to stop and lie down! That accomplished, I could work on more challenging routines that involved her going out to a group of ewes and bringing them in towards me. At first, progress was slow and I have to confess that I became frustrated at times. Unperturbed, Roy insisted that training a dog can't be rushed and our sessions needed to be kept short. That poor old group of

228

pet ewes must've got thoroughly sick of seeing us trudging up the field towards them for one of our regular sessions!

By the time it got around to the end of March, Tosh and I were becoming an effective team, unfortunately, frustratingly for us both, during lambing, I needed to keep Tosh away from ewes with lambs to avoid her getting attacked by defensive mums; ewes can be very aggressive when there's lambs about! So I kept Tosh safely tethered outside the lambing shed and used the odd free moment in practicing her skills, and mine, on rounding up a rather award group of tups in Cae Afon, a small field near a stream we often passed during our regular exercise walks.

Around this time, as Tosh and I bonded ever closer together, Sarah, intrigued by my letters to her that overflowed with news about our training sessions, decided that it was time for a sisterly bonding session. We settled on the first weekend of April for our little get together.

'Now Plum', she'd said, 'I don't want to just play the role of a guest when I visit, I want to help. Perhaps I can be your lambing mother and make sure you have a steady flow of sustenance on the go so you don't have to worry about it for a change.'

The lambing mother moniker stuck and Sarah was as good as her word. On the appointed Friday afternoon, having followed the signs from the road that directed visitors to the farm, I spotted her entering the back garden through the wicket gate from the sheds. Immediately I rushed out to her and we hugged.

'Well Plum, you've certainly landed on your feet here! I absolutely love the walled garden... I'm quite jealous, it's like something out of Country Living Magazine!'

I laughed; I could see her sizing it all up and readjusting her image of her younger sister as a woman with a home and a garden rather than a vagrant in a caravan. I said, 'Glad you like it. The best bit is there's a gardener and I even have that indispensable accessory of country living, a faithful collie dog!'

'Yes, Tosh, where is she? You haven't got her chained up inside some darkened shed, have you? I know you farming types are not overly sentimental when it comes to animals.'

I shook my head.

'No! She's got a bed in the hall by the kitchen door.' I paused for a moment thinking of a way to describe our relationship, but before I could come up with something that sounded professional, my heart beat me to it and I said, 'I love her.'

Sarah looked intently at me for a long moment. I could see she was getting quite emotional as well, but all she said was, 'C'mon sis, I'm dying for a cup of tea and one of the wonderful scones you've been promising!'

Partway through her second scone, Sarah drew breath after recounting a long list of her doings in London and got onto the subject of Sean, the new man in her life who she'd met at a New Year's Eve party.

'Well sis, we're getting on like a house on fire... so well, in fact, I'm pregnant! Sean's delighted as well and we've told his family, the Maloneys, and they're all thrilled. I'm just trying to decide when's the best time to tell Mummy. I'm on my way to visit her after leaving you. I can't think of any other way but to just come straight out with it!'

I'd been nodding along with her words. I wasn't surprised about her getting pregnant, my sister had always been impulsive, but I worried about the way she was going to suddenly spring the news on Esme. I knew my mother would deftly handle the news with her usual quiet diplomacy, but what about John? I said, 'That's fantastic news! Really, really happy for you!' We hugged, but I felt the need to give her some advice. So I said, 'Sarah... do you think it's wise to just spring the news on Esme like that?'

Sarah looked wary and said, 'She'll be fine, and I'm not going to just blurt it out you know.'

I nodded.

'It's just that John strikes me as a bit, well, conservative. It's likely to give him a bit of a shock.'

'Never mind John, it gave me a shock too when I found out!'

We both laughed at this, but I knew Sarah's news would land like the proverbial bombshell.

Later on, just as evening was starting to close in, I said I'd need to nip out with Tosh and check on some gimmer ewes that hadn't been served the previous October.[36] With all the attention the pregnant ewes were getting, I was concerned they were getting rather neglected. Sarah was just cracking open a bottle of Pinot Grigio that she'd described as "scrummy and on offer from Waitrose" when I said, 'Sis, I've just got to pop out with Tosh and check on some ewes on the top field, do you fancy coming along? It'd be a chance for you to see Tosh and me in action.'

Putting the bottle swiftly back in the fridge, she said, 'How could I refuse such an offer of a night out in the freezing cold, lead on!'

Perhaps inspired by having an audience, Tosh and I worked flawlessly together and I got the worst looking ewes into a group so I could get them in a pen and check their feet.

'Bravo!' Sarah clapped and said, 'Just like One Man and His Dog! You should try for an audition. I'm sure you'd be the only woman on the show — one in the eye for women's lib eh Plum!'

Sarah had then gone on to joke some more about the traditional male chauvinism she assumed would be rife at Glantnor. I'd stuck up for blokes I worked with, they were brilliant and I said so. However, the little show that Tosh and I put on for her had apparently left a deep impression because years later I found a letter of hers to Esme that waxed lyrical. In it she said,

"...*Went for a walk last night as Plum put Tosh through her sheepdog trials once more. The image of the two of them herding up sheep in the dark, stark against the dark grey sky, was very reminiscent of Thomas Hardy... we then spent a very pleasant evening in front of the fire catching up!*"

The admiring tone of Sarah's letter was extremely gratifying to me in that it was one of those rare times when a member of the family was able to appreciate what I did. It felt like I'd earned some much-needed cred with them, and Sarah in particular.

***

Whilst lambing time had been a bit frustrating for me and Tosh, we finally got a chance to try out our skills in earnest to bring a batch of sick

---

[36] Gimmer: A female sheep that has been weaned but not yet sheared, usually between six and fifteen months old.

hill ewes down from Tan-y-Grûg to minister to their feet. We'd been up on the hill to check on a group of lamb-less ewes that'd been let out onto the high slopes for spring and summer. They'd been rather neglected during lambing and were in rather a sorry state. When we arrived up there, one in particular had a very lame right foreleg. She was so bad I could see her old face was riven with pain as she looked beseechingly at me from behind a silage feeder. Due to the strong tendency for members of a flock to follow each other, the infection looked like it was spreading to quite a few of the others and I knew that, since they'd be doing more lying down to keep off their painful feet, the maggots were sure to get into their fleece and cause even more problems.

'C'mon Tosh, this is our chance to shine! Let's have a go at getting this lot down to the Cae Afon so's we can get them sorted out.' Tosh listened to my voice and I could almost see her nodding in agreement!

'All right then! Tosh, away!' off she shot towards the little group of ewes. I thought it would be a piece cake catching a bunch of crippled animals, but I was wrong. At the sight of Tosh pelting hell-for-leather towards them, they shot off in the other direction with surprising speed! 'Come by!' Tosh flawlessly circled to the left of the group and flopped down behind them when I shouted for her to 'lie down.' The sheep ambled towards me and then skittered past and headed off down towards the field gate; I was grinning from ear to ear. 'Here Tosh!' As she came towards me, I couldn't help kneeling and holding my arms out to give her a cuddle. We stayed like that for a minute, enjoying the moment, and then I remembered the sheep! Of course, they'd scattered, but at least they were still at the bottom of the field! Striding down the hill towards the sheep, Tosh ran forward. As I was now out of earshot, and my whistling skills hadn't improved any, I signalled with my arms to direct Tosh to push the group into a corner of the field near the gate and to wait whilst I caught them up. As I trotted towards them, Tosh turned her head in my direction, her tongue was out and she was panting. 'Well done, Tosh, well done girl!' in reply, Tosh barked and wagged her tail. On that day, when I finally felt like I'd become a professional shepherdess, I remember that I was happier than I'd ever been.

Chapter 28
Leave of absence

"Sometimes, the biggest risks are those we take with our hearts." Anon.

Now that Adam and Vanda had decided to stay on in Charagua for a further couple of years, this gave me the chance to plan a trip out to see them. Whilst the wilds of Peru and Bolivia sounded enticing, I didn't fancy travelling out there on my own, but whom could I ask to come along as my travelling companion? Many of the younger, unmarried guys on the estate were out of the question since, even if they could take the time off, they'd interpret an invitation to be my travel companion as the green light for a romantic relationship, and truth be known, I didn't fancy any of them! Therefore, my preference was for a woman, but who? While I was searching for a fellow traveller, I'd got a letter from Adam suggesting that November would be a good time to come out; the weather is warm, but not too hot and there's plenty of clear days that'd be ideal for catching sight of the Andes or going on a trek to that unmissable tourist icon, Peru's Inca citadel, Machu Picchu. So a plan slowly emerged. I'd fly into Peru's capital, Lima, and stay with family friends, John and Judy Crabtree. John was a Brit, and an expatriate working on a project funded by the UK Department for Overseas Development, but Judy was Peruvian. From Lima I would travel overland by bus to Cusco and use the town as a staging post for a trek up to Machu Picchu. Then on across Lake Titicaca, that straddles the border between Peru and Bolivia, to Bolivia's capital, La Paz and finally to Charagua. So that I'd see more of the country (and save money on internal flights) I decided to travel by road and rail the whole way; which was likely to be a challenge and all the more reason why I needed a solid travelling companion. After I'd spent several nights juggling with atlases and travel guides, I reckoned I needed about three months to do such a trip justice.

The next step was to have a chat with William. As luck would have it, I found an opportune moment whilst we were discussing a set of very promising figures from that year's lambing. For once, William was impressed and said, 'I have to say Debbie, these are amongst the best results we've had with the flock. With all his experience, even while Rhys Thomas was with us, we never achieved the improvement that we've seen this year. Both Roy and Tony are saying it's largely down to your efforts Debbie. I'd have to agree, you're turning into quite the shepherdess!'

Whilst he was speaking, I realised that there was never going to be a better moment to pop the question. So I took a deep breath and launched into it.

'Well, I can't take all the praise, Roy spent a lot of his own time helping me train Tosh, which has really helped me keep on top of the flock maintenance so's they're in good condition for tupping this year.' William was nodding and looked like he was lapping it up, now was the moment. 'Er... I was meaning to ask you something. Well, as you know, my brother, Adam, is working on a veterinary aid project in Bolivia and he's suggested that, since he's out there, it would be a good chance for me to visit. He reckons a good time would be during our downtime over Christmas. I've had a chat to Roy and he reckons that he and Tony could hold the fort whilst I'm away and Roy would be happy to look after Tosh.'

William looked thoughtful.

'Mmmh, well, you seem to have thought of everything. However, it can't be holiday, it'd have to be unpaid leave. And mind you come back to us now that Roy's gone to all the trouble to train you!' That last was said in jest, but I could tell he meant it in earnest. When I'd left the farm office, I punched the air, 'Yesss!'

***

Still wracking my brains about who could be travelling companion material, one Saturday, I was out shopping for a few bits and pieces in Berwen when I bumped into Cathy. She was pleased to see me, so as a treat, we had a natter over a coffee in the Red Lion. Cathy and I had first met at a Young Farmers' bash in Welshpool the previous year. Since she lived near Berwen, we'd kept in touch and we'd met a few times for drinks at the Talbot and we regularly played badminton whenever I could get over to Newtown where she lived. I'd recently invited her to one of my Garden Cottage get-togethers and it was then that I'd met her long-term partner Dan, who was a forester, who I got on with really well with. He had a great sense of humour and doted on Cathy who worked in the local garden centre. During the course of our conversation, Cathy had said she'd love to do a bit of travelling before she settled down and started a family. I mentioned that I'd fairly recently been out in California and had got a taste for hot tubs, which were really popular out there.

Cathy had then smiled broadly and said, 'Actually Debbie, if you like hot tubs, you're in luck! Dan's just finished building a hot tub at our place. In fact, I was wondering who to invite over for its inaugural lighting up! I've already got Madeleine coming over; she's married to my brother Alex — they run an off-licence in Llandod.[37]

I happily agreed. A soak in a hot tub in Wales sounded like a great idea, just the thing to relax aching shoulders after a day's work! In the end, Alex cried off, so Madeleine came on her own. Actually, I don't think hot tubs were Chris's thing. Cathy told me her brother "could be a bit of a stick-in-the-mud" and was "a bit traditional" when it came to anything out of the ordinary.

Cathy and Dan lived some distance out of Berwen on the edge of a wood that stood on a low embankment. On the night in question, we'd agreed to come over about eight p.m. for drinks and get the hot tub going so it'd be ready by the time it got dark so we could watch the stars. Petite and attractive with raven hair, Madeleine was quite quiet to start with which I assumed was because she was there on her own without Alex. However, once we got started on the Pimm's, she came out of her shell and became quite animated. She'd been born and brought up in Paris, her mother was Spanish and she was a fluent Spanish speaker. I remember thinking, 'Mmh, it'd be handy to have a Spanish-speaking travelling companion!' Whilst Dan fussed around getting the wood-burning stove going that heated the hot tub, I chatted to the two women. It was then that I decided to mention my planned trip to South America. Both of them loved it and I talked excitedly about arrangements and said that I was looking for a travelling companion.

---

[37] A commonly-used nickname for Llandrindod Wells, the county town of Powys.

The tub took a while to heat up, so we'd all had a fair amount to drink by the time it was ready and Dan finally announced, 'Ladies, your hot tub awaits!'

We all giggled and Cathy said, 'Dan darling, Debbie's just invited us girls to come with her to Bolivia, what do you think dear?'

Dan looked rather taken aback, but he nodded.

'It sounds like a fantastic idea!'

Without further ado, Madeleine stripped off her clothes. Standing in front of us completely naked, she then said, 'C'mon girls, get your kit off and join me in the tub!'

I suppose, being French and more comfortable in her own skin, Madeleine could have been expected to take the lead, but I could see that Cathy was quite taken aback. Not to be dissuaded, she said, 'If we're going to be travelling together, we might as well get used to seeing each other with no clothes on!' The drink helped, so Cathy and I managed to get down to our bra and panties easily enough. I then slid myself into the tub: Gawd it was lovely!

Cathy and Madeleine began laughing hysterically together as we all made the most of being in the hot tub. I felt sorry for Dan as we became more rowdy. At one point, Madeleine hopped out of the tub and paraded around stark naked whilst she poured us more wine and urged Dan to join us. You could see Dan was hesitant but Madeline egged him on almost as though she was flirting with him. Cathy looked concerned and jumped out of the tub to give Dan a protective hug and to perhaps save him from temptation.

Much later, when Cathy had gone upstairs and Madeleine had left, Dan took me to one side and said, 'Sorry if you found that embarrassing. You will keep an eye on Cathy if she decides to go travelling with you. She can get a bit over the top when she's had a few too many, especially when Madeleine's about; they tend to egg each other on. Come to think of it, I think you'd do well to keep an eye on both of them!'

Chapter 29
Lima

Peru is a realm of high mountains inhabited by ancient tribal cultures that were supplanted centuries ago by the Spanish Conquistadors. It's certainly a land of mystery (and birthplace of Paddington Bear!) even the name for Peru's capital, Lima, is often misconstrued as having been derived from its usurpers' word for lime, but actually the name has nothing to do with limes, but is named after an ancient tribal oracle, or Limaq, that used to live in the region where Lima now stands. Confusion aside, Lima is associated with limes; it's kind of the city of 'the Big Lime' that sits on the Pacific coast. Whilst reference to its over-achieving North American cousin, New York, sitting on the shores of the Atlantic, as being 'the Big Apple' conjures up a sweet and appealing vision that's associated with the city's history of horse racing and big money, Lima's association is also apt, but in a rather less appetising way. In common with the limes selling in its open markets, the exhaust fumes and pollution that clouds Lima's teeming streets certainly leaves a sour taste in your mouth, but it's the grinding poverty that tugs at your heartstrings.

***

Cathy, Madeleine and myself disembarked from a British Airways flight from Heathrow and were disgorged into the blinding light and blistering heat of a Peruvian early November morning. None of us knew what to expect, but since she spoke Spanish, Maddie took the lead and hailed a taxi from a long line of battered cars sitting outside arrivals. Leaving the bland international nowhere land of the airport, we dropped off a cultural cliff and were thrust into a honking, hooting frenzy of cars, thronging pavements and urgent street vendors. The only piece of solid ground we had was we were booked into a hotel called the Ramos for the night and the Crabtrees had said Judy's sister, Vicky Condon, was very keen to help be our "tour guide" for our short stay in Lima.

Having taken a seat in a taxi at the head of the queue and Maddie had told the driver the name of our hotel he indicated that we should give him our bags. He chucked these into the copious trunk of his car, which I noticed he then padlocked. Carefully, the driver eased off the curb and into the traffic, an apparently solid phalanx of cars. Once ensconced in the flow, our driver cranked up the volume on his car radio and picked up speed, swerving in and out of the traffic lanes.

Slightly fearful that we might crash any minute, the dulcet tones of what sounded like an old man singing a heart-breaking melody had a soothing effect and Maddie said knowledgeably, 'It's Cuban Bolero, very popular all over Latin America, apparently.' This crumb of knowledge suggested she'd probably done some research on the place. I suddenly realised I knew absolutely nothing about Peru or Bolivia, its people or its culture and here we were flying at a suicidal speed through Lima's Friday evening rush hour! Swerving off the main drag, the driver crept along a labyrinth of narrow streets that wouldn't have been out of place in Dickensian London. We all looked at each other and thought the same thing, 'we're being kidnapped!'

Maddie tapped the glass panel behind the taxi driver's head.

'Erm… queremos ir al Hotel Casa de Ramos. Está en Calle Pingoyo.'

The driver rather gruffly replied, 'Si, si, lo se, esta bien. Es el Día de Todos los Santos Vivos, el trafico es muy malo!' He then turned to us, laughed and wagged his head. 'Escogiste un mal momento para llegar a Lima señoras!'

Maddie promptly slumped back into the cracked vinyl of the back seat.

'Oh my God, it's the celebration of All Souls Day, basically, The Day of the Dead!' No wonder the traffic's murder!' Cathy and I giggled at her unintentional pun.

It made sense; we'd left the UK just the day before Halloween and I knew All Souls is on the first to the second of November. As if to confirm this, as we broke out onto the main thoroughfare, an ancient Ford Chevrolet crawled past us in the opposite direction with a man standing in the truck's load bed ornately dressed in a crimson and gold headdress holding a huge black crucifix.

At the sight of this macabre spectacle Cathy became quite animated and said, 'This looks amazing! We've just got to go out this evening for a look around!' I must've looked sceptical, because she pulled a face and said, 'C'mon Debbie, where's your sense of adventure!' I thought to myself, there's adventure and recklessness, and there's a thin dividing line between the two!

Arriving at the hotel, Maddie gave the taxi guy five US dollars; which I thought was quite a lot, but our driver looked disappointed and said, 'y la propina señora?' So Maddie gave him another couple of dollars.

I said, 'We'd better change some money, or we'll run out of dollars at this rate!'

We were pleasantly surprised that the hotel foyer was clean and tidy and the neighbourhood looked to be fairly upmarket. Encouraged by this, I decided to change five hundred dollars at reception. The woman at the desk raised an eyebrow, but she nodded. It then took her several minutes to count what turned out to be almost two and a half million Sols! I was flabbergasted, until I realised that a coffee and two beers cost us twenty-four thous, and five hundred sols and the denominations of the banknotes ranged from one thousand to five thousand. I was to later learn that hyperinflation meant that five-million-sol notes, weren't uncommon.

After a tepid shower and an encounter with a large cockroach that leapt out of my hotel room closet, I had a rather less sanguine opinion of our lodgings and its surroundings, so I suggested, 'We could just eat at the hotel, it'd be easier on our first night.'

But Cathy couldn't be deflected from her idea to have a Halloween night time walk and Maddie agreed with her and said, 'Did you see what they're serving in there? Some kind of dried meat and yucca. No, I'm with Cathy, let's have a look for a proper restaurant.'

Walking away from the hotel along the tree-lined street, our upscale surroundings quickly degraded into shambling dilapidated buildings and unnervingly large open spaces that looked increasingly uninviting in the gathering darkness. After a while, we were passing the dark shape of a church, when we caught sight of groups of people carrying candles and large wooden platters of what looked like food and drink into the graveyard. As we got closer, a macabre and unsettling tableau unfolded before us. Using the flat top of what was probably the lid of the family crypt as a table, a woman dressed in a flowing black robe and headscarf served food to a small group of diners sitting on the ground using nearby gravestones as backrests. It was like something out of a movie by Hammer House of Horror, The Return of the Mummy, or some such nonsense, but this was real! I was momentarily transfixed. We would've stayed longer, but it felt like we were intruding on a private ritual and I could see people's heads turning in our direction. Hurrying away from the church, we lost our bearings. Realising that we were actually walking back towards to the hotel, we unanimously decided to make do with the hotel restaurant after all. I think Maddie and Cathy's appetite for further cultural experience that night had been thoroughly appeased!

***

We seemed to have arrived in Lima during a busy month for festivals! The macabre rituals of All Souls Day had piqued our appetite for Peruvian culture, so we eagerly agreed to Vicky's suggestion that we experience another cultural must-see, the spectacle of La Feria del Señor de los Milagros, the largest bullfighting festival in Peru that ran in Lima on five consecutive Sundays in November. Up until then, my naïve understanding of a bullfight was that it was all show; the man versus beast equivalent of the BBC's wrestling contests between Big Daddy and Giant Haystacks that I used to watch on TV in the brief interregnum between Mass and Sunday lunch back at home. In other words, it was a carefully choreographed encounter in which the bullfighter (torero) wore a rather camp outfit and enraged the bull with his little red cape and nimbly dodged out of the way to the crowd's chant of 'olé' as el toro attempted to bring half a ton of muscle and sharp horns to bear on his human opponent.

Like All Souls, the bullfight is another popular import from Spain. The event is held in the Plaza de Toros de Acho, the oldest bullfighting arena in the Americas, which dominates one of Lima's historic quarters, the Rimac District on the other side of the city from where we were staying. After meeting up with Vicky and her parents at our hotel, an early-afternoon taxi ride took us past some of the most impoverished parts of the city. Partly finished buildings jostled with four-storey terraces that looked like they'd been bombed out if it wasn't that families were clearly living in them. Sewerage flowed in some of the streets we were passing, in others, heaping piles of refuse were being methodically dug through by groups of people looking for something to eat or sell. Up until that point, I'd never seen such abject poverty. It made me sick to my stomach to witness such human suffering.

With so many desperate people about, before exiting the relative safety of the taxi, Vicky gave us the kind of briefing an army sergeant might give his men before they went into battle.

'I would strongly advise taking off all jewellery, including rings, earrings, bangles and watches, and definitely no handbags!'

Replying on our behalf, Cathy said, 'Don't worry, any valuables we're carrying are in body belts pushed down into our trousers.' Vicky's parents, Eduardo and Maria nodded approvingly.

Thus reassured, we exited the taxi at the main entrance and entered the throng of people. Like the gladiatorial games of Ancient Rome, rich and poor appeared happy to rub shoulders. In fact, its huge size and numerous high-lintel entrances gave it the appearance of a single-storey version of the Colosseum itself. Climbing up to the second tier of seating in the arena, we stayed near one of the entrances so we could get a fairly uninterrupted view of the baked, bare earth circle of the arena. As we took our seats, the crowd roared as six toreros entered the ring and the announcer introduced each one in turn.

Vicky leaned over and said, 'Four of the men are from Spain, but two, wearing blue, are young local men, we are going to be cheering for them!'

According to tradition, one of the local men went first. A huddle of attendants goaded the bull before it was released into the arena; the crowd went quiet as the torero paced towards the pawing animal. I'm sure everyone in the crowd was rooting for the man, but I was on the bull's side as it charged toward the bullfighter's fluttering muleta (the red cape), 'olé!' As the matador quickly turned on his heel, the bull was right behind him, 'olé', and again, 'ole'. The bull paused and appeared to have momentarily lost its bearings, so the torero briefly bowed and the crowd roared again enraging the bull enough for it to charge again. After a break whilst the torero ducked into a protective slot in the arena wall, he stepped out again and there was a repeat of the first encounter, however, this time it ended with the torero thrusting a sharpened stick into the bull's shoulder. The animal bellowed, and it was then I realised this wasn't a show, but a fight to the death.

In pain, his flanks gleaming with blood and foaming with sweat in the sweltering heat, the bull took a run at the goading crowd that resulted in an injury to its foreleg as it crashed into the guard-wall. As we watched, the bull staggered slightly and the torero stepped up to the wall and took a sword from an attendant and sheathed it in his muleta. I couldn't watch. I'd begun crying, but I didn't want to embarrass Vicky and her parents. All my instincts urged me to I run out into the ring and to put an end to the brutality unfolding in front of me. Unable to watch, I heard the crowd screaming and I was forced to look up just as the torero thrust his sword into the bull's shoulders. Mercifully, the animal went down like a rock and made no further movement. Feeling trapped by etiquette and practicality which meant I was dependent on our hosts for transport, I was forced to sit through three more performances, but the other toreros failed to kill their bulls cleanly, and thankfully, Vicky's father, apparently disappointed by their performance, decided that we'd had enough.

Whilst Vicky and the Condons set about finding us a taxi, Cathy, Maddie and I formed a supportive huddle. We'd been pretty shaken up by the casual brutality of the bullfight. Cathy said, 'God! I hope the rest of the afternoon isn't as horrendous! From now on, we're organising our own tourist itinerary! Maddie and I laughed nervously.

Our next stop was the Cathedral of Lima, situated just over the Avenue Panamericana Norte and a short distance from the arena. We were going to evening Mass, but all I wanted to do was go for a beer to calm my jangled nerves. Anxious not to miss the beginning, Mr Condon grabbed a taxi rather than walking. It could have been a rerun of Best Sundays back in Hainested, except that the décor in the Cathedral of Lima was seriously over-the-top compared with Our Lady of Compassion in Saffron Walden. Actually, ornate wouldn't do the place justice, the main altar was vast and much of it encrusted with gold. Just before we went inside, Vicky, in a nod to our status as tourists, suggested that we shell out a couple of hundred sols each for a guided tour around the cathedral's crypt to pay our respects to the dead people down there. Visions of us propping up a few of the crypt's inhabitants and sitting down for a polite tea flashed into my head. Then, as if Cathy and Maddie had read my thoughts, unanimously, we politely declined!

In our rush, we'd actually arrived early, so while people started arriving, I took a tour around the cathedral. About midway around the nave, I spotted several huge glass cases. A closer look revealed that each contained a life-sized waxwork of Christ apparently in various Stations of the Cross. As I approached, I noticed a frail old man kneeling in front of a figure depicting "under the weight of the cross". Not wishing to intrude, but fascinated at the same time, I walked around the perimeter of the nave so that I was partially hidden by a case depicting Jesus' first fall. The old man had his rosary beads out and he was staring intently into the vivid blue eyes of the waxwork mannequin, the head of which was turned upwards and had the look of someone in extremis of suffering. I'd never seen anything like it before and I found it deeply disturbing. As I watched, my convent school tutor, Sister Scholastica's voice popped unbidden into my head reading the Ten Commandments, "thou shalt not make unto thee any graven image or any likeness that is in heaven above or that is in the earth beneath..." Whilst it wasn't an image of God, the waxwork's lifelike form was very unnerving. Returning the same way through the cathedral after Mass, I noticed the old man was still there. I felt pity for him, as though he'd fallen in love with Christ's image and would, like Narcissus who fell in love with his own reflection, waste away and die in front of it.

Chapter 30
Angel

It was noisy and fumes from the roaring traffic on a nearby freeway stung our eyes and boy it was hot! We'd said goodbye to our hosts, the Crabtrees and Condons, and had now taken the first step on a one thousand five-hundred-mile journey, first by road and then by rail, that would ultimately lead us to Charagua where Adam, Vanda and their family were completing their fifth and final year in Bolivia. At seven a.m. Lima's Atocongo bus station was a swirling mass of people. Some were wearing western-style business suits, others wouldn't be out of place in Armada Michigan and then there were a few, mostly women, wearing traditional dress. This traditional dress consisted of brightly coloured alpaca mantas (a simple poncho made from a square of cloth) over a jobona (small woollen jacket) and voluminous embroidered polleras (flowing skirts). All this was finished off with a trademark hat. For older women, this was often a traditional montera (colourful headgear that looks like a bowl full of flowers) or, if they were younger, it was more likely to be a bombin (essentially, a flat-topped bowler hat). The decorous and riotous colours of the women's traditional dress reminded me of the strange and exciting culture that lay ahead of us out there on the open road. Travelling the road was never easy though.

As the old adage goes, two's company and three's a crowd. For the few days we'd spent in Lima, that third person had been Cathy whose short haired, boyish features had started to habitually wear a petulant frown and today was no exception. I'd assumed she might be missing Dan and wished he was travelling with her, but it turned out that her moodiness was likely down to a 'tiff' between her and Maddie. As we stood in the bus station, having found the stand for Nazca, Cathy briefly went in search of some bottled water.

Whilst she was gone, Maddie took the chance to confide in me that she'd had "words" with Cathy a couple of nights ago.

'It's like this Debbie', she then moved her head closer to mine and continued, 'I couldn't keep it under the table any longer, Alex is having an affair and it's been going on for a while. I had been hoping it wasn't serious, but... look, I won't go into details but I think the woman he's seeing might've had an abortion. A couple of days ago, I mentioned it to Cathy, but she denied it and said that Alex wouldn't do such a thing. She's been moody with me ever since. To be honest, relations between Alex and me have been terrible recently. He hardly even touches me any more. I'm guessing he was secretly overjoyed when I told him I was disappearing off for three months! Basically, I'm not sure I want to go back to him...' She was cut short by Cathy's return. When Cathy approached, her face was like thunder and I suspected that she'd seen us talking conspiratorially.

Feeling rather awkward in the silence between us that followed, I was pleasantly surprised that Cathy's mood seemed to lift once we started leaving the city on a cleaner than expected bus headed for Nazca and a touristic stopover to trek up into surrounding hills to view the famous geoglyphs that'd been etched into the Nazca Desert sands by a civilisation that had thrived there in 500 BC. Discovered in the fifteenth century, the Nazca Lines were popularised in modern times by the Swiss author, Erich von Däniken. Däniken, incredulous that an ancient people would, or could, make such intricate patterns, including human forms, birds and other animals on such a huge scale (some are over one hundred and fifty feet square) postulated that the lines were evidence of contact between humanity and spacefaring aliens in antiquity. Not being a space-weirdo buff myself, I'd still got the book from the library before our trip, but had found it far too turbid to be a fun read.

Taking advice from Vicky, we'd planned to spend a couple of days on the desert plateau staying in the town of Nazca itself so we could take an early morning taxi to a low hill out in the desert to get a better view of the lines as the rising sun picked out the markings etched in the sand. On arrival, we checked into our hotel, the rather strangely named Hospedaje Secretos (which I sincerely hoped wasn't a front for a brothel), dumped our bags and headed out to the taxi rank outside.[38] The cheapest option was to join a group of tourists on a minibus tour. Crammed in with two starched and fragrant German couples and a

---

[38] Roughly translates as the Secrets Hotel.

dishevelled looking lone traveller with a thin beard and straggling long hair, we headed out along the gun-barrel straight Pan American Highway and into the desert. We were excited, and not sure what to expect. Cathy had lost her frown and became animated about the vast emptiness of the expanse around us as lengthening shadows and the austere desert landscape gave the impression that we'd landed on another planet.

Our destination, a low hill on our right that floated above the mirage caused by the heat shimmer, slowly materialised and the driver pulled in to a lay-by and said, 'Damas y caballeros. Hemos llegado al mirador. Regresaré en dos horas a eso de las cuatro y te llevaré de regreso a la ciudad. ¡disfruta tu día!'

'Okay, we've got until four o'clock when the driver will come back and pick us up. C'mon!'

Maddie headed off along a rough track heading out into the desert where we caught up on the mysterious loner. Drawing alongside him, I could see he was young, but had the careworn look of someone who'd seen something of life. As we plodded along in silence, a fan heater breeze ripped the sweat off exposed skin and dust rose from our feet as they churned up the fine red tilth. I imagined that Nazca farmers working this land thousands of years ago; it must've been fertile once. The silence was profound. The object of our curiosity remained quiet. I looked over at him, his features were tinged with melancholia, but he then met my gaze and winked; it was then that I saw a flash of his youthful light-heartedness.

'Buenas tardes!' I offered into the silence.

Already straining my nascent Spanish to the max, I was unsure how to continue, so I was relieved when he replied in English with a Spanish accent infused with an American twang, 'And good even'n to you!' He thrust out a thin, rather grubby hand from under his poncho, which we all shook in turn. This seemed to spur him to continue, 'M'name's Angel, not 'cos I'm angelic, but I picked up the name from the tribal peoples while I was in the Mato Grosso jungles.[39] I've been travel'n in South America for the last seven years, play'n music in clubs and bars to earn money. I'm near to get'n burned out though. I was hope'n to catch the

---

[39] Mato Grosso is a huge, largely undisturbed area of the Amazon Rainforest near the border with Bolivia.

vibe from these lines, y'know, maybe get a direction.' He fell silent again like this was his potted biog. he trotted out to strangers.

I could see that Maddie and Cathy were fascinated and started asking him a barrage of questions like he was the oracle on the mount and knower of all things, like 'do you know a great place to stay, drink, things to see in Cuzco, Machu Picchu, La Paz', etc, etc. He nodded and gave out small breadcrumbs of information that only led them to ask more questions. He was cool with it though and appeared to show no sign of irritation. At the conical summit of the farthest peak, we joined the German couple on a rather impractical circular steel bench with a steel pole protruding that could've been for a flagpole at some point. Angel walked on and stopped a short distance away, hunkered down on a ledge, fiddled with his tobacco pouch, and despite the warm, gusting wind, successfully managed to role a cigarette. The acrid aroma of marijuana was carried back to us on the breeze. He then stretched out his arms like a sorcerer casting a spell. Intrigued, I quietly walked over and sat down a short distance from him.

In answer to my unasked question, he said, 'I'm shake'n those big old hands out there, y'see'm out in the desert?

Straining against the glare of the sun, I could make out a network of spidery lines running out to the horizon and some angular shapes like someone had gone crazy on a sand-drawing table, but no hands. As my mind struggled to make sense of what I was seeing, five conjoined, finger-like shapes emerged from the confusion, like I'd unlocked a secret from a coded message.

'Yes, yes... I can see them now!'

Following Angel's example, I stretched out my hands and tried to place them into the 'fingers' of lines traced in the sand far below. The desert etchings seemed like a riddle within a conundrum. Were they a message to the Nazca's gods, a conjuring trick, or a coded labyrinth? I wondered what future generations, thousands of years from now, would make of our huge network of motorways mostly leading to London. Maybe they'd think the city was the epicentre of an ancient cult worshipping the Nasdaq and the FTSE 100. I chuckled to myself, closed my eyes and felt a rare and momentary sense of peace, or was it that Angel's spliff was getting to me!

***

That evening, back at our hotel, we crashed out in our rooms for a couple of hours, but agreed to meet down in the hotel bar at eight. Unable to sleep, I came down early and found Maddie in deep conversation with a rather handsome Peruvian guy. Once I'd joined them at their table she said, 'This is Miguel, he's offered to give us a lift up into the mountains for a better view of the lines early tomorrow before we leave town.' I thought to myself it's all rather sudden, gallivanting off in some stranger's car, so I had some reservations; but what the hell, there's three of us and only one of him!

When Cathy came down, I bought her a beer at the bar, burnished my nascent Spanish and asked the barman for, 'Cusqueña por favor.'

'Oh Debbie, your Spanish is coming on a treat! You still have that posh accent though!' Cathy chuckled at her own joke. The sleep had done her good. We joined Maddie and Miguel, but I could see she was reluctant to come with us for an evening meal, so we eventually left her to it.

Cathy and I had an enjoyable evening together with me recounting a few of my classic Glantnor legends. , but unfortunately, my brief period basking in Cathy's sunny mood evaporated the next morning at breakfast when we sat at a table together. Maddie was nowhere to be seen despite the fact we were supposed to be getting an early start. I could feel Cathy's frustration boiling over.

Unable to contain herself any longer, she broke off from a rather indigestible looking plate of Chicharrón de Chancho and said, 'I bet Maddie's been telling you that Alex is being unfaithful.[40] But I reckon it's 'cos she just wants to have an excuse to get laid by anyone she feels like while she's away. If that's what she wants to do it's up to her, I'm not standing in her way and I'm not going to hurt Alex by telling tales, but it makes me mad she's using some story about my brother being unfaithful as an excuse!'

I didn't want to take sides, but struggled to stay neutral during the ensuing discussions between the three of us when Maddie finally showed

---

[40] Deep fried chunks of pork.

up. The fact was all of us had come from a closeted existence in Wales where the daily routine had worn us down. We were young and wanted some excitement. In the end, after a lot of soul-searching, we all came to an unspoken understanding to accept that, as the North American Indians used to say, "What's said and done in the tepee stays in the tepee". Once we were okay with that, we collectively gave each other permission to get down to enjoying a rare and exhilarating time of freedom in our lives whilst still looking after each other like kind of "chaperones". If that freedom included seeing other men, that was our decision and it would be respected. As a result, at least for the time we were travelling together, a warmer sense of camaraderie emerged. But like all freedoms, they come at a cost. Unfortunately, at that point, we just didn't know yet how much the bill would come to.

Chapter 31
Cusco

"Romeo, Romeo, wherefore art thou Romeo?"[41] Shakespeare's Juliet may have wondered where her feckless lover may have got to, but judging by the voluminous pages of my diary written at the time that recounted a veritable tsunami wave of approaches from local men, you'd be forgiven for thinking that a fair few of Romeo's descendants seemed to have fled Italy and had come to live in Peru. Whether it was down to the vagaries of translation from Spanish into English, or that our would-be suitors had themselves borrowed their English from the great bard's flowery prose, some of the chat up lines, notes and letters we received from our Romeos would be amusing if they weren't so fervent. Here's a classic example of the type of fevered language they liked to use. It's from a note to me thrust under my hotel room door by a lovely chap called Lyca, and I quote,

"You arrived like the sun who takes away the [shadows] and [gives me] warmth, you arrived like [the] wind who takes away the clouds [to] let the sun through, you arrived like [the] magic of a simple song." And so on, I think you get the picture!

In hindsight, I think the reason why Cusco became the birthplace for several romances was that we'd decided to make this rather picturesque and charming town a base for our trek into Machu Picchu and to immerse ourselves in the vibrant taverna-based culture and partying we found there. Since we weren't travelling for a while, we were no longer moving targets, so the Romeos were able to get to work on us! Angel had been the source of much invaluable, and some rather questionable, information on where we should stay and what we should do whilst we were in Cusco, so clearly, he'd spent quite a bit of time there and liked the place. Therefore, I wasn't overly surprised when we recognised his gangling form lounging in an easy chair of the Wild Rover backpackers

---

[41] Romeo and Juliet, Act II, Scene II, Lines 33–36

when we checked in after our arrival off the train from Arequipa. Since we last saw him, Angel had acquired a flamboyant fedora with a crimson feather stuck in its hatband, which I thought rather suited him.

He also appeared to be a little drunk, but he recognised us and seemed pleased to see us.

'Bienvenidos a Cusco mis queridos! Veo que seguiste mi consejo!' He hugged and kissed our cheeks in turn, and then he switched to English.

'Sooo, you guys are gonna do Machu Picchu then? Hack your way through the jungle! I'm think'n of do'n the same thing. I'd love to tag along with you if that's okay. You're gonna need a Spaniard to act the part of one of those evil old Conquistadors!'

In a breathless conversation that ensued, Cathy spoke for all of us when she gladly welcomed Angel into our little cabal of wanderers. A journey to the Inca citadel of Machu Picchu, perched on the top of a seven-thousand-foot-high ridge in the Eastern Cordillera, required travellers to make an arduous three-to-four-day hike through a steamy jungle that culminated in a tough climb up to the ruins in the thin atmosphere. I reckon we all must've thought we might find the support of a seasoned jungle-dweller highly beneficial! For his part, Angel appeared to be lonely and wanted company. It was good to have him along, since he rounded off the edges of our sometimes-edgy threesome. For me, he quickly became a trusted companion and a male sounding board for ensuing romantic entanglements. Cathy came to treat him like an older brother and Maddie became very fond of him. In return, Angel kept us amused with his traveller's tales. He was writing a book about his experiences with the tribal peoples of the Amazon, some of whom hadn't previously had contact with westerners. Despite his swashbuckling appearance, and Maddie's fondness for him, he never made a pass at any of us. Instead, he was happy to remain as an observer, a guardian angel; perhaps that's how he'd acquired his moniker from the Gavião people in the Mato Grosso. In return for our company, Angel facilitated our travels, acting like a 'tour-guide' for all the stuff they don't put in travel books like, where to buy the best marijuana, how to catch a ride on a train without paying and what the black-market rate for American dollars should be, and so on.

Leaving Angel nursing his Pisco Sour in the bar, we climbed two flights of steps up to the women's dorm.[42] At over nine thousand feet, Cusco's thin atmosphere had us puffing like a bunch of geriatrics and I wondered what it'd be like climbing up to Machu Picchu. Like Goldilocks' bears, our narrow, triple room had three single beds lined up in a little row against the wall with a window at the far end that gave a stunning view out over the twinkling lights and illuminated church spires of the town below. Looking like huge bats in the gloom, knotted mosquito nets hung from the ceiling above each bed.

Sighing contentedly, Maddie threw her backpack on the middle of the three, and flopped down onto its firm but comfortable mattress.

'Home sweet home! At least for the next few days at any rate.' We'd certainly landed on our feet taking Angel's advice to stay at the Wild Rover. The hostel was clean and perched on a hill overlooking the historic centre of Cusco.

Cathy said, 'We should get something to eat before it gets too late.'

Maddie nodded, and replied, 'But let's get a shower first, we must stink!'

As I stripped off my sweat-stained clothes, I noticed how much weight I'd lost already, which was great news for me! My belly was looking tighter and my navel was beginning to stretch out nicely; I gave my stomach a satisfied pat and said, 'I'm losing weight! This Peruvian diet is doing me good!'

Cathy quipped, 'So, you're no longer going to be Aunty Plum by the time you get to Charagua; your brother's kids won't recognise you! But I think I'm going too far. I've gotta find some decent food otherwise I'm gonna waste away!' As if to demonstrate, she did a twirl and I could see her ribs showing and that her heavy backpack had left painful looking sores on her bony pelvis that jutted out on either side of her thin belly. We all laughed, wrapped ourselves in our towels and headed for the showers.

Opening the door to the shower room, we were met by clouds of steam and a solid wall of gregarious, naked Frenchwomen that wouldn't

---

[42] Having now reached the status of being the Peruvian national drink, the Pisco Sour is a cocktail that was actually invented by an American that lived in Lima. The Pisco Sour consists of a grape brandy, egg white, lime juice and a little sugar. It's actually very refreshing!

let us past to get to the stalls.

Maddie rolled her eyes, sighed, and rather out of character for her, said loudly, 'Merde! Je me sens parfois gêné d'être français!'

Hearing this, one of the women replied, 'Oh, ayez une vie!' The other women tittered in unison. We beat a hasty retreat and decided on eating first and showering later.

Chapter 32
Machu Picchu

'My friends, the only way to do this thing is on foot!' Angel made his point by alternately stamping his flip-flopped feet on the floor like he was walking. The wooden floorboards of the taverna boomed like a kettledrum. A group of women, sitting at a table opposite, turned anxiously around to find out what was going on; they were none other than the Frenchwomen we'd encountered in the shower.

Angel doffed his fedora graciously.

'Oh, excusez-moi mesdames, je fais juste un point!' Angel got several radiant smiles and some unintelligible but friendly-sounding comments in French, a very different reception to the one we got from them in the shower!

Maddie nudged him and said, 'Ne savais pas que tu pouvais parler Français!'

Angel smiled.

'Oh, j'ai plein de petits secrets mon cher!'

'C'mon you two, this is a group discussion, no French!' Maddie feigned like she was leaving, so Cathy qualified her statement.

'No speaking French I mean!' We all laughed.

I'm enjoying this new group dynamic; I really think it's prevented us from going our separate ways. We unanimously agreed to walk the whole trail, after all, it was only forty kilometres, or twenty-five miles, starting at Ollantaytambo, a little town accessible by train from Cusco.

To celebrate, we ordered a round of Cristal beer, but Angel had other ideas.

'If we're gonna do the Inca trail we need to toast with the traditional beer of the Andes, Chicha de Jora.'

The guy at the bar must've heard us because he said, 'Vale, cuatro chicha ya vienen!' Then, with much aplomb, the barman placed four large glasses of cloudy and slightly frothy liquid on the table.

'¡Salud!' Despite its resemblance to dirty washing-up water, it tasted sweet, but had a pleasant, bitter aftertaste.

Continuing our celebration, later that evening, we had a meal at the Kusikuy Restaurante, a traditional place in the historic centre serving local food that Angel had said was authentic and very good. Unexpectedly, he offered to order and pay for our meals.

'If you're gonna to be put'n' up with me in the next week or two, the least I can do is buy you all dinner!' He wouldn't hear of any of our protestations.

Cathy did make one stipulation though, and said, 'Okay, that's fine, but no cow's heels or cow's kneecaps!'

Angel nodded, and said, 'I promise'. He then went up to the cashier's booth and returned after a few minutes saying he'd got us a set meal for four.

The starter was something we all recognised and had eaten before several times already, sliced, boiled potatoes in a spicy sauce; so far, so good. Next up was something less recognisable. It was large, it was coated in a thick brown sauce and it was crouching in the centre of our plates surrounded by boiled potatoes and some more potatoes in what appeared to be a yoghurt sauce. We all just stared for a moment.

It was Maddie who broke the silence and voiced our inner fears

'What is it Angel? It looks like, erm, a large rat.' There was a round of involuntary gasps from all of us, surely not!

'Not a rat, chiquitas, it's cuy asado, roast cuy, a local delicacy. I'm not sure what you call it in English. All I know, is that farmers produce cuy for eating.'

Maddie stroked her chin.

'Mmh, I've not heard of it. It can't be Castilian Spanish, it must be a Peruvian word for a local farm animal.' We all agreed it tasted very good though. It had a delicate, sweet flesh. It was only later, when we checked our Latin Spanish that we discovered it was guinea pig! Cuy is Peruvian onomatopoeia for the plaintive sound they make.

***

Only twenty-five miles! By the end of day two of our trek along the Inca trail, I'd mentally removed the word 'only' as a prefix to the mileage and replaced it with gruelling. As we climbed steadily up a narrow path on our third day, the afternoon deluge started, first with a few drops until its intensity began to turn the roughly cobbled track into a stream. The rainy season had come early and emphatically! We were climbing through a particularly steep section. From the gloom-laden interior, a rich odour of decay wafted out of the dense cloud forest on either side of the path. We were climbing towards the aptly named 'Pase de mujer muerta' (Dead Woman's Pass) over three thousand feet of ascent to over thirteen thous, and before descending to our campsite at Pacaymayu for the night.

Incredibly, Angel was still only wearing his flip-flops. His only concession to the weather was a piece of clear plastic draped over his shoulders with a hole cut in it for his head that he said he'd often used as a shelter for the night. In fact, the entire sum of his equipment was contained within a large canvas satchel slung over his shoulders. Whilst we'd stored a lot of our gear at the Wild Rover, we, on the other hand were tottering under the weight of fifty-pound packs. Infuriatingly, Angel moved up the path as if he were floating, like an angel presumably.

As we stopped to refresh ourselves from our canteens, I saw that Angel was barely sweating. For some reason, I found this infuriating

'Aren't you even hot?' I asked querulously. 'It's thirty-five degrees and seventy-five percent humidity for goodness' sake!'

In answer, he held up his finger in an instructional manner.

'So many numbers! But if you calm your mind, still your thoughts and focus only on your footsteps, you can change the way your body communicates with your mind so you can embrace the heat rather than fighting it.'

'Ommmmm!' we turned around and saw Maddie coming up behind us. She giggled and said, 'All very transcendental!'

Angel laughed, then, addressing his comment to me, 'Or I can always throw water on my face and puff like an old woman if that'd make you feel better Debbie!' I chucked my sweat-laden bush hat at him. There's no winning an argument with Angel around!

However, I did take a moment to listen. The air was full of sounds, the rush of a stream running below us, a screech from one or more of the many species of brightly-coloured parrots fluttering in the treetops, an unearthly scream from a bird or a frog, the grunt of a monkey, and on the very edge of my hearing, was that a growl of a jaguar? This cacophony was bracketed by the constant white noise of cicada beetles. The thought of an unseen jaguar stealthily tracking us sent a shiver up my spine. Then I thought of the evening ahead. For our one hundred- and fifty-dollars' entry fee, we had the privilege of lying together under a large canvas tarpaulin with a communal meal provided by the park rangers and cooked over a charcoal stove with heat against the evening chill coming from a coal-burning stove, or 'jiko'. I thought, 'at least the fire will keep the jaguars at bay, right?'

***

Rising very early the next morning, we had the privilege of seeing a huge bird, possibly a condor, circling effortlessly above the rocky precipice above us as the first of the sun's shafts of light bathed the cliff-face in an otherworldly orange glow. It was relatively cold, but soon our walking and the sun's rays warmed us as it climbed higher into a cobalt-blue clear sky. We'd decided to rise before dawn so we could get up to Inti Punku (Sun Gate) for a spectacular view of the Machu Picchu citadel at dawn. I'm glad we did. I don't think I'll ever see a more incredible sight as the rising sun picked out the hundreds of stone structures laid out on the broad ridge below us. This time, we all followed Angel's example and sat together on a small ledge, closed our eyes and took deep breaths of the rarefied atmosphere. I tried to imagine the pageant and ceremony of the Inca emperor, Pachacuti, entering his city in the sky.

Chapter 33
Victor

On our return to the Wild Rover, I didn't feel right,
I felt rather dizzy and fell onto the floor,
I was helped up by the landlady and into a chair,
But my head was still spinning and I fell down once more!

I know, I know, it's a terrible parody! The Wild Rover is an old drinking song that was also a big hit for the Irish punk group, the Pogues who I was fleetingly into at the time of our trip to South America. My rendition commemorates my rather inauspicious arrival back in Cusco after our hike up to Machu Picchu. On the night of our return to the Wild Rover backpackers, I had a bout of fainting in a restaurant followed by an uncomfortably sleepless night. Feeling groggy all the next day, I tried to sleep it off whilst Cathy did some shopping in town for some supplies. On the other hand Maddie, who'd already got ahead of both of us in the 'dating' game and picked up a small posse of male admirers before we'd left for Machu Picchu, was out and about with Gose and Pepe, who she'd met in Chez Maggie's Pizzeria during a night out, and Edgar, who she'd met the previous evening in the Café Manuela. Rather than keeping her new friends to herself she'd been introducing them all to Cathy and myself, so we now had a kind of group friendship going on. It was actually Gose that came to see if I was all right after my spell of fainting the day before. To be honest, I think it was a touch of altitude sickness. A day's rest and rehydration had me back on my feet so I agreed to Gose's offer to accompany him as he walked over to where the others were meeting for dinner.

Slim and bronzed, Gose had studied in France. He was polite and quite charming; I could see why Maddie had taken a shine to him. After a ten-minute walk, we entered the Hotel Casa del Ande where, he said, Cathy and Maddie were having drinks with a guy called

Edgar who was staying there on business with a colleague. By the time we arrived at the bar, Edgar's associate, Victor, had decided to join what was now quite a convivial little gathering. As I'd come late to the 'party' Victor offered to buy me a drink. When he returned with my requested Coke, he sat next to me. From the start, I could see he'd taken an interest. A coiffured crop of frizzy hair and high cheekbones and a neat moustache gave him a distinguished look. He was a little older than me, which I found reassuring since I had little experience of men up to that point. Victor had travelled and worked in the US and I could tell that he'd likely switched into 'gringo' mode, being deferential rather than controlling as he might have been with a Peruvian woman. He fixed me with his eyes and we talked together late into the evening. He was a surveyor for the Ministerio de Vivienda, Construcción y Saneamiento the Peruvian Department of Housing and Sanitation). He'd studied for a masters in environmental health at Colorado State University. He loved Denver, it was clean, efficient and people were friendly. He'd done some hiking in the Rocky Mountain National Park nearby; it reminded him of the Andes.

I was envious, and said, 'I spent a whole year in the US with an agricultural exchange programme working my guts out on a dairy farm in Michigan and only got off the farm a few times for beers in Armada, a totally one-horse town!'

Victor laughed and reached out to ruffle my hair with his hand.

'You are in the wrong business mi querida! You need to get a government job like me. It gives me the chance to travel and do some business for my family company. A win-win as they say in America!'

Victor was tactile and attentive. He emphasised his points by brushing my shoulder, and a couple of times he stroked my thigh. I didn't find this repellent like I did with the wandering hand syndrome I'd experienced at college or on the farm, this felt different, assured; like he wanted all of me, not just my body. I felt like he wanted to devour me whole and I wanted him to; needed him to. I wanted to stay longer, and Victor wanted me to, but Cathy and Maddie insisted that we get back to the hostel. I left Victor with a scrap of paper with my name and where we were staying and left.

***

A sleepless night followed. I instantly regretted not staying longer at the hotel, why was I always so timid and shy? Why hadn't I just stayed there like I wanted to, taken control of the situation like Maddie did with her entourage? I tossed and turned and eventually gave it up and went down to the breakfast room intending to have a coffee to try and get my head straight; that was before I saw some other backpackers devouring huge plates of salchicha de huacho![43] Returning with some money, I noticed that Angel had come down and was sitting drinking an espresso and smoking one of his trademark roll-ups, so I grabbed my breakfast and joined him in a convivial huddle in the corner where he was sitting. Angel politely crushed out his cigarette and kissed my cheeks in turn. His loud 'mwah' sounds seemed to echo off the wall behind us.

I loved how Angel was so expressive and alive; this, after all, was still just five a.m! He said, '¡Muy buenos días a mi encantadora! Then, he went on, 'How was your evening? I hear that you met a man last night! Tell all to your uncle Angel.

I was taken aback.

'How on earth do you know already?'

He smiled, 'I'm floating above your head and keeping an eye on you remember!'

I kind of believed him!

'Well, if you know already, I don't need to tell you what happened!'

He smiled at this and said, 'You have come to confess something, not for me to tell you what happened because you already know.'

I thought, 'more riddles from the guru', so I went on.

'I've met this Peruvian guy. He's called Victor and after just an evening together, I have to confess I already fancy him!' It was like talking to an older brother, so I asked Angel's opinion on Peruvian men.

His answer was simple, and not what I wanted to hear. He just said, 'Like many Latinos, they're not one-woman guys. He's bound to have other chiquitas.[44] I should be careful with my heart; and have him wear a condom! If he's working for the government, he'll be travelling a lot

---

[43] Peruvian-style pork sausages.
[44] Sweethearts

260

and probably has a woman in every town.'

The great oracle had spoken! But I didn't want to believe what Angel was saying on this occasion; I therefore secretly resolved to ignore all of his advice!

So I decided to deflect the conversation away from my 'romance', and noticing that he had a thick dog-eared bundle of notebooks sitting in front of him, I said, 'Is that your book?'

He nodded uncertainly.

'It's in the early stages, but yes, it is. I'm writing it in English, for the international market. It'd be real helpful of you if you could check the English in a few passages. You went to private school, right?' I nodded.

'Well, in that case, you'd be great for this 'cos I want it to be native English, not American.'

It was a pretty thick wad of diaries tied together with string, so I set to work and spent an enchanting morning reading about Gavião tribal traditions and rites of passage.

***

Later that day, in the early evening, I was sitting on the hostel veranda still editing Angel's book when Maddie came over and said, 'Debbie, that guy you were talking to last night, he's come over and wants to see you.'

My heart seemed to physically leap out of my chest and I got up so rapidly, I knocked the coffee table over. Maddie patted my arm.

'It's okay, I'll sort this, and you go and see him before he changes his mind!' She smiled, and pushed me towards the sitting room door.

Standing in the hostel reception, Victor seemed smaller than he was when we were sitting together at the hotel. He was with Edgar and chatting to Cathy. I went to him and we pecked each other's cheeks politely, but inside my heart was pounding!

Victor guided us outside. A rather battered yellow Volkswagen Beetle was sitting in front of the hostel.

'I thought you and your friend might like some lunch and maybe a drive out around Cusco?' I nodded enthusiastically, but what I really wanted was to be alone with Victor so we could get to know each other.

During lunch, I briefly had a chance to talk to him whilst Edgar and Cathy were in deep conversation.

'Victor, there's a party going on at Ukuku's bar and club.'

Victor nodded, 'I know it well.'

'Our friend Angel is playing guitar and there'll be dancing and live music.' He seemed keen on the idea so we arranged to meet at eight.

Ukuku's was packed when we arrived and I offered to pay the one-thousand sols for entry for both of us, but Victor insisted on 'going Dutch' which I assumed meant he was firmly in gringo mode again! Angel was the first on, the warm-up act, to get people in the mood. He played some classic Spanish guitar starting with a couple of haunting melodies that became increasingly intense and technical, like he was urging his instrument on, tapping the body of the guitar with his fingers of one hand with his other on the strings. Victor was stomping his feet and clapping along: it was mesmerising. At some point, we started holding hands and I could feel Victor's fingers gliding through my hair. Angel's finale was flamenco. It got people up dancing, fast and furious, clapping, stamping, I could feel the passion building in the crowd around us, and in me. A group of mariachis followed. Their speciality was merengue. For a while, I watched the men moving the women, holding their waists, testing them, stretching their bodies, feeling their litheness. For their part, the women were giving in to the men, being guided by them, luring them with their bodies. I started to feel the restrained sexuality of the music. Victor asked me to dance. Fortunately, merengue is one of the easier Latin dance forms, so I was able to pick up the basic steps fairly quickly, the three Pisco Sours I'd just downed certainly helped though! Victor was patient, and guided me firmly by the waist. I felt he was testing my resolve to resist.

We danced for while, and then he pulled me close and whispered into my sweat-slicked neck, 'I have asked Edgar to sleep in another room this evening, we can be alone.' He'd known all along that I couldn't resist! We walked back to the Casa del Ande holding hands; occasionally Victor's arm was around my waist. I was nervous but intoxicated. Victor's room was quiet and empty when we walked in, but the bedside light was on as though it'd just been vacated.

Victor was reassuring.

'Don't worry, Edgar will not disturb us.' He closed the door. We kissed fully and deeply this time and while we did, I could feel Victor's expert fingers unbuckling the belt of my jeans, opening the waistband unzipping them and pushing his hand down to cup me between my legs. I wasn't able to resist. With the exception of Fred, other guys had just wanted to get the moment over with, but Victor took his time. He unbuttoned my blouse and pushing down my jeans. We broke off and I undressed leaving my panties on, but when I turned to look at Victor, he was naked. We were both tense, but eager. I explained that I had little experience with men and asked him to go slowly. We sat on the end of the bed and kissed for a long while before we lay down together. Our kissing became passionate and I lost my panties and all further inhibitions. We made love. Pleasure exploded in my belly; I'd never felt such happiness.

Chapter 34
Journey to Charagua

I awoke from a fitful slumber with a new and unusual addition to my morning routine, I had a man lying next to me in bed! Victor stirred and turned over to face me and whispered, 'Anoche te apasionaste cariño.' He kissed my shoulder and moved closer so I could accommodate his hips between my thighs. A passion consumed me, which I had never felt before with a man. This time our lovemaking was slower, more tender compared to the raw desire we'd experienced the night before and I was relaxed enough this time to experience immense pleasure. It was only when I was bathing in the afterglow that a small, sensible part of my brain briefly remembered Angel's admonishment and I thought, 'so much for wearing a condom!'

I was completely drained. It was still early morning, and checking his watch on the credenza, Victor said, 'I need to work today querida. I'm afraid I must go.' I must've looked pained by this, because he said, 'You are sad? We will see each other again in a couple of days when I return to Cusco.'

I shook my head

'Victor, I must go to Bolivia, remember? I told you we are travelling to see my brother in Charagua.'

Holding me tight again, he said, 'Then we must make the most of our time.' I thought we would make love again, I wanted us to, but he was spent and his face registered conflicting emotions, frustration, petulance, but I could also see sadness; he seemed to genuinely want me. 'Can you not change your plans?' I shook my head and said nothing. We parted then and Victor left without another word spoken between us.

The fact was, I was torn. I felt compelled to follow-through with our plans to go to Charagua, but my whole physical being just wanted to stay with Victor. I had his address and phone number, so I resolved to keep in touch. I couldn't get him out of my mind, and for the remainder of our travels, until I started my return journey, Victor was to become an obsession that filled me with joy and despair in equal measure. The French call it 'la petite mort', a small death. It refers to the post-orgasmic lethargy experienced by lovers. I too had experienced it myself and had "died and gone to heaven" when I came so hard with him inside me. I was hooked on the feeling, and like a drug addict, I wanted another 'shot'.

Leaving Victor's hotel, I wandered absently back towards the hostel, but noticing it was open, I entered the post office to check if there was anything for me in the poste restante. To my surprise, I found a postcard from Roy; it carried a photograph of a group of sheep in a snowy landscape. At that moment, my life back in Berwen seemed to be a world away from what I was experiencing now. Roy recounted that Simon and Tony sent their regards. He'd seemed to sense that I might be worried about Tosh and he assured me that she was okay and still working well. A memory of us rounding up hill ewes flashed into my mind. At that moment, I fervently wished Tosh could be here with me. My fond mental image reminded me that I loved her. In fact, I had so much love to give and realised I was falling in love with Victor, but how could this be after just one day and a night, no matter how torrid it'd been?

I headed back to the hostel and bumped into Maddie in the foyer, she looked concerned and said, 'I spoke with Victor. He came here looking for you. I was worried. He was in rather a strange mood; I guess you two spent the night together?'

I nodded, but I was too choked up to say anything.

***

I felt like I'd been torn away from Victor and what we might have developed between us, and had entered a race against time to cross the Peruvian border into Bolivia. Angel had heard from some Spanish backpackers at the Wild Rover that the border might close any day due to a general strike that was spreading paralysis across Bolivia. When we finally managed to tear ourselves away from Cusco, we'd left ourselves just twenty-four hours to get to the border at Puno, a distance of almost two hundred and fifty miles. Needing to get there fast, we rocked up at Cusco's San Pedro train station and searched its crowded halls for the

Peru Rail booking office. We'd arrived at six in the morning and the train was due to depart at eight.

After nervously waiting half an hour in a long queue, Maddie had asked for four standard class tickets, but the ticket clerk replied, 'Lo siento, ¡la clase estándar está llena! Todo lo que tengo son boletos para primera clase. son setecientos setenta y cinco mil soles.'

Maddie looked crestfallen and said, 'Jeez! There's no standard class tickets left, but there are spaces in first class for S/750,000! That's each, in case you were thinking it's for all of us.'

We had no choice. We all reached down into our jeans, tugged open our money belts and started pulling out wads of cash. Bizarrely, whilst we were groping in our undies, Angel smoothly removed an American Express gold card from what I thought was a witch doctor's pouch he always wore around his neck, and paid for all of us saying, 'Está en la casa queridos!'

The female ticket clerk beamed at him as he dropped his card onto the desk in front of her with a flourish; she seemed impressed. Maybe she thought he was some kind of business magnate travelling with his harem of concubines! As if to confirm the clerk's assumption, we all kissed his cheeks in turn and Maddie said, 'We owe you! You're not paying for a single thing from now on!'

Boarding the train ahead of all the other passengers waiting on the platform, I suddenly felt out of place in the relative opulence of our carriage, a bit like the old-style trains you got on British Rail. We couldn't fit our packs on the luggage racks, so had to pile them at one end of our compartment. Once we'd left Cusco, we headed along to the restaurant car for a celebratory beer.

After a few hours of listening to the somnolent 'chunk, chunk' of worn train wheels passing slowly over worn rails trying to avoid a derailment, we stopped at La Raya and took a chance to get out to stretch our legs. I felt short of breath at the high altitude. Local women had set up tables to sell their wares along the tracks near the station building. I suddenly realised that I'd been so preoccupied with Victor, that I'd forgotten to buy Christmas presents for Adam and Vandas' children. I knew that most of the presents they'd receive would be homemade, so anything that their aunty brought them would be extra special. Hurriedly,

I bought a couple of brightly painted wooden dolls that'd been clothed in little handmade jackets and dresses. The ladies must've overcharged me but I didn't care. They must've been ancient, they all gave me toothless grins; their faces were beyond wrinkled. I wished I could've received some their wisdom on life, I certainly needed some at that moment.

Then I noticed Angel sitting on a bench smoking. I joined him there. It occurred to me that, even though we'd spent the last three weeks together, we knew next to nothing about him, so I asked, 'Do you have family back in Spain?'

He nodded.

'Yeah, parents in Seville and a couple 'of kids with a girlfriend.' He shook his head slowly. 'Didn't work out from the start, but we ended up have'n' kids anyway.' I nodded; he didn't seem to want to talk about it. It was then I also realised that Angel must be quite a bit older than us. It made sense, he'd been travelling for years and he said he'd been to university in Granada, worked as a tourist guide in the Sierra Nevada and had travelled in the United States. Angel puffed out a few smoke rings and we watched the mist clear slightly on the snow-capped peaks opposite. Light played on the slopes, casting shadows across deep ravines. 'So, are you and Victor gonna make a go of it you think?' It was like, at that moment, he'd reached into my thoughts.

I shrugged my shoulders.

'We've only had a day and a night together...' I blushed, and went on. 'But I'd give everything up for him. It's totally crazy and I don't understand why I feel like this.'

Angel stroked his straggly beard, considered what I'd said, blew a few more smoke rings, and then replied, 'I've had my share of traveller's romances over the years. The closest I've come to settle'n' was with a Gavião woman, it's why I left the Mato Grosso and came back over to Peru. I was gett'n' in way over my head. All the other women I've been with, they've been beautiful, charming, sexual tigresses even! But she tugged at someth'n' in me from the first day I met her. The Tribal Elders had asked her to teach me Jê, but I learnt more from her than language, I learnt how to love with my soul. I'm go'n' back to her. If I can find her again, I'm never gonna go home; I'm not lose'n' her twice.' Angel's eyes misted over. This time, the great oracle didn't have any answers for me, just more questions.

***

In common with many border towns the world over, Puno was a dump. A port town on the shores of Lake Titicaca, the world's highest navigable lake, sounded exotic and mysterious, but it was far from it. Desperate to find a toilet, Cathy checked the facilities at the station. She came back with a report that the toilet pan was, quite literally, filled with excrement. Since she'd been suffering from a touch of dysentery, we quickly headed towards the port and found a hotel, the Hostel Virgin de las Nieves nearby. The name sounded enchanting, it translates as 'the Virgin of the snows', however, it belied its dilapidated exterior. We managed to a get a room with two double beds for thirty-eight thousand sols; which wasn't bad, but when we asked if there was somewhere good to eat close to the hotel, the woman at the reception desk suggested, El Casino de Oro del Inca. A casino? Maddie questioned this with her and she replied, saying it had pretty good food and the place was guarded by seguranças (bouncers), which were pretty handy as town could get a little rowdy at night. We were all intrigued.

The casino was in a backstreet off the main drag into town. Sure enough, two burly men were stationed on either side of the door. Seeing Angel's scraggy looks, they were stern looking at first, until they realised, he'd brought three young women with him. The promise of "fresh females" always opens doors. The interior walls were lined with the kind of silky flock wallpaper you get in Indian restaurants. Adjusting to the dim lighting, I could make out at least six baize-covered card tables, a roulette wheel, and right at the far end of the room, a craps table. Most were empty, but there was a gaggle of people playing craps. Seeing Angel, one of the girls who'd been hovering around the players detached herself from the group and sashayed over to him; she was wearing heels and not much else except a very small cocktail dress her breasts were falling out of. Noticing that he'd always got three women with him, she must've decided he had plenty of action already so she went to get a waitress instead.

Seeing this, Maddie said, 'Perdon, sonos cortarle las alas!'

Angel laughed and said, 'Ha! Nooo, you're not clipping my wings, she's not my type anyway!'

We had to admit that the food was good. There was quinoa soup, papas fritas on the side and for the main, trout! Expecting something more exotic we were very surprised until we consulted our guidebook and discovered that, one hundred years ago, lake trout had been introduced from the US to bolster indigenous fish stocks that were, and still are, becoming endangered due to overfishing and pollution. Lake trout is now one of the most invasive species in Peru! This magnificent stupidity was similar to the introduction of rabbits to Australia by British colonists for food and hunting. I mean, there wasn't anything else they could eat or hunt? When rabbit numbers got out of control, the same stupidos introduced foxes for hunting and to control the rabbits. Unfortunately, the foxes weren't bothered about eating rabbits; they ate the indigenous marsupials instead. Game, set and match, Australia's flora and fauna were screwed from then on!

Sewage, pollution and tawdriness aside, Puno did redeem itself: the sunset over Lake Titicaca with red light catching the snow-capped Andes was achingly beautiful. As a finale, the lake appeared to briefly turn purple and orange. Sunsets are one of the few things, humans haven't found a way of screwing up... yet!

***

There was one final notable occurrence on the way to Charagua: we lost Maddie. This would seem remiss to a casual bystander, but for us, it was an accident waiting to happen. After having had a truly hair-raising bus journey from Bolivia's present-day governmental capital, La Paz, via Cochabamba (a tropical paradise) through mountain passes at night, we arrived in Bolivia's constitutional capital, Sucre. To cut a long story short, we decided to take a break in la ciudad blanca, or the white city, for two reasons. The first was to rest and enjoy the pleasant climate and colonial architecture of the historic centre, and the second was to explore the neighbouring town of Potosi's silver mines, the source of the wealth on which Sucre was built and yet another sorry tale of colonial plunder, enslavement and death in the notorious silver mines of the Cerro Rico. If this all sounds wild and exciting, like the plot of John Huston's movie, The Treasure of the Sierra Madre, we were to find that the reality was far from it.

As a "treat" the day before Cathy's birthday on the ninth December, we took the bus from a small square on the outskirts of Sucre that, we'd been told, would take us up a mountain pass to the mines. We joined a group of what turned out to be miners, waiting at the bus-stand. Although the mine ran visitor tours, several of the men gave us hard stares, perhaps wondering why a group of gringas would consider a mine as a fun place to visit.

Feeling uncomfortable from the start, when we arrived at the quaintly named "mountain that eats men", we were informed by the guide that groups that included females in the party wouldn't be able to visit the working part of the mine. This was to preserve workers' dignity as many of the men worked naked in the heat of the lower levels where the silver deposits were still worth mining. What we saw around us was an entire mountain laid bare by the toil of human bone, muscle and sinew. A huge, gaping maw, deep and black, constituted the entrance to the mineshaft and the mine-workings hundreds of feet below. The story we heard from our guide of the slow and agonising genocide of thousands of local people, and in colonial times, African slaves who were forced to work down the mines, was disturbing. In the upper level of the mine, we were able to enter one of the many galleries where the miners had worked, often bent double, hacking at the seam with picks and shovels.

The human cost of mining at Potosi brought the ongoing British miners' strike and the struggle to save their livelihoods and improve their pay and conditions into stark relief. A transcript of an impassioned speech by the Miners' union president, Arthur Scargill, that he gave to a members' strike rally resonated with what we saw that day. In it, Scargill had said, *"Comrades, I salute you for your magnificent achievements and for your support — together, we cannot fail."* At the time, I fervently hoped that the British miners would prevail in their stand against the Establishment.[45] The price of greed and a colonial regime that placed

---

[45] The miners' strike of1984-85 was a defining moment in Britain's industrial relations that saw the defeat of the National Union of Mineworkers and its president, Arthur Scargill that ultimately led to closure of most the UK's coal mines and the diminishment of trade-unionism

wealth-creation above human dignity was laid out in front of us in the starkest possible way.

If our visit to the Cerro Rico had been a chilling reminder of humanity's brutality, the evening we spent in Sucre to celebrate Cathy's birthday was the complete antithesis. Keen to check out the nightlife, we passed a lively place, the Sabor Cubano, which had Cuban music blasting out of the doors.

'I've been here before!' Angel said. 'It sells the best Mojitos this side of La Paz.'

We all nodded, 'Let's go!'

A couple of hours in and a few Mojitos later, I was having a slow dance with Angel, when I noticed that Maddie and Cathy were in deep conversation in a booth with a couple of tall, slim black guys who were casually sprawled out on benches inside the booth. Angel and I looked at each other and moseyed over to check whether they were enjoying solicited or unsolicited attention. It turned out to be a bit of both. As we joined them, the taller guy switched to English and introduced himself as Lugo and his friend as Josué; both of them were Haitian. Before our trip to South America, if you were to tell me it was possible to meet, become attracted to and agree to stay with somebody after you'd only spent a couple of days with them, I'd have been rather shocked; that was naïve Debbie. The Debbie sitting in the Sabor Cubano several weeks and a night of unbridled passion later was a totally different beast! After talking endlessly, dancing and becoming increasingly inebriated on the periphery of Maddie's encounter with Lugo, Cathy and I decided to return to the hotel; after all it was two in morning. Angel said he was 'having some luck' with a barmaid, so would stay and keep an eye on Maddie, 'just in case.'

The following day, in his absence, Cathy and I officially "fired" Angel for having done a terrible babysitting job! Maddie was nowhere to be seen. We were mightily relieved when she reappeared later that morning with Lugo in tow; apparently, she'd agreed to stay overnight at his apartment. I felt she'd been irresponsible, but who was I to pour scorn? Maddie had only reprised what I'd done with Victor a few days earlier! It seemed like we were collectively throwing caution to the wind and giving in to unmet needs, for what? Excitement? Lust?

Later the same day, over lunch, while Lugo took a phone call at the bar, Maddie answered our unasked questions.

'I spent the night on his couch, if you must know!' She looked at both of us in turn, and then said, 'I can't vouch for Angel though. The last I saw of him, he was having a smoke outside with one of the women serving behind the bar!'

Much later, I was sitting on my own in the social room at the hotel, when Angel walked over and said, 'Sorry for going AWOL just then, but... well, since you chiquitas are having so much fun at the moment, I thought why not your uncle Angel as well?' We both laughed, and then he leaned over and fished a cellophane-coated packet out of his pocket, and winked, 'I took my own advice for once and wore a condom though!'

***

In an unexpected twist, our last three nights at Sucre were spent staying at Lugo's apartment. Lugo was very accommodating and said it was crazy for us to stay at a hostel when he had so much spare room. There was, in my opinion, an obvious flaw in this reasoning. Why would you take in a group of four unwashed backpackers and put them up in your home free of charge? The answer was also obvious: Lugo had his sights on Maddie. When we flew to Santa Cruz and travelled onwards to Charagua by train, Maddie stayed on in Sucre for a few more days with Lugo. She was tight-lipped about what had transpired, but I could tell, woman's intuition perhaps, that she'd gone further with Lugo than spending a few nights sleeping on his couch.

Chapter 35
Charagua at last!

"...[The] inefficiency and disaster... conveyed in our newsletters... [is not] my only impression of Bolivia — a laughingstock of post-colonial, post-revolutionary slapstick — but because it is so much easier for me to put together in writing, a collage of disaster and misfortune, so much easier to paint a written picture of comedy, than it is for me to convey the idea of hope, to express the positive aspects of struggle and construction, of survival and human goodness, despite all the prevailing difficulties, that we have witnessed, lived with and participated in over the last [three] years." Adam Best, Valentine's Day, 1985, Quepos, Costa Rica.

Our train journey from Santa Cruz to Charagua was never going to be straightforward. The train line was prone to natural disasters, including flooding and landslides, then there were derailments, and worryingly, bridges sometimes just collapsed! Whilst in Santa Cruz, I'd telegrammed Adam to say we'd arrive by train in Charagua at six in the evening on the seventeenth December. However, when we'd got to the station, the train failed to turn up and I began to fret over Adam having to wait for us. Holding up his hand in an 'I'll sort this' gesture, Angel, who'd stepped into Maddie's role as interpreter, found an official looking man with an ENFE cap badge standing outside the ticket office and asked him when the Yacuiba train was due.[46]

The guard shrugged, and said, 'Lo siento señor, es la huelga del tren. no habrá trenes hasta el jueves.'

Angel shook his head and said, 'No trains are running today, it's the strike. We're gonna have to wait.'

That was that, we went back to the grimy and overpriced hotel we'd been staying at, and waited. The train finally turned up two days later on Wednesday and was standing in the station when we arrived at six a.m.

---

[46] Peruvian National State Railway Company

Staring at the total chaos on the platform, I said to nobody in particular, 'We're never going to get in there, never mind get a seat!'

My loud English voice must have attracted the attention of a corpulent man standing beside us, who I'd noticed was sweating profusely, because he turned in my direction and spoke to me in English, 'No problem señorita, I have a carriage reservation, come with me.'

Sure enough, he apparently had a whole carriage to himself. I thought, 'how is this possible?' He didn't mind at all when our rucksacks and other paraphernalia virtually filled the remaining space in the carriage, he just blew out his cheeks and sat heavily down at a seat by the window and remained rather aloof and detached for the rest of the journey.

Angel attempted some small talk with our benefactor, but all he would say that he was in the 'import and export business.'

More than five hours passed with the scene out the window barely changing from flat scrub intermixed with farmland. However, on nearing a scheduled stop about halfway through our journey, the huge flanks of a mountain range started to come into view that I assumed were the eastern foothills of the Andes. As the train approached a small town, our carriage lurched violently and the train slowed from its already sloth-like crawl. We then clanked across a rusting iron bridge over the rushing, brown-coloured torrent of the Rio Grande and stopped at Abapó.

For some reason, crossing the Rio Grande conjured up in my mind powerful images of wild nature and rugged frontiersmen and women. Whereas in the US, the home of South America's northern cousin with the same name, my vision of the Wild West had been shattered by an apparently never-ending urban sprawl, it really did seem like we were entering a primal wilderness of cloud-topped mountains and swift-flowing rivers.

On the farther side of Abapó's straggling habitation, evidence of human activity became thinner on the ground. Eventually, as we slowed again, and our train's clanking and screeching heralded its approach to our next stop in Charagua, my heart missed a beat; we'd finally arrived! The three of us stepped down from the train to find the narrow platform thronging with local people either getting on or off. As we watched, a woman and a man, her husband presumably, made a start on loading crates of squawking chickens into the guard's van along with sacks of maize, luggage and passengers who were presumably unable to afford the ticket to travel in the carriages. The three of us stood back and allowed the scene to unfold. We then noticed that our weighty travelling companion had got out of his carriage and was shouting at one of the guards; he was red-faced and bawling at the top of his voice. The guard just shrugged and then spoke to the couple who then began removing the crates of chickens that they'd just stowed in the guard's van, and instead, stacked them in the passageway inside one of the already crowded carriages; it was quite extraordinary!

'Contraband', Angel said, 'I seen those comerciante guys before.[47] They trade in biscuits, soup, wine, cigarettes, stuff like that, that they buy in Argentina and Paraguay. I guess he's paid off the guard to keep an eye on what goes in the guard's van. It was probably handy to have a bunch of gringos in his carriage, it might've dissuaded the militia guys that got on at Abapó from trying to get a cut of the bribe money.' After ten minutes of frantic activity, a small baby was kissed by an old woman with a wonderfully toothless smile, and then passed through an open carriage window to her mother. The train hissed, the whistle was blown and the train clanked, creaked and groaned its way out of the station and continued on its long journey down to its final stop in Yacuiba in southern Bolivia near the Argentine border. The crowd dissipated and the platform returned to its, presumably, typically deserted and inert self. The show now being over, we walked through an arch and out onto a dusty patch of ground in front of the station to wait for Adam. The eastern foothills of the Andes Mountains now formed a spectacular craggy backdrop behind the low, sun-bleached station building.

I'd rehearsed the moment so many times in my head, but I was still overwhelmed when a khaki-coloured Toyota jeep drove into the square in front of the station and stopped in a cloud of dust. Adam stepped out, immediately saw us and came running over with his arms outstretched.

'Plum!' he said, 'you finally made it! I hugged him and started crying — I was overwhelmed. Time seemed to stand still for a moment. Adam had left England as a clean-shaven vet, but the man in front of me had been transformed. He'd grown a shaggy beard and his unkempt hair

---

[47] Merchants

had grown long. He'd lost quite a bit of weight, but he looked tanned and relaxed and there was something in his eyes, the assured look of a man that had found a place he felt he belonged. He hugged Cathy and shook Angel's hand. For once Angel remained quiet and appeared quite shy in Adam's presence. I could see he felt rather uncomfortable, like a guy who'd had his role as guardian and protector snatched suddenly away from him.

'What do you think Plum?' Adam patted the jeep. 'I bought this with a donation from the Saffron Walden Round Table, no less! I don't know what I'd have done without her this last year and a half, she's quite a beast.' Adam drove fast along the dusty roads up to their house, chickens squawked and ran from under the wheels and pigs trotted nonchalantly out of the way just in time. We held on tight and I wondered whether I'd recognise the girls, or they me. The last time I saw them, Alice was five going on six, and Daisy was just two. Then there was Marcus. Vanda, desperate for a son, had decided to adopt a local boy, a tiny baby, from a Catholic mission in La Paz. I'd heard something of the story about how they'd fallen in love with him from the first and had named him after the Catholic priest, Father Marcus, with whom they'd formed a strong bond of friendship during the adoption process. I guessed that Marcus would now be a two-year-old. I suddenly felt a pang of guilt that I'd not brought him a special present from home. I wondered why and realised that despite all the excitement I'd felt about seeing Adam and his family again, I hadn't yet thought of him as a family member. I inwardly chastised myself and vowed to be a proper aunty to little Marcus in future; he deserved all the love he could get after his difficult start in life.

As we left the station, we realised that Charagua was a portmanteau town composed of two settlements. The smaller of the two was where the train station was located and a second, larger one where Adam and Vanda lived was situated on the banks of the Parapetí River that rises in Bolivia's Cordillera Central. Passing through the centre, we continued out the other side beyond a final row of houses. We were tired, and my mind was in a spin.

It was Adam that broke the silence, he said, 'A bit different from Radwinter, eh Plum? There's nothing that we really miss though, except a decent pub! I'd kill for a pint of Abbot! On the plus side, there's the river to swim in and a friendly donkey to take us into town! The girls have pretty much free rein to do what they want. Everybody knows everybody else and we all keep an eye on the children. Alice and Daisy have gone quite feral!' He smiled at me and squeezed my shoulder, 'It's good to see you Plum!' And I felt like he really meant it. I thought to myself that he'd gone quite feral too; I was already enjoying this new, relaxed Adam immensely.

Arriving at the house, heavy raindrops started falling out of a menacing black cloud that was now obscuring the mountaintops. A girl ran from the house letting the door bang in the gust of wind you get just before a rainstorm. The drops turned into a deluge, but she didn't take any notice and shouted, 'Aunty Plum, Aunty Plum!' It was Alice, she remembered me, we just flew into each other's arms, it was a magical moment I'll never forget.

Chapter 36
Pigs!

After a week in Charagua, Adam woke me early one morning and said, 'Plum, I've got something for you to see that you might find interesting! I know you're a pig enthusiast, so you'll appreciate what we're doing to help campesino cooperatives to improve the health of pigs and increase production.' The mention of pigs brought me out of my slumber and I quickly dressed and joined Marcus and Daisy at the breakfast table where they resumed their hilarious game of trying to teach their aunt some Spanish. This consisted of Daisy pointing at things and Marcus laughing hysterically when I got the wrong word or mispronounced something.

Once I'd sat down and started munching on my jam and freshly-baked bread, Daisy continued the game and said slowly, so her dumb aunty could underst, and 'Tía… que es esto?' And pointed to a plate.

I said, 'Plato,' she clapped enthusiastically, and then pointed to a knife, 'cuchillo, more clapping then to an egg, 'huevo', more clapping, then to a dish of butter, 'mermelada' …

'¡No! tonto, es un mantequilla!' Marcus laughed even harder this time.

In the midst of this hilarity, Adam, who'd been packing stuff in the jeep, came back in to join me at the table at this point. He scowled at his daughter and said, 'Daisy, that's enough!' Daisy stuck her tongue out at her father, slid down from her chair and disappeared off into the kitchen with Marcus in tow. Adam shook his head and feigned a despairing look.

'Daisy hardly speaks any English; we'll need to remedy that before she starts at Radwinter Primary School! Where was I? Yes, pigs! Why don't you come with me to take a look at the project that we've set up at Pampa Redonda? Our in-country partner organisation in La Paz, CIPCA, is funding a pilot project where we're fattening the pigs with soya that the campesinos grow and harvest along with their other crops.[48] Usually pigs just eat household scraps and root around in the yard, but they grow and put on weight very slowly until they're about twelve months old and around forty to fifty kilos, then they tie them to a tree and feed them maize, yucca and pumpkin like Sumo wrestlers until they nearly burst with blubber. Then they're slaughtered. The reason for this last-minute generosity? Everyone needs a steady supply of pig fat for bread making and cooking. It's a pretty haphazard and not very profitable way to produce pig fat! The idea of the project is to try and change campesinos' minds so they see pig rearing as a way to make money; turn pig keeping into pig production. The pilot projects have been pretty successful.'

I jumped at the chance! It would mean being able to spend some time with Adam on his own, and then my heart sank again. Cathy and Angel came into the kitchen. Adam must've thought they'd also be interested in a trip up-country, because he said, '¡Hola chicos! ¿Ustedes dos quieren venir con nosotros a ver algunos de los proyectos?'

Angel glanced at Cathy and looked apologetic

'Nos encantaría Adam, pero tenemos otros planes amigo.' Angel then turned and winked at me, and said, 'yYu two have a great day!'

'Phew!' I thought, what a relief! Angel knew I was desperate to have time alone with my brother.

Adam turned back to me and said, 'Plum, you'd better pack some clothes, a washing kit and your sleeping bag, it's likely that we'll be two or three days on the road. The reason is I just remembered I need to check in on a couple of cattle projects, there's castration of a few bulls at a farm at Piedritas near Mboreti and we can also check on the progress of a women's cattle project in Eden. Then we can travel on to Camiri where we'll stay the night and continue up to the pig project at Pampa Redonda. How does that sound?' I thought it sounded exhausting! But I could see Adam was wired. He was itching to get out on the road and do the work he'd come here for.

**

---

[48] Centro de Investigación y Promoción del Campesinado Bolivia — loosely translates to, 'the centre for the improvement of subsistence farming

As the crow flies, Camiri is maybe seventy kilometres from Charagua; however, a spritely crow can fly across the cordillera. We, on the other hand, would have to make a detour around the mountains to the south that added on one hundred and fifty kilometres of hard driving in rough country. We headed south towards San Antonio del Parapeti, a town, Adam said, which was on the banks of another raging torrent, the Rio Parapeti, where there was, hopefully, a bridge still in place after the heavy rains.

The red dirt road stretched away through the vast expanse of scrubland ahead of us. As we passed the bloated carcass of a cow lying at the side of the road, we spooked a group of five black vultures that were dining on it.

Adam nodded in the direction of the unfortunate animal and said, 'That's what we want to prevent. The campesinos allow their cattle to roam free, it's all pretty hit or miss whether they survive or not, there's no concept of production. When they want to make some money, they just round a few up, slaughter them and sell the meat at the market. We want to help them make a decent living from their livestock; it's the main aim of most of what we're doing.'

I was awestruck by the grandeur of the scenery; it was wild and stunning. I craned my neck to take a look at the mountaintops that'd now cleared of cloud after the heavy rain the previous night. Adam interrupted my rubbernecking.

'What's the thing going on with the "silent Frenchman", as Vanda's taken to calling him.[49] Are he and Cathy an "item?"'

I shook my head.

'No, no, nothing like that; actually, Angel's Spanish. We met in Nazca when we did a touristic stop to see the Inca lines. He's been super helpful ever since. He's travelling, but seems to have lost his way for a while. You'd approve of this though! He's writing a book about the indigenous peoples of the Mato Grosso. I've seen his notebooks; it's pretty gripping from what I can make of it.'

Adam, who'd been nodding along to my story said, 'Mato Grosso, okay, that *is* remote! We think Charagua is off the beaten track, but

---

[49] Probably an oblique reference to a book by Jean Berthe, 'The Quiet Frenchman', the story of a French refugee in the First World War.

thousands of square miles of virgin jungle, is off the scale. I'd like to read his book when it's finished' I could see by the gleam in his eyes that even Adam was impressed!

Once we'd reached the end of the cordillera, we swung west and headed towards a town that Adam said was called Boyuibe, but before we skirted the little town to head up into the complex of sierras beyond, we had to make a rather hair-raising crossing of the Rio de Cuevo, which was in full spate.[50] Adam stopped the jeep a short distance from the rusting iron bridge, got out and said, 'I'd better take a look and see if it's safe after the rain we had yesterday!' I joined him and together we walked over to the river. The roaring sound of the cascade further up from the road was deafening. Water was rushing just below the bridge, lapping over the road deck and tugging mercilessly at the supports. I looked dubious, Adam struck the boards of the bridge with heel of his boot a few times and said, 'C'mon Plum, where's your spirit of adventure?' So saying, we got back into the car (we didn't strap into our seats in case the bridge collapsed into the river on our way over) and Adam sped across the bridge at high speed. Presumably the principle was to spend as little time as possible over the torrent below!

Climbing steadily, we came into the small town of Mboreti. Entering the square, Adam drove on a short distance into the scrub beyond the town and through the gates of a farm. As we came to a stop, a man who'd been standing by a corral examining some cattle waved and came over to meet us; Adam said his name was Gregorio. The man was pleased to see us and greeted Adam like an old friend, he said, 'Hola doctor Adam! ¿cómo estás? es bueno verte!' We both shook his hand and Adam introduced me, Gregorio beamed and nodded, 'Si, *hermanda* Debbie, okay!' I half wondered whether he thought Adam had brought along a girlfriend!

Introductions over, the two men consulted together in Spanish and Gregorio guided us towards a separate corral where three, quite good-looking young bulls were penned. These animals had recently been bought by the campesino cooperativa to improve the quality of their herd.[51] As Adam had explained, cattle in the subsistence farming

---

[50] Actually, the Sierra de Ocharagua.
[51] Farmers' cooperative

practiced in much of Bolivia were mostly allowed to run wild. Basically, any old bow-legged bull was able to breed with any cow it felt like, reducing the quality of the herd and lowering production, which, as Adam had drolly put it on our way over, 'Isn't really what puts the meat in Fray Bentos corned beef!'

As we approached their corral, I could see that the bulls were young and rather frisky and I became a little concerned for Adam. Two additional farmhands appeared and one of them lassoed the smallest of the three bulls and secured the rope to a post; the animal bucked and kicked violently. Gregorio used a bolas and expertly hobbled the beast by tying its rear legs together. Although the animal was effectively hog-tied he was still pretty frisky. As he was about to climb into the corral, I grabbed Adam's arm and said, 'Just watch yourself, they're a bit wild!'

Adam just patted my shoulder and replied, 'It's all right, sis, don't worry, I've done this quite a few times before!'

Normally, castration is performed on young bull calves, but not on young adults. Brandishing a large steel burdizzo, Adam crouched near the rear of the smaller bull's flank and deftly clamped the animal's testicles.[52] The movement was so quick and smooth I almost missed it. The same process was repeated with the other two. Job done, Adam winked at me as he climbed back out of the corral and said, 'Now that is how you do that!'

***

About forty kilometres further on, we came to another settlement Adam said was the comunidad of Eden near where the women's cattle improvement project was based.[53] By the time we got there the sun was slipping low in the sky. We'd been lucky that the afternoon rain had been light and even more so when the sun shone as we passed through the town of Camia and headed up into the hills around Eden.

Adam had met with the women's group just a week ago and he'd agreed to come back and castrate the young bulls they'd bought for their

---

52 A humane castration device that employs a large clamp used to break the testicular blood vessels, which leads to testicular shrinkage and necrosis.
53 Community

improvement project. When we arrived at the cooperativa, a group of young women, older couples and a few single men were sitting at a table set out in the shade of the farmhouse veranda drinking chicha out of old lard tins.[54]

A young woman rose from her chair rather unsteadily and came over to talk to us. Her breath was heavy with the smell of alcohol and she seemed pretty inebriated.

'¡Doctor Adam! Tengo buenas noticias. ¡Hemos construido el corral!' Adam smiled and seemed pleased. The woman then held his arm and shook her head and said, 'Pero los toros se han escapado. Mis amigas han ido a buscarlos!'

Adam smiled, shook his head, then turned to me and said, 'The good news is they've built the corral for the cattle, the bad news is, the young bulls I've come to castrate have escaped and there's a search party out looking for them! We can afford to wait for a bit until they find them. Even if I manage to castrate half of them, it's going save me time on another journey over here next week.' So we waited.

Presumably thinking that we might feel left out, a few members of the drinking party on the veranda waved us over and insisted we should join them in some chicha. Since we were just sitting waiting it seemed churlish to refuse. The turbid brew tasted pretty rough, but unexpectedly refreshing. Straining the maize grinds through our teeth, we managed to get through a couple of lard tins full before the 'hunting party' of six, or so, women triumphantly returned. Each woman was leading a bull with a rope through its nose ring to pacify its otherwise feisty bucking. This time the animals were more like the size and age of bull calves we would castrate back home.

By the time Adam had castrated the bullocks and extracted himself from the crowd of enthusiastic women, some of whom were now quite drunk, shadows were lengthening and the sun had started to dip behind the mountains. Once we were back on the road to Camiri, Adam smiled and said, 'What did you think of the chicha?'

I could see there was more to his question than met the eye, so I

---

54 Chicha is the standard campesino alcoholic beverage made using maize that's been fermented after being mixed with copious quantities of saliva in its preparation to aid in the pre-digestion of the maize flour before the fermentation process.

replied, 'Well, it would probably get the thumbs down from CAMRA!'[55]

Adam laughed, 'You're right there Plum. Chicha is fermented from maize flour that's been pre-digested using saliva.'

'Adam! Why didn't you tell me?'

I playfully punched his shoulder and he said, 'You seemed to be getting into it, so I didn't want to spoil your enjoyment!'

***

Camiri was a pretty large town. There was the obligatory slew of Catholic churches and even a cathedral. In addition to the copious number of places to worship God, Camiri also had a very fine example of that other place of worship close to many Latinos' hearts: there was a very impressive looking football ground. Actually, the stadium appeared to be by far the best maintained and cleanest building in town. Dwellings, shops and offices fitted into the typical low-rise blue and red painted white stucco formula that meant that one town looked much the same as another. Adam had obviously stayed in Camiri quite a few times, so he knew where he was going. After filling up with petrol at a La William's gas station, we checked into a hotel nearby that he reckoned was the only decent accommodation in town, the Hotel La Casona — it even had a small swimming pool!

Both of us were pretty tired at the end of a long day, so we crashed out early and rose at six the next morning for the long drive over to the pig project that had been set up in Pampa Redonda. As expected, Adam was already sitting in the breakfast room reading a copy of El Nuevo Día when I arrived. After I'd flopped into the chair opposite him, Adam went and got me a coffee and a little basket of empanadas.[56] Once I'd started on my breakfast, Adam leaned over towards me, lowered his voice and said, 'I know you guys at home think we've all become bearded little revolutionaries during our time out here. However, I know you have leftist leanings, so here's a fact that you might find interesting. One of the comunidades near Camiri is very close to Nancahuazu, where Che

---

[55] Campaign for Real Ale
[56] Similar to a small British pastie, empanadas are stuffed with beef, chicken, peas, potatoes, olives or eggs.

Guevara and his guerrilleros had their farm and their base.[57] Since then, the locals still look a little suspiciously at bearded foreigners!' We both chuckled at this. I looked over at Adam's bright, smiling face and fervently wished this trip we were making together would never end.

It was over one hundred and fifty kilometres from Camiri to Pampa Redonda, an area of vertiginous, scrub-covered mountains with a fertile vale of farmland along the floodplain of the Rio Pilcomayo. As we got closer to Mboreviti, a village were Adam had a cattle project with another campesino comunidad, he gave me some background about the work he was doing there.

'It's been a bit of a disaster with this project so far this year. Just at the moment of harvesting the soybean crop, that would easily have provided twelve thousand kilograms of grain, it started to rain and it continued non-stop until the whole crop rotted in the ground. All the campesinos could do was plough it all in and plant winter wheat. Fortunately, they were insured under a new CIPCA scheme so at least they could claim back the cost of production, but nothing can compensate for the all the work they'd put in. When we get to the farm where we're running the pig trial, two young lads I trained back in Charagua will meet us. They've hopefully taken on the management of the pig-fattening project. I hope they've also been able to share their training with other members of the cooperativa in Mboreviti that's the plan anyway. I left instructions for them to mix one thousand kilograms of soya with two thousand of maize to create enough feed to fatten the ten, twenty-kilogram piglets to one hundred kilograms. The aim of the trial is to rear robust piglets in enclosures where they can be provided with enough feed and water. If the trial catches on, I'm hoping that the volunteers that replace us will be able to roll it out to other comunidades next year. Once we've got improved pig management established, the next step will be to introduce pedigree boars adapted to the conditions here to improve the small-stature criollo pig they currently have.'

Hearing Adam map out the project made it seem so straightforward, but nothing is easy or can be taken for granted in the impoverished

---

[57] Ernesto "Che" Guevara was an Argentine Marxist revolutionary, physician, author, guerrilla leader, diplomat, and
military theorist. A major figure of the Cuban Revolution. He died in in 1967 in La Higuera, Bolivia.

campesino communities. When we got to the farm, it took us a while to eventually track down the two young lads, Ronaldo and Pepe, that Adam had been training. When we did find them, there were the usual greetings and pleasantries, after all, this was Adam's fifth visit, but I could see things weren't looking good. Adam had hoped to do the boar castrations, but the guys admitted that they'd allowed the pigs to go loose and were scattered who knows where! They could see Adam was rather upset and apologised profusely and said, 'Ha sido muy difícil llevar suficiente agua para los cerdos, así que dejamos que la consigan ellos mismos. ¡Lo sentimos mucho señor!'

There was nothing else to be done, so Adam and I smiled and shook their hands, but back in the jeep, I could see Adam was furious. He fumed, 'Basically, it was probably too much trouble carrying the water to the pigs, or them to the water each day; which I understand, but it's left me a little open-mouthed and speechless! Never mind, asi la vida![58] At least I don't have to be thinking about the pounds ticking up for every hour of my visit!'

***

A rather mysterious chain of events occurred on our way our back to Charagua that forced even Adam to briefly question his stoical disbelief in the superstitions of the local people. We'd successfully recrossed the Rio de Cuevo; which was rather less turbulent than it had been on our outward journey, when the jeep's headlights picked out the skeletal remains of the dead cow we'd passed a couple of days earlier. We both glanced at the carcass as we passed, however, when our eyes returned to the road ahead, a fox trotted across our path from right to left.
'Mmmh,' Adam said, 'that's a bad omen around these parts.'

I was intrigued, Adam had always given short shrift to any notions of religion or fate, which he tended to lump together under the amorphous banner of superstition, and so I said, 'A bit like a black cat?'

'Similar, but with a fox, it depends on the direction of travel. The native Guarani people around here reckon that if a fox crosses from left to right, it's good luck, but if it crosses in the other direction, as it did just

---

[58] That's life!

now, it's a bad omen.'

We thought nothing more of this until we arrived home. Adam had just shut down the engine and was getting out of the jeep when Alice rushed out of the house in a distressed state. As she ran towards us, dread clutched at my stomach and I thought something awful had happened. Adam scooped her up and kissed her grimy, tear-stained face and said, '¿Qué pasa Alicia?'

In between sobs, she said, 'Oh papá, es terrible, una de las vacas se ha caído. Mamá está tratando de ayudarla.'

Adam turned to me and said, 'C'mon Plum, one of our cows has gone down.' We jogged together up the field at the back of the house. Under the shade of a tree by the fence, a cow was flat out on the ground in the throes of agony. Adam knelt next to the poor animal and said, 'It looks like she's been poisoned; there's quite a few rather nasty euphorbia weeds around. Or maybe it's suffering from milk fever, staggers or ketosis, take your pick![59] Plum, run in the house and get a bucket of water and ask Vanda to find the stuff I need to administer calcium borogluconate intravenously. Also, bring some cooking oil, it looks as though it might be ketosis.'

Vanda and I rushed back with what Adam needed and we got to work setting up a cow emergency ward in the field. We'd just got the intravenous drip in when it started to drizzle. Adam huffed, 'That's all we need!'

I said, 'Don't worry, I'll set up a shelter over her, I've done this before when a cow's gone down in a field and she won't get up.'

Night fell, the rain intensified, but Adam refused to give up on her.

'C'mon girl, don't lie there and die on me,' he said while he stroked her ears.

However, in the early hours of the morning, the unfortunate beast gave one last shiver and died. Adam looked crestfallen, so I put an arm around his shoulder and said, 'You did all you could. You were brilliant!'

He replied, 'Thanks, sis', but I could see he didn't look convinced.

---

[59] Milk fever: a metabolic disorder caused by calcium deficiency; staggers: caused by low magnesium around calving; ketosis: basically, hypoglycaemia (low blood sugar) caused by the high energy demand placed on the cow's system by milk production. A baseline treatment with glycerol present in cooking oil is an effective way of quickly boosting blood glucose.

For Adam, the only result worth congratulation was success, not one hundred dollars' worth of dead cow.

As if one dead cow wasn't bad enough, another bizarre coincidence occurred the next day. Coming back from a fishing trip on the Rio Parapeti, a fox again crossed the track in front of us from right to left. I thought to myself, 'twice in a row, surely not!'

But fate it seemed wouldn't be denied. As we arrived at the house, Adam shouted, 'Look over there, now that's ominous!' The children and I looked over towards a copse that I knew was situated in one of the fields near the house and saw a group of black vultures sitting in the crown of one of the trees. Telling the children to go in the house, Adam and hurried up the field towards the copse. As we approached, I saw the dark form of a cow lying on the ground in the gathering gloom. Adam crouched by her flank, shook his head and said, 'She's gone. I'm not sure what's happened, but it looks like she might've asphyxiated — you see those petechiae (broken blood vessels) in her eyes? It's a sure sign of hypoxia (oxygen starvation) and laboured breathing.'

Adam carried out a post mortem the next day on both of the unfortunate cows. In the first, he concluded she'd died of a compacted omasum, a physical catastrophe in her stomach, and the second had died of asphyxiation after inhaling food into her lungs. Since neither of these conditions were infectious, the post mortems had continued to dismemberment and slicing of meat from the carcasses into thin strips which were then cured in salt and dried in the sun to make 'ch'arki', the Bolivian equivalent of beef jerky. Adam said, 'Waste not, want not! A cow's worth the equivalent of almost twice the annual earnings of a campesino around these parts.' Two cows make an awful lot of beef jerky though! The cha'rki was as tough as boot leather, but I have to admit, it was quite tasty!

After the incidents with the cows, I always paid close attention to direction of travel when a fox passed in front of me!

Chapter 37
Christmas in Charagua

Despite the poverty suffered by many campesinos, the festival of Chuntunquis on Christmas Eve was one of the big events of the year that not even drought, floods, or harvest disasters could disrupt.[60] We'd been told to expect a riotous party; we weren't disappointed. Since this was to be their final Christmas in Bolivia, Adam and Vanda filled their home to bursting-point with local people, fellow volunteers, like Elaine and Ruth, and expats like Don and Helen who were based in La Paz. Contrary to the happy mood of the visitors who'd come to stay for Christmas, preparations for the fiesta no doubt reminded Cathy and Maddie that they must soon return home to what they'd already admitted was their humdrum existence in rural Wales. Both women were also deeply unhappy with their partners, Maddie because of her husband's unfaithfulness and Cathy with what she referred to as her partner, Dan's, traditional attitudes and the "never-ending routine of his work with the Forestry Commission." As a result, both had become increasingly morose during our time in Charagua. I, on the other hand was struggling with my infatuation with Victor and how it might be resolved. Since leaving Cusco, I'd managed to send two postcards to his address in Lima and had received one card in return via Adam who'd attended a UNIS volunteer meeting in La Paz and had picked up my mail from the post restante. Victor's card confirmed that he would meet me in Nazca on my way back to Lima. In the meantime, I tried to live in the present, but my thoughts were filled with plans to stay in Peru and perhaps apply to be a volunteer on one of the aid programmes that Don and Helen were administrating. Diary entries made at the time read like the ramblings of a lovesick teenager and I find myself cringing at the naïveté of it all, but if writing this book has taught me anything it's not to disparage the hopes

---

[60] Chuntunqui (or Chuntuqui) is a style of Christmas song and dance which originated in Chuquisaqueña.

and dreams of my younger self.

Frustrations notwithstanding, of all of us in our band of travellers, I was most concerned about Cathy who'd basically said she didn't want to return with us and suggested that she was actively looking for a means by which she could stay in Bolivia or Peru indefinitely. In fact, I was so concerned, I had a quiet word with our resident travelling expert, Angel, to get his opinion on how we might dissuade her from doing something crazy.

'Well,' he said, 'I guess what you want is for me to give you an answer that you want to hear, but all I can say is that we all have different reasons for travelling. Some do it 'cos they want to see things they haven't seen before, others do it 'cos they've got time on their hands and they can't think of anything better to do and others are running away from something or someone. Once you've figured out which of these things Cathy is doing, then what she does next will make perfect sense.' The 'oracle' had spoken once again!

***

Navidad (Christmas) is celebrated in Bolivia from Christmas Eve to Epiphany on the sixth January. As the 'centrepiece' for their celebrations, Adam and Vanda had decided to pull out all the stops and slaughter one of the household's pigs. Since vets generally try and keep animals alive, rather than killing and butchering them, a neighbour, Manuel, took on the job slaughtering said pig and carrying out the basic preparation of the carcass. The pig that drew the 'short straw' was a poor-performing boar, which, like 'Hopeless Henry' at the Stamps' farm during my pre-college year, had been falling behind in his "duties". Unlike Henry, who couldn't actually mount the sows properly, his Bolivian counterpart had lost interest altogether! I love pigs and consoled myself that the one we'd chosen to be our Christmas dinner had led a happy life in the fields behind the house foraging for roots and tree mast in the same way that pigs back home in the New Forest had roamed for centuries in a tradition called Pannage, an ancient right that dates back to the region of William the Conqueror.[61]

Around mid-morning on Christmas Eve, Manuel brought the slain and gutted animal over and we got to work stuffing the beast. Meticulous as always, Adam had set up his outdoor charnel house more in the way of an operating theatre than a kitchen. I'm not sure whether that famous stalwart of BBC cook shows, Fanny Cradock, would have approved. Whilst still at school, I remember watching her show, Fanny Cooks for Christmas where she prepared a turkey. As I recall, she got her long-suffering husband Johnnie, to do the actual stuffing, in order, as she said, 'to avoid ruining my nails darling!' In our Bolivian-style cook show, Adam had used plastic sacks to cover the "operating" table. Knives, twine, skewers and a large steel rod that looked like the axle of an old car (cleaned of course) were neatly laid out on a separate table ready to use. Preparing a whole roast pig is messy business! As I was going to be his assistant (Cathy, Maddie and Angel had made themselves scarce) Adam brought me one of his green PVC veterinary aprons and a pair of long disposable gloves vets use to check cervical dilation in cows amongst other things. The first step was to get the pig onto the table and insert the rod; at well over seventy pounds in weight, it was like trying to lift a wet and slippery corpse. With a bit of swearing and brute force, we managed to force the rod through the beast's back passage and out through its mouth, a rather indelicate process, but the pig was, after all, dead, so he didn't mind too much! Once the pig was on the spit, we bound his legs to the rod and stuffed the body with herbs, chopped apples and onions. To complete the operation, Adam expertly closed the body cavity with suture stitches. I couldn't, at that moment, vouch for our patient's wellbeing, but I knew what the prognosis would be! We then placed the pig on the spit supports and left it to roast for the rest of the day.

The traditional Chuntunquis dance unexpectedly provided me with an opportunity to shine. I say unexpected, because the robust body-type I had as a child had rather held me back from excelling in ballet and other forms of dancing that was, and still is, all the rage in English public

---

[61] Pannage is the practice of releasing domestic pigs into a forest (also known as 'Common of mast'), and goes all the way back to the time of William the Conqueror, who founded The New Forest in 1079.

schools. Whilst prancing around in a tutu wasn't my thing, I had got into tap-dancing with Sue, a friend of Tony's at Glantnor where I'd actually done pretty well at a Young Farmers tap-dancing competition in Welshpool. When we got to the village square, most of the inhabitants of Charagua appeared to be there. At a cursory glance, Chuntunquis seemed to be very similar to Scottish ceilidh dancing, with a row of men facing their female partners in a long line; however, that's where the similarity ended. Instead of skipping around together, the dance was a mix of what looked like jive with tap-dancing thrown in, perfect! As soon as Maddie, Cathy and myself had shown up, we were taken in hand by a group of young local lads who were very keen to show us the moves. One of the older men in the group, who'd been dancing with his partner when we'd arrived, made a beeline for Cathy. He spoke some English and introduced himself as David and the woman he was with as Pilar, who, he said, was his girlfriend. Apparently unperturbed by this switch of partners, Pilar joined a larger group of local women and men and left him to it.

Later that night, I noticed David and Cathy deep in conversation sitting on a bench in a corner of the square, but that was the last we saw of her that evening and for the next three days. Getting rather worried, Maddie and I formed a search party and eventually found Cathy sitting outside a small annex of what turned out to be David's family home.

Somewhat concerned, I said to her, 'Are you okay? We were all starting to get worried.'

Cathy just scowled and replied, 'Well you've found me! I'm staying with David for a few days — it was all getting rather overcrowded at your brother's place anyway.'

We didn't get to say much more to her, because David came out of the annex with a jug of fruit juice and a couple of glasses. As he emerged, the door remained open and I could see the annex was actually a bedroom and inside there was a large unmade double bed that David and Cathy had clearly been sharing for the last few nights. Suddenly embarrassed that we might be intruding, we made our excuses and left.

As we walked away from them, I said to Maddie, 'Well, Vanda was right, Cathy *is* staying with David. She also said he's the son of a schoolteacher and knows some English, but not much. It must make communication difficult.'

Maddie smiled, 'It's past noon and they looked like they'd just got up, so I don't think much verbal communication is going on! I've spoken to a few of the local women and they're already saying that Cathy is David's "amante", or lover.'

Given my traditional and rather naïve take on relationships, I said, 'Well, I can't get my head around it! David has a girlfriend, right?'

Maddie shook her head and said, 'Debbie, Debbie... this is Latin America. Before they get married, and even when they *are* married, men play the field. It's kind of an unwritten law of the dating game. I guess women here might not like it, but so long as the man is fairly discreet, then I suppose she just puts up with it. It's a similar situation with Adam and Vandas' volunteer friend, Elaine. She lives with her local boyfriend, but she admitted to me that she knows he has at least one other local girlfriend.'

I nodded, but remained unconvinced. Then I thought, 'well, if that's the case, then Victor is probably doing the same thing.' I put the thought out of my mind. It was just too painful to contemplate.

***

In the week before Maddie, Cathy and I were due to leave Charagua at the end of December, it became clear that the fellowship of travellers that'd kept our little band together for the last two months was coming to an end as each of us struggled to decide which path we each must follow. The first to break our unspoken pact was Angel who'd seemed increasingly out of place in the all-encompassing family atmosphere that seemed to emanate from Adam and Vanda like an invisible force field that you were either inside or on the outside. Angel was no longer the centre of our little gang; he'd become an outsider, the silent Frenchman in fact. One evening, the children were playing by the river and I had assumed my Aunty Plum persona, ensuring that Marcus didn't stray too far from the riverbank to try and splash Alice and Daisy who were lying in the shallows in their underwear enjoying the sensation of the silt-laden water rushing over their bodies. It was an expression of childlike freedom, and I envied them for it. My childhood had been so regimented by the nuns at St Mary's that I had little or no unstructured time to just be myself, or to be a child in fact.

Deep in my reverie, I didn't notice Angel's approach and I jumped when he stopped beside me. For a moment we watched the children playing in silence and then he said, 'Kids are the same the world over, aren't they? The Gavião women used to wash their families' clothes in the river and the children would play in the water in just the same way. I had a dream last night that Tuitão, the woman I was bonded to, out of shame that she couldn't keep her man with her, had given birth to our child on her on her own in the jungle. At first, she was going to drown the baby in the river, but she spoke to me in the dream and begged me to return to her to be a father to our son. It was a powerful dream, like an omen. I need to go back there Debbie, back to her and my son.' At first, I thought Angel was joking with me or he'd been chewing too many coca leaves, but now I could see he was serious. 'I'm gonna head out on the bus tomorrow. I'm not sure how I'm gonna get back to the Mato Grosso, but I got there before and I'll find a way back somehow. I don't want to make a big deal out of it 'cos I hate goodbyes, but if you guys want to see me off you've all got to promise not to cry!' His little joke fell flat. My face must have looked sad, because he came over and hugged me, and for a while, we just stood like that and listened to the river and the children's laughter.

We'd all hoped that Angel's bus to Santa Cruz wouldn't be running. The previous day, our farewell had been postponed due to a train derailment that was serious enough to have brought rail transport to a grinding halt for the time being; however, Angel was determined. Since there were no trains, the square in Charagua that also served as a bus station was a seething mass of people. There were several buses going towards Santa Cruz, it didn't seem to matter to Angel which of these he travelled on, he was clearly anxious to leave. We'd all been quiet in the jeep whilst Adam had driven us the short distance to the centre of Charagua — for Maddie and me, it was like taking a condemned man to the scaffold. As I often do in stressful situations, I take comfort in food; after all, I'm called Plum for a good reason! My comfort eating can also extend to other people, sort of food therapy by proxy. I had, therefore, made Angel a huge packed lunch and squeezed sufficient oranges to fill a large glass bottle with juice. I'd then packed these things into a cotton bag that I planned to give to him to take on his journey. We stopped on the perimeter of the crowd and all of us got out of the jeep to form a sad little leaving committee.

Adam shook Angel's hand and said, 'Adiós amigo mío, y felices viajes. Espero que encuentres lo que estás buscando.' Angel nodded and Maddie started to cry; which set me off as well. Cathy remained stone-faced and impassive; she'd reacted badly to some of the oracle's advice about her love life that had gone down like a proverbial lead balloon. Angel gently disentangled himself from Maddie who'd been holding onto him tightly since we'd got out of the car.

Seeing my chance, I stepped forward to give him the food I'd prepared and realised that my packed lunch bag was almost as big as the satchel that contained the sum total of his belongings! I then recalled a conversation I'd had with Angel in which I'd asked how, after seven years of travelling, did he still only carry a small bag; didn't he have mementos, keepsakes? In answer, he'd tapped the side of his head with his forefinger and said, 'It's all up here mi querida amiga' and then he'd pressed the palm of his right hand to his chest, 'and here in my heart.'

Now Angel held out his arms to me and I got up on my toes so I could give him one last hug. I then passed him the cotton bag which he accepted saying, 'You have such a big heart Debbie, please take care of it — you have a habit of giving it out too easily.' Putting the palms of his hands together, Angel bowed; 'Namaste', he said, before walking away without hesitating or looking back and disappeared into the crowd.

Cathy got back into the jeep, but Maddie and I spent a few moments craning our necks to try and see where he'd gone, but to no avail. Maddie said, 'It's almost like he never existed. Maybe he was an angel after all.' It was then that we noticed he'd left the packed lunch bag I'd packed for him. While I was bending to pick it up, Maddie continued, 'It's as if he couldn't bear to carry a single thing more.'

I shook my head.

'I think it's something that started out as a habit and it's now become his credo. For Angel, memories are more important than things.' I thought, 'now I'm beginning to sound like Angel!' I smiled to myself and joined the others in the back of Adam's jeep and we drove away.

***

Our plans for departure were set, or at least I thought so. We'd agreed to catch a flight to London out of Lima on the 23rd January of what was now 1985. The replacement volunteers for the vet project, Robert and Monique had arrived in Charagua, therefore Adam and Vanda's attention had become focussed on handing over the various livestock and soybean projects. This meant Adam was busy introducing Robert to the heads of various cooperativas, so we hadn't been able to travel over to Camiri to visit Cathy who was now staying with David who lived and worked there as a technico helping to keep the cooperativa's maize hammer mills running.[62] Fortunately, Adam and Vanda had been able to take a message to her outlining our travel plans during one of their project visits.

Just two days before we were about to leave by train to Santa Cruz to catch a New Year's Day flight to La Paz, Cathy showed up at Adam and Vandas' house; we could see she was in a fuming temper. Whilst David made himself scarce in the kitchen, Cathy said, 'Vanda has been giving me some of her potted wisdom about Bolivian men. What would *she* know? She's been living with a husband and three kids for the last three and a half years! I suppose you put her up to it? Anyway, I've made my decision; I'm staying here. It's none of Vanda's business! Telling me that I'm breaking up David's relationship with Pilar and causing problems with his family. He's a grown-up and he can make his own decision which of us he wants to be with. If you must know, we want to settle down and have a family together.'

This last comment took me totally by surprise and stunned us into silence. However, after a few moments, I thought I'd better mention what, for me was the proverbial "elephant in the room", so I said, 'What about Dan? Does he know that you might not be coming home?' Cathy frowned at this in a way that suggested all thoughts of Dan and his feelings hadn't entered her mind. It was my turn to get angry, so I said, 'You do realise that Maddie and I will have the unpleasant task of explaining to Dan why you're not coming home? The least you can do is to let him know!'

Cathy's answer only made it worse, she said, 'Actually, truth be

---

[62] Mechanic or general handyman.

known, I don't intend to tell Dan anything, what he doesn't know won't hurt him. You can tell him what you like, just say I'm staying on in Bolivia to do a bit more travelling.'

I couldn't believe I what I was hearing, so I said, 'But you're talking about having a baby! Surely, he's going to notice that for Christ's sake!' That pretty much ended our conversation. Cathy flounced off to join David in the kitchen. The door then slammed and we saw the happy couple drive off into the sunset leaving us to deal with the situation.

Chapter 38
A brief encounter

Two down and two to go! It felt to me like we were haemorrhaging team members right and left, then Maddie dropped her own bombshell whilst we were waiting in the quaint little departure lounge of Santa Cruz airport. I remember that her words had a soundtrack of heart-rending Bolero music playing on the airport speakers in the background when she said, 'There's no other way of saying this, so I'll just tell it straight out… I've decided not to fly back to London with you when we get back to Lima. I've arranged with Vicky to stay with her for a while; I'm not sure how long to be honest. I've only had a couple of cards from Alex the whole time we've been out here. He didn't write much, but reading between the lines there's a bit of passive-aggressive language going on that suggests that he thinks *I've* run out on *him*. I think this means he might be thinking of leaving me altogether.' Maddie's face collapsed and she began crying, so I held her in my arms. 'It's so sad', she stammered, 'I've thought long and hard about this Debbie… I need more time to decide what to do. I've let Alex know I'm going to stay on in Peru, I just haven't said why.' I couldn't feel angry with her. She said she'd stick with me and support me through whatever happened with Victor, but her mind was made up. So now we were one! I alone would have to break the devastating news to Dan when I met him at Heathrow.

For now, I fervently hoped that when I met Victor again, he'd still be keen and willing to commit to a relationship. Whilst staying in Charagua, I'd even gone as far as sending an application to the International Institute for International Relations (CIIR) inquiring about the possibility of volunteering as a livestock development worker in Bolivia.[63] As we got closer to Nazca and my meeting with Victor, the achingly slow progress of our journey tormented me and I could think

---

[63] The CIIR, now known as Progresso, is an international development charity that enables poor communities to solve their own problems through support from skilled workers.

about nothing else. Like Cathy and Maddie, I too wanted to stay, to run away and leave behind what I had back home. But I couldn't let everyone down. I needed to go back to Glantnor and work towards returning to Bolivia as soon as I could. I comforted myself with the thought that it would soon be lambing time. It was my favourite time in the sheep's wheel of the year, it'd be hard work but that would take my mind off things. And then my stomach tightened, I missed Tosh. What would I do with her if I left Glantnor?

As I'd arranged, we found our way to the Hotel El Mirador when we got to Nazca. Checking in at reception, I realised only Maddie needed to get a room because I'd be sleeping with Victor. Butterflies fluttered in my stomach, and for once, I'd lost my appetite. It seemed like I was fully in the grip of a severe case of lovesickness. It was early evening when the 'cure' for my ailments walked through the door with a man he introduced as Peter, a work colleague, who, on seeing me, just waved and said he needed to go up to his room for a shower. Maddie had also left to do a bit more sightseeing around Nazca. I thought, 'bless her!' I'm not sure what as there was not much to see, the town was a just a domicile for tourists visiting the lines out in the desert. So that just left the two of us. We walked out to the swimming pool so we could be alone. All doubts I had evaporated as Victor took my hands across the low table between us. As he was speaking to me, I remembered Maddie had translated what Victor had said to her about his feelings for me when he briefly visited our hostel before he left Cusco.

She'd said, 'Look at that girl over there [talking about me] I am madly in love with every part of her. Look at her eyes, her face, but what can I do? I can't lock her up in a room and just look at her. She is free to do what she wants. I just wish she could understand [my words] in Spanish.'

'So' I thought, 'this man does love me!' It was the first time in my life that anyone had said that to me and I was transfixed by it. Victor then spoke of his plans for us. He asked about the possibility of getting work in England, or if I could stay in Peru? He was surprised that I had no boyfriend at home and wondered why Maddie would travel alone if she still loved her husband.

Then he said, 'We can be alone in my room. I have ordered room service for a meal for us so we can be together for the rest of the evening.' I felt nervous and excited holding his hand as we went to his room and sat together on a large double bed. Victor gently kissed me and slowly removed my clothes like he was unwrapping a precious gift. We were more relaxed than we were in Cusco. I had lost my nerves; he caressed my body and we held each other tightly and took our time to explore each other's bodies. We made love until we were completely sated and a feeling of warm contentment spread throughout my body. My earlier doubts were forgotten; surely our love was real? We made arrangements to meet in Lima a few days hence.

***

Finally, back in Lima, and with our combined financial resources running low, I'll always be thankful to John and Judy Crabtree, and Judy's sister Vicky, for putting us up at their respective homes whilst Maddie and myself tried to unpick the skein of emotional turmoil in which both of us had become entangled. With some difficulty, and after several attempts, I managed to get hold of Victor on the phone number he'd given me. His voice seemed hesitant and nervous, as though he was trying to avoid someone else from overhearing. From the very start of our conversation, my hackles rose and I could feel the cold trickle of doubt infuse my being.

After some initial chit-chat, I came out with what I wanted to say, which was, 'Look, Victor, we need to speak to each other face to face. You know how I feel for you. I cannot explain it or understand it, but you must already know that I've fallen in love with you. I'm willing to do everything I can to stay in Lima for as long as possible so we can work something out. I'll give up everything for us Victor, please just let me know truthfully how you feel.' Tears stung my eyes and I momentarily lost my power of speech.

As tears rolled down my cheeks, I could hear a long sigh from Victor down the crackly line. Finally, he said, 'Darling, I am so sorry to have caused you this pain you are feeling, but you must know something. If we stay in my country, we will need to conform, I'm sorry; I do not know the right word in English. I will need to be, what do you say, macho. I will need to show that I'm in control of you in front of friends and family.

My culture will not allow us to live in any other way.'

I'd found my words again at this point, so I interrupted and said, 'But Victor, we could look at ways for you to come to England. I have a job and a house. We could find work for you.'

Another long sigh from Victor was followed by a tapping sound that sounded like he was impatiently drumming his fingers on his telephone receiver, 'Look Debbie, mi querida, I love you, you know that, but I have a good job here with the government and I have... certain family commitments that would make it difficult to leave Peru at the moment.'

At this point, it felt like Victor was getting cold feet. No matter how hard I tried to explain my feelings for him, he'd come back with some new cockamamie answer. It was like I was desperately giving mouth-to-mouth resuscitation to my dreams of love and happy ever after only to find that my patient was stubbornly refusing my help and just wanted to die. Finally, we agreed to meet at a little café at the seafront that we both knew in a couple of days' time, however, this was easier said than done since I wasn't able to get Victor back on the phone.

Finally, in exasperation, and with time running out before my flight left on January 23rd, I took the bull by the horns, so to speak, and Maddie and I took a taxi over to the address Victor had given me for his home in Lima. Sitting in the back of the swaying vehicle, Maddie reached over and held onto my hands that I was anxiously wringing in my lap. She gently stopped my hands moving and said, 'Debbie, we will sort this out with Victor. Either way, I'm staying with you to make sure you're okay. If it's any consolation, I know how you're feeling; I've been there before. Men are all the same; they have their pride and their independence that they feel they're giving away to a woman. And their precious ego, that's often the hardest to deal with. Alex has been cheating on me for months. I know it for sure, and yet he doesn't have the decency to come out and admit it. I guess if he admits it, it's like accepting that he's in the wrong. But all I want to do is for us to get over this and make it right again with us... eeragh! Men!' We both laughed at this.

The tension eased a bit and then the driver said, 'Señoras, estamos aquí en Santa Isabel. ¿Cuál es la calle y el número de la casa?' Maddie took the piece of paper with Victor's address I was holding and spoke to the driver, who nodded and we drove on.

Maddie gave me a hug and said, 'We're almost there, it'll be fine.'

I gave her a grim smile and said, 'You know what fine stands for in the US? F***ked up, insecure, neurotic and emotional!'

Cruising along the main street, it seemed like Pueblo Libre looked like a fairly upscale precinct of Lima. Houses were clean, tidy and generally squared away and roofs were festooned with razor wire and notices on gates warning of fierce dogs. If you've got money in Lima, I guessed the place was thick with thieves trying to steal it. We stopped outside number one hundred and forty-three, Sant Isabel and we got out. The terraced house overlooked a small, fairly well-kept park. I nervously tapped on the door and we stood back and waited. Dogs snarled and yapped on the other side of the door and I thought, 'oh great, they have savage dogs!'

The door then opened a crack and a woman's voice said querulously, '¿Quién eres y qué quieres?'

Maddie replied, 'Somos amigos de Victor. ¿Está él en casa?'

There was a harrumphing sound followed by the woman shouting at the top of her voice, 'Victor, Victor, hay una mujer en la puerta!' More shuffling, and then Victor appeared in the doorway followed by two white poodle lapdogs that yapped incessantly. He looked small, sheepish and rather surprised, but he motioned to us that we should follow him inside. We each sat in separate chairs in a smartly furnished living room.

Victor broke the silence and said, 'It is the house of my mother. It is where I stay when I'm working in Lima. I'm very sorry Debbie, but this isn't a good time to talk.' As if to reinforce this statement, Mrs Rodrigues re-entered the room and said something inaudible. Victor immediately stood up like he'd been bitten by something, and without saying anything, passed me the two poodles he'd been holding onto. Both of them then left together and closed the door.

After a short pause, the flimsy nature of the walls allowed us to overhear everything they were saying in the next room. The most strident voice was that of Mrs Rodrigues, and she didn't sound happy. In a shrill, hectoring tone that sounded like she was berating him like a schoolboy, she said, '¡Me avergüenzas trayendo tus dos putas Americanas aquí, a mi casa! ¡Cómo te atreves! No me digas que amas a esta mujer? Ella no es nada. ¡Ella no tiene familia, ni crianza, ni español!' The two poodles I was holding started yapping petulantly on my lap. Looking even more sheepish, Victor came back into the room; he looked dejected and crestfallen.

Maddie said, 'Let's find a café, you two can talk there while I take a few turns around the block.' Victor nodded and left the room to fetch the little leather pouch he always carried.

I whispered to Maddie, 'What was she saying?'

Maddie drew a deep breath and said, 'You don't want to know; it wasn't good! Basically, she called us American whores.'

We walked in silence past the manicured park and along a residential street until we came to a six-lane highway, which we crossed to a rather nice little café called the Panera Espresso Bar. Maddie squeezed my hand and whispered, 'Bon chance' and kissed my cheek before she continued on down the road towards a rather unappealing group of car dealerships. Once inside the café, we took a seat by the window and Victor bought us coffee and a couple of sandwiches with some unappetising meat inside which he called chicharron.[64] We sat opposite each other and held hands across the table. I stared at Victor's face where a mixture of emotions, sadness, anxiety, exasperation, played across his features. I didn't have anything much more to say. My heart ached and emotion welled up inside me. All I wanted to do was cling to him and not let go. I felt it was Victor's turn to give an explanation, to offer hope, but he seemed to offer none, except to continue as we had done. Leaving off from a list of places we could visit and hotels we could stay in, and perhaps thinking that he needed to offer some kind of material evidence that he cared for me, Victor delved into his little leather pouch and produced a pocket-sized white plastic plaque with the words, "I love Debbie. From Victor" embossed on it in ornate black script. After he'd laid it carefully on the table between us, I stared at it for a while. It reminded me of the temporary markers placed by undertakers on a newly occupied grave in lieu of a proper gravestone. Perhaps this was the final nail in the coffin so to speak? The futility of the gesture filled me with ineffable sadness. Registering that his offering hadn't had the effect he was looking for, Victor said, 'I am so sorry, sorry, to have caused you so much sadness. Can you not stay a few more days? Maybe we can stay at a local hotel?'

---

[64] Pork crackling.

I shook my head and replied, 'Victor, my plane ticket is booked for the 23rd January; I have to leave then. I cannot afford to stay here any longer. I have to go back to work. I don't know what else to do!' A few heads turned of people sitting at neighbouring tables. I saw a woman opposite look at us with concern and pity in her eyes, like she knew what was happening.

When it came, Victor's reply sounded final.

'I cannot offer you what you want now, but maybe in a few months, you can return. We will keep in touch.' And that, as they say, was that. We sat for a few minutes longer holding hands.

Then, like the final words of a condemned convict desperately wishing to postpone the inevitable for a few moments longer, I offered my own futile gesture in the form of a long list of platitudes. I told him I loved him over and over again. When this seemed to have no effect, I said that I'd felt closer to him the previous evening than I'd ever done before. Then I thought, 'what does the word "ever" mean when you've only been with a person for three days?' It was my turn to resign myself to the futility of the situation.

I started crying and said, 'At least we have the memories of the lovely time we had together.' It sounded trite, like I was trying to put a positive spin on a disaster.

I got up and we hugged for a long while. Then, as I left Victor sitting at the table staring after me, Jim Morrison's fateful words echoed in my head like a dreadful mind-worm, his voice singing over and over, "this is the end…"[65] A heavy weight felt like it had come to rest on my chest and I found it difficult to breathe as I walked out into the crowds on the pavement and away from the café and from Victor forever.

So, just a few days after we'd shared a night of unbridled passion, the house of cards I'd built around my relationship with Victor had come tumbling down. I was devastated.

***

It was early morning and the air, for once, was pollution-free and crystal-

---

[65] Jim Morrison, the lead singer of the American rock band, and The Doors, famously sang, The End, a song he wrote about the break up with his girlfriend Mary Werbelow.

clear as the plane rushed down the runway, and for a one hundred and eighty tonne plane, rather exuberantly threw itself into the air. I was pulled back into my seat as the pilot opened up the Boeing 747's massive engines to blast us along a steep trajectory into the dazzling blue vault of the sky. The luggage cabinets above our heads vibrated and I briefly thought of what it must be like to be an astronaut taking off from Cape Canaveral, the noise and vibration might be similar, but I didn't feel their sense of exhilaration and wonder, just the reality that I was returning home. For once, I'd been blessed with a window seat, so I was able to watch out of the portal as Lima receded below me. As it did so, the South Pacific came into view gleaming and sparkling. I could recognise Lake Titicaca, the Andes and the vivid green of the apparently endless Amazon Basin. We flew north, and finally, I could make out the familiar reddish-grey shape of the South American continent nestling in the vast expanse of the world's oceans; it was an awe-inspiring sight. As I watched the spectacle unfolding far below, I wondered if I'd ever return, or see Victor once more, or whether I'd ever experience such emotions again. We levelled off at cruising altitude.

Sometime later, as fluffy little clouds and the snow-capped Andes passed beneath us, a cabin attendant brought around the drinks trolley. I went for large prosecco and made a quiet toast to Victor, to Angel, to Maddie and Cathy, to my brother Adam and his family and I clinked my wineglass on the window pane. I then pondered what story I was going to tell Dan, as he'd be waiting at Heathrow Airport expecting it to be reunited with Cathy…

'You-all making a toast to somebody? Is it someone special?'

I turned and met the smiling and friendly face of the woman who was sitting next to me, and replied, 'Yes, I've been travelling for three months in Peru and Bolivia to see my brother who's been working in Charagua. There were three of us travelling together, but I'm the only one leaving. I met someone, but I don't know how it'll turn out.'

I must have looked sad, because the woman said, 'It'll work out honey. It always does eventually. Time is a great healer y'know.' She patted my arm and I felt glad to have such a friendly travelling companion on what was going to be a long and dismal journey back to London.

At some point during the "night", or the restless tossing and turning you do in the cheap seats during the pseudo-night imposed on passengers so they don't drink too much, I woke and found the contents of my dream still floating around in the space above my head. In my confused state, I tried to push away the leering head of a beast that seemed intent on trying to molest me; I could feel its urgent fingers pawing my flesh. I thought I was awake, I could see the headrest in front of me, the luggage lockers above, but the leering eyes of the beast remained hanging in mid-air like the Cheshire Cat's smile before it finally disappeared altogether.[66] I didn't feel a calming, post-sleep fuzziness; I'd woken up straight into the clutches of my gnawing anxiety and on the horns of a dilemma. What should I do about Glantnor? Should I try and make a go of it? It felt like I'd made a life there, and yet, I had dreams of being with Victor, or was I deluding myself into thinking he felt the same for me as I did for him? What about Tosh and Roy? I'd let them down if I left now. What would people think if I went gallivanting off again? That I couldn't hold down a steady job? That I was a fly-by-night, or a flibbertigibbet that chattered away about one fleeting fancy before latching onto another but never sticking with anything, and more immediately, what about Dan? Should I feed him a candy-coated version of Cathy's lies, or give him the hard-boiled truth? I felt so torn and so overwhelmed by conflicting emotions and priorities. I couldn't even decide whether I was going to be relieved that my long journey home had ended when we arrived at Heathrow, or not. The dread I felt about the hard conversation I was going to have with Dan made me wish that I could fly on indefinitely in some kind of limbo state, neither leaving Lima nor arriving in London. I liked the idea of a limbo state; it would've given me time. I needed more time to decide on what to do, but life isn't like that, it can't be put on hold. Instead, after fifteen hours in the air, and a stop in Madrid, we bumped and bounced and yawed as we came down hard onto the tarmac at Heathrow. One of the male cabin attendants solemnly announced that the forecast was for heavy rain and the temperature was currently 7 ^{0}C. Then, assuming a more upbeat tone, he said, 'Have a nice day, and we look forward to you

---

[66] A reference to one of Lewis Carroll's characters in Alice's Adventures in Wonderland. Rather aptly considering my state of mind at the time, the Cheshire Cat is believed to be a product of Alice's schizophrenia since he appears and disappears at will, leaving confusion and madness in his wake.

travelling with us again on Iberian Airways.' His Spanish accent reminded me of Victor. Everything seemed to remind me of Victor. A pang of sadness pricked my heart again. I was in no hurry to get out of my seat, so I sat and watched the other passengers fussing with luggage and shuffling along the aisle.

***

After walking along the endless corridors of the arrivals lounge, I stood in the British and EU passengers' queue in the passport check area and rehearsed the yarn I was going to spin to Dan. I'm a hopeless liar, so I had to check my story for flaws and remembered the old adage that, "the best lies are always based as much as possible on the truth."

I cruised through the 'nothing to declare' area and felt the hard stares of the customs staff boring into me. I'm sure they were thinking, 'c'mon, surely you have something to declare after spending all that time in dodgy parts of South America!'

'Yes', I thought in reply, 'I do have something to declare. My unrequited love for someone I met there.'

Speaking of unrequited love, as I emerged from the customs area, I saw Dan leaning on the stainless-steel railings in front of the automatic doors. I could see he'd spotted me and was searching the crowd for Cathy. I walked up to him, dumped my bags and we hugged, he said, 'Debbie! Hi! Great to see you!' Dan was elated, no doubt looking forward to being reunited with his girlfriend, followed by a meal out perhaps, and then a long night of catching up in bed together.

After our hug, I said, 'Dan... Cathy didn't travel back with me, she's still in Bolivia.'

Dan was stunned for a moment while he processed this, then he said, 'So, she's coming back later on with Maddie? Alex told me that Maddie was staying a bit longer in Lima to do some sightseeing.'

Dan imperceptibly nodded his head, which I took as a cue for me to continue with an explanation, but instead I said, 'Look, let's find a café so we can have a cuppa, I'm gagging for a decent cup of tea.' I tried a laugh, but it fell flat and had the effect of causing a look of anxiety to appear on Dan's face. I wanted to do this in a neutral area, preferably a public space, rather than in Dan's car. I think it was cowardice on my part, but I didn't want to be trapped so I'd be forced to deal with his emotions. If things got really bad, I could make a run for it and catch the train instead. I wasn't feeling brave that day, just exhausted.

We found a comfortable seat at the back of a stylish-looking Wimpy. Eerily, the geometry of the way Dan and I placed ourselves at the table was a recapitulation of the one I'd shared with Victor in Lima; we didn't hold hands though. I went first.

'Look'... Then I completely lost the thread of my carefully composed lie and I just blurted out, 'Cathy's staying with a guy she met in Charagua.' That was it, I'd blown the pooch, so I just continued and said, 'They met while we were staying at Adam and Vandas'; at a party actually... She was probably drunk.' I thought, so was that mitigating circumstances? Probably not, so I continued with, 'I think Cathy's just confused, emotional, y'know, mid-life crisis'. I could see Dan wasn't convinced, she was, after all, only twenty-seven, but he was nodding, so I kept going with the mitigating stuff and said, 'I'm certain, she'll come back once she's got her head straight.'

I briefly paused at this point so Dan interrupted my flow and said, 'this guy she met... is she sleeping with him? I mean, does she... you know...'

I could see that Dan was forcing back tears, so I finished his sentence with, 'No, no, nothing like that I'm sure of it, it's just a friendship...'

Dan interrupted again, this time he spoke more forcefully, spelling it out for me like I hadn't understood his question the first time.

'Is... she... sleeping... with... him?'

I drew a deep breath and said, 'Yes, I think she is... look, I'm so sorry to be the bearer of bad tidings', God! I thought, I'm slipping into some kind of Shakespeare soliloquy, snap out of it, but before I could think of anything else to say, I looked up and saw that Dan was holding his head in the palms of his cupped hands. He was sobbing uncontrollably, his body had assumed the posture of someone in the throes of the most abject sadness and grief. People around us were looking over in our direction, probably thinking I was in some way responsible. Ignoring their stares, I moved my chair around to Dan's side of the table and held him in my arms. My body reverberated to the flow of Dan's sobbing. For the moment, there was nothing more to be said.

***

I travelled back to Berwen in the passenger seat of Dan's car. Mostly he drove in silence, although occasionally he'd ask the odd question to probe deeper into what had happened. It was like he could only deal with hearing small bits of the story at once. So I fed it to him in small bite-sized chunks, 'Yes, he's about the same age. Sort of average looking. No, he can't speak much English. She looked well, very thin though…' and so on. The hours passed and it got dark. Like going backwards towards a river's source, the motorways gave way to trunk roads, then 'B' roads, until we were winding our way through sunken lanes and large woods. I offered to stay at Dan's house, which he accepted. I was relieved because I wanted to make sure he was all right. I was unsure of his mental state. He was, after all, a forester and there were all kinds of sharp tools, chainsaws and shotguns lying around just waiting to be snatched up in a fit of despair by a desperately unhappy man. I left after a couple of days so I could get back to Garden Cottage, scrape the frost off the inside of the windows and get the fire going to try and chase away the chilling dampness. I looked in on Dan once in a while, but to be honest, I needed to leave him to his grief and find my own way to get through the next few weeks and months. I also needed to try and find a way to heal the heartache I'd brought back with me from South America.

Chapter 39
Farewell to Glantnor

To say that I'd arrived back at Glantnor with a bump would be an understatement. The sound of sheep on the hills was he same, the friendly voices of the birds were the same, my motorbike's dodgy kick-start was the same (and I received a bruise on my shin to prove it) and the people around me were the same. The only thing that had changed was me. Tosh still recognised me and she was very happy to be back with me in my warm kitchen. I treasured her bark and her presence even more than I had before I left on my travels. I loved her and I now understood what that meant, what the essence of love was. My experiences in South America had profoundly changed me, but everything else had stayed the same. I wanted to feel that fusion of emotions again, and now I knew I would never feel it at Glantnor. So I threw myself into work and reached out to friends and family. I needed a distraction from grief over my lost love. I no longer wanted to spend more years in the 'wilderness' as a lost sheep.

During the year after my return, Garden Cottage became something of a social hub to family and friends. This was a pure delight to a person like me. I liked nothing better than getting friends together for a party and watching their faces light up as they shed their inhibitions, and enjoyed some of the cakes and scones I loved to bake for them. I'd lived in so many temporary accommodations, lonely places and freezing caravans that I once thought I'd never get a chance to entertain and have friends to stay. However, whilst I worked hard and organised parties, I was planning my next move. Part of the plan was to get more qualifications, so I signed up for an Open University course in World Politics. I also searched through newspapers, magazines and the local library jobs resources looking for opportunities to work abroad and volunteer for aid organisations. Adam's experiences in Charagua, and mine, had opened my eyes to the world's injustices. I wanted to do something. I knew I had skills to offer. I was inspired, I saw that, for want of a better word, my destiny lay elsewhere; I just wasn't sure where, yet!

It was February, and from where I was standing at my kitchen sink, I watched as cold rain, intermingled with sleet, drifted past the window. The walled garden was fully in the clutches of one of those deepest, darkest days that only mid Wales could muster. The house was, as usual, cold and damp, so I'd moved Tosh's bed into the kitchen near the Superser gas heater that was purring away merrily in the corner. It added to the damp of course, but there was no choice, the house was literally freezing and an icy sheen had formed on the inside of the upstairs windows; Irish double-glazing Babs used to call it. But I was happy! Why? It was Friday evening, the day's work fixing the stock fencing was finished, and… it was the Young Farmers' tap-dancing competition at Newtown the next day! Everybody was going to be there, and afterwards, I'd organised a party, so I'd have a full house in the evening. To get me in the mood, I'd put my favourite Christmas record on the turntable, and the familiar strains of one of my father's favourite musicals was playing. If you're getting long in the tooth yourself, you'd know the music and lyrics immediately, good ol' Fred Astaire 'n' Ginger Rogers in Singin' in the Rain. If you're chronologically challenged as I now am, you'd also remember that Singin' in the Rain used to get trotted out every year on Christmas television along with other favourites like *Gone With the Wind*, *Journey to the Centre of the Earth*, *Quatermass* and the *Pit*, and the marvellously ancient sci-fi flick, *Forbidden Planet*. Bought as a Christmas present to myself, the recording didn't include the percussion of Fred and Gingers' tapping feet, but my mind filled in the gaps and I danced the steps around the kitchen. The music was doubly apt, it was raining, but I'd also decided that Fred's *Singin' in the Rain* dance routine was also going to be my entry for the tap-dancing competition. The event was to be at the Maesmawr Hall Hotel in Newtown, a rather pretentious mock Tudor place that just happened to have a large and very elegant ballroom it rented out for weddings and other functions. The music was still playing on my record player, and I was just getting to the bit where I was going to need a lamp post to swing myself around, when the phone rang. It was my good friend Sue. In between running a dairy and sheep farm near Berwen with her husband Rob, she somehow managed to organise events for the local Young Farmers. Her voice on the phone was concerned and she said, 'The snow, it's really coming down out there — the driving conditions are going to be pretty grim Debbie! Our four-wheels on the blink, so Tony's offered to drive us there in his Land Rover. How's the dance practice going? Oh, and have you got your dress back from the cleaners yet?' Sue loved to mother me occasionally and I just gave into it like snuggling into a great big fluffy marshmallow. However, she finished by saying, 'Snow, or no snow, the show must go on!'

As you've probably gathered by now, farms, farmers and farm workers exist in an alternate universe where the time clock is set somewhere in a chronological never-never land in which a trailing moment of the present day remains forever locked into the past. Even in the 1980s tap-dancing would be regarded as a pastime for old folks, but the competition was an annual fixture in the Young Farmers' calendar where the average age of members was twenty-two. Actually, there's some Best family history with tap-dancing. As I've already mentioned, my father, Dougie, was a film director, but he started out as an actor, in fact, he played a walk-on part in the movie, Angels One Five where he played the part of a pilot in a sequence where he rushed into the airmen's mess and uttered the immortal words, 'Scramble chaps' in an exceedingly posh BBC English accent![67] Part of my father's training at the RADA acting school must've included dance, specifically, tap dance.[68] This was, presumably, some kind of backup plan so if you weren't able to get work as an actor, you could maybe earn a few bob dancing on a street corner. Even though it wasn't to be his destined career, Dougie took tap-dancing pretty seriously and used to give impromptu performances at our neighbours, the Oars', house at Christmas time. I say impromptu, but actually, he'd go the whole nine yards with a set-up that included a small wooden floor to give the right tapping resonance, and the full tux and top hat. I guess I was just following in his footsteps.

For the competition I'd dug out an old favourite, a rather risqué red

---

[67] A 1952 British war film staring Jack Hawkins that tells a classic boy's own story from The Battle of Britain during WWII
[68] The Royal Academy of Dramatic Art in London

cocktail dress that I'd worn at a party during my first year at WAC. Recently, it'd been relegated to the back of the wardrobe due to an upward weight fluctuation, but a diet of yucca and boiled potatoes in South America meant I'd reacquired what's referred to as a bikini-ready body complete with a residual tan. I twirled in front of the mirror and gave a little sigh of satisfaction. It's not often that I've been at peace with my body shape.

***

Despite nine inches of snow, Tony did get us all to the ball on time, but it was touch and go until we'd got onto the ploughed main roads. I'd invited a little group of friends as a kind of groupie fan club that I'd arranged to have sitting near the front. This group, had all assembled on time, except for Shân and Nigel. Until recently, Nigel had been a rather shadowy figure who'd not yet been brought into the full glare of a friends gathering, so their absence was not wholly unexpected. And then there was the snow to add further difficulty in getting over from their farm near Hay-on-Wye. After lunch, and about halfway through the competition, Shân and Ni both appeared at the back of the room, and rather embarrassed, they did that stooping walk you do in cinemas to avoid being seen, and made their way to their seats near the front. They were just in time for my big finale, so I looked over at them, smiled and waved. It was then that I noticed how smartly dressed they were. Most of the audience were in their usual grungy farm outfits, definitely not their best bib and tucker reserved for weddings and funerals, but a notch up from farmyard wear. So Shân and Ni stuck out like proverbial sore thumbs, so much so that I briefly thought they'd entered themselves for the competition and I'd be upstaged by the two of them doing a racy Fred and Ginger number together! I needn't have worried; they stayed firmly in the audience throughout. In the end, I got third prize, so not bad all round!

After the performance, I briefly bumped into them over drinks. It was packed and noisy, so I could barely hear what Shân was saying, but I could see she had something to tell me.

It was only when they arrived at Garden Cottage, still attired in all their finery, that I finally managed to ask the obvious question, so I said, 'Shân, what's with the posh get-up? You both look fantastic, but a bit over the top for a Young Farmers' do!'

'Well,' she said, 'I'd been meaning to tell you,' (which in Shân-speak means, I'd not got around to saying anything) ', but me and Ni just tied the knot this afternoon at the registry in Welshpool.'

This, I felt, was quite an omission even for Shân who liked to play things close to her chest. I thought to myself, 'who would get married and not tell anyone?' Well, Shân and Ni obviously. So, now I was going to be playing host to a couple of newly-weds in my freezing cold and damp house! Whilst everyone was tucking into some homemade sausage rolls, I quickly nipped upstairs to change the bed sheets and put out fresh towels and some of the little bottles of smellies I'd collected from various stays in hotels. I also put the Superser up there, but then I thought better of it, I didn't want their first night together to be in a hospital bed suffering from carbon monoxide poisoning!

***

Fast forward a few weeks, spring was on its way at last and notions to find work overseas were beginning to crystallise into plans, but opportunities to work in South America were limited due to my lack of fluency in Spanish. After weeks of fruitlessly searching, despite the many affectionate letters we had sent reach other, I resigned myself to never seing Victor again and I started to cast the net a bit wider. It was then that I noticed an advert by Voluntary Service Overseas in the Guardian jobs supplement. It'd caught my eye right away because it mentioned that there were places available for agricultural specialists in East Africa. 'Mmmh' I thought, so I read on. One posting in particular, at a place near Thika, caught my eye. It certainly ticked all the boxes in terms of my qualifications and experience with the added benefit that I would, for once, be running the show. I thought, nothing ventured, nothing gained, so I decided to apply for it — but whom could I ask to provide a reference? I didn't want to alert William to the possibility of me leaving again; he'd have a fit, so my mind involuntarily drifted back over my previous farming jobs and employers. It was a motley crew that included

Mr Stamp, a possible since he'd already given me a good reference, Mr Trick, definitely not, Mrs Northridge, another possible. I just needed a third reference for my character — then I thought of Paul Oar. Yes, of course! He was a company director and his transport business had interests in East Africa, so he'd know the score out there. He'd also, quite literally, known me since I was a baby, so his would be a perfect character reference. He didn't let me down. In fact, Paul wrote a reference from the heart that still remains my most glowing ever. From the very first sentence, Paul heaped generous praise not only on me, but also on us Bests in general. It had been provided as a reference, but it also revealed the high regard in which he held our family. In it he wrote, *"Deb is to me a remarkable woman... from her early childhood she has been both loving and considerate but clearly independent. As she grew up, she determined for herself a chosen career in agriculture and pursued her training logically and with considerable success... she has been independent physically, financially and of mind from a very young age... supported by the knowledge of the high regard and affection in which she is held by her family and many friends... Deb's impact on others is fundamentally twofold. She has an immediate friendly response and secondly, she inspires confidence... there is a strong element of service to others in the makeup of the entire family."* It doesn't get any better than that!

I didn't hear anything back from VSO for several weeks. Then in July, when we'd just finished shearing, I got a letter from their recruitment office offering me an interview. I was thrilled and left in no doubt that Paul's glowing character reference had been pivotal in their decision. I shall always be grateful to him for his faith in me.

***

Since being invited for an interview, I'd been keeping my VSO plans under wraps, so my trip to the London VSO office in Belgrave Square was ostensibly to visit Sarah who'd recently given birth to Abigail with her partner, Sean. It had all happened very quickly! Looking back, sudden gestalt-like switches from one state of life homeostasis to another wholly different one seemed to be a defining characteristic of us Best

315

girls! In the space of eighteen months, Sarah had started out bemoaning all men after she'd just split up with her long-term partner, Steve. She'd said matter-of-factly, 'All men are total bastards!' Still in the aftermath of my emotional turmoil with Victor, I'd been wholeheartedly in agreement. Then, a few months later, she met Sean at a New Year party in London. Both of them fell in love and Sarah had fallen pregnant. Despite the speed of her romance and suddenly changed status, Sarah appeared to be very happy in her new role as mother and homemaker. So my visit to London killed two birds with one stone so to speak.

During the interview with VSO, I spent most of my one-hour slot regaling the selection panel about the various jobs, problems overcome and skills I'd picked up along the way. When I'd finished, the chair announced that I'd been the most well-qualified of their candidates so far, and they'd definitely be in touch! I was elated and felt like I was walking a few inches off the ground as I made my way back to the Hyde Park Corner tube station. It occurred to me that, up until now, nobody had really taken me seriously, that my choice to become a farm worker had been unwise, ridiculous even. However, I'd just spent an hour with people who believed I was competent, skilled and had a contribution to make. The VSO offices were right in the beating heart of London, a stone's throw away from Buckingham Palace, the Saatchi Gallery and swish Knightsbridge where Esme and Dougie used to have their London flat. It felt like I was at the centre of it all. Suddenly captivated by it, instead of heading into the tube, I walked through Hyde Park, and portentously, happened upon the Kenyan High Commission as I walked towards Regents Park to catch the tube at Baker Street; I remember thinking it might've been a good omen.

My offer letter from VSO came through a month later. Now it was time to make a difficult decision.

***

A few days after receiving the offer from VSO, Tony and I were gathering ewes into the 'maternity' field. The first rays of April sunshine were warming our backs. I momentarily stood still for a moment to inhale the atmosphere, imbibe the sense of place and its peacefulness. On a day like today, it was hard to imagine doing anything else, and yet I'd accepted VSO's offer. The old adage that, "you can't live off a view" is very true, but what a view! I'd been up half the previous night with a couple of difficult lambings, but I was in the moment and contented myself with listening to the lambs' bleating and to the red kite's soulful cry as it circled far above us. Tosh was working with Tony's dogs, Pip and Meg, to bring the ewes into the shed. We needed to be careful with them now to avoid stress, so we kept the dogs at a distance.

After I'd put some concentrate out for them in the feeders, we went back into the shed so I could give the orphan lambs their milk substitute while Tony loaded Pip and Meg into the back of his Land Rover. He returned carrying his battered old lunch bag and said, 'Bait time Debbie?' Then he shook his head in exasperation, 'So many cade lambs.[69] It's a bit of a balls-up, isn't it?'

I had to agree with him

'Yeah, it's the set-up in here. It's nigh-on impossible to keep the lambs with their mums especially at night, or when there's been a lot of twins and triplets. We've managed to get a few orphans onto ewes with stillbirths with the old woolly jumper trick, but I'm hopeless at it.'[70]

Tony exhaled sharply.

'Buggered by your own success then! You'd think with all 'is money, William could invest in a better set-up, improve the stock. I've been tell'n' 'im till I'm blue in the face. I should take 'im over to my place, I can't wait to see what price I get for my Charollais lambs, they're looking well so far.' As we sat down for our breakfast sandwiches, Tony winced and cried out in pain. I rushed over to him, but he motioned me away. 'It's okay Debbie, my bloody knee's give'n' me some gyp! It always swells up bad during lambing.'

It was just Tony and me for elevenses that morning, so, seeing my chance, I decided to tell him about my VSO plans. I wanted Tony to be the first to know. But his twinging knee, almost certainly the start of arthritis, just made me feel like I was leaving him and the others in the lurch. I guess I was looking for some reassurance that they'd be able to

---

[69] Orphaned, or bottle-fed lambs

[70] When a ewe has multiple births but doesn't mother all her lambs, it's often possible to foster orphan lambs onto ewes that have lost lambs, or have only gone a singleton by skinning the dead lamb to create a woolly 'jumper' for the foster.

cope. The disorganisation I'd had to deal with at times and the make do and mend attitude was infuriating, especially since there was so much money floating around the estate. I knew I could do things better if I just had a chance. I took a deep breath and said, 'Tony…'

He sighed and then he said, 'You're leaving, aren't you?'

'Yes', I said. 'I had this big speech, but I can't remember it now. I got an offer from Voluntary Service Overseas to work in Kenya. It's a two-year posting. I'll have to hand in my notice. I wanted you to be the first to know. I feel so bad, like I'm letting you all down again, but I want to have a go at doing things right, y'know, on my own terms for once.'

I started crying and Tony said, 'C'mon Debbie, you're not letting us down. We'll manage. William will just have to get things sorted out. We'll miss you… I'll miss you. You've been a breath of fresh air in this place. You'll have to be sure to come and organise another one of your parties mind!'

We both laughed, and Tony continued in his usual flippant tone, I could see he was upset, but he'd never show it.

***

I had to admit to feeling rather a fraud! I was about to become a celebrity shepherdess just weeks before I was about to jet off to East Africa! The Lady magazine, apparently England's longest-running weekly magazine for women, contacted me and asked whether I'd be interested in doing an interview that would be published in March the following year. I'd be twelve thousand miles away in March 1986, but what the hell! A bit of publicity wouldn't hurt my job search when I returned home. I wondered where they'd got my name from, but then I remembered. I'd appeared in the Montgomeryshire County Times in a photograph taken of William along with a couple of the judges of the Young Farmers Open Sheep Competition. Tony's wife, Sue, had sent me a cutting with the photo. In it, I was standing next to William, who had his shirt unbuttoned to his navel. At the time, this affectation had apparently gone unnoticed, but tap-dancing Sue reckoned it was because he thought of himself as, 'a bit of a ladies' man!' We'd both had a giggle at that.

On Sunday morning, a couple of weeks later, I had a tap on the front door. Expecting a reporter from The Lady to be a starchy old gran with a blue rinse, I was surprised when I opened the door to a tall, thirty-something woman that had the slim, athletic looks I associated with horsey-types. She held out her hand and said, 'Mair Unsworth, pleased to meet you, Debbie!' After fixing her a cup of tea, she got to work.

'So Debbie, how did you get started as a shepherdess? How many sheep do you look after? When's your busiest time?' And so on. When she asked about what it was like to work in such a male-dominated industry, 'Do they doubt your ability, or your physical strength to handle heavy sheep?' I thought about this for a while. Up until I'd come to Glantnor, I might have answered this question rather differently since my experiences as a woman on farms had been mixed and sometimes unpleasant. My time at Glantnor had changed all that. So I meant it when I said that I'd been accepted for who I was. I'd been treated like an equal and I'd enjoyed the genuine friendship of the other farm and estate workers. , but when Mair asked if I would consider marrying a farmer, my answer to that was an emphatic, no!

***

Since our fateful encounter at Heathrow back at the end of January, I'd kept in touch with Dan and had visited him a couple of times to make sure he was okay. During one of these 'pastoral' calls I made during lambing, he mentioned that he'd received a letter from Cathy saying she was coming home. In it she said she'd "finally got her head straight" and that their separation had made her "appreciate what they had together". Dan appeared willing to take her back without question. At the time, I remember thinking that you could never really understand what went on in people's relationships. It seemed incredible to me that somebody could just forgive and forget such disloyalty. I just couldn't get the vision of Cathy and David's unmade bed out of my mind. I thought if Dan had seen for himself this evidence of her unfaithfulness, he would feel differently about taking her back. I've always held the trait of loyalty in high regard and I couldn't see how somebody in Dan's position could overlook such a transgression. How could he ever trust Cathy again? Perhaps he didn't care? Maybe he'd done some long-winded cost-benefit analysis, weighed the pros and cons of taking her back and had come to the conclusion that he simply couldn't live without her and if she was willing to come back to him, he'd have her back, no questions asked. Later, I heard through the Glantnor 'jungle telegraph' that Cathy had indeed returned home. In due course, I got an invitation for their wedding in June with a request that I play the organ. I thought to myself, 'perhaps marriage was one of Dan's "conditions" for taking her back?'

***

In the weeks following the receipt of my little silvery-lettered invitation, I had thought no more about Cathy and Dan's upcoming wedding or my part in it. The unending grind associated with the sheep wheel of the year put paid to thoughts of anything else but work. It seemed at the time like William was squeezing every last drop of work out of me before I left. Admittedly, he had been rather taken aback when I handed in my resignation, whereupon he'd assumed a wounded, "after all I've done for you" attitude. This was followed three weeks later by a very strained visit from his wife, Kate. Completely ignoring the fact that the house had been morbidly damp throughout my tenure, she took the classic landlady attitude and had gone around the house, checking things off on an itinerary of contents as though I'd be running off with the mouldy carpets, the mouldy settee with its little community of mice and the bedraggled, moth-eaten curtains! Finally, she'd got around to the kitchen and the cooker.

'It was nearly new you know,' she said. Opening first the grill and then the oven, she made a small guttural noise, which I assumed was shock and revulsion, and said, 'Goodness! This *is* in a mess! I hope you will give it a good clean before you move out!' Kate then left, taking her self-righteous indignation with her, but leaving behind a hefty waft of Chanel perfume. I was fuming. I'd worked for the Wynn-Jones' for more than three years, six or seven days a week, often more than ten hours a day and this is all the thanks I get!

The languid odour of Kate's perfume was still malevolently hanging in the air when I got another knock at the door. I thought Kate had returned for round two, but Cathy was standing there. She said, 'I hope

I'm not coming at a bad time, I just saw Kate leaving. Has she been giving you a hard time?'

'You could say that,' I said, and then we hugged each other. It seemed the natural thing to do. Cathy appeared to be a different person, like she'd been transformed. She was warm and open, whereas before she'd been cold and aloof. I wondered whether she was thinking the same thing about me. For my part, I felt I'd just become more cynical.

Cathy said, 'I've heard all about you being accepted by VSO, from Dan. You must be excited!'

I nodded rather unconvincingly. The fact was I'd become overwhelmed by the enormity of the task ahead, the packing, the VSO training course, and all this had to be done whilst I was still working. Then, quite unexpectedly, Cathy said, 'Look, I know how busy you must be. I have some time on my hands at the moment, so before I get much bigger…' She then paused and caressed her stomach, like pregnant women do, before going on to say, 'I'm happy to give you a hand with tidying up the cottage. When the time comes, Dan's also happy to help move your furniture out, or arrange to put it in storage once you've gone. It'll be one less thing for you to think about.'

A wave of relief flowed over me and I said, 'Thank you so much! That would be really, really helpful. My mum had offered to come and do some tidying, but she's really not physically up to it and neither is her husband, John. That'd be such a weight off my mind, thank you!' Before continuing, I glanced at her belly, and realised that she had, indeed, put on weight, so I put two and two together. However, you can never be sure about these things, so I said, 'Did you just say you're getting bigger?'

Cathy nodded.

'Didn't you know? I reckon I'm about two months' gone.' Unintentionally, I started doing the mental arithmetic in my head. I hadn't meant to, but it's a kind of natural female thing to do. However, I've never been very quick at maths, so I think my face must've gone blank for a moment because Cathy said, 'In case you're wondering, I'm pretty certain it's Dan's. We had loads of sex when I got back.' She smiled ruefully and then said, 'It wasn't for the want of trying with David though. He wouldn't use contraception for "religious" reasons, but we were talking about having a baby so I didn't use any either — I must've

321

been mad! But I'd lost so much weight; I was down to seven stone. My periods just stopped. I think that was why I didn't get pregnant.' Cathy paused, and then, with a distant look on her face, she said, 'It was something about the place, the people, the freedom from reality, family and having to conform. There were no "rules", it seemed like anything was possible. Even while David and I were supposedly making a baby, I just kept thinking, if I get pregnant, maybe I could pass it off as Dan's. I wasn't thinking straight, I was all over the place emotionally…' Cathy paused, and like a swimmer who was fighting against the tide, she came up for air, took a deep breath, and continued, 'I think we were all suffering from a collective insanity, right? I mean, Maddie was with Lugo and you had Victor. But what snapped me out of it was a visit from David's girlfriend, Pilar. One night, she came over to David's place in Camiri. She was banging on the door and screaming at the top of her voice. She was demanding to see him. Finally, we let her in. I could see that David still had feelings for her and hated seeing her so upset. She swore and called me a bitch, but she eventually started crying and wouldn't stop. When she left, the day after, I thought to myself, this is madness. I thought, here I am, risking getting pregnant with a guy who could just dump me and then where would I be? It shook me out of my dream world and made me see sense, thank God!' Cathy took a break from her confessional, got up and poured herself another cup of tea. Then she stood with her back to me so I couldn't see her face and said, 'I really appreciate that you've been there for Dan these last few months. I've been a real shit to him; I accept that now. The least I can do is help you out when you leave for Kenya.' Her words caught in her throat and she fell silent. I felt then that we'd made our peace.

Over the years, since coming back from Africa, we lost touch. I'd forgiven her, but I never forgot how she'd treated Dan.

***

Having said goodbyes to all my friends at Glantnor and sent cards and letters to others telling them of my plans for the next couple of years, it was just left for me to say farewell to one other person in my life, well, not a person perhaps, but a trusted and much-loved companion, Tosh.

During my final few weeks at Glantnor, before the hectic whirl of VSO training courses started and I moved out of Garden Cottage to stay with Esme and John at Cleobury Mortimer in the final few days before I flew out to Kenya, Roy suggested that I should take Tosh over to his farm and leave her with him and his other dogs so she could get used to her new surroundings again. Part of me wanted to delay our parting for as long as possible, but I knew it was the right thing to do. I also knew Tosh would be in good hands, and in any case, I wouldn't have had the time to look after her properly in those final weeks. When we left my kitchen and went through the wicket gate that's the side entrance to the walled garden, I knew that Tosh would be thinking we'd be heading up the fields to work with the sheep. As always, she was excited, but obedient, but when we were approaching the back of Roy's fields and began to walk over to his house, Tosh stopped just ahead of me and I knelt down and stroked her head. I think she knew something was going to happen, so we had our final moment, just us two, under the willow trees by the little bridge over the brook. The sheep were bleating in the fields like they always had, always will, but I knew I'd never be there with her again. I cried long and hard, dampening her fur with my tears. Training Tosh had been a milestone, a signpost along my long hard path to becoming a professional. She was my companion when I most needed one. I shall never forget her. Her memory will live in my heart for the rest of my life.

Part 8
VSO

"The truth is that everyone should be aware of third-world problems for how else are we to live in a well-governed, peaceful world? But now you do — you and Adam are examples to youth the world over. You will probably find your husband now that your aims are so clarified — I hope you recognise him..." Margaret Orensson, Wakefield, Rhode Isl, and January, 1986

Chapter 40
Motorbikes and boiler suits

You could've summed up what I knew about Bristol on the back of a postage stamp! It had been a centre of heavy industry, and during the Second World War the Beaufighter light bomber aircraft was built there by the Bristol Aeroplane Company. This was the reason why the German Luftwaffe had raised much of Bristol to the ground in WWII, and was probably why the place still looked so terribly run down in the mid-eighties. What prompted VSO to select Bristol as the epicentre for their motorbike training courses, we'll never know, but Bristol was, and still is, one of my favourite places in all the world. Why? It's where I met Nick. The course lasted two days, so participants had to stay overnight at bed and breakfast accommodation. On such small things does the fate of individuals sometimes rest. If we'd simply come for the day, course participants wouldn't have needed go out for a meal together, or travel together in a minibus to the training centre, or for that matter, have a few well-deserved pints together down the local pub. Also, the course was mandatory, so you couldn't wheedle out of it even if you'd wanted to. Whether you were a seasoned biker (like me I suppose, if a hairy biker would deign to call a 50cc moped, or a 125cc Honda proper motorbikes) or a complete newbie, you had to attend and pass the course. If you had ridden a motorbike, the driving part of the course was a breeze, however, if you were a newbie, it represented a steep learning curve. From many previous Saturday morning shopping trips, I'd learnt that motorcyclists are almost invisible to most of the gormless people driving cars in the UK. At the time I remember thinking if people in Britain had a blasé attitude to a motorcyclist's safety, I couldn't imagine that they'd be much better in Kenya; maybe they'd just knock you down for fun — just kidding! Intriguingly, the course joining instructions informed us that we'd be learning "defensive motor biking skills". Which sounded cool, like they'd be throwing in some martial arts moves as well. Actually, as it turned out, being able to fell somebody with a single blow would've been a useful skill to have during my two-year posting in Kenya.

***

On the 16th of December, I was still working out my notice period at Glantnor. It was also my birthday. I'd received some cards from family and a few friends, but my "present" was going to have to be a couple of nights at the Arundel House B&B in the Bath Road near the Bristol Temple Meads railway station. It was a cold but clear evening when I exited the station, so I decided to save money and walk instead of getting a taxi. Walking through an industrial area past some pavement rubbish bins near a string of fast-food shops, I disturbed a group of what looked like black rats that were foraging there. Recoiling in revulsion at the unexpected sight, I crossed the road and quickened my step. I remember thinking that the streets of Lima had been cleaner, at least there hadn't been food waste and wrappers blowing around. I shuddered and walked on.

Fortunately, the welcome I got from Mr and Mrs Steadings at the Arundel more than made up for the dismal surrounds. Mrs Steadings showed me up to my room in a cosy little corner of the hotel on the third floor from where I just about had a view of the river. I was excited and very much looking forward to meeting the other volunteers, so I quickly freshened up and went down to the reception area to watch out for the others arriving. We'd all been told to say that we were with the VSO training course, so it'd be easy to pick them out as they checked in. The next couple of people through the door were both volunteers, Mel Woods and Jon Potter; they'd travelled separately, but arrived together. Mel was clearly a bit of a live wire. She was petite, and had a boyish short-back-and-sides hairstyle. Perhaps in an attempt to counterbalance her slight stature, she wore a huge pair of Dr Marten bovver boots, a flamboyant caftan and a red beret. Her outgoing personality also made her seem much taller than her five-foot stature. Mel said she'd been posted to Tanzania. She then nodded over to Jon who was standing nearby, and said, 'Same as Jon!' taking his cue, Jon smiled and said he'd be working on a project in northern Tanzania near Kilimanjaro. In complete contrast to Mel, Jon was tall, ginger-haired and seemed quite shy. It was then that the reality hit me, I was going to Africa; the thrill of it was almost intoxicating. When Jon had mentioned Kilimanjaro, I thought of Ernest Hemingway's book, The Snows of Kilimanjaro. It hadn't been a happy read, but it'd been one of the books about Africa I'd managed to pick up in a recent troll through second-hand bookstores in Welshpool. In it, whilst Hemingway evokes the majesty of the central character's surroundings, it's a claustrophobic, semi-autobiographical tale of a writer dying of gangrene, lovely!

The next two VSOs to come through the door arrived as a couple. They were Tony Banks and Tracy Armstrong. They'd met on a VSO country orientation course a few weeks previously and had been together ever since. They were going out to Kenya, and as luck would have it, had been posted quite close by in the Rift Valley near Nakuru. All of us were going to work as extension workers on agriculture projects and needed to use motorbikes to get out to the villages where we were going to work. We were one of the few groups of volunteers thought to need their own transport, so we were the lucky ones! Thinking we'd all now arrived, we made plans to have a meal out together. Tony and Tracy said they'd seen what looked like a decent balti house down the road, so we all crammed ourselves in the little restaurant and had a very enjoyable first evening together.

There was, however, one further person still to join our party. Having travelled further than the rest of us, I had to wait until the following morning to meet Nick. The first I knew that we had another addition to our group was when we assembled outside the B&B to wait for the minibus that'd been organised to shuttle us to and from the Bristol Motorcycle Training Centre situated to the north of the city. Nick was already talking to Jon when I joined everyone on the pavement outside the B&B, so I had time to observe our late arrival before actually meeting him. Nick was dressed in, what looked like, military fatigues. He had on an army-style combat jacket and a commodious pair of khaki cargo trousers. On his feet were, what turned out to be, a pair of very sturdy parade-ground army boots, into which his trouser-ends were firmly tucked. On his head was a khaki hat, complete with ear warmers that hung down on either side of his face. His hair was long and straggly and he sported an unkempt beard. From what little of his face that remained unobscured by hair, I could just about discern a pair of piercing blue eyes, and what I considered to be quite handsome features. My interest was firmly piqued, so I made sure I got a seat near him on the minibus.

Seated opposite, now that Nick had removed his hat, I noticed that his hair was rather greasy and probably unwashed. Mmmh, I thought, 'this guy certainly doesn't bother much about his appearance!' Despite this, from what I could overhear from his conversion with Jon, he was well spoken, polite and friendly, so I persevered and said, 'Hi, Nick, is it? I'm Debbie Best.'

For want of any other sort of greeting, I rather formally held out my hand across the aisle of the bus, which he promptly shook and said, 'Nick Gosman. I got in from Edinburgh late last night and just went straight to bed I'm afraid!'

My first impressions were of a shy, but kind person. Nick and I chatted all the way to the training centre. He was still living with his parents, so not independent which was, for me, a bad sign. Hugely on the plus side though, Nick had recently come back from a nine-month cycling trip to Tanzania that had taken him across Europe, Egypt, Sudan, Uganda and northern Kenya, so I reckoned he must have some go about him…, and I remember thinking, he must also have a very nice body! He'd also tried and failed to climb Kilimanjaro and had suffered numerous bouts of malaria. He'd studied at university, had a degree in plant science, but no practical agricultural experience (a bad sign) and yet he seemed better prepared than any of us to work in Africa; he even spoke some Swahili.

Despite his appearance, I was immediately drawn to Nick's warm personality and his self-deprecating sense of humour. An example of this came after our instructor had gone through the health and safely preliminaries and we prepared to go out to familiarise ourselves with our motorbikes. It was then that Nick revealed the pièce de résistance of his wardrobe, an enormous blue boiler suit. Once he'd got it on, it was so commodious that the only thing preventing it from sagging everywhere and acting like a windbreak on the motorbike was a large belt around its middle. It was a comedic sight and I couldn't help laughing. Nick said, 'I know, it's ridiculous right? You can probably see that I do most of my shopping at an army-navy shop.' Still laughing, I just nodded. 'This', he

330

said giving us a twirl, 'is a WWII RAF issue airman's flying overall. I'll have you know, I actually did my glider flying training in these overalls when I was in the Air Cadets at school!' His explanation didn't make his garb any less amusing, but it did make him seem rather adorable, at least it did to me at any rate!

We'd been blessed with a fine, clear morning of winter sunshine. There was frost on the ground and the roads looked icy, but Ben, our instructor, said that the ice would've melted by the time we got through the preliminaries and got out onto the road. Seated in the little training room next to the centre's workshops, it soon became clear that I was the only one who knew how to ride a motorcycle. Whilst Ben was explaining the motorbike's controls, everyone was taking notes and I could see that Mel was carefully sketching a bike with the various levers on her notepad. I thought to myself, blimey, we've only got two days for these guys to learn the whole thing from how to control the bike right through to driving on the road *and* there's motorbike maintenance and mechanics! However, Ben had a very easy-going manner and delivery. Rotund, short and completely bald, Ben had a large bulbous head, a round face and a ready smile, a bit like the little laughing Buddhas you see in Chinese restaurants.

Liberally sprinkled with amusing asides to illustrate important points, Ben's health and safety talk, delivered in a strong Birmingham accent, was a tour de force in getting a message across in a way that was memorable and totally non-patronising, a far cry from some of the mechanics lecturers at WAC. So when we did get onto the subject of motorcycle maintenance, I was able to listen and take it all in without feeling my hackles rising at the condescending tone in the tutor's voice every time someone asked a question. Nevertheless, the insides of the bike's engine and clutch remained somewhat of a mystery even after Ben's simplified explanation. Perhaps seeing the puzzlement on our faces when he was describing how the clutch worked, Ben stopped and fixed us all with an amused expression and said, 'Look, it's terribly, terribly easy right. Some of you are into livestock, yeah? Look, all you need to remember is to feed your bike what it needs and check nothin's leak'n' from where it shouldn't, see? Here's a handy way of remembering yer daily checks, just think VOLTS, right! "V" for visual, "O" for oil,

"L" for lights, "T" for tyres and brakes, "S" for steering and suspension. And when you're riding, especially at night, be aware of what's com'n' at you from all sides, not just pedestrians, cyclists, cars 'n' the like, but protruding branches and stuff lying on the road like bricks, they'll all have you of yer bike in a jiffy if you let 'em! And not just the road, mind how you go when coming into yer back yard! One night we'd left the washing line up. It was only when I was slowly being pushed off me bike backwards that I realised somethin' was up. I landed heavy on me bum think'n' it was me neighbour playing silly buggers until I saw me missus' knickers and bras hang'n' above me 'ed!'

Thank goodness we weren't in the centre of Bristol or the first speeding motorist that happened along would have cleaned us all up! There was wobbling, looking down at the clutch shift, stalling, mistaking the clutch lever for the brake, the list was endless. In the cloistered confines of the training centre car park, people were making all the mistakes you could possibly make, and some new ones I hadn't seen before. This is where Ben's Zen approach came to the fore. He breezed around everyone laughing and joking, tirelessly demonstrating and repeating explanations over and over. After we broke for lunch, we started all over again, but eventually, from confusion there emerged understanding, and even a measure of confidence. Out of all of them, I was most surprised at how Nick had managed to pick up the balance and control of the bike so easily. Clad in his ridiculously floppy boiler suit, he glided around with apparent ease.

'It's all the mountain-biking I've done.' And then he said rather grandly, 'If you've crossed the Nubian Desert on a fully-loaded bicycle, you can ride anything!'

An hour or so before it got dark, Ben said, 'All right, come on, let's go for a quick spin before it gets completely dark.' And so we did. Wearing high vis jackets with a huge 'L' plate design front and back, we headed out over a motorway flyover near the training centre and along a pleasant ride around Woodlands Country Club and back along a relatively quiet 'B' road. When we'd all got back to the training centre car park in one piece everyone was elated. Ben just beamed and said, 'Well done folks, see yer nice 'n' early tomorrow, we've got a lot to get through!'

***

Sitting in the Bath Road Crown, we were all talking ten to the dozen about our experiences that day. Mel said, 'That Ben, he was a laugh. I started calling him the "baby Buddha". All I wanted to do was give him a cuddle. He was lovely!' Everyone laughed at that. It turned out that we all had shared the same impression!

To accommodate our group, we'd pulled a couple of tables together. Sitting at one end with Nick, I realised that we'd either consciously, or unconsciously, paired off. There was Tony and Tracy, of course, but Mel and Jon were also sitting together and getting inexorably closer as the evening wore on. By the time we'd had a couple more pints and Nick and I had finished off a huge plate of pub food, we were all virtually sitting in each other's laps. We'd all joined VSO to find something that we were missing, but maybe it was that special someone? I'd never thought of VSO as a dating agency, but maybe they should consider it as a side-line!

Nick and I had been shy with each other to start with, but soon discovered that we had a lot in common. We'd both gone to public school, Nick had an overbearing mother and I, an overbearing father. We'd both been painfully shy as children and young teens and neither of us had much experience with the opposite sex. Actually, I turned out to be the more experienced of the two of us having at least had romantic encounters with a couple of men, if somewhat fleetingly. Nick admitted he'd had just a single encounter with a woman he'd met on a climbing holiday in Norway. He'd wanted to keep in touch with her, but his mother always made it very difficult for him to make phone calls at the house. As a result, he felt a deep guilt every time he picked up the phone to call her — "phonophobia" he'd called it. In the end, he'd bottled it, so his burgeoning romance had fizzled out before it'd started. That was more than six years ago! So then, compared with Nick, I was an inveterate man-eater!

Arriving back at our B&B, we all stood prevaricating in the reception before going up to our rooms, but the little bar was closed and there was nowhere for us all to sit. Mel smiled and said, 'Right you lot,

333

I'm going to be checking to see that everyone stays in their own room this evening!' We laughed, but actually what I really wanted to do was to spend some time with Nick, but in response to Mel's little joke, he promptly said his goodbyes and headed up to his room. I could see he wanted to stay chatting, however I knew that neither of us were confident enough to suggest it.

The final afternoon of the motorbike course saw us all driving through some moderate traffic and tackling a large roundabout that even I found quite scary. In the end we all passed the course with flying colours; I was amazed. That evening, walking together along the Bath Road towards the train station, I said to Nick, 'Why don't you come over to Glantnor? It'd be a great chance for you to meet everyone and understand more about my life there.' Nick appeared conflicted. I could see he would like to say yes, but going on what he'd been telling me about his mother, I reckoned he'd have to think of some kind of cast iron excuse. A vision sprang to mind of Norman Bates in Psycho listening deferentially while his mother, rocking in her chair, said to him, 'Mind you don't speak to any of those tarty girls while you're away! They're all trash!' And Nick replying, 'Yes mother.' The image was disturbing and I remember wondering what damage Nick's domineering mother had inflicted on his mental health over the years.

***

Our parting at Bristol Temple Meads Station, like that of the previous evening, was chastened, but we'd swapped phone numbers. Even so, I was surprised when I received a call from him a few days later. Hearing the phone at Garden Cottage was a relatively rare event, so I dashed out of the kitchen and into the hall in case it stopped ringing. I remember feeling a prickle of excitement when I lifted the receiver and said, 'Hello, Debbie Best speaking.'

There was then a pause followed by the 'peep, peep, peep, sound of a public callbox. 'Hello? … It's Nick, hi sorry, I'm calling from a callbox up the road, actually the nearest one is over at Buckstone shops, but I've gone to a more private one at the other end of our estate.'

I thought to myself, 'it's like he's avoiding capture by the FBI or maybe Special Branch had put a tap on his phone!'

He said, 'I'd love to come and see you. How about this weekend? I've finished with my sales job at the portable building company, so I'm pretty free at the moment.' I was taken aback that he wanted to see me again and said yes immediately.

I knew then that I wanted to find out more about him, show him my home, introduce him to the people I knew so that I could somehow weave him into the fabric of my life as much as possible in the short time we had before we flew out to our postings. Nick would be based near Tabora in central Tanzania and I in Thika, Kenya, a distance of more than five hundred miles on who knew what sort of public transport system. It wasn't even clear whether it was possible to cross between the two countries. The border had been closed between Kenya and Tanzania several times over the last few years as a result of various political disputes. Also, it seemed like I was, as Angel had put it, 'giving my heart away too easily' yet again. But I didn't care, this felt different. I felt a connection that wasn't there with Fred and Victor. Like there was a feeling of warmth and trust between us that could catch fire into something more. I just wished we had more time!

***

The train from Shrewsbury was half an hour late. I was standing waiting at the disused, soon-to-be closed Welshpool Station whilst a strong, freezing January wind blew sleet almost horizontally before it. The station buildings, such as they then were, acted more like a wind tunnel than providing any meaningful shelter from the elements.

Eventually, out of the gloom and drizzle, a train chugged and wheezed its way slowly to a stop, the 11.43 a.m. from Shrewsbury was arriving almost forty minutes late, I was freezing, but my stomach tightened with the thrill of anticipation. I thought, 'let's hope he's on the train. Maybe his mother had got wind of it and had locked and barred him in his room!' But no, Nick's dishevelled head appeared at one of the carriage windows, it looked like he was struggling with the door, so I rushed over, and through our combined efforts, we wrenched it open. Once he was standing on the platform, I could see that Nick had tried

335

harder with his appearance this time.

He was wearing a passable-looking, if rather formal, dark blue double-breasted overcoat and a clean pair of chunky, brown corduroy trousers, which definitely looked like a "mummy-buy". Not waiting for him to decide what to do, I leaned in, hugged him and his arms went around my shoulders for our first proper embrace. Standing back appraisingly, I said, 'Well, you look smart!'

Nick shook his head and said, 'It's still mostly from the army-navy store. This', pointing at his jacket, 'is a Swedish submariner's dress coat — the trousers are Marks & Spencer's though. I'm afraid my mum does most of my clothes shopping.'

'Oh God', I thought, 'I was right about the trousers. We'll definitely have to do something about that!'

Then he said, 'If I'd come dressed any smarter, Mum would've suspected something. I'm supposed to be visiting an old friend from university called Bill.'

I was thinking, 'it's even worse than I thought! He's completely controlled by his mother.' Well, a woman has ways and means of turning a man's head, and that's just what I was going to do! I smiled to myself, but then, just as we were walking out of the station, I remembered I'd come off the pill. After returning from South America, I'd been pining over Victor and there was nobody at Glantnor I even remotely fancied, so why bother with tedious visits to the doctor to get more contraceptives? Damn! I thought, 'we'll just have to be a bit more creative in that department!'

Walking into the car park where our rather insubstantial means of transport awaited, the snow was beginning to quickly settle on the ground. Recently, Lucy had "sold" me her Dad's old Citroën. I say sold because she'd actually almost given it to me for free.

Handing me the keys she wished me luck, saying, 'Hopefully, there's some life in the old girl!' Actually, for a cast-off, the old Citroën was pretty swish by my standards and it meant that I could proactively visit friends rather than waiting for them to come to me.

So, as we approached its frog-like yellow form, I said proudly, 'Ta-da! My wheels; one up on a motorbike, eh!'

Nick looked unimpressed, 'Mmmh, French, eh? Aren't they a bit unreliable? My dad used to be a mechanic. He doesn't think French cars are up to much; says they're rust buckets. He reckons Italian cars are worse though. He jokes that Fiat stands for "fix it again Tony".

Sorry, not very PC, I know! I used to drive around in an old Hillman Imp, the body was more Polyfilla and fibreglass than metal though. We bought it off a scrap dealer friend of Dad's.'

I giggled, and said, 'You're criticising *this* car, and you're driving around in a wreck from a scrap heap!'

He shook his head.

'Used to drive, it's gone to the car graveyard — the cambelt broke.'

By the time we got back to Glantnor, the snow was getting quite deep. We slithered our way along the estate tracks and almost came off into a ditch, which would've been a great way to start the weekend! As I opened the front door, we were met by a chilly blast of damp air. I had taken the risk of leaving the gas fire on, but it'd run out of gas — thwarted again! I said, 'How are you at lighting fires?'

Nick smiled broadly.

'I'm a pro! I've spent years in the Boy Scouts, man and boy.' Nick confidently approached the fireplace and got to work. It took him half an hour and most of a box of matches to get a feeble blaze going. Nick excused this apparent poor performance by saying, 'The matches were damp and so's the wood!'

'Story of my life', I thought. That morning I'd awoken with visions of deep fireside conversation over a bottle of red and a few nibbles followed by some getting to know you time, but now we'd be risking hypothermia to remove our coats, never mind getting down to business in our undies! So I quickly changed plan.

'Tell you what, let's bank up the fire with a load of coal and walk over to Roy's house to keep warm, we'll freeze if we sit around here. Hopefully the place will've heated up a bit by the time we get back. How are you with dogs?'

'Well,' he said, 'I'm not a big fan. Dogs are the bane of a cyclist's existence. I've received a few bites and several close shaves with dogs. The worst was being chased by a rabid-looking dog in Greece. They always wait until you're going uphill before attacking. Oh, and there was the time we were stalked by a pack of wild dogs in Egypt.'

I nodded.

'Fair do's, but Tosh, my sheepdog, is very well-trained and friendly, so I'm sure you'll get on fine.'

Roy and Judy had been half expecting me to drop by and see Tosh, and sure enough, she was waiting for me in the snowy lane. I knelt down and waited whilst she ran towards us and into my arms. Her fur was full of melting snow crystals. Nick bent down and stroked her head and she licked his hand. Introductions over, we walked on up to the farm and knocked on the back door.

'Come in Debbie. Try and fight your way through the wellies, just push them to one side.' Judy must've seen us coming because she already had a fresh pot of tea on the go. She said, 'Roy's busy up at the estate helping to clear a tree that's come down. He's probably going to be late back. He'll be sorry he missed you.' I introduced her to Nick and we spent a while chatting. Judy would normally have asked whether I'd heard from Victor, but fortunately she didn't mention him. It felt like I'd turned a corner with my infatuation and had moved to the excitement of a new relationship. Life was full of possibilities again!

The coal we'd put on the fire had done its job. Since we'd been over at Roy and Judys', the temperature had perceptibly increased, so I brought out some bottles of ale and fixed us some oatcakes with salmon. We carried these through to the living room and arranged the settee so it was directly in front of the fire. We didn't get past the hors d'oeuvre. A couple of bottles of beer later, we were deep in the throes of passionate kissing and cuddling and it was clear where it was going, so, despite what my my body was telling me I'd like to do, I managed to blurt out, 'I'm not on the pill.' Then, after a few moments of consideration, I said, 'it'll just have to be heavy petting I'm afraid, but that doesn't mean we can't enjoy ourselves!' As a girl, I'd always wondered about the meaning of signs in public swimming baths warning against heavy petting. That night, we took heavy petting to its limits and back again! Refreshingly, unlike my previous encounters, I had to lead the way and gently guide Nick around my body, it was an unexpected and a deeply moving experience.

That night in bed together, I thrilled to the touch and feel of our bodies lying together. It felt like it was my first meaningful night with a man. Despite my contraception malfunction, we decided not to risk using condoms in case I got pregnant. We both felt that now wasn't the time for a sexual relationship. We needed to see through our postings in Africa; we owed it to VSO and the aid agencies we were going to be working for. Nick respected my wishes and our need to wait. It was then that I realised we both shared a strong sense of responsibility.

Nick's visit to Glantnor had prompted me to organise an impromptu farewell get together down at the Talbot. Tony, Di and Simon would be there and Roy said he might pop in later. I was a little nervous bringing my freshly baked relationship under such close scrutiny, but the guys were keen to meet "the new man" in my life. I assumed everyone, secretly, would think I'd gone completely mad. Who, but Debbie Best, would start a relationship just a few weeks before shipping out to Africa to spend the next two years in neighbouring, but separate countries? I'd expected some tut-tutting and a few questioning comments at bait times, but everyone was very positive and wanted to meet the man of mystery who'd whisked me off my feet whilst so many others had failed!

The Talbot was fairly quiet, probably because of the new fall of snow, but Tony and the others were already down there holding forth at a large table opposite the fire. Di and Simon were playing pool, so Tony got the first pints in. I could see that he was sizing up my new man, so when Nick went up to the bar to get the next round of drinks, Tony said, 'He seems like a nice chap Debbie. You said he was from Scotland, but he doesn't have a Scots accent, but we won't hold that against 'im! So this is the man of your dreams then? It's a pity you didn't meet 'im sooner!' we both laughed heartily at the irony of it all. Tony made it clear he was happy for me. I felt I'd got his 'official' seal of approval and it meant a lot to me.

I'd prepared more drinks and nibbles back at Garden Cottage, so everyone came back there. Roy showed up and so did Duncan, and for a short time, Marilyn with her first child, a little lad that was now crawling around and getting into everything, and their new baby, a girl. I'd been so out of touch with things, that I was surprised.

Marilyn said, 'Hadn't you heard I was having another?

I shook my head.

'I think you mentioned in a card you sent me whilst I was in Bolivia that you were trying for another, but I didn't know you'd given birth! Congratulations, you must be so happy.'

Before replying, Marilyn checked where Duncan was and said, 'Actually, it's Duncan's this time. We didn't want our lad to be an only child, so we took the plunge again and this time it happened naturally. Duncan dotes on the kids, he really does, so I think it's all going to work out in the end.'

I was so relieved and happy for them, but I wanted my relationship with Nick to be based on honesty, no secrets.

***

With just a couple of weeks left before flying out to Kenya, VSO had booked me into a week-long country orientation course at Reading University. It all seemed to be such a rush. To be honest, I was head over heels in love and I wasn't thinking straight. In the end, I had to leave the final packing up of Garden Cottage and sale of my old car for my mother to organise. She'd accepted the challenge without complaint. Since remarrying, it seemed like I'd got the old Esme back at last. She'd shaken off her alcoholism and despair and become the mother I felt I'd never had when I was younger. It was such a relief to know that her life was back on track and one less thing for me to worry about whilst I was out in Africa. Esme's help meant that I could stay at Garden Cottage almost until I had to fly out to Nairobi. So I was able to travel over to Reading by car.

Driving onto the campus, the Faculty of Agriculture seemed like a low-key kind of a place situated in a leafy suburb and nothing like the huge citadel and grand open spaces I saw at Ohio State. I'd never been at a UK university before, but first impressions of the place were rather underwhelming. There were square concrete 1950s blockhouses, presumably science laboratories, then, opposite the car park and nearer the centre of the campus, there were older red-brick buildings that looked like they dated back to the Victorian era. Walking towards main reception, I passed the refectory and copped a huge waft of boiled cabbage, as usual, the smell triggered memories of St Mary's, so I scuttled quickly past and hoped there was another smaller sandwich place where we could have lunch during the course. We'd been told to check into the main reception on arrival where we'd be assigned our rooms.

These were in the student dorms that looked much like the blocks where we were housed at WAC, only much bigger and a bit better appointed. The big plus of the course was that Nick would be there along with the group I'd already met at the motorbike course plus a few new faces, mostly English teachers. There were twenty of us, all soon to be shipping out to countries in Africa and all points around the globe.

The studious university atmosphere, plus being surrounded by teachers, doctors and nurses, I felt that my status had finally changed. From being a lowly farm worker, I was now able to apply the knowledge I'd acquired into training others. It was a really huge confidence boost. To be honest, I really didn't take in much of what was said in the training sessions, I was too distracted, however one group discussion we had really brought home the potential risks we were taking by working in such completely different cultures. In particular, as women working in the traditional cultures we'd be encountering, we had to ensure we were completely professional at all times so as to avoid giving out the "wrong" signals to men. This meant that we needed to be culturally sensitive in the way we dressed and how we addressed men and women socially and at work. Whilst attacks on volunteers were very rare, the instructor had been very clear about how women in particular needed to protect themselves from unwanted attention. Sobering stuff!

In addition to training, that one heady week was also filled with socialising and partying, but like all good things, it had to end and it seemed like no time before I was driving to Reading Station to see Nick off on the train. As we sat together in my battered old car, it seemed like we were acting out a scene that I'd done too many times before. I loved this man, and yet we had to say goodbye and live hundreds of miles apart for the next two years, it seemed like we had an emotional mountain to climb, and Nick didn't look as though he was up to the task. For him, the shock of finding someone was even greater than mine. I'd already experienced two long-distance relationships and knew that, even though it would be tough, I could handle it. But for Nick, it was his first time. He looked like a lost sheep when he finally boarded the train for the long journey back up to Edinburgh. I wished I could alleviate his misery, but it was something he had to come to terms with on his own.

When I arrived back at Garden Cottage, amongst cards from friends wishing me well, there was a letter from big old Uncle Tim waiting for me. Tim and I had kept in touch ever since I'd stayed a month with him at Watersplace near Ware as part of that trio of lambing after coming back from the US. He was quite a bit older and I think he'd taken a brotherly interest in me. In it he sounded a note of caution on my current romance by saying, "... *if you want my honest opinion, I think you sum people up too quickly — remember the Peruvian guy — much better to take a level-headed approach. But then I'm different and that sort of comment probably makes you scorch at the ears.*" At the time, Chris's words reached out and dealt me a firm rebuff. I had wondered then whether I was being foolish chasing after another man when it could all end in more heartache, but I needed more than anything to be loved for who I was. I wasn't ready to hear any criticism from anyone about my life choices. At the time he wrote to me warning against being too hasty in matters of the heart. Tim was deliberating long and hard, and had misgivings about, his feelings for a woman who'd recently come into his life. I felt at the time that he was being too deliberate, taking too long to make a decision and might lose his chance for love. I, on the other hand, have always been impulsive and live in the moment. I thought, 'Chris, you go your way, I'll go mine.' Carpe diem![71]

***

Bizarrely, the final act to our little melodrama came in London during a night at the opera on the very last evening before I was due to fly out to Nairobi. Nick and I were staying with Sarah at the flat in London she now shared with Sean and their daughter Abigail. We needed a distraction to get us through our emotional turmoil that evening, so Sarah suggested a night on the town to enjoy the carefully choreographed emotional turmoil of Mozart's Don Giovanni, a moralistic tale of the doom a licentious villain brings upon himself in the pursuit of his relentless womanising. I wondered whether this was a fit tale for two star-crossed lovers to be watching on the eve of a long separation? Who knows, but it *was* distracting! Our cheap seats at the Royal Opera House

---

[71] Roughly translates as seize the day! A phrase in Latin used by the Roman poet Horace to express the idea that one should enjoy life while one can.

were so far back, in order for us to see anything at all, required the liberal use of our opera glasses. Despite a few dull moments in the middle where we completely lost track of the plot, as expected, in the end, the licentious Don was dragged down into hell by a ghostly statue of the avenging father of a woman he brutally murdered earlier in the opera. As the villain got his just deserts, we held hands and cried, not for the fate of the hapless Giovanni, but for the journey of separation that lay before us. I hoped we'd both be strong enough to make it through to a happier ending than the one we were watching! Since that evening, music from Don Giovanni always conjures up that night of destiny and hope. Oh, the pathos, oh the love!

Chapter 41
VSO expects

Nowadays, connectivity is king. In the twenty-first century we have more ways to connect with each other than ever before. Sitting in an armchair, we can take a virtual 'flight' from one place to another with Google Earth and interact with the features we find there; it's been a useful tool in writing this book, but more than thirty years ago, all we had were landline phones and telegrams. For instance, there was such a delay between one person speaking and the other answering that, during an international call between UK and Australia for example, a beep sound filled in the blank, just like it did when Neil Armstrong was speaking to mission control from the lunar surface! Therefore, the creaky, or non-existent phone network in Africa meant that communication with family, friends and Nick was reliant on letters. As I've already mentioned, I'm a hoarder, so you won't be surprised to learn that I have several huge box files of Africa letters sitting in my trusty wooden chest that I've spent many a happy hour rereading whilst piecing together events for this book. Meeting Nick during VSO training, of course, meant that my time in Kenya often seemed to resemble a low budget remake of the movie, Out of Africa, the true-life story of Karen Blixen's bittersweet romance with both East Africa and her lover, big game hunter Denys Finch-Hatton (played in the movie by Meryl Streep and Robert Redford).[72] Nick wasn't a swave big game hunter, but he had spent a considerable amount of time risking life and limb rock climbing and mountaineering, and he'd also learnt to fly when he was an RAF cadet at school, so there was some similarity to Redford's character.[73] I, on the other hand, was going out to Africa to work with dairy cows, but like Blixon, we both ended up doing something rather different. In Blixon's case, her feckless and unfaithful husband Bror, spent the money she gave him to buy a dairy farm on

---

[72] The movie was actually released while we were having our own African romance!
[73] If you haven't seen the movie I shan't say anything more, but it did involve a plane.

philandering and purchasing a loss-making coffee plantation instead. Similarly, I arrived at Muka Mukuu expecting to be advising local farmers on livestock production but wound up doing something else entirely!

Similarities between my African adventures with stories from the silver screen didn't end with romance. There was also plenty of cloak-and-dagger intrigue, plotting and counter-plotting going on at the project, and since Muka Mukuu was based near Thika, there were some obvious parallels between my experiences and those portrayed in Elspeth Huxley's romantic, colonial-era confection, The Flame Trees of Thika, a story of a British family's experiences in British East Africa, now known as Kenya. Just as the BBC's dramatized version was being aired on television in seven episodes, I was on my way to Thika, or close to there, to start my two-year VSO posting. The scars from the injustices imposed by colonial rule in Kenya, like those in neighbouring Tanzania, seemed to have healed over, but rather imperfectly. On the plus side, the British left behind a passable infrastructure that included a basic system of all-season tarmac roads and railway lines, electricity, water and sewage systems to some urban centres and a rudimentary telecommunications network. On the down side, the Kenyans have inherited a bureaucracy of Byzantine complexity that is modelled on the British civil service. It was this bureaucracy that, at times, threatened to drive me insane.

***

Nairobi, Nairobi, Nairobi! The self-proclaimed capital of East Africa and the nerve centre of western influence in a region that encompasses old colonial British East Africa is a swaggering parody of affluence. I say parody, because the multi-storey confidence of the city's central business district hides a grim secret. The notorious suburb of the city, Kibera, which holds the dubious record of being one of Africa's largest and most populous slums with more than one million people eking out a squalid living just a stone's throw from affluence that wouldn't be out of place in Europe or North America. Unfortunately, whilst a modest amount of the wealth tends to trickle down via taxes in many parts of the world, the powers that be, and an elite retinue of western businesses, including many aid agencies, conspire in a kind of wealth constipation whereby cash and resources flow in to Nairobi whilst only a tiny trickle makes it out into the largely poverty-stricken rural areas where the volunteers worked. Nairobi is, however, blessed by having a pleasant microclimate. Geographically, the city sits at the southern tip of the Kenyan Central Plateau above the searing heat of the Athi Plains on the eastern, cool, wet side of the Rift Valley peaks known as the Ngong Hills close to where Blixon had her farm.

My first encounter with Nairobi happened on Thursday, January 2nd 1986 after I'd travelled straight down for over eight and a half hours on a journey from London Heathrow. With just a plus three-hour time-difference, you could be fooled into thinking you'd arrived in a sunnier part of Europe, however, latitude is the key. In those eight hours, I'd travelled more or less straight down from 51.5074° N in London to 1.2921° S, so I was now, more or less, on the equator. And what a difference fifty plus degrees of latitude makes! Feeling like a drunk with a hangover, I woke from an exhausted slumber that had lasted pretty much for the whole flight. At that moment, the plane banked steeply over an arid brown-scape that ended abruptly, giving way to my first view of the city as the rising sun glinted on the glass and adamantine steel of Nairobi's skyscrapers. From photographs Nick had shown me of the city, I was able to pick out a few of the larger monoliths as they came into view like the Kenyatta Convention Centre with its characteristic saucer-shaped hat and a gleaming glass monstrosity that housed the Co-operative Bank. I was travelling with fellow volunteers, Tony and Tracy, who I met on the motorbike training course in Bristol. Seated further back in the plane, I'd passed them on the way to the toilets a couple of times. On both occasions, they were being overly affectionate with each other and I felt a pang of jealously as I passed them. I also wondered how they'd get anything done when they finally arrived at their postings as they seemed so distracted with each other.

On arrival, the Kenya VSO field officer, Peter Gilbert, had arranged for a taxi to pick us up at the airport and take us over to meet the field director, Chris Robertson, at his home on the outskirts of Nairobi. Emerging from arrivals, we easily found our driver. He was wearing a dark suit and tie, smiling broadly and standing holding a large official-looking board with VSO written in green lettering. It was whilst James, our driver, checked us off on his list, that we discovered there were two additional people in our party. These turned out to be an older couple, Arnold and Megan, who'd paid for upgraded seats nearer the front of the plane, as Megan explained, 'to avoid Arnold's knee completely locking-up on him.' The extra room may have been beneficial, but Arnold still hobbled badly when they walked over to us. In the taxi, Megan explained that they'd been posted as teachers to a school in western Kenya, she said, 'All our kids have flown the nest, all six of them, thank goodness! We'd always wanted to do something more positive with our lives, y'know, put something back, so this was our chance. We're really out in the sticks, so VSO's going to provide us with a motorbike for transport, Arnold was quite a biker in his day!'

Arnold interrupted at that point and said, 'That was over forty years ago dear! I'm going to need brush up my skills.'

Megan then said, gleefully, 'I'll be riding pillion again after all these years. How exciting!'

I found it rather worrying that VSO hadn't put them both on the motorbike training course to at least check Arnold's proficiency, so I said, 'I'm surprised VSO didn't book you on the Bristol motorbike course. I've used a motorbike quite a bit as part of my shepherding job. I'm more than happy to help give you a bit of a refresher when we're at our language and orientation course in Kitui if you like.'

Arnold nodded.

'That would be very useful. I'm not sure how good my balance will be with my dodgy knee!'

I sat back in my seat and shook my head and thought, 'oh boy, they're an accident waiting to happen!'

Our journey from Jomo Kenyatta Airport to the south took us right through the centre of Nairobi, affording us an opportunity for a backpacker's tour of the city, no stopping, just passing through. Driving on the left, there was copious, unpotholed tarmac, gleaming concrete and glass buildings, yellow lines, parking meters and traffic wardens; we could have been in London! In a final flourish, we left the city centre via Kenyatta Avenue's palm-lined opulence and passed the Stanley and Intercontinental hotels. Chris Robertson's house was situated in a plush neighbourhood to the north of the city called Runda. Road signs indicting turnings for diplomatic residences, various embassies and the United Nations Secretariat suggested that, in Runda, Kenya's wealthy elite rubbed shoulders with expatriates working for various funding agencies that included the World Bank. Whilst such agencies were channelling much-needed aid into the country, there appeared to be no intention of integrating with the local people, preferring opulence to simplicity. Inclined avenues took us through a scented, lush green iridescence of tropical vegetation sprinkled with red flame trees, pink bougainvillea and purple jacaranda. Looking beyond the electronic gates, some manned by armed sentries, presumably cheaper than lawnmowers, armies of men wielding hooked-shaped pangas swinging like metronomes were patiently traversing acres of verdant lawns.[74] It felt like we'd travelled back in time to colonial East Africa, or perhaps it never left entirely, but lived on in discrete enclaves like the one we were passing through.

In a nod to utility and the more grass roots approach taken to aid by VSO, the front garden of Chris's rather less than grand villa was festooned with a small crowd of Honda 125cc mud bikes. I smiled to myself and wondered what the posh residents of Runda thought of such an overt display of so much practical transportation. Perhaps there was much tut-tutting and wagging of heads that Chis was allowed to bring down the neighbourhood in such a way. However, such toys were of great value in a country where purchase of a motorbike would consume the annual wages of an average Kenyan. So, in common with the grander residences, a guard, called an Askari, was stationed in a little clapperboard sentry box by the gate.

As we stepped into the house, Chris's wife Marion welcomed us all warmly, and bustled around serving us all coffee accompanied by little pink wafer biscuits while her husband Chis held forth with a tired old doggerel, a welcome speech and pep talk that he must've trotted hundreds, if not, thousands, of times during his long tenure in the job. It was a mixture of 'pleasure to meet you', 'VSO expects' and the 'vision thing' all rolled into one. Handshakes, refreshments, speech, job done, Peter ushered us out and we carried on our way to Kitui, a little town situated in the parched scrubland that covers much of Kenya, and the

---

[74] Machetes

Catholic Pastoral Centre where we would spend the next four weeks imbibing VSO lore and Kiswahili in a spartan environment of early mornings whilst feeding on copious quantities of maize meal. I was soon to learn that ground maize, a staple in East Africa, is served in one of two forms, both revolting, a stiff sludge known as ugali and runny sludge known as uji.

It finally felt like I'd landed. Evening had come by the time we arrived at the pastoral centre, and since several volunteers would be arriving late, the start of our training programme was delayed until the following day, which was why I was idling away some time to exploring our surroundings. Stepping off the concrete walkway, I took my sandals off and walked on the grass at the back of the centre. Before stepping onto it, the grass had looked lush, but it was actually quite hard and bristly, the tightly packed sward giving way only reluctantly under my bare feet. The early evening air was laden with the sweet scent of bougainvillea infused with a pungent metallic undertone. Just then, the sprinklers came on and I realised why the lower portion of the white walls near the lawn were ochre in colour. The water was almost orange, infused with iron deposits from the borehole. Above my head, there was a clamorous twittering. Expecting to see something more exotic, I was rather disappointed to find the sound was coming from a group of house sparrows. I nodded and said 'Hi there, not so strange, strangers!' Seeing them chattering, reminded me of the UK and then of Nick. He'd be at his language and orientation course in Kent. Peter Gilbert had passed a letter from him to me when we'd arrived at the pastoral centre. In it Nick had complained of the freezing cold at the priory where his own language and orientation course was being held. So, we were both currently in chastened monastic surroundings. I thought, 'how apt!'

Before I could get any more morose thinking about my love affair that'd been put on hold almost before it'd started, Peter called us into the front room of the centre. As we were all taking a seat, a youngish blonde-haired woman joined him, who he introduced as the assistant field officer.

'Now', he said, 'Carol here will bring the final few recruits over from the airport tomorrow. Then, she'll be your drill sergeant for the next four weeks.' Then he guffawed at his own little joke and said, 'Just kidding!'

While Peter was talking, I noticed Carol had turned her head in Peter's direction and was giving him an icy stare. Since we'd met him earlier in the morning, Peter had oozed good humour, sprinkling his conversation with numerous little witticisms that were already becoming predictable, but otherwise he seemed harmless in a buffoonish kind of a way, at least in front of the volunteers. My experience of such people is that they usually use this type of avuncular good humour as a cover for shyness. Before handing over to Carol, and perhaps in response to her icy stare, Peter finished by saying, 'Joking aside, Carol has kindly delayed her departure from the VSO field office so as she can be the facilitator for your introductory course. She was a volunteer herself for several years working as a midwife and nurse in Wajir County in north-eastern Kenya. It's tough country up there where droughts aren't uncommon and neither is starvation nor its effects. She, more than anyone in the Kenyan field office, knows what it's like to be a volunteer and we'll be sorry to see her leave us. To work for Oxfam in Biafra, am I right Carol?'

Carol nodded, and taking her cue from Peter, she stepped up and began arranging the pages of a large flip chart standing behind her on which was written a summary of the course content. Carol was the complete antithesis of Peter's schoolboy-like charm. She positively bristled with a rancour that suggested training greenhorn volunteers was a task that had been imposed upon her against her will; perhaps that was why she was leaving. Carol looked like she was thirty-five going on forty-five. Her face was reasonably unlined and young but a pointed, bird-like nose seemed to draw her lean face inwards to give her features a look of hawkish malevolence that belied her age. Her long, sun-bleached hair was scraped back into a ponytail that was fixed in place by a rubber band. Her body was painfully thin, and without any sign of breasts, she looked almost boyish, dressed as she was in military-style jungle fatigues that suggested she, like Nick, probably did most of her clothes shopping at an army-navy store. Taken together, her features and appearance, hinted at a woman whose femininity had been washed out of her, maybe by what she'd seen and perhaps by the harsh injustices of the world. I'd met her kind many times in farming. Carol actually reminded me of the bitter old harridan of a farmer's wife, Mrs Owen,

350

who I'd had the displeasure of meeting during my sandwich year at Llover Gyfall. I wondered what she'd look like when she was her age. However, I wasn't proposing to warn her that, as granny used to say, 'If you keep frowning like that, your face will stay like it!'

Before speaking to us, Carol rocked back on her heels like a proverbial drill sergeant, cast her steely gaze over us and said, 'As Peter mentioned, more volunteers will be arriving tomorrow. There'll be seventeen of you in total. Whilst cooking and washing up will be taken care of by the centre's staff, we expect you to help with duties including assisting during mealtimes and with general cleaning. It's part of the ethos of the pastoral centre — tidiness close to Goodliness and all that. Local food only is on the menu, there's no point in eating a western diet when you all, or many of you, will be going to remote rural communities where such food will not be available. Cooking bananas, dried beans, cassava, arrowroot, some bread and potatoes; that's the very simple diet over most of East Africa. For those of you who might struggle with cooking,' here she paused and looked pointedly at the males in the room before she went on, 'I'll be giving some demonstrations on how to prepare these raw ingredients and how to keep safe if you're lucky enough to find some meat. By and large, you'll mostly be eating a vegetarian diet plus eggs when you can get hold of them. Our days here start at six thirty a.m. sharp. If you're more than half an hour later than that, you'll miss breakfast. Sister Immaculata will ring the chapel bell for reveille at five thirty a.m. I can vouch for the fact that it's quite loud and better than any alarm clock!' There were some giggles from a couple of the women sitting at the front, however, Carol just stared, she was *not* amused.

'Dammit!' I thought, 'I'm back in a bloody convent. I've travelled seven thousand miles to end up back where I started!'

***

Two weeks later and our diet of early mornings and Carol's blunt demeanour and harsh tongue was making all our lives a misery. It was like sitting through lessons from my hard-nosed nemesis, Sister Scholastica, at St Mary's. In the morning, whilst the sun rose to paint the plains below with its orange glow, we were at our desks for four hours of

Kiswahili tuition. Our tutor, Maria, a trainee nun, or novice, was one of the bright spots in our day. She was friendly, warm and tirelessly patient, saying, 'This is such a great chance to test my teaching skills! You learn so quickly and are much more obedient than the school children I teach in the villages!' Maria's white veil framed her ebony skin and matched the brilliance of her teeth as she smiled. Where Carol was gaunt and austere, Maria was bright, bouncy and endlessly patient. We all loved her immediately and we learnt quickly. Also, as I discovered, she could be a shoulder to cry on.

Towards the end of our stay at Kitui, via the VSO field office, I received a letter of doom and gloom from Nick's mother of all people, who I had never met or had any contact with previously. In it, I read four pages of her spidery longhand in which Nick's mother reeled off a list of her son's misdemeanours and gave an insight into a household where her son "kept [her] in the dark." In a nutshell, it sounded like Nick had lied to his parents about where he was during his stay with me at Garden Cottage. It was a letter full of self-righteous indignation about a son who'd gone to the bad and off the rails. It was a masterful piece of character assassination that even had me wondering what I might be letting myself into. After reading it, I was confused, but also saddened that Nick's mother had felt the need to resort to denigrating her son in a letter to a complete stranger. After rereading the letter several times, I was moved to tears. Was it for Nick's mother or for Nick himself, I wasn't sure.

I was holding the pages of the letter in my hand and sitting on a bench when Sister Maria emerged from the chapel opposite where I was sitting. When she saw how distressed I was she came over, sat down quietly next to me, gently squeezed my hand and said, 'You don't need to say what it is that's making you so sad, but sometimes it can help to just talk about it. I think that the VSO is a calling, and like my calling to do God's work, it can be a hard, lonely path to follow.'

Maria smiled at me and I said, 'Sister, I fell in love before I came out to Kenya. I met a lovely man who loves me. It seems so cruel that after all my years of being alone working on farms that I should finally find someone just when I joined VSO. We will not see each other for a year, maybe more…' my voice trailed off and my sobs took over.

Maria said, 'When God tests us, it is always for a reason. Meeting a man has opened your heart. Let it also help you open your heart to the people you have come here to help. They too need your compassion, your knowledge, and your understanding. Do not fight against this separation, instead, you need to embrace it and learn from it. Nothing worthwhile ever comes without suffering.'

Sister Maria's words were generous and loving, the opposite of Sister Thomas's stern lecture on food and the world's poor she used when she tried to force me to eat that revolting meal back in the refectory at St Mary's. In that moment, my view of nuns was, if not completely transformed, modified.

I took a deep breath, smiled at her, and said, 'Thank you!' And I really meant it. If Carol Mann's experience of suffering had turned her into a bitter woman that appeared to have aged beyond her years, Sister Maria, on the other hand, radiated magnanimity and hope, and was a lesson and example to us all.

***

I wasn't just a pupil during my time at Kitui, I also became a teacher, or should I say, motorcycling instructor, for Arnold. Worried that Arnold might do himself, and Megan riding pillion, serious harm, I'd managed to persuade Peter to let me give him a few driving lessons. For the final two weeks of our stay at the pastoral centre, every afternoon after our dose of cultural orientation, Arnold and I had gone out together, at first on the service roads around the centre and then out onto the quiet lanes and dirt tracks nearby. At first, it looked like I was getting somewhere, and Arnold's motorbike handling had improved, but only up to a certain point. It seemed like he was fine riding on the open road with no obstacles or crossroads to negotiate, but when he tangled with anything more than a simple stop and start manoeuvre, he became unpredictable and unstable. In the end, he'd admitted that his balance was decidedly worse than it was thirty years ago and his dodgy knee was making it difficult for him to hold the motorbike upright when he stopped. But he was an old stalwart and wouldn't be beaten, or ask VSO for help.

'I don't want to make a fuss', he said. In the end, I said I'd have a word with Peter.

Unfortunately, as the course was drawing to a close, Peter had needed to travel upcountry, so I rolled up my sleeves, girded my loins and had a word with Carol instead. During the last three and a half weeks, Carol had become moderately well disposed towards me. Secretly, I think she was rather impressed by the fact that I'd worked on farms in the physically demanding world of men. So, when I asked if I could have a word about Arnold's lack of motorcycling prowess, she did at least listen to what I had to say. When she'd heard me out, she said, 'Why doesn't he come and talk to me himself? Surely, he's old enough to speak for himself, he must be in his sixties! Look, Debbie, we can't make an exception. VSO has limited funds. It's hard enough finding the money for motorbikes let alone pickup trucks! If they're not up to the job, then they should go home. Better now than months down the line with time and money wasted. I'm gonna talk to Peter about it.'

I shook my head.

'I'm not saying he can't do his posting, it's just his balance isn't good enough! Megan and Arnold would make great teachers. Arnold's been a real father figure to some of the younger volunteers while he's been here.' But Carol wouldn't hear anything more about it and started walking away, so I said, 'You're not being fair, they deserve a chance.'

Carol then turned and said, 'A chance to do what? Waste our critical time and resources? Why are you so supportive of him, he's not your dad for Christ's sake! He's just some old bloke who's past his sell-by date, that's all.'

At that, Carol stormed off and wouldn't speak to me for the rest of our time at Kitui. I did have a word with Peter, though, and I managed to convince him that Megan and Arnold needed a pickup instead of a motorbike. He said, 'I agree with you Debbie, they deserve a chance. After all, VSO is about inclusion as well and we need to show that all ages can make a contribution. Life experience is often a key factor for success when the going gets tough.'

For once, Peter showed his metal and convinced Chris Robertson to sign off on a pickup truck. Apparently, Carol was fuming!

Chapter 42
One [wo]man, two guvnors

They say that in Kenya you can grow just about anything. I'm sure the old adage is right, but judging by the thin dusty soil that covers most of the country, there needs to be caveats, and those are, if you're *high* enough above sea level and the soil is *fertile* enough you can grow *anything*. The stark reality is that, although farming is the most important and widespread economic activity in Kenya, only twenty percent of the land is used for crop and animal feed production, of which just eight percent is suitable for cultivation. In colonial times, that eight percent was owned and controlled by a tiny number of wealthy foreign nationals, mostly British businessmen and landed gentry that controlled interests in East Africa. One of these, a certain Sir William Northrup McMillan, an American multimillionaire, secured a ninety-nine-year lease on ten thousand acres of prime land including, and encompassing, the highlands around the foot of a seven-thousand-foot massif known locally as Ol Donyo Sabuk in Ki Maasai.[75]

The property and farmhouse were known as Juja Farm by the McMillans, but to the local people, Ol Donyo Sabuk, or Kilimambogo in Ki Swahili, is a sacred mountain with life-giving powers. In its rain-shadow lies the dry and dusty expanse of the Athi Plains, but in the lee of its nourishing and life-giving slopes, rain clouds form and water issues from springs on the mountain which ultimately contribute to the Athi River far below, that forms the border between the Thika and Machakos districts. Near the town of Thika, the river passes over fourteen consecutive rapids, which together are known as Fourteen Falls. The McMillans' farm, nestling between a swift-flowing river and a mighty mountain, enjoys the best of both worlds; it is here that you really can grow anything.

In the 1950s and in failing health, McMillan sold his farm, which, in

---

[75] The Maasai language

turn, after the country's independence, came into the possession of the Kenyan Ministry of Cooperative Development. Having by this time expanded to its current area of twenty-eight thousand acres, with many hundreds of cooperative members farming on demarcated plots, the scheme became unmanageable and the Kenyan government, for some reason best known to itself, called on the assistance of a German aid organisation, GAT, who proposed an eight-million-pound plan to develop a farm and settlement scheme. Profits from the farm, which includes coffee, sisal and citrus plantations, flow into the Kenyan government coffers and individual members of the cooperative share profits from the settlement scheme.

To begin with, it took a while to get my head around the complexity of the project, but when I arrived at Muka Mukuu, the GAT scheme manager, Theo Döeffler, attempted to set me straight on where I fitted into this gargantuan organisational stew. In a nutshell, I was going to be employed as a female version of one man with two guvnors. In Richard Bean's comedic play of the same name, the hero becomes separately employed by two men, one a gangster and the other, for want of a better word, is an upper-class twit. Whilst there wasn't a strict equivalent for either of these two guvnors at Muka Mukuu, I was destined to try and please both the settlement manager, Mr Willi Mbenge and polytechnic manageress, Josephine Matuku, a task that, like the hapless hero of Bean's play, was almost impossible to achieve.

Urbane, in a way that only Germanic men can achieve, during our meeting on my first morning, Döeffler suavely ushered me into a rattan chair in front of an expansive desk that resembled a battleship under full sail. My impression of this huge teak edifice was that it positively bristled with importance. There were two telephones, a tottering in tray and an equally tottering out tray. There was a coffee machine, a fax machine, and on a separate little table, a telex machine hummed patiently away in a corner. With such a vast array of distractions, it was a wonder Döeffler got anything done, but at his level in the food chain, I assumed he had a host of subordinates and minions he could call on to actually *do* things, he just had to decide *what* they did and when.

Once I was settled in the rattan chair, sipping the coffee he'd graciously poured for me, Döeffler fixed me with his impassive grey eyes and launched into his spiel.

'So Debbie, welcome to Muka Mukuu at last! VSO has told me that you have practical experience of a large number of different farm animals. I think your CV is very impressive. But I think VSO have rather misunderstood the role when we agreed your posting with them.'

Here, he paused momentarily for effect and I thought, 'Here it comes', I've heard this type of preamble before. Two people, organisations in this case, identified a need. They weren't clear what that need was, but by the time the person employed to fulfil that need arrives, they've come to the conclusion that they actually need two people to do two separate jobs. But we now have just one person, so let's see if (s)he can do both jobs at the same time. 'Perfect' they both say. We can save time and money and both people/organisations are happy. Now we see the logic of one man, two guvnors!

Döeffler tented his fingertips and absently tapped them together before launching into the nitty-gritty.

'So... I had a discussion with VSO and we decided that part of your job will be to teach animal husbandry to the students at the society's polytechnic and other part will be to set up and run a zero-grazing demonstration project for the extension team. You seem to have the right experience for both roles, so, as it turns out, you are perfect for this challenging joint role!' Döeffler seemed genuinely happy and looked like a man that saw that yet another little problem had been solved. He then made a little self-congratulatory hmm-ing noise before continuing. 'Well Debbie, have you got any questions?'

At this point, what I should have said was, 'Does Muka Mukuu, by any chance, exist in some kind of warp in space-time that allows for days that are longer than twenty-four hours?' But what I actually said was, 'Right, yes, I do have some of the right experience that's true...'

But before I could say anything else, Döeffler had got up from his desk and was ushering me out saying, 'Great Debbie. Mr Kubaru, the head of the extension team, will arrange for you to be transported up to your accommodation. You're in luck you know. The house where you'll be staying has a VSO volunteer already living there to help you settle in, and I'm told, the veranda affords a very nice view of the surrounding countryside.'

And so, that, as they say, was that!

***

Thunder was rolling around Ol Donyo Sabuk mountain and I was buffeted by a gusting wind that whipped up eddies of red dust as I walked down the broad estate track leading down to the Muka Mukuu workshops. John Maddox, fellow VSO volunteer and alternative technologist, had declined to give me a ride down to the estate compound saying he was 'far too busy to waste time running errands this morning.' So, during my three-mile walk, I had time to reflect on my current predicament.

We're told that our opinion of a person is built up, not from hundreds of interactions and instances of behaviour over time, but in an instant; thirty seconds apparently. My opinion had already been formed two weeks previously when, after my meeting with Döeffler, Joseph Kubaru had driven me over to my accommodation and dropped me off in front of its veranda where a forty-something year-old man with unkempt hair and a straggling beard was sitting. After a rather perfunctory exchange of greetings, I learned that the man was indeed my erstwhile living companion, John Maddox. At first, I assumed that Joseph's rather hasty departure was because he was busy, or was anxious to get to another appointment, but now I suspect he simply didn't like John. Under normal circumstances, the arrival of a fellow human being would be the prompt for a normal person to rise from their porch lounger, walk across to that person and perform some kind of greeting ceremony commensurate with that individual's cultural norms, however strange they may be, for example, 'Me Tarzan, you Jane' or 'Livingstone, I presume', followed by a handshake. Failing that, a simple 'Hi' would do. But John Maddox, I have now come to understand is not a normal person, and instead I was greeted by moody indifference. Mumbling something that might have been 'Come in, I'll show you your room', John disappeared inside allowing the insect screen to bang in my face. By the time I'd levered the screen open, and dragged my heavy bags inside, he was nowhere to be seen. As I entered a long hallway with red-coloured concrete flooring and walls painted in the kind of green colour you get in hospitals, a sense of deep foreboding pervaded my senses. It felt like I was entering a creature's lair, Kurtz's brooding character in Conrad's Heart of Darkness sprang to mind. Not that I'm suggesting John was some kind of Machiavellian evil genius, but I'd immediately recognised a wildness about him, an impassive intent that, I was soon to learn, could quickly flare into rage. The lack of conversation during our initial meeting had forced me to weigh up various possibilities, (1) like Dr Livingstone, John had become a recluse, (2) John was indeed a Machiavellian evil genius, or (3) John was a combination of the above. However, after two weeks of living with him, I decided that he was none of these; he was something much worse, a self-opinionated male chauvinist who delighted in the sound of his own voice and putting others down.

John was a Scot, a cousin of the singer-songwriter Annie Maddox, and, though likely now retired, a nuclear submarine engineer based at the Rosyth Royal Naval Dockyard on the Firth of Forth. Perhaps it was his time on submarines and lengthy fraternisation with submariners, which had caused John to be obsessively tidy, to endlessly brood over missing items of personal property and deal so offhandedly with women. Or maybe it was because he was Scots. I don't want to be disingenuous to an entire race of people just because I'd met two miscreant examples, but up until I met Nick (a Scot hailing from Edinburgh), my opinion of Scots was not good. At Wyddial Bury Farm, during my first job after graduating from WAC, I'd had the dubious pleasure of working with another Scot, and human powder keg, Andrew Geddes. Geddes, you might remember, was in the habit of beating his wife when he exploded into rage. So, since he'd already shown he was obsessive, offhand and moody, I was naturally concerned whether John shared Geddes' violent temperament. These thoughts swirled around my head as I finally walked through the gate of the wire mesh fenced compound and over to a garage where a brand new, white Suzuki 125cc motorbike was standing. Noticing that I'd walked into his yard, a smiling man emerged from the workshop office and introduced himself as Charles Mburu, the head extension worker. When I handed him the kibali I'd been given by Döeffler approving the release of the bike to me, his surprise had been a picture to see.[76]

---

[76] Official approval document.

Whilst he didn't actually question whether a motorbike was a suitable or dignified mode of transport for a woman to use, Mburu did ask, 'You have passed your driving test and you have ridden a pikipiki before?'[77]

I nodded.

'Yes, I've used a motorbike for years to drive up the field and around the farm when I was working as a shepherd in England.' I then smiled reassuringly at him, donned my helmet and leather gloves and climbed aboard. I could see that Mburu was about to show me the controls, but in order to provide further reassurance, I switched on the ignition and kick-started the bike. Unlike my old Suzuki back at Glantnor, the engine immediately burst into life and I revved it a couple of times for good measure. I then thanked Mburu profusely, smiled sweetly and drove off and out of the compound towards the road leading up the mountain. I was determined to see what the bike could do!

The threat of rain had passed and the sun shone as I accelerated up the track leading towards the summit of Ol Donyo Sabuk. Climbing steadily for about twenty minutes, I rode into a clearing and shut down the engine. Dismounting, I hung my helmet on the handlebars and walked over to the summit edge. For once, the view to the horizon was crystal clear, as earlier rain had cleared dust from the air. To the northeast, I could see the rocky summit of Mount Kenya with snow lingering in its rugged gullies. Then, looking far to the south, I could make out the white, snow-clad dome of Mount Kilimanjaro, a 'gift' by Queen Victoria to Kaizer Wilhelm of Germany for his birthday.[78] It was an exhilarating and uplifting sight. I felt the thrill of Africa beginning to seep into my being. As I took it all in, words from a wonderfully poetic letter from Maddie came to mind. She, herself, had fallen in love with Africa whist growing

---

[77] Swahili for motorbike.

[78] A reference to the fact that Queen Victoria 'gifted' Mt. Kilimanjaro to Germany which, at the time, imposed colonial rule over Tanzania, by shifting Kenya's border exclude the mountain. Reportedly Victoria had said that, 'it had seemed rather unfair that I should have two mountains when cousin Willie has none.' Later, after WWI, Britain confiscated Tanzania from Germany and brought it under its own colonial jurisdiction. And so it was, that the fate of the world used to be dictated by the whim of distant superpowers. However, after independence was granted to both countries, Kilimanjaro still remains in Tanzania, no doubt much to the chagrin of Kenya's tourist industry!

360

up on the Ivory Coast. In what seemed like a stream of consciousness that'd just flowed out of her, she said, "*have you noticed how [the African] people, despite their poverty [and] suffering, [just] enjoy life? Everything is so beautiful... look at the nature Debbie... the trees [talk] to you, [look] at their flowers. How, before a storm, it's so powerful, you feel it deep inside... nature is full of anxiety and tension, and then, after the storm, you can feel the relaxation, the flowers reopen and the [animals] come alive again.*" It felt like I too had come through a storm. My intense relationship with Victor had seared my heart and I'd experienced a deep despair that I might never love again. But I'd come through it. Unhealthy infatuation had been supplanted by a more equal and nourishing relationship with Nick. As Maddie had so eloquently put it in her letter, "*[in Lima] your heart had been doing all the talking and there was no little door for the reason to filter through.*" But now that 'little door' had been reopened and I felt whole again.

Then, like I'd been holding my breath for a long while, I exhaled. The tension I'd been holding was lifted from my shoulders. I'd broken free from the past. I was ready to take on whatever lay in the future, but what did it hold? With Kilimanjaro still in view, I reflected that, just beyond it, was the great expanse of the Serengeti and beyond that, and more than five hundred miles to the southwest, was Tabora Region and the village of Urambo where Nick was posted and would spend the next two years. I sighed with melancholy. Here at the top of a mountain where I was privileged to have two of East Africa's, and indeed, the world's, great mountains in my sights, all I could think about was how terrible our separation was going to be.

The exhilaration I'd experienced whilst riding up had fallen rather flat, so I slowly walked back to my motorcycle and headed into Muka Mukuu and back to the house I was sharing with John Maddox, a fellow Scot, but Nick's morose antithesis.

***

Eighty pairs of eyes were fixed firmly on me as I walked into a huge, barn-like classroom. Whereas many students at WAC had often treated our lecturers with a combination of drink-induced lethargy or bored indifference, I looked around and saw a room full of youngsters that were eager to learn. The problem? I'd basically spent four weeks at Kitui studying the basics of Kiswahili, a language which, I was soon to find out, came only a poor third behind my students' tribal language, Kikamba and then English. Fortunately, many of the students were passably trilingual, using Kikamba to communicate between each other, English as a language of commerce, and in their case, learning, and the sorry third, Kiswahili, to communicate between tribes. The solution might've been for me to learn Kikamba, but I soon discovered that, in common with the Welsh, the students tended to switch to a language I couldn't understand to continue talking to each other when I came into the room, so basically, it would have been futile. However, if I'd been teaching in school or college in the coastal region of East Africa, I'd have been in luck. It just happens that Kiswahili is the lingua franca of the East African coastal region that includes Kenya and Tanzania. Basically, their Kiswahili is excellent, they have no other tribal language, and at least in Kenya, their English is usually pretty good. Mind you, the coast is a stronghold of Islam, so they'd probably just switch to Arabic, a language they have to learn for the mosque, so you just can't win!

As you might expect, basic language misunderstandings were fairly common. For instance, here's an example of the difficulties. One morning, I was giving a talk about problems suffered by dairy cows and got onto the subject of milk fever and mastitis. Naturally, because of the subject matter, I'd have to talk about udders and milk, but unsurprisingly, I saw rows of blank faces because nobody knew what the hell an udder was, so, instead, I used the Kiswahili word, 'kiwele'. Like a person who'd just played what they thought was a winning card in poker only to find it was to no avail, I was momentarily flummoxed, so instead, I blurted out the Kiswahili word for milk, maziwa. I then immediately got a response, but not the one I was expecting, everyone burst out laughing. By using an incorrect pronunciation, I'd just said the word for woman's breasts, or it could also be lakes, it just depended on context. Unfortunately, many Bantu languages, including Kiswahili and Kikamba are rife with homonyms, or multiple-meaning words; it's a minefield, which often provided much humour and amusement for the students!

Whilst homonym slip-ups could be amusing, there was one language faux pas I made early on in my lecturing "career" that I never made again. This time it wasn't a homonym; it was a mispronunciation of the Kiswahili word for the number ten, or kumi. In my first frustrating week of teaching, I'd already reduced my speed of delivery from an average of about one hundred words per minute to a crawl of less than half that. So I assumed, like many Brits trying to communicate with people from other countries, that if someone doesn't understand something when you speak slowly you just have to repeat the word louder. Thus, when I saw looks of incomprehension when I was talking about the litter size and the number of teats a sow has, I repeated the number ten in English a few times and then had a brainwave and switched to the Kiswahili word kumi. I then repeated the word kumi several times, getting louder and louder in my frustration as the students at the front looked more and more blank. Then it occurred to me that there was a gender difference in the looks I was getting in which the boys appeared to be trying to stifle their hilarity whilst the girls looked totally shocked. Eventually, one of the older girls, actually a mature student, quietly came over to me and said, 'Please Ms Debbie, but I think you are speaking the word kumi wrongly.' She then moved closer and said, 'It sounds like you are shouting the Swahili word for vagina!' She then giggled and said, 'I think it is funny, but some of the girls will be quite embarrassed!' It was then my turn to look very embarrassed, and my face and neck went completely red. Being unfamiliar with such a rapid skin colour change, it takes a trained eye to spot when a black person is blushing, the woman who'd just put me straight about kumi got quite concerned and rushed to my aid and helped me to a chair thinking I was suffering a fit or a stroke of some kind!

***

Rather than sitting in a classroom and listening to me wittering on for hours, an excellent alternative way for the students to learn was through practicals. Three livestock projects were ongoing at the polytechnic when I arrived, dairy cows, fodder crop production and rabbit keeping. Rabbit projects were one of the longest established, so, naturally, I was able to organise a student project from the outset. The German aid organisation running Muka Mukuu, GAT, was very keen on rabbits as an alternative source of animal-based protein in a diet that was, by and large, largely protein-deficient; remember my earlier introduction to the stodgy maize-meal staple, ugali and uji, that I encountered when I was up in Kitui? Rabbits required simple housing that was small and easy to construct. Rabbits could also put on weight and produce meat rapidly with minimal fodder intake, an important factor when you consider that, as individual farmer plot size continued to fall as existing family plots, or shambas, were subdivided between family members, access to fodder was a severe problem because most, or all of a family's one or two-acre plot was required for food production. Rabbit keeping seemed like a great way to improve diets, so I thought, why didn't everybody eat rabbits as a staple?

My first foray into rabbits involved a feeding and meat-production trial where I had the students set up an experiment that involved two breeds of rabbits that had been supplied by the Ngong Farmers Training Centre. Results from previous trials with improved New Zealand bunnies had been quite poor so I thought they hadn't properly considered different aspects of husbandry including fodder type, age of bunnies and the genetic quality of bucks (males) and does (females). Throwing all this into the pot, or in this case rabbit stew, we came up with a trial involving ten cages and three different sources of feed, household slops, local weeds and grasses and specially produced fodder crops including protein-rich leaves from the leguminous shrub, Leucaena. All fine and dandy I thought, the trial would demonstrate the value of specially produced forage, or a mixture of forage with household feed. With the addition of improved bucks and does, we should get a decent increase in production. The trial was a disaster and demonstrated that it really didn't matter what you did, production stayed the same. That was until I discovered the real reason.

GAT and the polytechnic extension staff had been pushing the benefits of rabbit for meat production for years, but nobody had stopped to think why rabbit keeping hadn't become widespread. So I decided to ask around and listen to the answers I got from students. What I discovered was, that for Kamba people, rabbit keeping was the preserve of children of the family, usually under ten years old, so, basically the rabbit trials were being performed by kids that didn't care about production, they were just keeping rabbits for fun or because they'd been told to. The second reason involved black magic. Stretching across the continent from West Africa, through Nigeria, Cameroon, and more recently, East Africa, rabbits amongst other animals with paws, like cats, are bad juju. Evidence of this comes from the ongoing slaughter of lions for their paws, which are then used in magic potions in occult rituals. Going back in time, cats and the occult have been linked with witchcraft in Europe and the UK for hundreds of years; just think of Halloween and a witch's familiar, the black cat. So, basically, for many African people, eating a rabbit is about as taboo as Mrs Jones killing and preparing Timmy her faithful moggy as an evening meal!

***

It was Sunday, and supposedly my day off, but I'd spent all morning, and most of the afternoon, at my desk. With the consequences of my dual role already beginning to bite, I had to work in what little spare time I had just to keep up. Since there was no formal syllabus for the classes I'd been asked to teach on animal husbandry at the polytechnic, for the first month I'd had to devise one on the hoof, so to speak. However, I desperately needed something written down that I could use for planning and to leave behind as a legacy for others, perhaps for VSOs that might follow me. Around me on the desk were dozens of texts on fodder, cattle breeds and ruminant digestion that I'd found in the polytechnic library. I've never been very good at speed reading texts, so I had to methodically read through the relevant sections and make notes; at least the books were in English! Earlier, the sound of the front door slamming indicated that John had left for his intended evening drinking session down at the Chairman's Bar, so as it began to get dark at around six p.m. I thought, what the hell, and decided to join him.

Hopping on my Suzuki, I cruised down the hill and into the gathering evening air. The short rains were well and truly over and I was heading towards my first Easter in East Africa. As I entered the town, I needed to carefully avoid the snarling packs of dogs, crowds of chickens and excited children running into my path. As always, the bustling town of Ol Donyo Sabuk invaded my senses, and demanded my attention. I'd been a fairly regular sight around town for the last three months, but I still received wide-eyed, incredulous looks from groups of women and shrieks of delight from children as I rode by. I thought to myself, 'guys, get over it! Yes, I'm a woman, and yes, I'm driving a motorbike!'

The Chairman's Bar was really just a sagging, rectangular mud-brick building like all the structures around it. The place was painted bright blue and it invariably had Zairian dance music blaring out of a couple of speakers near the entrance. You could choose to sit at one of the tables outside, slump at the bar or sit at one of the tables inside. There were three fridges, two contained crates of beer, one of Tusker, the other of White Cap. The third fridge was filled with crates of Cola-Cola. Oh, and you could get food. Usually this consisted of a fried, sugar-coated doughy thing called a mandazi. Or, if you were lucky, somebody was frying chicken on a charcoal stove (jiko) nearby, so you could get kuku ya choma, or roast chicken, a bit like Kentucky fried chicken, but it tasted a lot better. It was a simple formula, but it worked, and on occasion, it got you rather drunk so you had to walk home up the hill instead of driving.

Sure enough, John was sitting at a table outside with Sato, a jovial, and somewhat irreverent, JICA volunteer.[79] Like VSO, JICA provided volunteers for grassroots-based projects in Africa and elsewhere. And like me, Sato was an extension worker who'd been thrown in at the deep end as an agricultural instructor at the polytechnic, so we were kind of kindred spirits. I said he was jovial, but unlike other JICA volunteers at Muka Mukuu, Sato's sense of humour went way beyond what would be considered normal by the standards of most JICA volunteers, and probably most Japanese for that matter. I had the impression that Sato was, what they used to call a 'star ship captain' a person immersed in drug taking to a level that had inflicted lasting, mind-altering effects!

No sooner had I joined them at their table with a bottle of cold Tusker, a cow burst out of the butcher's shop opposite followed by a shouting group of six men wielding pangas in hot pursuit.[80] I was quite taken aback by the sudden appearance of an angry mob in the street, however, Sato, who continued to puff on his cigarette, appeared

---

[79] Japanese International Cooperation Agency
[80] Machetes.

366

unperturbed by this macabre scene, just said, 'You see Debbie, this is how they make the Kenyan version of Sushi around here. It's better to eat the meat raw, cooking it just makes it more tough.'

John interjected.

'This guy's crazy,' he said in the calm, cultured version of his Scots accent that sounded like Sean Connery. 'You're the equivalent of a bloody culinary Kamikaze pilot Sato! You'll get worms or worse!'

I'm shocked by John's rather non-PC comment, but Sato's not offended and just laughs saying, 'There is worse John, it's not just food, I think I'm becoming a sexual Kamikaze!'

He'd definitely grabbed our attention. John raised his eyebrows and said, 'Go on, please tell us the gory details.'

'I shouldn't say this,' he said, 'but I have been seeing one or two of the "ladies of the night", as you call them, when I've been in Nairobi.'

Becoming somewhat outraged, I said, 'Sato! That's far too much information for me thank you!'

They both laughed, but I was mortified and would have said more, but John cut me off and reverting to the previous subject, he said. 'Sato, my friend, I keep telling you, you need to *pressure cook* the meat before eating it, otherwise it's like trying to eat boot leather and you'll end up with a tapeworm the size of an elephant.'

Whilst he was speaking, the men who'd been chasing the cow, returned with the eviscerated, bleeding and fly-covered carcass suspended by its legs and tied to a wooden pole that was being carried between four of them. After all this excitement, and the revelation that he'd been regularly using prostitutes on his visits to Nairobi, Sato decided to change the subject and entertain us with a lost in translation story he'd heard about a very serious Japanese volunteer who'd lived with his housemate at Muka Mukuu. He said, 'This volunteer's name was Kuma Moto. He was working at an agricultural extension project to improve rice production around Kisumu near Lake Victoria. He had asked the elders to introduce him to a group of farmers, but he became very angry when they had refused. Since this went against Japanese protocol, he had ordered them to do so. The youngest of the elders was, therefore, told to introduce him. But when he said the volunteer's name, Mr Kuma Moto, there was a shocked silence from the farmers. One or two of the younger men began to laugh. The volunteer was outraged and he asked why his name was so funny. One of the elders took him aside and said that kuma moto is Kiswahili for hot vagina!' John had evidently heard Sato's story before, however, I'd already had my own vagina moment in front of the polytechnic students, so I really felt for the guy!

Wishing to change the subject and get away from the currently male-centred jocularity of our conversation, I decided to mention a letter I'd received from Alan, a fellow VSO volunteer and previous occupant of the house I was now sharing with John. I'd briefly met Alan before he finished his posting and returned to England. Alan had confided in me then that he and John had 'agreed to disagree' on most topics, including the polytechnic and life in general. Reading between the lines, I could see that they'd had a rather strained relationship. To avoid conflict, it sounded like they'd basically kept themselves to themselves, and in any case, John had spent most weekends in Nairobi with his Kenyan girlfriend, Dorothy (Dot). However, Alan's letter was really quite singular. He'd started by urging me to "read and then destroy, or eat it" which had piqued my interest! Thinking he was being droll by referring to the TV show, Mission Impossible and its famous tagline, *"this tape will self-destruct in five seconds..."* but after reading it, I'd decided he was being serious! Besides some further "health warnings" about John's moodiness and tantrums, Alan had gone into great detail about his suspicions regarding corruption and nepotism at both the cooperative and the polytechnic. One person in particular came in for criticism, the settlement manager, Willi Mbenge. Since Mbenge was going to be key influencer on what breed of cows we were going to purchase for the zero-grazing demonstration project, I was interested to know what I was going to be up against, so I leaned in conspiratorially and casually said, 'What do you guys think of Mbenge the settlement manager?'

The two men were quiet for a moment, then Sato began to speak, but John cut him off.

'I know what you're going to say Sato, you're going to be all polite and Japanese, but I'm going say it how it is, Mbenge is a thief! He's been misappropriating funds from the settlement for years. By all accounts, he's a US dollar millionaire and he's in cahoots with several influential members of the cooperative, including two permanent secretaries in

KANU, a few senior governmental advisors and a retired general in the Kenyan armed forces no less.[81] You might ask why, when most members are subsistence farmers, are such people interested in Muka Mukuu when most of them live in swanky houses on the outskirts of Nairobi? The answer is that, as members, they can influence money coming into the project from Kenyan and foreign governments. There's two thousand five hundred members, so there's plenty of scope for money to go missing!' Then even John lowered his voice and continued, 'I've heard that Moi himself takes an interest in the estate, so it doesn't get any higher up the food chain than that!'

Sato shook his head and said, 'John, man, you need to watch what you say. It's not just out of politeness that I avoid saying anything; it's not safe to be so critical. You ask Chege, he's the Kenyan guy who's staying with Noboro and me,' Sato turned to me and said, 'Noboro's another JICA volunteer, I don't think you've met him yet. Chege is doing research at the estate; he's got a PhD at the University of Nairobi. He's really nervous about saying anything about senior people at Muka Mukuu in general. His dad, Professor Henry Njenga, was recently arrested for supporting the opposition party. Chege's basically hiding out at our house until things settle down. He's really nervous about political stuff. You might think Mbenge is what you call a buffoon in public, but he dislikes mzungus and I just don't trust him.'[82]

In response to Sato's last comment, John lapsed in the Glaswegian brogue he used when he was having one of his tantrums and said, 'Bollocks te the lot of 'em, I'm no afraid o' them, they kin go an' stuff themsels for all I care! They don't know bugger all. They'd probably argue aboot the colour o' sh*te if they did'na talk so much of it themselves!' With that, John pushed back his chair, but as he headed towards the bar, he turned and said, 'Are we here to drink or what! What are you hav'n Sato?'

While John was at the bar, Sato said, 'John's making himself a lot of enemies Debbie. He's rude to the students and they dislike him. He needs

---

[81] Kenyan African National Party. In 1986, its president was Daniel arap Moi. Moi ruled Kenya with an iron hand for twenty-four years and ruthlessly suppressed all opposition, including the unofficial opposition party, Mwakenya.
[82] Kiswahili for white people, or westerners. The term is used in a mildly deprecating way.

to watch what he says.' Then, lowering his voice further, Sato continued, 'He wouldn't be the first white person to simply disappear around here. The Kenyans remember the old days and what the white settlers did to them. I'm sure that some of them would like to get their own back if they could.' And with that sobering thought, we had another round of beers and I allowed the conversation to go back to male jocularity, it was much safer!

Chapter 43
An unexpected visitor

Late Saturday afternoon. With the help of three of the polytechnic students, I'd spent all day, and off and on during the previous two weeks, harvesting the zero-grazing unit fodder trial project. It had been a disaster from the outset. Planted on waterlogged ground at the start of the short rains in the December before I arrived, the soil's low oxygen content meant that many of the seeds didn't germinate and those that did grew badly. But I'd continued the trial because I was worried that we might not have enough stored fodder for the cows when the extension team selection committee, headed by Mbenge and his cronies, finally got around to deciding on which breed to purchase. Over the last three weeks, the temperature and humidity had been steadily climbing as we approached the long rains that were due to start towards the end of April. All day, mosquitoes had buzzed and sweat had poured down my back and dripped from my brow into the headband of my straw hat as we used hand-sickles to cut plots of lucerne, bana and napier grass. Helping me was a group of polytechnic students, Peter, Mary and Agnes. They were using cheap sickles imported from China that might have been made from recycled tin cans, as they seemed to bend at the slightest provocation. I, on the other hand was using an almost new serrated Japanese sickle that Sato had lent me. I'd thought this would give me an advantage, but they were still going faster than I was! Even though I was wearing gloves, the sharp fronds, particularly of the napier grass, chaffed my forearms, it was a bit like repeatedly receiving a paper cut. Sweat then aggravated the cuts and gave me a rash, but pulling down my shirt sleeves just made me sweat more! Just as I was cursing this classic vicious cycle, raucous bird sound made me look up. A flock of lilac-breasted roller birds had landed in the trees, presumably to feed on the cloud of insects we were raising from the grass plots. Their grating calls sounded like they were laughing at us, as well they might! Who but a foolish mzungu would go out in thirty-five degrees heat and wrestle with huge clumps of six-foot high grass armed with just a sickle? Noël Coward's little ditty mocking the colonial British in India sprung to mind, *"mad dogs and Englishmen go out in the mid-day sun!"* As I watched, the rollers took off and wheeled overhead, but one of them landed on a clump of grass nearby and cocked a questioning eye at me. Fixing him with a hard stare, I put my hands on my hips and shouted, 'And what are you staring at!'

Peter nudged the two girls and said, 'Miss Debbie has had too much sun, she's talking to the birds!' They all laughed, and finally seeing the funny side, I joined in.

At two o'clock, once we'd finished cutting the last of the bana grass plots, we stopped for a break before loading the trailer. I handed around some flapjacks I'd made using oats I'd found on a shopping trip to Nairobi. Mixed with molasses, I thought the oats made a very passable flapjack.

Peter bit into one and said, 'These are very good, are they mkate wa sinia?'[83]

Unsure what that was, I said, 'They're made from oats and molasses.'

At that, Peter stopped eating his.

'We use molasses to make silage for the cows! You eat the same food as cows in England!'

I laughed and shook my head.

'No, well it's sort of the same, but they taste good right?' Everyone nodded; at least we were agreed on that.

After we'd fed the grass we'd harvested through hand-operated chaff cutters, we added the molasses and sheeted the silage clamps. Phew, job finally done! I was exhausted and ready for a shower and a cold beer. I thanked my helpers and they disappeared back to their dormitories for an evening meal. I didn't envy them their piles of stodgy ugali, but it would've been nice to think that John and Dot might've cooked something. I thought, dream on Debbie!

Back at the house, I entered the kitchen to be confronted by piles of washing up. All the pans had been used and so had most of the plates. It looked like John and Dot had been having another one of their duvet days

---

[83] Rice cakes, a popular Kenyan dessert.

and had left everything lying in the sink. Just as I was surveying the wreckage, as if to confirm my suspicions, Dot appeared at the door of John's room wrapped in her kanga, and ignoring me completely, she padded across the hall to the bathroom and banged the door. I checked the fridge, there weren't any leftovers to eat and now Dot had locked herself in the bathroom, so I couldn't freshen up. John's pet name for her was Malaika, meaning angel in Kiswahili, but in John's presence, she acted more like the Queen of Sheba, leaving her clothes lying around the washing basket and her dirty dishes in the sink. The place was starting to resemble a college student dorm. Dot's visits had now become a weekly occurrence. Previously, they'd stayed at her family home in Nairobi at weekends, but I guess they could be more relaxed together here. I could understand it, but John needed to contribute something to the household finances on her behalf, and do the bloody washing-up!

A couple of weeks ago, I'd had enough. I'd confronted John and asked that he contribute something to the household kitty for Dot's food and expenses. Predictably, he'd exploded in rage and I was concerned that he might become violent. Even though Dot was staying, it was unlikely she'd have intervened, she and John seemed to have a very traditional relationship, and in Kenya, the man is the top dog. That afternoon, when they'd gone out, I'd phoned the field director, Chris Robertson, to explain the situation. He gave me a sympathetic ear, but he said, 'Debbie, I really think you need to build bridges with John and try harder to live together. You know that John has requested an extension to his posting?' I was shocked. I could've put up with the situation for six months, but now I'd be sharing with John for another year at least. It was clear that VSO wasn't going to help and Chris didn't show any inclination towards understanding my predicament.

In another bizarre twist, I'd been warned by Tamsin, a Dutch veterinary nurse volunteer, that the Muka Mukuu rumour-mill had been going into overdrive about the fact that I, a single woman, was sharing a house with two single men, John plus our recently-arrived German interim, called Gerhard. As a result, it now seemed like the men on the estate had decided I was "fair game" and would go with anyone. As if to confirm this, a few days ago, one of the estate accountants, Thomas Mburu, asked me to meet him in his office on the pretext that he wanted to discuss project finances and the upcoming purchase of the cows. Whilst we were discussing suppliers and the cost of different breeds, at some point in our conversation, Thomas started stroking my thigh. Trying desperately to ignore it in the hope he'd stop or get the message when I didn't react, he then asked me out on a date. I was mortified. I made it clear that I had a boyfriend who would be visiting soon, but all he'd said was, 'You have so many men, why can't I be one of them!'

'Christ!' I thought, 'I'm assailed on all sides either by men that want sexual favours, or controlling men that seem hell-bent on driving me crazy with their pedantic fussing.'

Whilst I was mulling over my predicament, Gerhard walked into the kitchen and said, 'Are you all right Debbie? I hope you don't mind, I've taken your clothes off the washing line and put them in your basket so I could hang mine out.' He passed me my basket. All my clothes had been neatly folded. Then, being a kindly soul, Gerhard suggested we go for something to eat in the Blue Post Hotel in Fourteen Falls. 'Sato will be there with Chege.' Pausing, he looked around the bomb site of a kitchen, and said, 'It looks like you need to drown your sorrows!'

An hour later, we were sitting outside the Blue Post wolfing down Kuku choma na wali accompanied by a cold beer.[84] This side of Nairobi, it didn't get better than that! Sato paid for all of us. The fact was Sato and the other JICA volunteers got reasonably good salaries, so he saw it as his "duty" to be generous, but when I thought about it, compared to what I actually took home from some of the jobs I'd had as a farm worker in the UK, the money wasn't that bad. On several farms, I'd had to pay for my accommodation. Then there were bills and food. On one occasion, I'd even had to pay for milk while I was working on a dairy farm! Whereas, at Muka Mukuu, accommodation was free, transport, electricity and so on was all thrown in, all I needed to pay for was food and the occasional beer. I even had holiday and the odd weekend off; I was actually saving money!

Arriving a little late, Chege introduced himself. He was slim, well-dressed in expensive, American-branded clothing and his English was excellent. Sato had mentioned that he was doing some research, so when I asked him about it, he said, 'It's really just a study on what impact the

---

[84] Roast chicken with rice.

Muka Mukuu cooperative has had on living conditions of cooperative members and the contribution it's made to the region as a whole.' Apparently not wanting to say anything more about what he was doing, he changed the subject and said, 'Before I did my PhD, I studied for a Master's degree in Politics and International Relations at Oxford University. I have hopes of getting into politics, but the current situation in Kenya makes it very difficult. Basically, if you're opposed to what KANU is doing, you're in danger of being arrested. It's pretty much a one-party system here in Kenya. Elections are rigged. There's no secret ballot, on election day, you have to literally line up behind your chosen candidate, there's bullying and intimidation, so most people line up behind the KANU candidate. It's a terrible situation.' Whilst he was speaking, Chege's eyes were constantly swivelling from right to left, checking to see if anyone was trying to listen in to our conversation. I'd never thought of Kenya as a dangerous or secretive country, but a few minutes listening to Chege was changing my mind.

I was in the process of making my own surreptitious sweep around to check on passers-by, when Peter, one of the crew of polytechnic students I'd been working alongside earlier in the day, rushed up and said, 'Miss Debbie, there is someone, an English man, looking for you. He was asking about you at a shop down the road, so I came to find you.' I couldn't imagine who it was, but guessed it might be somebody from the VSO field office, after all, I'd recently made a complaint about John, but it was rather late for them to come calling.

By now, it was fully dark, so I followed Peter through the throng of people who always seemed to come out to socialise in the evening. Sure enough, there was a white guy standing outside a row of shops. In the light of the multi-coloured bulbs strung above the doors, I could just about make out that he was dishevelled-looking and wearing... military-style clothing, 'oh my God', I thought, 'it's Nick!' I shouted his name, but when he turned towards me, I was doubly shocked, his face was so pale and gaunt I hardly recognised him as the same man I last saw more than three months ago. We hugged each other, and for a moment, the outside world no longer mattered. People, motorbikes, dogs, children, hooting cars and the whole crazy world of Kenya swirled around us, but we didn't care.

***

'Damn!' In the mauve half-light that often came before an African dawn, I was rummaging around the kitchen shelves where I should've found some pots and pans. After ten minutes of fruitless searching, I concluded that John had locked all the kitchen utensils in his room. Recently, this had become a routine occurrence every time John was aggrieved about some wrongdoing on my behalf. You might think such behaviour was quite childish if it wasn't that it had a serious intent, namely, to cause me aggravation. In this case, my misdemeanour was to bring a man into "his" house. Perhaps this, in some way, threatened his alpha male status, who knows? Initially, my plan had been simple, leave Nick sleeping the slumber of the dead whilst I cooked us some pancakes for breakfast, but now it had become complicated, a mission, where I needed to first find some pans, cutlery, and cooking spoons before I could even start. Rather than lose my temper, I did the little counting to ten routine I'd learnt during my early days on farms. By the time I'd reached seven, I'd come up with a solution, rather than play John's little game by knocking on his bedroom door and asking ever so politely if I could, at his lordship's earliest convenience, please can I have some of the GOD DAMN KITCHEN EQUIPMENT YOU'VE GOT STASHED IN YOUR ROOM! I'd be ever so grateful! 'Sod that', I thought. 'I'll borrow the stuff I need from Sato.'

It was still early, but since he was a hard-working soul, I knew Sato would be up and about, so I drove over to his place. Sato, Noboro and Chege lived a few miles away in a rather palatial old colonial house on the other side of the estate near the McMillan castle. It was a pleasant drive in the coolness and already dazzling sunshine of the early morning. On the equator, dawn, and nightfall for that matter, came with unwonted speed at six o'clock sharp. It was either light or dark, like somebody switching a light switch. To be honest, I missed the gloaming you get in England where the half-light of early morning or late evening gives you time to prepare for the daily transition into day or night. But hey, the all-year-round great weather in Kenya certainly made up for this minor defect! Sato's had been one of the managers' houses back when the

McMillans ran the estate. Part of the McMillan castle was used by the Muka Mukuu Cooperative as its HQ; Döeffler had an office in the castle and also a house nearby that he shared with his wife Annette. Within the same little enclave of luxurious colonial dwellings lived the estate consultant, Mike Norris and his wife, Pippa with their playful Dalmatian, Terror. Mike and Pippa were one hundred percent gold-plated remnants of Britain's colonial past. They were fourth generation white Kenyans. Mike's great grandfather, like many others at the time, had been lured over to East Africa by easy money and the promise of freedom from the strictures of a Victorian England where war with Germany had loomed large. According to Mike, whilst Europe endured the ravages of the First World War, colonial residents of Happy Valley, a moniker coined by McMillan himself for the sunny vales along the Athi River, enjoyed a life of drug-taking and easy morals that included wild wife-swapping orgies. To this day, Kenyans puzzle over why, as a childless couple, the McMillans needed a house with eleven bedrooms. 'Well,' I thought, 'that would be to accommodate wild, wife-swapping parties of course!' As I passed the castle, I wondered whether McMillan's decision to sell the estate into Kenyan ownership was a last-ditch attempt at redemption as the Pearly Gates beckoned, who knows.

Arriving at Sato's house, I shut down the motorbike and cautiously called out, 'hodi.'

To which I got an answering 'karibu' from the Askari guarding the house.

During this little ritual, a visitor is basically saying, 'Hi, friend, I'm here' to which your would-be host replies, 'Welcome'. This procedure reduces the chance of there being a misunderstanding that might result in you getting shot dead by the Askari, or the residents for that matter! Well, possibly not shot. To avoid the tiresome business of getting a firearms certificate that required you to part with about one thousand Kenyan shillings plus pay the usual bribes, Askaris used a simple bow and arrow as their weapon of choice. Apparently, they were quite accurate, and they're silent. After all, there's no need to wake the whole household whilst you deal with a band of marauding thieves! As I walked over to the house, the now disarmed and friendly Askari approached, smiled and waved at me whilst I politely knocked on the back door fly-screen. When Sato's unkempt-looking face appeared out of the gloom of the kitchen, I apologised profusely. It looked like he was recovering from a hard night on the bottle; however, he still managed to give me a buffoonish grin.

'Oh, Debbie. Wait, I'll come out to you, I don't want to wake the others.' Sato shoved on a pair of boots and shuffled outside. Still swaying slightly, he said, 'After the Blue Post, I went over to Mike's house last night to have a few more beers. All was okay until he brought out a bottle of Scotch whisky.' He paused and shook his head, 'Then it got really bad... Oh, I heard already that you have a visitor.'

'Wow! The jungle telegraph works fast! How did you know so fast? I thought I'd managed to sneak him away without anyone noticing!'

Sato laughed and winked.

'Y'know, smoke signals, we have our ways.'

I chuckled to myself and said, 'You won't believe this, my boyfriend turned up unexpectedly at the Blue Post.' It sounded strange and exciting to talk about "my boyfriend", but I suppose it was official: Debbie had a boyfriend.

While Sato reflected on this for a moment, a mixture of emotions played across his usually jovial face. Eventually, he said, 'Mmmh, I think this is true love Debbie. For him to come all this way for you; it's romantic, yeah?' Then, he sighed and said, 'I'm sort of envious. I mean, when I go back to Japan, my family will force me into an arranged marriage, it's terrible.' Then his familiar smile returned and he said, 'That's why I'm having such a great time now!'

We both laughed and I said, 'Look, sorry to be a pain, but John's locked the kitchen stuff in his room again and I want to cook Nick some breakfast. Would it be okay to borrow some pans and cooking spoons?'

Sato threw his arms in the air in a comical show of acquiescence and said, 'Go right ahead and take what you need Debbie. You already have the makings of an excellent wife; cooking breakfast for your man after a night together, how romantic!'

I shook my head.

'Hardly romantic, he was exhausted and slept like a baby all night.' Sato wasn't convinced, so he just winked and gave me a knowing look.

As I was leaving with a clanking cargo of cooking stuff in my rucksack, Sato called out, 'You lovebirds enjoy yourselves!'

When I returned to the house, I stuck my head around my bedroom door. Nick was propped up in bed like a recovering hospital patient. He was pale, but he looked more like his usual self, so I walked over, kissed the top of his head, hugged him close and said, 'I love you.'

Nick smiled and replied, 'I love you.'

We'd exchanged just three words, but in that moment the world I knew before changed forever. I had a love and a partner to share my life. As we held each other, I thought to myself, 'if we don't have another person to witness our lives, do we ever really live?' When you live on your own, there's a kind of ambivalence, you're living, but there's nobody to share your triumphs, offer encouragement to you when you're down, or carry you when it feels like you can't go on any longer. With a partner you can both say, 'yes, we lived, yes, we struggled, yes, we came through together and that's all that matters!' In other words, in that moment, it felt like my life was complete.

***

Thika bus-stand on the Wednesday afternoon before Easter Sunday, that was, at least in 1987, on the 17th April. I'd managed to convince my two guvnors, Döeffler and Josephine, that, since it was Easter, the polytechnic was closed and construction of the zero-grazing unit would be temporarily halted for the public holiday, Muka Mukuu could do without me for a few days. So, with a few precious days ahead of us, Nick and I planned a trip to Kisumu. Situated on the shores of Lake Victoria, Kisumu is Kenya's third-largest town after Nairobi and a port that services a lake steamer that runs between Kenya and Tanzania. Our journey would essentially kill two birds with one stone. The first bird was rather practical. We wanted to test out an alternative route we could use to make further journeys to visit each other that wouldn't involve hours of riding on buses and taxis. The second bird was much less practical but more enjoyable, we were going to spend some much-wished for time together. The only fly in the ointment with the second bird was that I hadn't yet started taking birth control. Reasoning that it would be a year at least before we would see each other, I thought there wouldn't be any point in going on the pill. Oh well, at least VSO had come to the rescue by very thoughtfully including condoms in the volunteer welcome pack I'd received when I checked in at their offices in Nairobi. It was a pack of thirty, so I just hoped it was enough!

It'd been easy enough to locate the bus-stand; we just followed the crowds and the din made by bus boys as they shouted their destinations like touts at the Grand National, 'Naaairobi, Nairobi, Nairobi, Nairobi, Nairobi, Nairobi, Nairobiii…' Herds of white or riotously painted Nissan and Isuzu minibuses vied with each other to pick up potential passengers whilst the bus boys hung dangerously from the running boards. I say twelve-seaters, but buses crammed with many more people than that, swayed dangerously from side to side under the strain. It wasn't just matatus, peddlers of all descriptions and ages were hawking their wares.[85] There were old men selling packs of 'Sportsman' cigarettes from wooden boxes attached to string around their necks like ice cream sellers in the cinema. Then there were women in brightly coloured kangas carrying hundreds of little cellophane bags of roasted karanga piled high in large steel bowls balanced precariously on their heads.[86] Finally, small boys rushed around selling packs of boiled sweets and chewing gum.

There was also entertainment to be had. In amongst this mayhem, on the ground in a corner of the dirt square that constituted the bus-stand a group of cheering spectators were sitting in a circle around a man wearing a taqiya and a flowing white jalabiya.[87] He was seated on a little stool that raised him above his audience whilst he played a snake charmer's pungi. Fascinated by the spectacle, we approached, and sure enough, we could make out the distinctive hood of a king cobra. The snake was swaying backwards and forwards, apparently following the swaying motion of the charmer's pungi as he played his hypnotic music. We were enthralled. So enthralled in fact, that we missed our matatu to Nairobi, but there was always another, so we bought some chai from a

---

[85] An almost mythical creature in Kenya, the matatu is essentially a mini-cab taxi. But it's much more than that, it's a lifeline transporting people and things to villages and towns. Living, as I still do, in rural England I often used to comment that public transport in rural Africa is miles better than it is back home where you're lucky if you see a bus pass though the village more than twice a week!

[86] Peanuts.

[87] The skullcaps worn by Moslem men.

little brightly-painted café, one of several that fringed the bus-stand. Before travelling to Africa, if you'd offered me some strong, milky tea that was laden with spice and up to five heaped spoons of sugar, that's per cup, I'd have said, 'no thanks' in no uncertain terms! But out here, the flavour of ginger, cinnamon and cardamom mingled pleasantly with that of the tealeaves imbuing the resulting drink with life-giving properties. Kenya seemed to, quite literally, run on chai; it's a meal and a stimulant in a cup. To accompany our drinks, Nick, asked a passing cake seller if they had vitumbua, or rice cakes, but she shook her head, and said 'Hamna. Vitumbua siyo na Kenya, ni chakula ya Tanzania!' She laughed and sold him two mandazis instead.

Nick said, 'Wow, these guys speak terrible Swahili! She said that they don't make vitumbua in Kenya. Well, they don't make mandazis in Tanzania.' Biting into his sugary square of dough he said, 'Correction, mandazis are the same as caki in Tanzania.' With that culinary mystery solved, we sat holding hands and contentedly munched our mandazis and sipped our tea. We were in calorific heaven!

***

Having dropped us off at our destination, dust and gravel spurted violently from the wheels of our matatu as it sped off down the road back towards Nakuru. When we'd said that we wanted to visit the lake, the driver had very obligingly made a special detour to drop us off at one of the entrances to the Nakuru National Park that led down to the lake itself. Beads of sweat immediately prickled my skin as we transitioned from the matatu's air-conditioned comfort to the baking heat of a Kenyan afternoon in the Rift Valley. Shading my eyes and peering ahead of us, the distance to the lake seemed a lot further than it looked on the map. Nick pointed out this wasn't surprising since it was a 1:500,000-scale map, so estimating distances from it was like using a school atlas for a walking trip! Also, for some unaccountable reason, neither of us had brought a hat, so I was worried that we'd suffer from serious sunburn or worse.

As we walked, Nick added to my mounting list of concerns about our impromptu and ill-planned first safari together by mentioning that the bus boy had warned us to watch out for "nyoka kubwa sana", or huge snakes. Apparently, he'd been quite graphic, saying that they'd been known to eat small children and animals in their sleep! We thought this was probably the product of his fevered imagination until we twigged that it might be pythons he was talking about. Nick said, 'Mind you, you'd have to be pretty careless, very drunk or exceedingly small to be swallowed by a python, so I don't think we need to worry about them. I'd be more concerned about the hyena and rhinos!'

'Oh great', I thought, well that's all right then!

Ahead of us as we walked, I noticed that the shimmering mirage caused by the intense heat was tinged by a pink mist that appeared to hover above the lake's aquamarine-coloured surface. As we drew closer, the 'mist' resolved itself into hundreds, or probably thousands of pink flamingos wading in the shallow waters. As this incredible spectacle became clearer, a wall of sound met us that I can only describe as resembling a countless number of human conversations melded together into a continuous cacophony. Fringing the lake was what appeared to be a dense woodland where we would find a shelter from the hot sun. However, as we got closer, the woodland turned out to be a rather spiny mix of acacia and cactus-like euphorbia trees. That they existed at all in such a harsh, arid environment seemed like a miracle, but they provided us with some much-needed shade. Under their prickly boughs, it was remarkably cool, so we found a suitable spot near a sandy beach so we could watch the comings and goings of a little colony of weaver birds who'd tethered their neat little basket-like homes to the waving stems of the lake's fringing reed-bed. Stretching away in front of us, little groups of flamingos strutted comically around in the shallow water like dancers in the Bolshoi Ballet. As if to enhance the illusion of ballet dancers, beaks held high, the haughty-looking birds swivelled their heads from left to right in unison with their striding legs like a choreographed dance routine. The life-giving alkaline waters of the soda lake seemed to literally teem with life, a birder's dream in fact. We'd brought a packed lunch of sorts. Our accommodation, the Nakuru Piccalilli Hoteli (we'd both immediately liked the name) didn't sell food or have a restaurant, so we'd cobbled together a few snacks from what we'd been able to buy from street sellers. There was karanga, mandazis and salted, fried cassava chips. As a stroke of genius, we'd asked a chai seller to fill Nick's thermos flask. As we sat contentedly munching, I realised that, up until now, I hadn't yet had the chance to just *be* in Africa. I'd been working non-stop, seven days a week, since I arrived. This was my first chance to actually take in my surroundings; I revelled in the moment. 'More chai darling?' Nick grinned. Getting the irony, I giggled. To a passer-by, we probably looked and sounded like an old married couple already! But we weren't old and we weren't married. The romance of the place momentarily overcame us and kissing would have led to lovemaking if we hadn't been so concerned about the herd of wildebeest heading in our direction!

Back at our room at the Piccalilli, we gave in to our carnal desires. Incredibly, up until that point, we hadn't yet given full rein to our lovemaking. On my mouldy old settee in Garden Cottage, we'd nibbled around the edges so to speak, but we hadn't actually done *it*. Neither had we gone "all the way" at Sarah and Seans' flat in London, even after a serious injection of romance from our night at the opera because at that point we'd been too miserable at the prospect of our parting the next morning. So this was our first time. Like the room, our bed was small, just marginally bigger than a single; this might make sleeping difficult later on, but that wasn't a problem for what we had in mind now. What did concern me was, when Nick undressed, I noticed how much weight he'd lost. He'd been slim before, but after two bouts of malaria since he'd arrived in country plus a meagre diet of rice and beans, I feared that he might be wasting away. As we got into bed together, I had an attack of nerves. Up to this point, I hadn't appreciated how inexperienced Nick was. Fred and Victor had confidently taken control of the situation, but I could see that Nick was hesitant and unsure of what to do, so we sat propped up in bed whilst I talked ten to the dozen about my problems with John and Dot. After a few minutes of this, I realised he'd gone silent. Wanting to reassure myself that this wasn't a completely one-sided conversation, I met Nick's gaze and his piercing blue eyes that were intently focussed on my face. My heart seemed to miss a beat and I took a long breath. Nobody had ever looked at me like that before. Working on farms, I'd had plenty of lecherous glances at my breasts, but nobody had taken the time to *look* at me and see who I was. That was how Nick was looking at that moment. I couldn't resist any longer, so I made the first move and we just melted into each other. Although Nick was still recovering from malaria, he had plenty of energy where it mattered!

Our bodies satisfied, at least for the time being, we once again sat together propped up in bed. In lieu of the then customary post-coital cigarette you used to see actors having in movies, we compared notes instead, so I asked Nick how things were going for him in Tanzania.

'Where should I start? My posting was nothing like I expected it to be. As you know, I'm based in Urambo. But it's more than fifty miles from the provincial town, Tabora, so I'm right out on a limb. There's nowhere to buy petrol out there, so I have to carry jerry cans of fuel in my rucksack when I visit Tabora, so I'm like a human firebomb on my motorbike when I return to Urambo! Then there's Susan the Peace Corps volunteer. She's been working on the Dumuzi project in Urambo for over three years! Nobody from VSO said anything about her being there, but I would've been lost without her. I didn't get my piki-piki for several weeks after I arrived, so I've had to rely on Sue to take me out to villages and introduce me to the mabalozi, otherwise I wouldn't have been able to do anything.[88] I'd have literally gone insane! Sue's been a saviour, but the downside is she's been having a long-running affair with a middle-aged married British expat, Peter Gerry, who lives in Tabora and acts as an advisor to the Dumuzi project — you couldn't make it up! I wouldn't mind, except Peter comes over to stay with Sue occasionally and I have to listen to them going at it in her room at the end of the hall. Then there's the Tabora 'set'. Basically, a clique of VSO volunteers and expats, including Peter Gerry, that live at the Tabora expat compound, a paradise of electricity, running water complete with a swimming pool where Jill, a three-year veteran VSO volunteer, rules the roost. The Dumuzi project, funded by the FAO, is a pest eradication programme involving the application of permethrin insecticide powder to shelled maize to reduce damage from an introduced insect pest, the greater grain borer beetle. Its local name is Dumuzi, or Scania beetle after the make of the lorries that transported Dumuzi-infested maize shipments from the US during a famine in the late 1970s. It's been a serious storage pest in Tanzania ever since. Anyway, I immediately made myself unpopular by questioning

[88] Village elders.

384

whether we should be advising people to put permethrin on food. It's fairly toxic. Also, the company that produces the chemical is part-funding the VSO project — it stinks! Anyway, like Susan has been doing, I'm going my own way and advising the farmers to shell their maize to make it less appetising to Dumuzi. The big problem is that the Wasukuma, a nomadic tribe that's essentially looked down on by the majority of Wanyamwezi farmers, also shell their maize and store it in baskets. Basically, the Wanyamwezi won't be seen dead doing the same thing, so at the moment we have an impasse. But my Tanzanian counterpart came up with a plan to construct kihenge, little mud-brick storage structures that he'd seen being used by one or two of the farmers. He reckons it's a way past the problem. Anyway, I'm a pariah as far as the Tabora set are concerned! So, after just few weeks in country, I've already made myself unpopular, it's got to be some kind of record! There's more! Susan introduced me to her friends in Urambo, who've now become my friends, so I kind of inherited them from her. There's Tchi-Tchi the tailor who's been making me these snazzy shirts, the storekeeper, Patel, who sells just about anything, and Una, and her family from Eritrea who own the Urambo Stores. Back in Tabora, there's Jeff, a crazy Californian Peace Corps volunteer and his Tanzanian girlfriend, Tabu, Jeff's fellow Peace Corps, Katrine Swartz who's going out with a colourful local character called Charles Kisco who works in the Kilimo's (Agriculture Department) office. Recently, I met Charles. He said that he'd broken his leg badly in a piki-piki accident. The Peace Corps volunteers in Tabora clubbed together to pay for Charles' private hospital treatment, otherwise he would've had to have his leg amputated for sure. But you know what, Katrine said that when she asked the Brits if they could contribute, they refused point blank, how mean is that?'

'Phew!' I thought. It all sounded much more interesting than my posting at Muka Mukuu! First-time nerves gone, and our initial urgency dissipated, we fell back to lovemaking. After a while we finally came up for air. Nick's face radiated a pure joy I hadn't seen before. He said, 'I love you so much my darling. Sometimes I don't know how to express it. It drives me mad. I guess I'm insanely in love!'

Cupping his face with my hands, I said, 'It's the same for me. I've never been so sure of anything.'

Then Nick kissed me and said, 'Let's get married when we get back home.' Startled at first, I immediately realised that this was what I'd wanted him to say from the first time we met, but for once, words failed me and all I could find to say was, 'yes!'

***

Back in the day, the wives and sweethearts of seamen and lovers separated by war, exchanged locks of hair or silhouettes mounted in sliver lockets. On our final evening together back in London, we must have experienced something like the same sense of impending loss and wanted to exchange something that would act as a reminder. After all, if that seafaring hero and philandering cad, Lord Horatio Nelson, could do it, so could we! However, short of time and cash, we weren't able to run to the kind of elaborate and expensive engraved gold lockets that Horatio exchanged with his mistress, Lady Hamilton.[89] Instead, we exchanged cherished personal items, I, a silver neck chain that I'd worn for years, and Nick, his wristwatch; much to the chagrin of his mother who'd apparently given it to him for his birthday! That was over five months ago and we'd come a long way since then. Now that Nick had 'popped the question' so to speak, we felt fully justified in spending a pleasantly romantic afternoon looking for a pair of affordable rings that would serve to celebrate our engagement. Like the pair of lovesick college preppies in the 1970s weepy, Love Story, we scoured the shops in Kisumu's bustling markets on the shores of Lake Victoria. Despite the town's rather dusty and dilapidated appearance, a romantic setting for wedding engagement ring-buying could probably not be found anywhere else in the world; anyway, at least we thought so. Apart from being a port providing sporadic and rather unreliable passenger and cargo services to Mwanza in Tanzania, the region is steeped in the kind of romanticised history that you can only find in Africa. Since Speke and Burton first set eyes on it and correctly deduced that it was indeed the long-searched for source of the Nile River, the lake has become the backdrop of hundreds of books and thousands more wild stories. Sitting, as it does, at the confluence of national boundaries between Kenya and Tanzania, it also

---

[89] Which recently sold at Sotheby's for an eye watering £44,000!

includes part of the border with landlocked Uganda. As such, the lake forms a natural trading route linking the Indian Ocean with the interior of Africa; if only successive governments of the three countries could see it like that. Once hailed by the first president of Tanzania, Julius Nyerere, as having the potential to be the nexus of a trading bloc, a kind of East African EEC, the national borders encompassed by the lake were more often closed than open during the 1960s up until the end of the '80s. In fact, in the case of Tanzania, the lake became a resupply route for Idi Amin's forces during Uganda's ill-fated attempt to invade the country in 1978. Of course, all this chaos simply provided a fertile breeding-ground for crime, spawning groups of smugglers and pirates who did, and still do, operate on the lake.

So, we have famous explorers, tales of albeit illegal derring-do, and the odd war, the perfect backdrop for our burgeoning romance! But it's more than human activity that imbues the lake with romance, there's a staggering array of flora and fauna that live on, in, and above its waters. However, not all of this wildlife is fun or beautiful to behold. On a longer than intended walk on our first evening, we stumbled upon a beautiful little wooded bay we later discovered was called Hippo Point.

Suffering from the heat and humidity, I noticed a gregarious group of small boys swimming from a rowing boat that had been moored out in the lake. Feeling the urge for a paddle coming on, I said, 'What a great idea, I could just do with a cooling bathe in the lake.'

At this point, Nick's scientific training reared its sometimes romance-crushing head and he said, 'Mmmh, you notice that big pipe that goes into the lake, I bet that's attached to the sewage plant we can smell. Plus, during our VSO country training we were told to avoid swimming in most, or all of East Africa's lakes, including this one.'

Doubting the first part and noticing an obvious flaw in the second part of Nick's reasoning, I said, 'But those boys are swimming in the lake.'

Nick nodded.

'Yes, but they're swimming from a boat that's out in deeper water. The problem is bilharzia. The parasite undergoes part of its lifecycle in water snails that live in the shallows, but further out, it's safe to swim because you don't make contact with the lake bottom.' Nick then went into an overly detailed description of what bilharzia does to you that was enough to put me off my lunch, let alone swimming! So, Lake Victoria and Kisumu are romantic, just don't go swimming!

Later, as we walked along the town's busy main street in search of somewhere to buy our rings, I despaired that we'd ever find anywhere selling something as non-functional as a pair of engagement rings. If we'd wanted to get our oil changed, or our rear shock absorbers repaired, we'd have been in luck, crowds of mechanical fundis worked on a huge variety of clapped-out cars and vans all along the highway, but as we got nearer the town centre, we struck lucky down a busy side street.[90] In common with towns and cities the world over, shops of a similar type tend to herd together, and Kisumu was no exception. Turning off onto the Gumbi road, we struck the proverbial crock of gold and found a whole street of jewellery shops. Whilst the practicalities seemed to be taken care of by local Kenyans, the sale of gold and precious stones appeared to be the preserve of Arab and Indian storekeepers who imported their stuff from outside Kenya, but we wanted something locally-made, so we persevered. Eventually, after what seemed like hours of fruitless searching, we came upon a group of Maasai women who were selling children's dolls, wood carvings and... beadwork jewellery. As we walked towards them, one of the younger women carrying a baby strapped to her back smiled broadly and said, 'Wapenzi' as she nudged the others and giggled.[91]

Nick said, 'Ndio, wapenzi.' The women giggled some more, while Nick continued and said, 'Tunajaribu kununua...' He paused, and pointed to the ring on the younger woman's finger, 'kwa ruhusi wetu.'

The woman nodded and patted the beaded strings on her neck bracelet and said, 'kwa ruhusi yangu.'

Nick turned to me and said, 'They don't have wedding rings, the Maasai wear wedding necklaces.'

With an excited look on her face, the young woman tapped Nick's arm, and said, 'Nitakufanyia pete maalum ya harusi... rudi baadaye.'

Nick grinned and said, 'Sawa, sawa, baadaye.' The woman nodded and Nick made to walk away.

---

[90] Experts/technicians/people that fix things.
[91] Lovers

By this time, I was getting rather frustrated that I couldn't understand what was going on and said, 'What did she say?'

Nick was beaming.

'She's going to make us a couple of rings specially. She's very sweet. I just hope we can afford the price she comes up with!'

While we waited, we found a coffee shop over the road so we could keep the Maasai in sight. I could see that the young woman was crouching down and had already got to work. By the time we'd finished a couple of very good samosas, I noticed that she looked up and saw us. She then wondered over to where we were sitting. In the palm of her hand were two colourful beaded rings; one slightly smaller than the other, which she indicated was mine. We put them on; they were a perfect fit. Nick smiled at her and said, 'Shilingi ngapi?'

Smiling broadly the woman replied, 'Mia mbili.' Even I could understand that she'd said two hundred shillings, which sounded a lot, but Nick had already paid her. Patting Nick's arm, she smiled broadly and touched her chest with the palm of her hand saying, 'Bahati nzuri na wewe wote' and then she walked away and disappeared into the crowd.

Nick, quite overcome with emotion said, 'She wished us luck. She was lovely, so friendly…' thinking he was going to say something else, I looked into Nick's face and I could see tears in his eyes. I hugged him tight and my eyes began to mist over as well.

'Blimey,' I thought, 'what a pair of old soft-soaps we are!'

***

Standing on the jetty in the early afternoon of our last day together, the scene across the lake was breathtakingly beautiful. The huge expanse of fresh water stretching to the horizon reminded me of Michigan's Lake Huron until I noticed the eyes and ears of a group of hippos bobbing up out of the water. As I watched, high in the sky, a small group of storks flapped ponderously southwards in the direction of Tanzania, where the steamer would soon be heading. At the thought of the steamer leaving, my heart literally seemed to ache and the now familiar weight descended onto my chest. In my pocket, I fiddled with the unaccustomed ring on my left hand. However, this parting was very different from the one I'd experienced when I left Victor sitting in a café in Lima. Now I knew what real love was all about. Nick's letters and now this unexpected visit against all the odds followed by his proposal of marriage, left me in no doubt that we would be together for the rest of our lives once our VSO postings were over. Convinced that our love was rock solid, I worried about the various hazards that abounded, especially when on safari in Africa. My gaze was drawn to the huge white and red painted bulk of the lake steamer as it sagged against the quayside. Like a column of safari ants, crowds of people swarmed up the quay, along the gangway and into the ship where things were being packed, stowed below and piled on the decks. I wondered what the cargo limit was for a ship of this size and asked Nick whether he reckoned it was safe. In answer, he peered over the side of the quay and pointed at a symbol, a circle with a horizontal line though it, painted on the hull of the ship that was just showing above the waterline and said, 'That's the Plimsoll line. My grandfather, George, was in the RAF Air-Sea Rescue Service stationed in Malta during the war, so he knew his stuff when it came to ships. He told me that mark indicates the maximum depth which a vessel can be safely loaded to.' I could see that it was already partially submerged, so it kind of answered my question. I would've been overjoyed if Nick had said it was maybe too dangerous, after all, previous Lake Victoria steamers had sunk with all hands at least twice before. It then struck me that our future travels to see each other over the next year and a half weren't going to be without risk. Buses and matatus crashed and lake steamers sank. Then there were the attacks of malaria, marauding pirates and other wrongdoers to contend with. It felt like we'd barely started our postings, in fact, there were almost two years still to go. I felt deeply concerned that we might not see each other again.

From the depth of my despair, I tried to be cheerful and optimistic, so I said, 'Remember to call in on Mel when you get to Mwanza', Nick looked puzzled, so I explained, 'Y'know, the woman we met on the motorbike course.'

Nick's face lit up.

'Yes, crazy Mel! I wonder how she's getting on. She and Jonathan looked like they were an item by the time we'd finished the course in Reading. There's also Tony and Tracy, the couple that were all over each

390

other before they'd even arrived at the motorbike course! At least we know we aren't alone.'

We hugged and then the ship's horn sounded two long blasts. I nearly jumped out of my skin. It was like the crack of doom sounding on Judgement Day. I held onto Nick for as long as I dared, but worried he'd miss the boat. I let go, but Nick held on like he was never going to find the strength to leave, so I took the lead, gently stepped back from him and said, 'We will see each other again soon, I promise. I'm going to come down to Tanzania in August, that's only three months. We'll both be so busy the time will fly by.'

The fact was I would be insanely busy once the cows arrived, but I worried that Nick was struggling to find enough to do from day-to-day due to slow progress on his project and an endless list of practical setbacks that seemed to impede progress. Like he'd said, "it was like walking through treacle."

Two more blasts from the ship's horn seemed to galvanise Nick into action. His body stiffened, and shouldering his enormous rucksack, he turned to go. After his final wave from the gangplank, I expected to see him emerge at the stern rails, but there was no sign by the time the ship finally pushed away from the quay and turned to head out into the lake. I scanned the starboard rails, no Nick, just a huge crowd of people that seemed to fill every conceivable space on the ship's decks so he probably couldn't get onto the upper decks even if he wanted to. Then, as the ship steamed into the middle of the bay, I saw him at the stern rails at last. My heart leapt and I jumped up and down whilst I waved furiously. The steamer was visible for a long time as it crept slowly out of the bay, but finally it disappeared from view around the point. Only then did I allow myself to cry.

Chapter 44
First milk

During a rare escape from Muka Mukuu, I was travelling in the White Highlands. Not the snowy uplands of Scotl, and but the preserve of the few remaining colonial-era white Kenyan dairy farmers that still remained in the Rift Valley. For almost sixty years, between 1902 and 1962, the central uplands of Kenya were administered for the exclusive use of European, mostly British, settlers. The Rift, home to several volcanoes, is a place of geological conflict; essentially, it's a giant tear in the earth's crust. For not such a lengthy period, the Rift has also been the focus of human conflict. A bone of contention since Kenya's independence, successive Kenyan governments have staunchly resisted calls from opposition groups for a Zimbabwean-style land grab that would have seen white settlers evicted from their lands years ago. In the 1980s, with KANU still firmly in control, such dissenting voices were drowned out by a ruling elite in Nairobi that may have viewed the white farmers with distain, but took a more sanguine approach when it came to the revenue their farms generated in taxes, "better to allow them to die out than drive them out."

On the subject of highlanders, I was travelling with John Maddox as my mechanic fundi. Whilst he didn't hail from the Scottish Highlands, he was Scots and he looked characteristically dour as we rumbled along in the society's old seven and a half tonne Bedford truck with me at the wheel. I was driving, firstly, because I'd had much more experience in handling farm trailers and large vehicles than he had, and secondly, he'd been unable to successfully back the lorry out from where it was parked outside the Muka Mukuu offices, much to the amusement of Sato and a few others that happened to be watching. That was why he was dour, I'd shown him up, but really, I had no intention of doing so, it's just that we had an appointment to keep and we were running out of time. The reason for our trip? We were travelling to a pedigree dairy farm situated in the heart of the White Highlands, at Rongai near Nakuru, where I was going to give the trio of pedigree Jersey cows purchased by the society a visual once-over to make sure they were sound in wind and limb before we transported them back to Muka Mukuu and installed them in their luxurious accommodations at the newly-completed zero-grazing unit.

The lead-up to this momentous event had, as usual, been long and tortuous. It had all started with my involvement in the selection process for the zero-grazing unit manager and ended with the decision to purchase three pedigree Jersey cows. On the face of it, this might sound straightforward, but it's the bit in the middle that was hard, and the devil is, as they say, in the detail. As a candidate for the post of zero-grazing manager[ess], Josephine Mwendwa was remarkable in many respects. First, she was a female, when all the other twelve candidates were male. Secondly, and related to the first aspect, she had reached the relatively ripe old age of twenty-six, yet remained unmarried and childless. Thirdly, she'd been educated at the Muka Mukuu polytechnic and had the skills, local knowledge and training that put her head and shoulders above the other candidates. She did, however, have one drawback, she wasn't related to Willi Mbenge the settlement manager or the polytechnic manageress, Josephine Matuku. Nepotism on the estate being rife, this put her at a serious disadvantage, but I'd fought hard for her and had finally won out when Döeffler supported me with his casting vote. Strike one for Debbie!

I didn't get so lucky on the choice of breed though, that was where Mbenge had really put his foot down. I'd argued that we should be cautious. Purchase some hardy local breed in the first instance so we could experiment with them to get over any initial teething problems. But Mbenge and the extension workers wouldn't hear of it. They wanted purebred exotic cows, Ayrshires, Jerseys or exotic crossbreds. In the end, they voted to purchase pedigree Jerseys. They're small, good milk producers and have fast-growing calves, perfect in the role of a house cow in the relatively cool and closeted environment I'd seen at Steven and Sallys' smallholding when I visited Margaret in Rhode Island, and but a disaster out in Kenya where even the merest whiff of an exotic cow sends the local tsetse fly and tick populations into a frenzy of excitement! Just keeping the poor beasts free of them would require full-immersion dipping once a week, quite a chore for a local farmer, but without it, exotics invariably die within a few months. On the other hand local breeds have some resistance.

Once you've got your cow(s) another problem is water. On an average subsistence shamba, or smallholding, every drop would have to be carried from a well and they'd need a lot of water to keep exotic cows' milk production up. If this wasn't difficult enough, intensive zero-grazing production would require farmers to grow fodder crops to feed the cows, which would significantly erode the area left for food and cash crops. Whilst a zero-grazing set-up with three cows could, in theory, produce as much milk as twelve under normal grazing providing excess milk for sale, the set-up would likely be impractical for most families, especially with exotic cows. If the polytechnic zero-grazing unit was to be truly experimental, we needed to work with different breeds as well as with different housing set-ups. During the crunch meeting where we decided on breed for the unit, my arguments were ignored to the point where I was talking to myself whilst everyone else made their decision. After the meeting I had a quiet word with Döeffler to at least state my case fully for the record.

His response was classic and an object lesson in laissez-faire-ism if there is such a word. He simply said, 'You may very well be right Debbie, but they need to make their own mistakes.'

'Oh well,' I thought, 'at least I tried!'

If the decision-making around breed of cow had been tortuous, the actual purchase had also been excruciatingly slow, included nine steps and took more than a month to complete. After my time in Kenya, I never again felt justified in complaining about requisition processes in places I've worked since! Following the Muka Mukuu purchasing process, you sometimes felt like a traveller in a mythical land searching for something impossibly rare and difficult to find, like a dragon's tooth, or a crock of gold at the end of a rainbow. The start-point was an itemised requisition order that included a reason for the purchase. This then needed to be signed by the polytechnic manager, then signed by the polytechnic committee, signed by the treasurer of the society committee, signed by the general manager of Muka Mukuu, signed by an accountant, signed by the extension team manager, signed by the society chairman and then, and only then, when you had all these signatories in your possession (bear in mind, it took just twenty-five barons to legalise the Magna Carta!) could you actually purchase something. The process was the same whether you were paying three hundred thousand shillings for three pedigree cows or fifty shillings for a pitchfork!

With the nightmare of the purchasing process behind me, we return to where we were at the start of my story and our journey up into the dairy-lands of the Rift Valley to collect the cows. As you climb up into the Rift, the first thing you notice is how the increased altitude transforms the landscape. The grey and rusty-brown palette of the Athi Plains gives way to verdant pastures of Boma Rhodes grass and lush green fields of maize and lucerne. A rich smell of silage, cow muck and drying hay wafted through my open window; this was dairy country. If one ignored pink flamingos on the lakes and the odd volcano, for all intents and purposes we could have been bowling along a lane in rural England. I looked across at the passenger seat and was pleasantly surprised that John had fallen asleep. Boots resting on the dashboard, head slumped back, mouth open and the now familiar Yankees baseball cap pulled firmly down over his eyes, even in the depth of his slumbers John's body language oozed an objectionable insouciance. Focusing back to the road after checking on my passenger, a sign for Rongai flashed past. Damn! John was supposed to be giving me directions; after all, he and Sato had been up to the farm at the end of the previous year when the dairy project started. Needing to pump the brake pedal several times to get a response, the front wheels suddenly locked up and the old truck lurched to one side before coming to a halt causing a trucker cruising behind to give me three belligerent blasts on his air horn. As he slowly passed, the driver leaned out of his window and shouted something unintelligible, and then, realising that a female mzungu was driving, his scowl changed to a tooth-filled smile like that of a Nile crocodile. He slowed almost to a halt beside me on the road, and probably would've stopped for a closer look and a chat. Then he must've noticed John slumped next to me. Immediately the trucker's smile vanished, and he decided to drive on. I chuckled to myself and thought, 'John does have his uses after all.' For future road journeys, perhaps I could create a kind of scarecrow version of John out of straw that I could use to ward off unwanted attention from other drivers.

'What?'

John's monosyllabic contribution to our current navigational problem was unhelpful, but at least he was awake, so I said, 'We've just passed a sign for Rongai, I remember you saying the farm's near there.'

John leant over, peered out of my window and said, 'Yeah, you missed the turn. You'll need to do a U-turn and then take the next left. Once you get through Salgaa, there's a sign. Keep go'n', you can't miss the farm, it's huge.'

Following his directions, I turned off the main road and followed a rutted dirt track that threaded through a small settlement consisting of dilapidated shacks with rusted tin roofs surrounded by stands of withered-looking maize and small fields planted with beans and what looked like sweet potatoes and cassava. The habitations were squalid and the faces of the people that watched us pass had the haunted look of the grindingly poor. These were the people that lived on the other side of the tracks from the white highlanders. A mile or so further on, I spotted a large wooden sign standing next to a pair of tall, white gateposts that formed an arch above the entrance to a farm drive. Underneath a beautifully hand-painted image of a dairy cow, the sign informed me that, "Barina Jerseys were 'breeders of top-quality pedigree Jerseys and Holsteins". I turned into the entrance and followed a long, straight and smoothly graded track that took me past a couple of forty-acre fields, one of maize and the other, a field of cut boma grass, was being worked by ten or more men gathering the hay with pitchforks and stacking it neatly into stooks for drying. To our right, on a small tree-clad rise, stood a grand-looking building that you might've called a mansion house save for the fact that its roof was covered by green-painted corrugated iron rather than tiles. At the end of the track, we passed through another pair of white gateposts and entered an expansive farmyard. Along the opposite side of the yard, was a row of six huge cowsheds. As we passed the one closest to us, I could see a long row of stalls with the familiar bobbing heads of Jersey cows munching contentedly on feed that had just been put out for them. While I was parking the truck, a white Toyota Land Cruiser stopped nearby and woman wearing green overalls got out. Her silvery hair was neatly tied back in a ponytail under her straw hat. As I jumped down from the truck to meet her, I noticed she was tall with a ramrod straight back and that the sleeves of her overalls were rolled up.

This woman looked like she was the boss and she meant business.

'Debbie Best?' she said, but before I could answer, she smiled and said, 'Janet Mills, good to meet you at last.' We shook hands. Up close, I could see that Janet was quite elderly, possibly more than seventy, but she'd worn well. Her tanned face had the fine features and high cheekbones of a woman that, in her youth, must have been very beautiful. Even now, her lively green eyes were striking. In a clipped accent that was somewhere between English home counties posh with an Afrikaans twang to it, she said, 'I'd heard that Muka Mukuu estate had the good sense to employ an experienced stock-woman. Your reputation travels ahead of you Debbie. Mike Norris was here a few weeks ago and he mentioned that you were already trying to inject some practical sense into the training programme at the polytechnic.' She smiled and her eyes flashed. Clearly Mrs Mills wasn't averse to speaking her mind.

At this point, the door of our Bedford truck banged and John wandered towards us yawning and stretching like somebody who'd spent a long journey sleeping, which he had. Looking over my head, and in his direction, Janet scowled as though he were somehow intruding on our convivial tête-à-tête. I could see by the set of her jaw that Janet's first impressions of John were rather unfavourable. As he approached, I said, 'This is John Maddox. He's our alternative technologist at the Muka Mukuu polytechnic.'

Having overheard me introduce him, John shook Janet's proffered hand and said, 'Yeah, I'm the guy with the dubious honour of managing the build'n' of the polytechnic's zero-grazing unit at the moment.'

Janet nodded and said, 'Have you any practical experience of farming Mr Maddox? I'm told you were a submarine mechanic before coming out to Kenya. I think it would be wise for you to have a look at our set-up before you finalise your plans.'

John snorted in derision.

'Not necessary, it's already been built, and besides, it's just a showcase for the cooperative's half-baked ideas on improving dairy production for subsistence farmers.'

'Well, half-baked or not, the buildings have to be fit for purpose. Are you sure you have constructed the floors properly so that slurry can be cleared away efficiently? What about the feeders, are they at the right height?'

Another snort from John, but rather than get into any more detail, he just shrugged his shoulders, stuck his hands defensively in his pockets and said, 'I'm go'n' to wait by the truck, herding cows isn't my thing.' Then, jabbing his chin in my direction, he said, 'I'm just here to help her out, if somethin' goes wrong with truck.'

As John sidled back to the lorry, Janet said, 'Mmh, well, I don't like *his* attitude! Oh well, come on Debbie, let me show you our set-up and introduce you to the cows.'

We walked past the sheds, to a small corral with crush pens at one end where three Jersey cows were sitting patiently on a bed of straw. Reaching into the pen and patting the closest one on the head she said, 'This smaller one's Cleopatra and the other two are Tsavo and Numbari. All of them have had their vaccinations against foot and mouth and anthrax. When we're in the farm office I'll give you a copy of the paperwork. I'll also give you a copy of their details from the herd book. As I said in my letter, Tsavo's in calf. Normally, I wouldn't recommend that you transport her, but since the journey's not too long and on decent roads, I think she'll be all right.'

Even though she knew that John was waiting in the truck, Janet took her time and invited me into the house for refreshments. Through the main door, a long entrance hallway gave onto a large front room with dark, wood-panelled walls that gave a solid and cosseted feeling to the room. Framed old black and white family photographs hung from the kind of special mouldings in the wooden panelling that you often see in stately homes. There was a huge painting of the house over the fire. Everything radiated a reassuring solidity. Leaving the front room, Janet unlocked a door into an annex at the back that was obviously her private study. Shelves full of books lined the walls. A pile of huge ledgers sat on a large wooden desk, which she shifted out of the way to make room for a leather record book she took out of a shelf beside her desk. She then came around to the front of her desk and sat next to me at a coffee table. While Janet was talking me through the cows' records, there was a knock at the door and a maid in a white pinny like you see servants wearing in Victorian melodramas like Upstairs, Downstairs, entered and placed an ornately decorated pewter tray carrying tea and cakes on the coffee table.

I remember thinking that Janet's inner sanctum had a silent old-world feel about it that reminded me of Granny's house, Top Farm.

After we'd finished our tea, Janet checked her watch and said, 'Right Debbie! With Mr Maddox's help, Joseph and Matthew will have loaded the cows into your truck by now, so we shouldn't keep the girls hanging around in there any longer than needs be. If you have any questions, just call me on the numbers I gave you; I usually check in at the farm office from around six thirty in the morning and I'm back at the house around seven in the evening, the rest of the time I'm out and about. Since my husband Reggie died I've had my hands pretty full. With more than two thousand acres of fodder and cash crops and more than hundred workers, the farm's a bit of a handful to say the least. After your VSO posting, if you fancy staying on in Kenya, I could certainly do with the help of a competent young herds-person.' At this, she winked at me and said, 'I think you could fit the bill, Debbie!'

Walking back to the truck, I thought about Janet and her offer and wondered about what she'd be like to work for. But knowing farmers like I do, a cosy business chat is one thing, but working for them is quite another. Janet reminded me of the formidable Mrs Northridge and Northridge's farm where I did some harvest tractor driving my first year after college. I concluded that she'd likely be a very hard taskmistress and extremely difficult to please! However, I appreciated her confidence in me.

***

A couple of days after we'd settled the cows into their new home, I decided I'd have to tackle John about some of the zero-grazing unit's shortcomings. Needless to say, I got the expected reaction.

'That's absolute bollocks! You've bin take'n' far too much notice of that stuck-up old bag Janet Mills. Have you any idea how much work's involved in creating a slant and drain-away under the floor? And where's it supposed to go, once it's gone down into the drain?'

'John,' I said, trying to get a word in, 'the slurry needs to go into a lagoon where it can be stored before it's spread on the land. If we don't have a drain-away, we are going to have to shovel everything manually.

It'll be so time-consuming.'

Whilst we'd been having this philosophical exchange of views, John, Josephine and I were standing up to our ankles in slurry. Early on in the construction of the sheds, I'd noticed how water would build up in the cows' stalls when it rained. With any farm animals that are penned inside for long periods, what goes in must, inevitably, come out, and in the case of our three cows, it was coming out in spades! I knew from first-hand experience how quickly cows' feet could deteriorate if they were fared to standing in slurry for long periods. Plus, a few days previously, Tsavo had given birth to a dead calf. It was difficult to tell what had caused it, but I felt it might've been the result of stress caused by having to adapt to the less than ideal conditions of our set-up. Luckily, it was a bull calf, so not too great a loss, but I worried about the two others. Cleopatra was due to calf in a month's time, and Numbari a month or so after that, so they needed to be pampered to maximise our chances of success. Because they were either stoking themselves before calving or, in Tsavo's case, coming to the peak of their lactation cycle, all three cows were eating their heads off and consuming copious quantities of water. Milk yields were about twelve litres per cow per day, which wasn't bad, but it could have been better, and we needed to ensure they had sufficient water. I hadn't yet broached the subject of shade or our problems with the newly installed water supply that often wasn't working, or when it did, the pressure was abysmally low. In the dry season, when the rain storage pans were empty, this would mean that we would have to manually transport water in a bowser mounted on a hand cart from a well much further away. Fortunately, at the end of May, we were coming into the cool dry season, which would hopefully reduce stress on the animals, but we'd need these problems ironed out when temperature and humidity started to increase as we moved into the short rains. Actually, and I wasn't going to mention it, but to assist with cooling, the roofs of the shed really needed to be much higher and the sheds themselves orientated east-west to create a larger shaded area for the cows during the day. Obviously, the latter would require the sheds to be knocked down and rebuilt; which I doubted anyone would agree to, let alone John! I just wished I'd been around when the plans for the buildings were being made in the first place. I had tried reasoning with

John. Now we had the cows actually in the stalls, it was obvious where the deficiencies were, but all John could see and appreciate was how much work he would have to do to rectify it. I also suspected that a lot of vehemence in his attitude was again down to pride and his damned ego that seemed to get in the way of anything.

As I was getting nowhere with my softly-softly approach, my anger finally boiled over and I said, 'John! You are not making these changes for my benefit! I'm only concerned for the well-being of the cows. I thought I could make you understand that changes must be made otherwise the system will become unworkable later in the season. I now have no alternative but to speak to Döeffler about this.'

My threat to go over his head touched a raw nerve. John struck one of the roof supports with his fist and stepped up so he was standing just a few inches from me and shouted in my face, 'Do you hear me! I DO NOT have time to make all these changes. I have other more important things to do. You go and see Döeffler if you want, that's up to you. But I don't have to listen to this!'

With that, John turned on his heel and stalked off. I was shaking and needed to sit down. Josephine, who'd been in one of the pens with Cleopatra, was wide-eyed with fear. I really thought John was going to become violent, where oh where was Tony? I wished he could have been here; he would definitely have brought John down a peg or two! I was reaching the end of my tether.

A few days later, and with John still vehemently refusing to consider any modifications, I had a word with Döeffler. He was sympathetic, but said, 'Debbie, I understand your concerns, but the dairy demonstration unit took six months to construct. We cannot commit more time or money to this project just now. Also, we need John and his team to complete the work on some new classrooms for the polytechnic before term starts. I don't want that work to stop in order to do more on the zero-grazing project.'

I thought, 'why the hell are people to worried about stepping on John's toes? What are they so afraid of?' He was just a VSO volunteer like me, yet everybody was always tiptoeing around him the whole time. It was driving me crazy!

So, with new, but less than adequate housing arrangements,

Josephine, Jonjo, a very capable estate worker that'd been assigned to us by the extension team, and Samuel, a polytechnic student that was very keen to learn, started a grinding daily routine that started at seven in the morning and ended at seven at night. In the cool of the morning, we cut bana and napier grass and transported it to the zero-grazing unit where it was chopped into pieces that were small enough for the cows to eat using manual chaff cutters, basically, a heavy, hand-cranked wheel that drove a set of cutting blades. Whilst this was going on, someone started transporting water from a well up near the polytechnic. Once the cows were fed and watered, we then got on with milking, cleaning down the sheds, scraping out and milling the feed corn for the concentrated feed we gave the cows in the evening. At around nine a.m. I left Josephine in charge whilst I went up to the polytechnic to teach the students up until three in the afternoon, at which point, I helped Josephine and Jonjo clean the dairy, wash out the returned milk bottles and prepare everything for the next day.

One day, I returned from the polytechnic to find Josephine and Jonjo pouring milk down the drain. I've always hated to see food wasted, so I was incensed and said to Josephine, 'What on earth are you doing?'

Shrugging her shoulders, she said, 'I am sorry Debbie, but the milk just isn't selling. Every day, Jonjo and I take it up to the cooperative shop to sell. Either Jonjo or I stay and try and sell the milk in the morning. If we have not sold it, we take it over to the polytechnic, but they use dried milk powder in the kitchen. The trouble is, everyone buys the government-subsidised dried milk and so people ask why they should pay more for our milk.'

Jonjo agreed, 'I am sorry too Miss Debbie, I know how much you work, but if we do not sell it, we have to throw it away after two days, there just isn't anywhere to store it.'

Then I had a brainwave. If people won't come to buy our milk, I'll take it to them. So I reprised the friendly milk delivery service I provided whilst working for the Faulkners in my pre-college year. I borrowed an estate Land Rover and did a milk round to cafés and shops in Muka Mukuu and Fourteen Falls. I became known as the, mjakazi wa maziwa [milkmaid]! But with help from Josephine, we finally made a breakthrough. A queue started to form at the polytechnic shop every morning. This turned into a crowd and then we had people trying to reserve milk. We then became victims of our own success and couldn't keep up with demand. But the popularity for creamy, tasty Jersey milk, and the fact that people were prepared to pay a price premium for it, seemed to vindicate what we were doing at the zero-grazing unit. Our milk became the talk of the town and word of its marvellous life-giving properties even reached as far as Thika! Whilst a few big local businessmen caught onto the idea and began investing serious money to construct a dairy operation, based on milk production from exotic cows for hotels and restaurants, it remained to be seen whether any sane farmer would turn a significant portion of their shamba over to milk production; but at least we'd proved the principle.

***

'Miss Debbie! Miss Debbie! It's Numbari, I think there is something wrong!' It was Josephine. She was in a terrible state and almost in tears. It was ten o'clock at night, and I'd just arrived at the cowsheds of the zero-grazing unit. When you look after animals, you develop a sixth sense, and perhaps even a seventh and an eighth. I'd been on the verge of retiring to bed when my good old sixth sense had started twitching, so, instead of a well-earned rest, I decided to go down and check on Numbari. I hadn't seen her as a particular calving risk. Her pelvis had no signs of deformity; she had a sturdy frame and was in excellent health, so what was there to go wrong? Everything, I suppose!

Once I'd got off my motorcycle, Josephine took my hand and towed me towards the cowsheds. As I approached Numbari's stall, a feeling of dread crept through me; perhaps she'd died. Instead, she was lying down and her eyes were wild with pain. In a state of abject misery, Josephine knelt beside the stricken animal and stroked her ears.

'Miss Debbie, I think the calf is stuck inside. I checked her this evening at six and I saw she had started her labour, so I stayed with her. She was pushing and I could see the calf, but then, when it didn't come out, I got worried.'

In the uncertain light of the oil lamps that Josephine had hung from the ceiling joists, I could just about make out what was probably the top of the calf's head showing, but there was no sign of the forelegs. A normal birth happens when the calf sits in the uterus with its forelimbs and nose pointing in the direction of travel so to speak. It wasn't a breech, or rear first, because the calf's head was visible, that meant it was most likely to be a flexion, where one, or both of the forelimbs remain in the uterus, a position which usually had the effect of pulling the head down so that the calf was well and truly stuck in Numbari's birth canal. Normally, in these circumstances, you'd call the friendly neighbourhood vet who'd be on call twenty-four seven, but this was Muka Mukuu, not Radwinter and the one and only local vet based down in Thika kept to regular hours and didn't work weekends; Adam would've been aghast! There would have been head-shaking and tut-tutting, then he'd have said, 'Not even available on call Plum! What sort of a vet does he call himself!

If I were going to save the calf, and probably the mother as well, I'd have to quite literally roll my sleeves up and get stuck in. I'd dealt with fore and hind-limb flexions and breech deliveries before with ewes, but never with cows, so I was going into uncharted water, so I asked Josephine, 'How long do you think she's been in labour?'

She looked up and she turned her miserable tear-stained face towards me and said, 'It must be more than three hours. I thought she would manage by herself at first, but then the calf didn't come…'

I didn't ask the obvious question, 'Why didn't you come and get me sooner?' I just washed my hands and forearms in a bucket of water and placed my hand gently on the calf's head. Numbari was tiring, but still trying to push. I therefore had to work against her contractions and push the calf along her birth canal and back into her uterus so I could try and get the calf's legs out in front. The first thing I had to contend with was the length of the cow's birth canal, which is significantly longer than a ewe's. With my forearm disappearing, I had the peculiar sensation of being drawn down inside and of my arm being firmly, almost painfully, squeezed by Numbari's contractions, but I succeeded in pushing the calf back into her uterus. By this time, Numbari appeared to have given up the struggle and just lay panting. Withdrawing my arm, I said, 'Josephine, we're going to need to give her some help to push out the calf. Could you find me a length of rope?' Glad to have something to do, Josephine rushed off and returned a few moments later with some sisal twine. Tying one end to my forefinger of my left hand I slid my arm back in and felt for the calf's head. It was now a fight against time. In cows, the lucky beasts, if all went well, labour was usually less than an hour and usually only thirty minutes. Anything much more than an hour and a half and you have a dead calf, so I didn't have much time. Once I'd located the calf's head, I threaded the string behind its ears and pulled it around the head and back out of the birth canal. Then we pulled on the string. Pulling was quite hard physically. I thought of Adam struggling in the same situation when I'd visited with him on a farm in Radwinter. I willed myself to remember any words of advice he might've given me at the time. Eventually the calf's legs appeared and I tied string on each of them so that Josephine could give me more help with pulling. We were sweating hard and I could feel myself tiring, never mind Numbari! Just as I was thinking we'd need to call on some more help, Numbari gave one last push and the calf emerged. We were soaked from head to foot with amniotic fluid, but we both whooped with delight! I cleared the mucus from the calf's mouth and realised that it was breathing. We hugged each other and both of us burst into tears of relief and joy.

Using a little kerosene stove, Josephine made us some hot sweet tea. We relaxed in a couple of chairs whilst Numbari nuzzled her new calf while it latched onto its mother and started sucking. It was a heifer; so there was even more reason to celebrate. After a while, we fell into conversation about our lives. Josephine said she was the eldest of four sisters. Her father was a drunk, didn't go out to work and was violent to her mother.

I thought to myself, 'how often have I heard this same old story?' I said, 'Y'know, after my father died, my mother was an alcoholic, probably still is, you can never really be free from it. But she turned her life around when she married again. He is a much older man, but he's given her back her life.'

Josephine said, 'I wish my mother could leave him, but she has no money and her family would reject her if she left my father. So you see, I really needed to get this job, we were desperate for money.' Josephine then went silent. I thought she'd finished her story or didn't want to say anything more, but then she said, 'I thought I would never tell anyone this, I feel so ashamed, but... after the interview, the extension team

405

manager, Mr Kubaru, came to see me. He said I had done well and the decision was a close one. So he said he would support me, but only if I slept with him. Oh Debbie! I did it with him. I have been so ashamed, but I got the job. I haven't been able to tell anybody. I thought if we lost another calf I could lose my job. I've been so worried.'

I hugged her and we sat together for a long while until we could see the first glow of dawn appearing over the mountain. I didn't say anything about what really happened. That, in reality, it was Döeffler and myself who'd pushed for her to be hired on her own merits. Women really were treated so badly in Kenya, but was it so different in the UK? At Glantnor, I'd suffered the fear of attack when Rhys threatened to use the raddling stick on me. And then there was the odious Mr Trick and his "natural payment" system for rent. But there were always decent people around to help, like Tony and the other men at Glantnor who looked out for me. Cared for me. But in Josephine's case, there was nobody in her corner. 'Well,' I thought, 'I'm in her corner now, and, at least while I'm here, I can make sure she's secure in her job.' And then I thought, 'But heaven knows what would happen after I left.'

Next morning, very tired, I was having a bucket wash in the bath when John banged hard on the bathroom door. I was completely naked, and afraid that he might come in, but instead, he shouted, 'Hey! I've got a bone to pick with you! You've burnt some't on my best pans! I've had it up to here with you, you lazy bitch!' There was then a loud banging and clattering outside the door like he'd thrown the pans on the floor.

After twenty minutes, and hoping that John had gone out to work, I opened the door to be greeted by a pile of dirty dishes and pans strewn on the floor. John was waiting for me. He launched himself out of his room and along the corridor to the bathroom where he squared up to me. He was in extremis of rage. Aware that I was wearing just my towel and really quite vulnerable, something snapped in my head and anger drove away my fear. I said, 'There was no need to do that! Have you gone completely crazy! They're just some old pans.'

John was incensed, 'No! They're my pans that I let you use! You'll clean them properly in future! I've had enough of you. I've made a complaint to Mbenge. I swear to God, I'm gonna get you out of here if it's the last thing I do!'

I was in a spin. My nerves had become like the overwound spring of a clockwork mechanism that was about ready to burst. I found myself grinding my teeth and hyperventilating with a fury I'd never experienced before. I said 'You can't do that John! It's not up to you. Why are you doing this to me? I've done nothing to you!'

John just turned, marched back into his bedroom and slammed the door so hard the walls shook and the plaster cracked. I dressed quickly and found myself back in the kitchen, that's when I noticed the knife block sitting on the countertop. I don't think I'd ever been so angry, I was shaking, and I felt I couldn't control myself around the knife block, it seemed to be beckoning me. Then I had the giddy, stomach-churning feeling you sometimes experience on the edge of a cliff when you think you might jump. A dark image floated into my mind, and a voice in my head said, 'I'll show you John Lennox! I'll finish you!' I recoiled from the thought. I had to go outside and cool off before I did something I'd regret.

Once I was outside on the front porch, warm air caressed my face. Familiar nature sounds flooded my senses and had a soothing effect. After a while I was calm enough to notice the crickets chirping and the rushing sound of cicadas. My shoulders relaxed; my rage had passed.

I'd spent a lot of time in faraway places, Charagua, Michigan, Glantnor even, and now here. After a while you become susceptible to local beliefs and superstitions; I felt that now. Africa was a place where the local people gave strong credence to the existence of supernatural powers and unseen spirits. The dark shadows of the house seemed to exert an almost palpable effect on my mood and I considered with some degree of seriousness whether they harboured some kind of evil that had seeped into the fabric of the place. Something that was lying in wait to be evoked for mayhem, or worse.

I can't remember anything of what happened during the rest of the day, but when I returned to the house, I found that John had changed the locks. Maybe he'd sensed that I'd become unhinged. All I had were the clothes I was wearing, my motorcycle and a few shillings in my pocket. It was after six in the evening. Darkness would soon come. John was nowhere to be seen. I thought perhaps he'd gone to Nairobi. Maybe he was staying with Dot, who knew! I was completely stuck. Then I thought,

'Sato… at least Sato will help.'

While I drove down the familiar track, past the McMillan castle, I tried to decide on the story I was going to tell Sato. In the end, it was easy. The man himself was sitting in the shade of the big old mango tree that grew at the back of the house. He was puffing on a cigarette and walked over to me while I was getting off my motorcycle. He said, 'Great to see you, Debbie.' He stopped his amiable welcome when he saw my face and reassuringly hugged my shoulders, 'What is the matter? You look like you have been crying.'

I blurted it all out.

'It's John,' I wailed, 'he's thrown me out! Changed the locks so I can't get back into the house. He's nowhere to be found, so I didn't know what else I could do but to come over to you.'

Sato settled me in his lawn chair and grabbed another. I cried long and hard while Sato repeated over and over, 'I'm so, so sorry Debbie, so sorry.'

The next day, Sato and Chege collected some of my things from the house. They said John wouldn't speak to them about the incident, but he let them in so they could go into my room. It was so humiliating to think that John had been able to do this to me and get away with it.

I called the VSO office in Nairobi. I thought at least Peter Gilbert would be supportive, but it seemed that John had got in before me and told his story. Instead of getting some encouraging words and an undertaking to do something about it, he said, 'Chris has had a word with me already about this. He says you called him a few weeks back to complain about John. I think we're in agreement that you needed to have done more to work out your issues with John; we can't be seen to be taking sides, or become involved in every single dispute between volunteers. After all, we aren't a nannying service.'

I thought, 'a nannying service, I nearly shoved one of the sanctimonious little git's knives between his ribs!' In the end, I said, 'So where am I supposed to live? I'm staying with the JICA volunteers over at the old estate manager's house at the moment…'

'Well, if that's a solution for the time being, then I would stick with it. I'll make the arrangements with the settlement manager, Mr Mbenge, and have the payments for your accommodation adjusted accordingly.'

And that was that! I'd effectively been evicted from my house. The house I was entitled to be in. I felt totally let down by VSO. Just before she'd left, Carol, the assistant field officer, had been supportive of my difficult situation with John and I think she put in a request to have me transferred to alternative, all female accommodation, but there just hadn't been any to be had near enough to my posting. She said, 'Privately, I think that VSO head office in London believes that, with his abilities and skill set, John has become a pivotal part of VSO's involvement in Muka Mukuu, which is seen as a bit of a flagship project.' I got the impression that I was, therefore, expendable. Oh well, so much for VSO's spirit of fairness and gender equality! Subsequently, I became a very active representative for VSOC, the volunteers' 'union'. Amongst the letters I used to get from volunteers with suggestions for things to bring up at regular VSOC meetings in Kitui, one was from a woman posted along with a male volunteer who had already attempted to molest her and continued giving her unwanted attention. In her case, I managed to get her moved somewhere else and to get an agreement from VSO to stop posting male and female volunteers together. I often think that my time as a VSOC rep marked the beginning of my involvement with trade unionism when I got back to England. So, whilst Adam's experiences in Charagua didn't quite turn him into a 'bearded revolutionary', my trade union work did subsequently earn me the moniker of 'Red Deb' by farming friends!

The dictum, out of the frying pan and into the fire, very neatly described the situation I found myself in in my new accommodations. Whilst I no longer had to put up with John's tirades, I now had Sato's Japanese housemate Noboro to contend with. On my second morning, Sato came into the kitchen to find me reading a notice that Noboro had stuck on the door of his private storage cupboard. 'What can I say? He's very Japanese!' Sato grinned and I just shook my head. The notice was written in Japanese for Sato's benefit, and underneath, likely the same thing was written in Kiswahili, presumably for Chege's benefit. Now, since I'd arrived, Noboro had added to his notice in English, but running out of space, he'd just written "please keep out!" Feeling childishly inquisitive, I couldn't resist having a peek inside. It was a huge cupboard, but even so, it was filled to capacity with Japanese food. I could see vacuum-packed dried seaweed, soy sauce, packs of noodles, and so on. Registering my amusement, Sato said, 'His mother sends him regular food parcels.'

Since I'd arrived, the presence of a woman had sent Noboro into a flat spin. According to Sato, in a new development, he now kept his bedroom door securely locked with all his possessions stowed inside. If we met in a corridor or the kitchen, all I got was a brief nod and 'Hi', before he turned around and went back to his room to wait until I'd finished. Perhaps he thought that western woman had such loose morals that, given the chance, I'd sneak into his room and into his bed where I'd tempt him into carnal lust! Or perhaps westerners were too freewheeling for him, unhinged even. Certainly not tied to the strictures demanded by Japanese culture. It seemed like he was piloting a rudderless ship across treacherous waters and just hoping it would all soon be over. In truth, I wasn't sure why Noboro had volunteered to work in Kenya. He seemed so unsuitable for a posting abroad since it was clear that he couldn't deal with European culture, never mind Kenyan. Sato previously told me he'd studied for a PhD in alternative technology at Kyoto University. Now, having invented a special kind of super-efficient jiko that burned less charcoal, he'd volunteered to test his creation and help set up its local manufacture. All fine and dandy, and useful to boot, but why, coming from the ultra-tech world of Japan, would you study a subject that might result in you having to travel to foreign countries when it was so clear that Noboro couldn't cope? It would be like doing a PhD in Marxist-Leninist doctrine and then taking a job in banking! Normally, I would've found all this rather amusing, but in the circumstances, I just thought, 'Oh God! Now I have to deal with another guy's insecurities.' But at least he was superficially polite and didn't shout!

Chapter 45
From Kenya, with love

"What a difference a day makes." Dinah Washington's dulcet tones were echoing through my brain while I brushed my teeth. I was happy, elated, excited. But it was going to take more than "twenty-four little hours" to get to where I was going. In fact, it was going to take at least seventy-two long hours to travel the six hundred miles I needed to cover to visit Nick in Urambo. Six hundred miles, plus change! It felt like I was going into the unknown, yet I wasn't going alone; there would be a lot of company on the bone-shaking buses, people-stuffed matatus and dodgy taxis. Probably too much company! As with all long trips, it's best to start at first light, and this journey was no exception.

For the first leg of my safari, I was going to have a lift. Chege was making a secret trip to visit his mother in Nairobi. Belying the convention of male chauvinism, Chege had asked me to drive the estate Land Rover he'd borrowed. Handing me the keys, he said, 'There's less chance of us being stopped at police checks outside Nairobi if they see a mzungu woman driving, and much less chance of us having to pay a bribe.' Basically, the police force in Kenya is institutionally corrupt. Traffic cops regularly set up roadblocks on major highways. Ostensibly, their purpose was to check on overcrowding in matatus or to confiscate contraband. The real reason was more to do with augmentation of their meagre salaries. So, rather than resulting in safer matatus or fewer duty-free cigarettes entering the country, everybody just paid a bribe, usually a fifty-shilling note placed inside the driver's licence when they handed it over for 'checking'. But for some reason, if you were white, you were somehow exempt. The coyness of Kenya's police force around mzungus is deep rooted and dates back to a time when well-connected whites could, and did, raise a stink if they smelt a whiff of corruption. Fortunately for us, old habits die hard, and at the expected police checkpoint outside Thika, the police officer just smiled and waved us through.

What, you may ask, was the reason for all this subterfuge on Chege's part? Actually, it was well founded. In 1986-87, student rioting had led to temporary closure of the University of Nairobi. The institution had become a hotbed of unrest and a base for the unofficial opposition group Mwakenya, or the Union of Nationalists to Liberate Kenya. There had been many recent arrests, and Chege's father, a university professor, had just been thrown in jail. 'You see Debbie, we are a Kikuyu family, but Moi is Luo, so there is some conflict in government with many Kikuyu losing the status they had under Kenyatta — it's kind of an "ethnic cleansing".' As if to reinforce what Chege was saying, as we entered the city outskirts, a fleet of armoured cars passed us, presumably on their way to the university. Each of them was equipped with a machine gun and a water cannon. I shuddered, and wondered which of these weapons they'd be using to subdue the students. Chege dropped me at the country bus-stand on the south side of the city centre. Uncharacteristically, as I got out and we passed each other in front of the bonnet, he hugged me and said, 'Take care and be careful. There are plenty of thieves and vagabonds about.' I was rather touched. His quaint use of language was reminiscent of what you might read in an ancient Boy's Own magazine. Perhaps that's where he'd picked up the phrase, from one of the many old books that got shipped to Africa by Oxfam or some such. At the time, I'd laughed, but I could see he was serious. Then I wondered what I was letting myself in for.

What I was 'in for' was a 'touristic' detour. My plan had been to ride on a bus to Kisumu on the nice, smooth tarmac roads along the Rift. Then, I would get the steamer to Mwanza, Tanzania's port on Lake Victoria. From there, I was going to travel by road to Tabora via Shinyanga. On my atlas-sized map of Kenya, it'd looked like the quickest route, and in April, when Nick had gone the same way on his return home, he'd said it was, and I quote, "not too bad". His journey was during the long rains in April, so I was expecting no problems with roads being washed out since I'd be travelling during the dry season in August. That was before reality kicked in, and as I was soon to learn, the Scots had a similar propensity for understatement as the Africans!

The first blow to my plans came at Kisumu where I was told the steamer had broken down and was "mbovu sana."[92] The chap I spoke to at the harbour office said this with some relish. I always felt there was something fatalistic about the African psyche, like, if the steamer had just mildly broken down, that would be somehow disappointing. Whereas mbovu sana implied an irrevocable mishap had occurred that was something you could really get your teeth into. Part of this fatalism commonly manifested itself as the use of gross understatement during friendly greetings between friends and even strangers. For example, one might politely enquire, 'habari gani', what's your news? To which you would get the reply, 'nzuri sana', all's good, or 'safi' meaning fresh/clean/generally fab, or the more street hip reply of 'mambo bam, bam!' To this day, I have no idea what the phrase means but it's about things being bam, bam, whatever that is! However, this wholehearted affirmation of being fine often came with a caveat that started with, 'lakini', meaning, but followed by, 'my wife has just died', or 'my house has just burned down', and so on. So, being at that time still rather unaware of Africans' fatalistic streak, I was kind of waiting for the harbour office guy to qualify his statement, like, it's broken, but it'll be fixed by tomorrow, but instead, he said it had sunk during a storm near Mwanza. Thankfully, he followed up by saying that most people escaped to the shore. I thought that probably qualified for a ten on the scale of one to ten of African understatement!

With no steamer, the only alternative was to travel by road along the eastern side of the lake. So, two days into my touristic diversion had, thus far, involved encounters with ruts so huge you could lose a bus in them and mud so deep that one of the passengers, a small boy, had to be rescued from drowning when everybody had been asked to get out and push. This incident had occurred shortly after crossing a river near Musoma. As we approached the Mara River, actually a deep and wide estuary of Lake Victoria, the rickety-looking bridge appeared to have been damaged. The lake had flooded its banks, much to the delight of hosts of egrets and a large group of hippos that were revelling in the shallow water. The driver, who'd been at the wheel for more than eight hours straight, came down the bus and asked us to get out. As he passed me, I noticed that the whites of his eyes were huge, the iris and pupils

---

[92] Totally broken.

413

resembling the bullseye in the middle of a dartboard. I was concerned for his state of health. But then, when we filed out of the bus, I noticed a huge paper bag of what looked like coca leaves sitting on the driver's dashboard. I thought, 'ah! That's how the bus drivers can stay awake, they're as high as kites, that's reassuring!' Nick later informed me that pretty much all drivers in Tanzania chew, not coca, but khat leaves. It's so effective as a stimulant, that even after a long shift, some drivers can't sleep for several days even though they're physically exhausted! Basically, the driver asked us all to walk across the bridge just in case it collapsed. I thought this was a very noble gesture by the driver, however, if it had collapsed while we were crossing on foot we'd probably have been trampled by hippos or eaten by crocodiles anyway! After getting safely over the river, the bus foundered on the ruts and mud that had formed near the bridge and needed pushing. It was at this point that a small boy disappeared from sight down what had appeared on the surface to be a small puddle but was actually some kind of deep sump hole. It was like a magic trick, one minute he was there and the next minute he'd gone. People immediately formed a human chain, each holding onto each other's coat-tails while the man at its head threw his jacket towards the floundering boy. Although everyone appeared to be thoroughly relieved that the lad was saved, their general nonchalance about the incident suggested that this was just another day in Tanzania and nothing to get worked up about. By now I was already beginning to appreciate the difference between Tanzanians and Kenyans. In Kenya, this sort of incident would probably be followed by vociferous brow-beating of the driver plus a general wailing and gnashing of teeth, but the Tanzanians simply shrugged, saying 'hayo ni maisha', that's life!

Shinyanga is a town that's out of place in both time and space. A sprawling collection of tin roofs in a wilderness of flat scrubland that stretches from one horizon to another. It's a place that's miles from other places, and invariably not the place you're going to. One young man I spoke to on the bus, who said he lived in Mwanza, reckoned the only good thing about Shinyanga was the recently constructed airport, which begged the question, 'so the place had absolutely nothing going for it before?' That was the town whose lights now beckoned. In the darkness, a few isolated streetlights picked out a wide dusty thoroughfare that served as the main street. Unfortunately, the friendly, English-speaking Tanzanian I'd been talking to got out shortly after we'd crossed the Mara River to try his luck on an alternative route to Mwanza along the lakeside. Although I wasn't missing his barrage of negativity about his home country, I was missing his friendly travel advice.

In a letter Nick had sent a few weeks previously, he said he'd meet me at the Malaika Hotel situated on the Old Shinyanga Road. Malaika, 'mmmh', I thought, 'the Angel Hotel'. John's pet name for Dot when applied to a hotel sounded a bit dodgy. Perhaps it was a brothel! Nick said a friend, an expat in Tabora called Roger White, had recommended it as being one of the better places to stay. He'd also mentioned that Roger was single and had spent the last twenty years working in Africa, so it could well be a brothel! Getting out at the dusty and ill-lit bus-stand I must've looked confused and lost, because a large smiling woman in a bright orange and black kanga sporting the words, "harusi hii iwe ya kheri na Baraka", who'd been travelling with six children, intervened and prevented me from ambling aimlessly off into the night.[93] She said, 'Jambo mama, unenda wapi? Una kukaa hotelini?'

Catching onto the word, hoteli, I nodded and said, 'Ndiyo, Malaika Hotel.' I was greatly relieved when she just nodded and didn't seem in the least bit shocked like she might have been if I'd just asked for directions to the nearest brothel.

What she did next was even more helpful. With her six children in tow, she guided me over to a huge old Peugeot 505, which she referred to as a dala-dala.[94] Sitting beside me, she smiled, patted my arm and said, 'tunaenda hoteli yako.' After about five minutes, when it looked like we were about to leave town, I spotted a pair of streetlights illuminating the hotel sign and two cheesy-looking manikins dressed in tribal costume standing at either side of the entrance. Once I'd been deposited outside the reception, I offered to pay the woman, but I had no local currency and she refused to accept the five-dollar bill I held out to her. I was beginning to like Tanzania and its people immensely!

As one problem resolved itself, another reared its ugly head. It had rapidly become clear that hardly anybody spoke English in Tanzania, so

---

[93] "A wedding is full of blessings".
[94] A Tanzanian onomatopoeic name for a taxi.

I was going to have to use pigeon Swahili to try and explain I was staying with a friend at the hotel. But for once I was in luck, Nick was sitting reading a book in a chair opposite the reception desk. I just threw myself into his arms. Then, like women tend to do, I stood back for a moment and gave him an appraising once-over. The first thing I noticed was that his hair and beard had grown even longer since the last time I'd seen him. The second thing I noticed, and perhaps more importantly, his hair may have been long, but it had been recently washed; I was making progress! Even so, he was beginning to resemble the old man of the north!

Rather disconcertingly, Nick seemed totally nonplussed by my arrival. Like it'd been something he'd fervently hoped for, but hadn't really expected to happen. He explained it like this: 'In Tanzania, journeys are, quite literally, undertaken on a wing and a prayer. A successful journey is one where nobody is injured, robbed or dies; arrival at your intended destination is icing on the cake rather than the expected outcome from the outset!'

Having now arrived, Nick collected his room key from the smiling woman at the hotel reception who gave us both an emphatic thumbs up sign. Despite the friendly welcome and fancy adornments at the hotel gates, my visions of hotel-style opulence, or even a cosy ambiance were quickly shattered. The institutional green paint on the walls and bare concrete floors wouldn't have been out of place in a hospital. Nick's room was bare and functional in the extreme containing just a small hard-looking double bed, two chairs and a table. Seeing my disappointment, Nick said, 'Yeah, what can I say? This is probably one of the nicer hotels in town. At least the room doors lock and there's a flushing toilet. By the way, don't drink from the taps and brush your teeth in bottled water. Oh, and there's no beer and the swimming pool's out of action; incidentally, watch you don't fall in at night, it's been drained of water!'

I smiled and said, 'Don't ever consider a career in sales or in the hotel business, you're definitely not selling this place to me!'

I like to think I always live in hope, so despite Nick's anti-sales pitch that emphasised the lack of just about everything you might expect in a hotel, we headed to the bar on the off chance there might be something we might drink to celebrate our second sojourn together. Sure enough, where a huge variety of alcoholic beverages should have been sitting in serried ranks, there were just three brown-coloured bottles that'd been tastefully arranged in the centre of a very long empty shelf behind the bar. As we arrived, the same friendly woman who'd been sitting at a reception desk when I arrived came over and positioned herself behind the bar. Giving me an impish grin, Nick said, 'I'm going to do something very Tanzanian; watch and learn!' Then, turning to the receptionist-cum-barperson, Nick said, 'Habari za jioni! Umepata bia?'

The woman politley shook her head, 'hatuna yoyote'

'Vipi kuhusu wini nyekundu?'

Another head shake, 'Hatuna yoyote.'

'Wini mweupe?'

'Hatuna yoyote... lakini tuna Konyagi!'

It was like a choreographed double act where Nick would ask for something and the woman would say there wasn't any. I began giggling uncontrollably; perhaps exhaustion was finally kicking in.

Nick turned to me and nodded towards the three brown bottles sitting on the shelf at the back of the bar and said, 'They don't have beer, or wine, but they do have Konyagi. I've not tried it yet, but my friend Roger, back in Tabora, warned me about the stuff... it's dynamite!'

Unperturbed by its reputation, Nick smiled at the woman and said, 'Konyagi mbili kubwa tafadhali.'

The woman poured out two large glasses of Konyagi and left the bottle on the counter. I thought it was a classic "whisky, leave the bottle" moment! We clinked glasses, 'Cheers!'

Three glasses in, I began to lose sensation in my lips and had an out of body experience where, in my mind, what I was saying made perfect sense, but it was coming out of my mouth as pure gibberish. After a bout of giggling where I thought I wasn't going to be able to stop, Nick kissed me and said, 'I think you're experiencing a "tears of the lion" moment! You're laughing uncontrollably and not making any sense! The Tanzanians mysteriously refer to Konyagi as the tears of the lion, but maybe it's actually a truth serum invented by the Tanzanian secret police; you've been going on about goodness knows what for the last ten minutes!' Sensibly, we went to bed shortly after that!

Groggy and utterly hungover the next morning, we must've slept in because we were woken by a loud knocking on our door. Nick said,

'That'll be housekeeping wanting to clean our room.'

Turning onto my side I said belligerently, 'Can't they wait?'

I was just about to ignore the knocking and lurch over to the bathroom for a much needed visit to the loo, when two women, presumably housekeeping, entered the room and began emptying our bins and bustling about cleaning the sink and washing the floor. I was flabbergasted. We were both completely naked and lying in bed! Eventually, Nick managed to get them to leave, but they seemed very reluctant to go. Personally, I thought it was a ruse in order to see what mzungus looked like without any clothes on; I hope we didn't disappoint them!

***

After a whole day on the bus, we finally arrived in Tabora in the late afternoon. Quite unlike the dusty makeshift feel of Shinyanga, Tabora has a fading grandeur that comes to a place that's played a role in history, good and bad. First entering western consciousness as an administrative centre for colonial Tanganyika during the country's time under German rule, Tabora has variously been a way point on a slaving route that stretched from as far away as the Congo, a place of rest for weary British explorers, Speke and Burton, during their search for the source of the Nile and a backdrop for a skirmish between competing colonial rulers, Germany and Belgium, during the First World War. For the keen observer, many traces of each of these historic landmarks (or should they be called pockmarks?) have been left behind. Since the time of the slavers, Tabora has been an important trading centre, so it isn't surprising to find there's still a vibrant community and spice market at its centre. Then there's the architecture. Along its busy streets, the fading, stucco-clad homes of rich Arab merchants are juxtaposed with colonial-era buildings complete with fans rotating languidly from high ceilings that wouldn't be out of place in the movie Casablanca. Finally, there's the overgrown cemetery where the bones of soldiers that fell in the Battle of Tabora lie mouldering in their graves as a testament to the hubris of military superpowers that fought over a land that wasn't theirs in the first place.

My lasting first impression of the town was the shady, tree-lined streets that radiate out from the centre towards the administrative buildings on the outskirts that include the Boma ya Kilimo, or the Tanzanian Department of Agriculture's offices... and the expat compound. Encompassed by a twelve-foot-high chain link fence, the expat compound was a fragment of first world convenience and luxury that'd been transplanted into a place, at least in the 1980s, that had only recently been connected to the electric grid and where the sound of a fax machine or the beep of a computer terminal was as rare as a grunt from a critically endangered white rhino. I have to admit that Nick's description of the people I'd find there hadn't been positive. At the top of his list of those he referred to as dirty rotten scoundrels, were two VSO volunteers, Jane and her henchman, Alexandro, closely followed by fellow Brit and expat, Peter. As mentioned previously, like Nick, all three worked on the FAO-funded Greater Grain Borer Beetle, or Dumuzi project. Not one to base my opinion of someone on hearsay, as we walked through the main gate of the compound, I was prepared to draw my own conclusions. So when Nick shouted the customary 'hodi', knocked and then entered Jane's house, and she'd shouted 'karibu', I thought we were potentially off to a good start.

A slim, blonde-haired woman that I assumed was Jane, appeared at the door of the comfortably-furnished front room and would likely have continued her conversation with Nick, when she spotted me, and said instead, 'Oh, I see, this is the Debbie you've been talking about so much!' She then fell silent for a moment whilst I was appraised from head to toe by her cold, green eyes. Apparently I'd come out wanting, because the next thing she said was, 'Mmmh, well I don't really have room for you both to stay with me overnight because Alexandro is here already. , but since it's so late, I don't know what you're going to do...'

Taking the hint, Nick said, 'Don't worry, once I've picked up my piki, we can go back into town and stay with Jeff and Tabu.' By the time we'd quaffed the offered glass of orange juice and made our excuses to leave, I'd made up my mind about Jane; she was an ice-cold, unfriendly bitch!

Returning to the centre of Tabora, the dense foliage of the trees cast dark shadows in the gathering dusk. It had quietened down and the crowds that had thronged the marketplace had disappeared. As we approached what appeared to be some administrative offices, we turned right off a main street, crossed a little bridge over a huge storm drain and stopped in a sandy courtyard.

Nick said, 'This is where Jeff lives now. He had been posted to a village called Kiloleni in Nzega district, but it didn't work out — he still refers to it as a "coffin of a place", unquote!' Nick tapped at the large wooden door of a pleasant-looking old annex building.

Almost immediately, a beautiful Tanzanian woman opened the door. Her mobile features were at once playful and petulant, but the mixture of both was compelling and I could see why such an exotic mixture might attract a young western man.

She said, 'Niki! Karibu sana,' and then she noticed me and repeated herself in the Kiswahili plural, 'karibuni sana!' As we entered, she shouted into the interior of the house, 'Jefu, Niki'... then there was a pause while she giggled, 'na mpenzi yake a me kuja.'

A tall, slim man, with sandy-coloured hair appeared behind Tabu and squeezed her waist. Jeff was the epitome of Californian beach charm: he was very handsome and reminded me of Fred.

'Come on in guys! Tabu likes to think she owns the place.'

He squeezed her again, and although she clearly didn't understand what he'd said in English, she knew he'd made a joke at her expense and she playfully elbowed him in the ribs and said, 'Jefu, unanidhihaki kila wakati!'[95]

Jeff's accommodations were small and spartan, but comfortable. The main room had a little kitchen where there was a single paraffin stove for cooking. The electric lights were on, but covered with wickerwork shades that looked like dunces' caps. While he made us chai, Jeff nodded towards the light shades.

'You like 'em? They're actually pombe strainers.[96] They're like Tabora "chic". The wazungus up at the expat compound came up with the idea.' I made a note of this idea as a possible decorative embellishment I might try when we got to Nick's place in Urambo! Tabu

---

[95] 'You're always making fun of me!'
[96] Pombe: a local beer made out in the villages from maize. After brewing, the mash is separated from the liquid using basketweave strainers.

sat talking to Nick in Kiswahili; it was clear that she didn't know any English, so to grease the social wheels, Jeff said, 'Hey Tabu, tell Debbie and Nick how you got your name.'

After Jeff translated for her, she comically rolled her eyes and said, 'mama yangu wakati alinizaa, ilikuwa ngumu sana, ilimchukua siku nzima. Na, wakati, mimi nilipotoka, alisema, 'huyo alikuwa tabu sana!' kwa hivyo nikapata jina langu, Tabu!' She'd likely told the story many times before, but she still gave an embarrassed giggle.

Nick said, 'Tabu's mother had such a difficult time giving birth to her, she decided to call her Tabu, the Kiswahili for trouble!'

Jeff chimed in, 'Yeah, and she's still a lot of trouble!' Then, translating for Tabu, he said, 'Na yeye ana bado shida nyingi!' Tabu feigned a comical pout.

Whilst Jeff was cooking food for us, Tabu danced around the room to some African music playing on a small tape recorder. I loved her unselfconscious way of being. It was clear for anyone to see that Tabu doted on Jeff. Then I realised I'd never really thought about how Africans might behave when they were in love; what were the signs? Up until that point, I'd only ever encountered Kenyans in a work environment where, at least in public, contact between men and women was formal, chastened even. Whilst the women tended to stick together in gregarious groups, in their interactions with one another, the men often appeared impassive, inscrutable even. As a consequence, particularly for a western female, Kenyan men's emotions were often difficult to read. In contrast, Tabu was very tactile around Jeff, so as she busied herself helping him fix us some food, there would a brush of the arm here, a stroke of the back of the neck there. I rapidly concluded that she was in love, but there was something missing, not from Tabu, but from Jeff. Perhaps I flatter myself too much when I say that, by that point, I was starting to recognise some of the signs when it comes to men. Applying these nascent intuitive powers to Jeff, I could see that he loved her company, but wasn't *in love*.

As though he'd read my thoughts and wanted to change the subject, Jeff broke through my musings and said, 'Do you guys like Zairian music?' We both nodded, so Jeff continued, 'Cool. Okay, there's a great place in town called the Silent Inn. After we've eaten our omelette, why don't we go down there and see who's play'n'? Nick, you've maybe not met Katrine, she's another Peace Corps, she's gonna be down there with her boyfriend, Charles. Y'all will love her, she's got an antsy Jewish sense of humour! Charles is pretty cool too. He works up at the Offici ya Kilimo. He crashed his piki recently and broke his shinbone real bad. He would've lost his leg, but Katrine and us Peace Corps pulled together the cash needed to send him to private hospital. The Brits up at the compound wouldn't help.'

Nick shook his head.

'Yeah, I know. Those guys are mean! We've just been up there and got the cold shoulder from Jane.'

Jeff laughed.

'Oh, I see, we're just the backup team. If y'can't get a bed up there, it's down to dependable ol' Jeff, right!' We all laughed heartily. Now no longer dancing, I noticed that Tabu was twiddling her thumbs and looking rather bored with all this talk in English. I suddenly felt bad that we interrupted their evening.

Tabu and I rode pillion on Nick and Jeffs' pikis. My first time on the back of a motorbike was rather unnerving. Of course, I'd driven a bike for years, but having to follow the driver's lead around corners made my stomach lurch. Instinctively, my knees tightened against Nick's hips; which caused him to reach down and pat my knee reassuringly, but all I wished he'd do was keep his hands on the handlebars and his eyes on the road! Ahead of us, I could see Tabu's yellow and orange kanga flapping in the wind. Totally fearless, I could hear her singing and waving her arms in the air in pure delight. I thought, 'perhaps what I need is more faith in my man.' So, not quite following her example, I relaxed a bit and cuddled into Nick's back.

The Silent Inn had sounded romantic, strange and exciting. In reality, from what I could make out in the dark, it was a steel construction with a corrugated iron roof that wasn't too far removed from a cow-barn. However, unlike a cow-barn, it was lit with huge banks of powerful lights like you'd find in a football stadium and the corrugated steel fencing around it was festooned with strings of multi-coloured light bulbs. We each paid a one-hundred-shilling fee at the entrance and stepped into a Tanzanian version of Shangri-La that consisted of a red dirt courtyard filled with tables that each sat under their own little grass-roofed pagoda.

At the far end, a huge raised stage illuminated by disco-style strobe lighting occupied the whole width of the courtyard. In front of the stage was a large expanse of wooden dance flooring that was already almost filled by couples. The band up on stage was playing electric guitars, drums and maracas. Out front, were a couple of guys that were dressed like, and wouldn't have looked out of place as, one of Gladys Knight's Pips, but instead of dancing, one was playing a saxophone and the other a trumpet. The music resembled the Cuban Son I'd loved so much when I was in South America. I was somewhat puzzled and surprised by this unexpected clash of musical cultures. Again, Jeff answered my unasked question like he could read my mind — I reckoned that I needed to watch what I was thinking whist I was around him! Bending down so his head was next to mine, he shouted, 'It's Congolese Rumba. They're a Congolese-Tanzanian band called Mezembe. Actually, they're quite famous. It's the reason we had to come tonight, I hope you guys don't mind!' Nick bought a round of beers, ice-cold bottles of 'Safari' lager accompanied by a big bowl of roasted karanga. The party had started!

The beat of the music was powerful, like it was vibrating deep inside my being. In his element, Jeff was shaking hands with various of Tabu's friends, when a young guy using a stick to walk, sneaked up and grabbed him from behind in a mock ambush. I guessed he must've been Charles. 'Hey! Can I join you guys?' A young woman wearing glasses and sporting a huge head of shoulder-length ringlets sat down next to me. 'I'm Katrine Swartz, and you must Debbie and Nick! It looked like you guys have a little romantic huddle go'n' on! Jeff says the two of you met on a VSO motorbike training course, how cool is that! We were hope'n' that Terry would be here tonight. Have you guys met Terry?'

Nick said, 'Jeff talks about him a lot, but I've never seen him.'

Katrine nodded.

'Yeah, he's become a recluse. I guess Jeff mentioned that he's a Nam Vet who's been working over in a place called Igunga. Man! It's the boonies out there. The village is more than one hundred miles out from Tabora. We've bin getting worried about his mental health and reckon Peace Corps haven't recognised that he might have problems. Since returning from Nam, he'd been living with his mom in a trailer park outside Beltsville, a real poor town in Maryland. The worst thing is

423

there's not even enough work out there for him to do so he's kinda retreated into himself.' Then, shaking her head, she said, 'I reckon some of those guys never really got home from Nam.'

Nick gave a sympathetic nod.

'Yeah, I know what it must be like for him. It's the same for me in Urambo. Then there's Jeff, he had the same situation in his village. You can't just parachute a person into the back of beyond and expect miracles to happen.'

There's agreement all round on that.

Katrine said, 'Have you spoken with Tabu much?' Nick shook his head, so she continued and said, 'She's got quite a back-story. Did you know she had a kid, a daughter, when she was fourteen? Reading between the lines, it sounded like a friend of the family raped her. An aunt adopted the baby so Tabu wouldn't bring shame on her family; can you believe that! I'm working on a women's health and well-being project in the villages around Tabora. Man, it's like the Stone Age out there! The men take multiple wives and then complain when they have multiple children. Providing women with contraceptives and advice on sexual health is a major part of what we do. There's a lot of ignorance. There's no proper sex education at school. For instance, not long after I started, a young woman, who can't have been more than eighteen, came to the clinic for contraceptive advice. She already had four kids with a fifth on the way. She'd tried the contraceptive pill, but nobody had the sense to make sure she knew how to use it. Basically, like she would with medicine from a witch doctor, she'd been holding the dawa in her hand whilst she was having unprotected sex.[97] Of course, she kept getting pregnant, so she'd stopped bothering with contraception. When she came to us, she was desperate. I managed to convince her to have an IUD fitted by one of the nurses and to keep coming back to the clinic for regular check-ups. That was my first success story; she's now gone almost a whole year without getting pregnant! The toughest part is trying to give women the confidence to challenge the men who won't wear a condom when they're sleeping around. AIDS is rife; slim they call it 'cos people lose so much weight before they die. It's an epidemic actually. We reckon that ten percent, or more, of people in Tanzania are infected. It's a human

---

[97] General Kiswahili term for medicine.

disaster! I wanna stay here, y'know, see this thing through, to try and help stop so many people dying.' Katrine's passion for what she was doing had the intensity of a person that had found her calling in life; I envied her. She would have said more, but Charles waved her over to meet a group of his friends. She said, 'Gotta go,' she then made a quotation marks gesture and said, 'my "husband" is calling me!'

As we watched her walk over to hug Charles and shake hands with his friends, I said, 'Katrine, she's quite a live-wire!'

Nick replied, 'I don't think she's going to leave when her posting finishes. Jeff says she's applied for a job with the Tanzanian Health Department. This is a place you either love or you hate; like Marmite. Me, I love Tanzania. The people are friendly and helpful and always positive. Like malaria, Africa got into my blood when I cycled down here, it's just that I don't want to be here on my own any more.' With that, he reached over and hugged me tight and we decided that it was time for a dance. As we approached the dance floor, the music became almost impossibly loud, and yet I could hear the accompanying rhythmical swishing sound created by hundreds of feet sliding on the wooden floor in time to the beat. This was the famous Zairian shuffle. In contrast to the inane arm-waving and leg-flailing we do on disco dance floors when we don't know what else to do, Tanzanian couples had refined this rather exhausting spectacle into a sedate and pleasingly straightforward shuffle whilst they held each other around the waist. With such a simple dance routine to follow, Nick and I joined the crowd and did our own version by adding a few samba moves, which we henceforth called the Tabora shuffle! Whilst we were dancing, one thing became clear to me, Nick's posting might be physically tougher with greater hardships, but the people here, locals and even some of the mzungus, had heart. There was a feeling of human warmth and a belonging that I hadn't yet experienced in Kenya.

***

Early morning outside the Caltex petrol station in Tabora. We arrived around six thirty a.m. and joined the end of a queue that'd already formed outside a chained-off area where the pumps were standing. Ahead of us were a couple of battered Isuzu trucks, a Hilux pickup and a couple of bwana shambas on pikis.[98] Just as we arrived, a mzungu guy, who turned out to be a French padre, pulled up behind us on what was known by the locals as a tuku-tuku. When it comes to motor vehicles, the Tanzanians loved onomatopoeia, so here's a quick recap and translation. Piki-piki, you know, it's a small motorbike. Then there's a tuku-tuku, that's a big motorbike. Moving to cars, there's the dala-dala, a big old diesel estate that's often used as a taxi. When they run out of sounds-like words, Tanzanians have adopted a modified version of the English words colonial British settlers would've used. Since the settlers were rather posh-sounding, their rather hoity-toity pronunciation has been rather amusingly 'fossilised' in Tanzanian Kiswahili. For example, there's trektor for tractor and treni for train. Try pronouncing trektor, and you'll see what I mean about being posh!

At seven thirty, the petrol pump attendant opened the chain across the forecourt and everybody in the queue started up their vehicles expectantly. First, each driver handed over their kibali, or signed requisition order for fuel. If you were lucky, this was read, countersigned by the attendant and retained. If you were unlucky the kibali was returned and the driver went away empty-handed. This usually happened when there wasn't enough fuel to fulfil the kibali, or the request exceeded the monthly fuel allocation for that company or organisation. It was frustrating and a complete lottery, but in 1980s Tanzania fuel was desperately scarce and very very expensive. Diesel must've run out because all the trucks and lorries were turned away, but the bwana shambas were in luck. They both looked overjoyed, like they'd won a golden ticket for a tour around Willy Wonka's chocolate factory! We were next. The attendant took the kibali from Nick who smiled and poured on the charm. It must've worked because we got to go forward. I then unshouldered the huge rucksack I'd been carrying and Nick proceeded to take out a little group of five, five litre plastic jerry cans.

He said, 'I hadn't previously mentioned anything about this because I thought you might disapprove, but… er, how can I say this, we, or more accurately, you, will be carrying five jerry cans full of petrol on your back

---

[98] Literally, 'Mr farming' in Kiswahili, bwana shamba is a general term for an agricultural extension worker.

on our way back to Urambo.'

While Nick methodically unscrewed the caps from each can and neatly lined them up in front of the petrol pump, I pondered my fate.

'Would it hurt more to just crash and die, or to crash and burn and then die?' I guessed the latter would be worse and that what we were about to do was tantamount to suicide!

Pondering these two fates, an idea suggested itself for a contribution to the 'Love is' series of greetings cards. Have you, dear reader, ever received one of those corny cards from your beloved on Valentine's Day with a cartoon of a cute, child-like little naked couple that has the words 'Love is...' in the top corner and in the opposite corner there's a corresponding answer? Well in my case, 'love [was]... carrying twenty litres of petrol on your back whilst you ride pillion on a motorbike!' I could have asked the padre standing behind us in the queue for a benediction, but I had faith in my man. So, with Nick's help, I put the heavy rucksack on my back and we saddled up for our little fifty-mile jaunt over to Urambo.

The first part of the journey was on degraded tarmac where we played 'chicken' with oncoming drivers as they swerved to avoid huge potholes. Then the tarmac came to an end and gave way to a gun-barrel straight dirt track that disappeared in the heat shimmer over the horizon. With no fields or other obstacles in the way, why bother with corners? Counter-intuitively, as we bumped off the tarmac and onto the sand Nick accelerated. Perhaps feeling this required some kind of explanation, he turned his head slightly and shouted, 'If you go too slowly, the vibration you get from the corrugations is horrendous. Literally screws and nuts and bolts fall out of the bike and you get a very sore bum, but if you get up to just a smidgen over fifty miles per hour, it's as smooth as silk because you kind of glide over the top of the corrugations.'

As our speed increased, I could feel the vibration becoming intolerable and then worrying. I held on tight to the pillion's 'scaredy bar' at the back of the bike, but sure enough, we finally broke free of this 'turbulence' and began to glide over the corrugations. [99] Of course,

---

[99] Tough, hairy bikers refer to the bar at the back of a motorbike that forms part of the load-carrying rack as the scaredy bar. A real '[wo]man' shuns such safety measures, and instead, nonchalantly sits with his/her hands on his/her lap no matter how exciting it gets.

reduced contact with the road as we skimmed over the sandy surface made steering rather vague, but as with many things in life, whenever there's an upside, there's always a corresponding downside waiting to catch you unawares. Unfortunately, that downside was quick in coming and took the form of the Urambo-Tabora bus which we saw coming hell-for-leather towards us around the first bend in the road. Under normal circumstances, the road would be wide enough for the bus to pass us without mishap, but this was no ordinary bus. This was a Tanzanian bus with a bent chassis. Being bent meant that, rather than travelling in a straight line, the back of the bus crabbed sideways at a twenty-degree angle which had the effect of increasing the amount of room it needed on the road. As this land-based leviathan bore down upon us, I remembered what Paul Oar had said about the buses in East Africa where his transport company operated not being totally in good working order. Here was one coming straight for us! I thought, 'how ironic if a member of the Best family was mown down by a bus owned by one of our friendly neighbours in Hainested!'

As Nick slowed, like the Star Trek Enterprise dropping out of light speed, we experienced vibration as the effect of the corrugations kicked in. This vibration intensified as we slowed further. Just as the bus was almost about to hit us, Nick expertly flicked the bike over the berm of sand that ran along the side of the road and stopped. It was just in time. The bus thundered past and the passengers smiled and waved at us! Again, as an explanation, this time for an apparently unnecessarily close encounter with forty tons of speeding bus, Nick said, 'Sorry about that, but if I'd have slowed down too quickly, we might have come off in front of the bus, and well, we'd have…'

Probably in recognition of what he thought might be more delicate sensibilities on my part, he hesitated, so I finished his sentence for him.

'You mean we would've crashed and burned?'

Nodding, he said, 'Yes, that's exactly right!'

Having made it around the first bend in the road, we'd covered about thirty miles and had entered the Urambo Forest. The word 'forest' conjures up densely packed trees soaring above your head, but actually, like Sherwood Forest, Urambo's dense miombo woodlands had been destroyed. In mediaeval times, the hearts of oak from Sherwood Forest were mostly harvested to build ships for the British Navy, however, in Urambo's case, British settlers cleared the trees so the people back home would be assured of a steady supply of tobacco for their fags. In the 1930s, as part of a huge project funded by the British Colonial Office, four thousand square miles of dense scrubland in what is now Urambo district, was cleared using chains stretched between tanks that had likely been used during the First World War. Wishing, no doubt, to swell national coffers after a costly war, another arm of the British government, the Meteorological Office, declared that, from a climatic perspective, the area around Urambo in central Tanzania was an excellent place for tobacco growing. An expedition sent to Tanzania to test the soil, confirmed that it did indeed rain between the months of October and May. Thus assured, for the price of a cheap car in today's money, the British government offered the chance to buy two hundred acres of land to all and sundry. What they got was a rush of would-be tobacco farmers flocking to the region hoping to get rich quick. In common with all colonial enterprises, there was a gargantuan marshal plan.

Piggybacking on an earlier railroad that was under construction by the German colonial government before the First War, the completion of the Tabora railway in 1923 meant that supplies of building materials could be shipped down from Kenya to Mwanza on Lake Victoria and then transported by rail to Tabora. In Urambo, water pumps were built, as were dams, houses and tarmac roads. Administrative buildings were constructed and the settlers used the ready supply of recently felled timber to build their farms and fence off their land. The planning was epic, the expense was enormous and the farmers bet their proverbial shirts on the outcome, but as they were to find out, Tabora experiences extreme seasonal variation in monthly rainfall even during the rainy season. Whilst rainfall in an average year is more than adequate to support tobacco production, it isn't always. One thing however is pretty constant, average temperatures are always high. The rains failed in the full first year of production and were sporadic in the years thereafter or fell at the wrong time to establish the crop. The settlers went bust one by one and eventually left. Many went bankrupt. Some died and remain buried somewhere out in the dense scrub that grew back in place of the miombo woodland.

Since independence, and despite its own burden of grinding poverty, Tanzania has long been a country that has been willing to offer safe haven to those in trouble. Fittingly, the area around Urambo that was once a site of an epic money-making project has since become (and still is) a place of refuge for more than one hundred and sixty thousand Tutsi refugees who fled from a civil war that raged for more than ten years in neighbouring Burundi in which the dominant Tutsi minority began a brutal programme of ethnic cleansing. Not content with sheltering non-combatant civilians, Urambo District played a rather less well-publicised, and more controversial role as a training ground for South African freedom fighters during their struggle to liberate their country from apartheid in the 1990s. So, despite its present-day reputation as being a sleepy backwater, the people of Urambo have played a significant part in support of their country's creed known as Ujamaa, a Kiswahili word for extended family, a socialist and economic policy instigated by Tanzania's founding father and first president, Julius Nyerere. So, as they say in the US, in your face Tabora!

Fast forward to 1986 and the culmination of my first epic journey to visit Nick. Apart from the bus, the first sign that we were re-entering civilisation was a huge steel water tower that came into view on our right. After passing this rusting colonial-era relic, and without further ado or further announcement in the form of a sign saying 'Welcome to Urambo' or some such, we turned a left corner and onto Urambo's main thoroughfare. On our right we passed Patel's general store that occupied a commanding position at the head of the street. On the left was the Urambo Hoteli and bar. Further along from that, there were a few shops, the Urambo Stores, a few other little establishments selling odds and bobs, and that was it.

As we slowed to take a sharp left, I shouted, 'Where do you buy your food?'

Nick shrugged and said, 'There's a market three days a week. Patel sells luxury goodies like Double Cola, toilet roll and even beer occasionally. You can buy tinned stuff at the Urambo stores, but that's about it. Oh, there are the kuku choma ladies that sometimes sell roasted chicken outside the Urambo Hoteli. I'm their best customer. It's the closest you'll get to fast food this side of Tabora!

I thought, 'no wonder he's losing weight!'

Slowing further, we took a right down a rough track into some woodland that gave onto an area where a few people were tending crops in their shambas. They all waved enthusiastically at us as we bumped over the ruts and swung sharply left onto a track leading to a long, low building constructed out of concrete bricks with a tin roof. Pulling up in a bare and dusty courtyard between the main building and a much smaller corrugated iron shelter opposite, Nick shouted 'Home sweet home!'

Stepping off the bike, I dusted myself down and surveyed Nick's 'homestead' whilst he busied himself trying to open the padlock on the rather insubstantial-looking wooden front door. At the far-right corner of the courtyard, there was an unroofed adobe-walled structure that looked like a squat-loo. The main building was the epitome of functionality. In lieu of glass, wire mesh grilles were mounted in each of three windows. Behind the grilles, somebody had thoughtfully constructed some wooden window frames that were covered in clear polythene, so at least you could reduce the influx of dust or rain when it was stormy. Following Nick inside, there was a kitchen with an aluminium structure at the far end that served as shelving. Besides some pots and pans and a primus stove, there was nothing else.

Through the main door and to the left, the kitchen gave straight into what appeared to be the main room that housed a single wooden table and two chairs. I sat down heavily in one of these, looked around the bare room and said, 'God! It's pretty dismal, isn't it?

'Nick nodded.

'Yeah, there's no point in giving you a tour, there's only two more pieces of furniture to look at; both are beds fortunately!'

While Nick got the paraffin stove going for some tea, I wondered down the long corridor that connected the main room with what was likely to be Nick's bedroom that contained just a bed with a mosquito net hanging above it. Then there was a bathroom with a bath and a broken toilet. In the bathroom, and to my right, was an almost full bath of water with… I flinched. There was a dead rat floating in the water. I shouted, 'There's a rat in the bath!'

Nick drolly answered, 'What's it doing? The breast stroke?'

'No', I said, 'it's dead and it's decomposing!'

'Aah, blast!' Came Nick's reply. 'That means we'll need to get rid of the rat and bail it out. That also means unless they switch the pump on there's no stored water for this evening's meal. When Susan was living here, her first bit of advice was, if you were going to be away, to keep the plug in and the bath tap on so if the water pump was switched on you could at least have some stored water to use when you got back. But she didn't mention how many rats there are running about!'

So, instead of a nice cup of tea, we spent half an hour emptying and cleaning the bath and disposing of the rat. After we were finished, Nick said, 'I think we're in luck though. I spotted the kuku choma ladies outside the Urambo Hoteli. We also have some bread in that paper bag sitting on top of the little wall in the front room. We can have a snack with that along with some peanut butter I made a while back.'

Doing as Nick suggested, and fearing a confrontation with a live rather than a dead rat, I gingerly opened the large paper bag sitting in a basket by the table. As I did so, a huge crowd of tiny ants fell out of the bag along with the bread. Ants were crawling inside and out. 'The bread's full of ants darling.'

'Yeah, sisimizi. Those little tiny ants get into everything. On the subject of ants, the zungu-zungu seem to like marching through the latrine outside, so be careful when you go out there at night!'[100]

Feeling parched and hungry, we retired to bed completely exhausted shortly after eight. Perhaps it was the unfamiliar night sounds that woke me during the night, but once I was awake, I needed to pee. Trying not to wake Nick, I crept outside holding a torch and made my way cautiously over to the loo. The almost full moon cast silvery shadows. Above my head, the sky seemed almost impossibly crowded with stars with a vaporescent Milky Way swirling across its vastness. As I took in this stunning heavenly display, I became aware of a movement in the shadows under the roof of the little outhouse. I froze mid-stride and instinctively crouched down like a small animal trying to make itself inconspicuous to a predator. As I held my breath, a man's shadow detached itself from that of the outhouse and walked away and around the back of the house and disappeared. Since I was wearing just a tee shirt with no underwear, I peed where I was squatting and hurried back

---

[100] Army ants.

into the house and bolted the door. Back in bed, I shook Nick's shoulders and whispered, 'There's a man wandering about outside!'

'Oh gosh! Sorry, I should have mentioned I have an askari. I had a break-in at the house a while back and the town council found me a guard. His name's Matthew, I actually doubted whether he actually showed up or not.'

'Robberies, askaris, army ants, rats as big as cats, is there anything else you haven't told me?'

'No, I think that's about it. Oh, there is one other thing...'

'What! There's marauding elephants and killer bees?'

'No... just that I love you.'

We made love, long and slow taking our time. We both fell soundly asleep this time and slept through to the morning.

***

Having bought some fresh bread the previous day, for breakfast, I was preparing a thick slice for myself and spreading it with some of Nick's surprisingly tasty homemade peanut butter and frying some eggs when I heard a woman outside shout the, now familiar, 'Hodi! Hodi!' 'I'm here' greeting.

I was actually glad of the distraction. Ignoring Nick's advice of floating all eggs in a bowl of water before cracking them open, the last two I'd tried had both contained foetal chicks and I was wondering whether I could stomach another attempt. Nick had left shortly after dawn to deliver a stack of kihenge grain shoots to some villages some distance away from Urambo. Since the back of his piki had been stacked with wooden frames and little door latches, we decided that I'd accompany him on his next trip.

Having finally decided to chicken out (geddit?) on cracking another egg, I shouted. 'Karibu!'

When I opened the door, a smartly dressed, slim young woman wearing a kanga tied at her waist as a skirt, a pressed white blouse and an orange headscarf greeted me with a friendly smile. Holding her hand was a girl of about fourteen, obviously her daughter, who smiled broadly at me and said, 'Shika miguu', which, translated literally, means 'I hold your feet.'

Used as a token of respect by a younger person or child to an adult or village elder, I found this uniquely Tanzanian form of greeting to be rather fraught with uncertainty around when I should use it and to whom. As always, Nick had developed a rule of thumb to help him negotiate the social maze. He said, 'Use it only if the person is older than you, or if you know they're of high status, e.g., the president of Tanzania for example.'

As they both entered, the woman shook my hand and said, 'Habari gani! Unaitwa Debbie?'

Since I'd heard her use my name, I assumed she'd asked whether I was called Debbie. Therefore, in reply, I rolled out one of the few stock-and-trade answers I could remember from my language training in Kitui and replied, 'Ndio, naitwa Debbie.'

Encouraged by my apparent grasp of Kiswahili, she said, 'Aaah, Miss Debbie! Karibu sana Urambo Debbie. Mimi, nimeitwa Mentewab, na hapa,' here, she pointed at the little girl and said, 'ni binti yangu anaitwa Sisi.'

Sisi smiled and curtsied and again said 'shika miguu', but this time she really threw herself into the 'shhhh' giving it a long shushing sound that was followed by a fit of girlish laughter.

Mentawab said, 'Mr Niki ipo?'

I shook my head and confessed, 'Samahani, Kiswahili yangu ni mbaya sana!'

The woman nodded, and then, to my surprise, broke into fluent English and said, 'Is Mr Niki at home today?'

I shook my head.

'No, he went out to the villages early this morning.'

'Sawa,' she said, and then explained, 'my daughter Sisi helps Mr Niki with his Kiswahili on Thursdays and Fridays. We will come back later.' She was about to leave, but feeling a little embarrassed, I asked them in for chai.

When they were seated in the only two chairs in the room, Sisi pointed at the pombe strainers I'd tied onto the ceiling lights as lampshades and said, 'Mama, vichungi via bia!'

Mentewab laughed and said, 'Sisi likes the way you have used the strainers! It's a better use than beer making. There are too many drunks in this village!' After I'd poured them some tea, Mentewab reached over and gently held my arm and said, 'Mr Niki, he is a very kind man. I am so glad he will marry. We will miss him. You know, he has not taken any other women into the house. He is a good man, Debbie. You will be very happy.' She smiled and gave my arm a squeeze.

As I registered what Mentewab had said, I felt a surge of love. I was very touched by her words. When Nick returned, I told him about Mentewab and Sisis' visit. He said, 'Blast! I totally forgot! Having you here has totally ruined my routine; in a nice way of course!' We kissed for a long moment. Despite of, or maybe because of, the shabbiness of his tawdry old accommodation building and the loneliness of his posting, it was clear that the local people had taken Nick to their hearts, just like I had.

***

Wider than a street, but rather narrow for it to be a market square, the main drag in Urambo sits somewhere in between these two functions. Taking central place at the head of the main street, or square, depending on how you looked at it, Patel's general store took pride of place. Like the old couples you sometimes see driving vintage cars that they can honestly claim to have had 'only one careful owner', Patel's life and that of his store were inextricably entwined together. Before there was Patel's store, there was no Patel, and vice versa, and both have become a seemingly permanent fixture within the very fabric of Urambo and its history. In the 1930s Patel set up his business to serve a large community of white settlers that had bought tobacco plantations to provide them what they needed from Kenya, or further afield. He'd watched the settlers arrive with dreams and high hopes and then leave with barely a shirt to wear on their backs. He had outstayed them all.

The store itself was large, but hardly out of the ordinary. Like so many in Tanzania, it was painted white and blue, and out front, there was a wide veranda. However, unlike the other shops in town, Patel's veranda was home to a small army of fundis, or makers. First, there were the tailors and clothes menders, then there were men making sandals out of old car tyres, and finally, there was a group of women weaving, amongst other things, the large, multi-coloured shopping baskets called kikapu, the quintessential practical item used by mostly everybody that had something to carry. Each maker paid obedience to Patel in the form of a monthly rent for his or her pitch on his veranda. Those near the main door and next to the, mostly empty, Caltex petrol pump paid the highest rent, whilst those who occupied pitches near either end occupied the 'cheap seats'.

At three in the afternoon, it was almost unbearably hot as we walked slowly up the road. Several passers-by and shopkeepers waved to us, but we were being inexorably drawn onward, as though Patel's store exerted an irresistible magnetism that you weren't able to resist, or was it the thought of a cold Double Cola, the Tanzanian rip-off of Coca-Cola, that, in the thirty-eight-degree heat, no sane person with fifty shillings to spare in their pocket could resist? As we got closer, I could see the man himself, leaning forward with his forearms resting on the glass-topped counter reeling us in with a Svengali-like stare that seemed to be almost speaking to me and saying, 'Come to me, come to me, come and spend your money!'

As we stepped onto the creaking floorboards of the veranda, one of the tailors next to the main entrance gave us a thousand-watt smile and got up from his sewing machine to shake Nick's hand. As their palms made a satisfying smack sound, the tailor said, 'karibu sana rafiki yangu![101] I see you have brought Debbie!'

As he leaned over and shook my hand Nick said, 'This is Chichi, my best friend and tailor!'

Chichi bowed slightly and said, 'Welcome Debbie! Nick has talked a lot about you and misses you very much.'

Chichi rolled his eyes comically and we all laughed, then Nick said, 'How's the Christmas shirt going?' Nick had told me that Chichi was making a shirt for him to wear when he came up to spend Christmas with me in Kenya with sister Sarah and her partner Sean. It had obviously become a big deal since we were only just getting to the end of August. But in Tanzania, plans had to be made well in advance, as progress was always glacially slow.

---

[101] Welcome my friend!

Chichi looked like he was pleased with himself. He bent down, and with a flourish, produced a bolt of cloth from behind his sewing machine. He said, 'I have it here, just like the one you wanted.' As he unfurled the cloth, I could see that the red pattern on a white background resembled the markings of a zebra. I thought it was a strange design to choose, but it was undoubtedly distinctive!

While Nick was talking to Chichi, I stepped up to Patel's time-honoured counter and ordered a couple of Double Colas. Patel, who had a kindly smile on his baggy old face, said, 'Nick must be very happy you have come Debbie. We often worry about how lonely he must be.' Patel waved my money away when I made to pay for the colas, and said, 'as they say in England, they're on the house.' Joining me at the counter, Nick squeezed my waist and thanked Patel who said, 'Actually, you're in luck, my son, Rajiv and his wife, Sonia, are visiting from London! If you come over, we can offer you a special curry.' Patel winked at me and we arranged to go round for dinner later that week.

Having earlier met Nick's neighbour Mentewab, and now Chichi and Patel, there was just one final member of Nick's support network that I hadn't met, Mushi, the District Executive Director. Known to everyone by the rather ominous acronym, the DED, Mushi was many things to many people, however, in Nick's opinion, he was an affable crook. Having taken quite a shine to Susan, Nick's predecessor in Urambo, Mushi, mistakenly, saw Nick as one of the last remaining, if rather tenuous, links with her, so he was always good for a beer if there was any to be had.

Sure enough, as we passed the Urambo Hoteli on the way back home, somebody shouted, 'Mr Nick!' at the top of his voice from somewhere inside the building.

Nick whispered, 'That is almost certainly the DED. The Urambo Hoteli is virtually his second home. I don't think I've ever seen him in his office! If the DED's around, there must be some beer available.'

The shadows inside the hotel were a welcome relief from the stifling heat. Passing an unmanned bar that looked like it'd been constructed from shipping pallets, we walked through to a courtyard and back out into the sunshine. Sitting under one of the little pagodas that seemed to be standard furnishings for bars in Tanzania, was a short, rotund-looking man wearing thick, horn-rimmed glasses and what was known in 1980s East Africa as a Kaunda suit, a type of lapel-less, short-sleeved formal garb made famous by Dr Kenneth Kaunda, the then president of Zambia. Like a president, Mushi, for it was he, was surrounded by a large retinue of acolytes that Nick had referred to as his cronies. Mushi rather formally stood up and kissed rather than shook my proffered hand. Having never experienced such a greeting before, I was unsure what to do in return, but in the end, I plumped for, 'Very pleased to meet you Mr Mushi!'

Taking this as an invitation to sit down, Mushi pushed a couple of bottles of ice-cold Safari beer in our direction and returned to his seat. 'So, Mr Nick, this must be your Debbie?' Then, turning to me, he said with a chuckle, 'You know, I've been teaching Mr Nick how to speak Kichagga.'

Taking his cue, Nick said, 'Mwanga luka!'

Mushi chuckled again and replied, 'Na chi cha!'

There was uproarious laughter from all sitting around the table. Nick just shook his head like someone who'd replayed the same old joke many times before. Not content with just beers, Mushi had also ordered a round of roasted chicken. A group of three young women that Nick said were the kuku choma ladies who inhabited the front terrace of the usually moribund hotel, trooped in with large quantities of their delectable chicken pieces. Immediately recognising Nick, their faces lit up, and forgetting the person who'd ordered the chicken in the first place, they came shimmying over and surrounded us in a tight little giggling huddle. I nodded to myself, and thought, 'here's Nick's little fan club. No wonder he always stops off and pays exorbitant prices for what is essentially just barbecued chicken!'

Much later, after our group had quaffed what appeared to be several crates of Safari, I vaguely remember us leaving the hotel and staggering back home where we both tripped over the mantrap that the Urambo Town Council had inconsiderately positioned in the path to Nick's door. I remember Nick saying he'd lost count how many times he'd tripped, or worse, driven over, the water stop cock that protruded from the ground in the middle of the back yard. At least we injured different feet, Nick his left and me my right, which meant that between us we had a serviceable pair of legs to get us up the step and into the house!

Later in the week, as we approached Patel's house for our dinner date, I could immediately see it didn't look like anything else in Urambo, at least that remained above ground and hadn't been eaten away by the voracious hordes of termites that'd no doubt seen off all the other colonial-era buildings years ago. The house could've been transported from the McMillan estate Muka Mukuu. For a start, there was a discernible lawn and discernible back and front gardens. There was a drive with a large white Toyota Land-cruiser sitting in it. Finally, there was a large painted corrugated iron roof sheltering a rambling single-story house with a veranda where there was a group of people sitting around a table having drinks. Nick had said that, to his knowledge, apart from Patel's senior employees, hardly anyone in Urambo had been to the house never mind seen inside. As we got closer, two Askaris who'd been huddling out of the heat in a small mud-brick shelter stood up and gave us a friendly wave with their bow and arrows. I guessed that, so long as there were no arrows notched on their bowstrings, there shouldn't be any nasty mishaps!

Patel welcomed us and introduced us to Rajiv and Sonia. If I'd shut my eyes, I could have imagined I was back in London! They both had Cockney accents and said they lived near the Finsbury Park tube station. Whilst Raj and Sonia chattered away like a couple at a dinner party, Mrs Patel senior seemed timid and rather nervous around visitors. Nick had said that Susan, one of the few outsiders to have ever met Patel's wife, said she spent most of her time in the house, almost as though she were in a self-imposed purdah. Unlike the lively interest her husband was taking in proceedings, Mrs Patel had the haunted look of a captive. I tried to imagine a reason for this. Looking at the house itself, it had every comfort that was on offer in a region so off the beaten track. In fact, it wouldn't have looked out of place in a suburb of a city in the US, except it was in a street by itself, like the first building in a planned new housing estate that never got completed through lack of funds.

Patel told us that his grandfather had followed British settlers and other Indian traders as they migrated to Tanzania from Kenya after

Germany was defeated in the First World War. When he'd moved to Tabora region at the start of the British tobacco debacle, Patel spoke of a thriving community. However, when he got onto ticking off a long list of moans about the state of the nation and how much better things were when the British were running things, I'd begun to disengage from the conversation, until he came to a story closer to home, well actually, Nick's current home.

As though he were following the time-honoured British tradition where stories are swapped after a convivial evening around a roaring fire during family gatherings, Patel said to Nick, 'You probably have not heard this story, but when I first came to Urambo, I became friendly with the man and his wife that built the house where you are now staying. His name was Liam McDonald and his wife was called Bertha. Liam said his family were landowners in Scotland. The youngest of three sons, Liam had come to Africa to seek his fortune after his father died leaving most of the family estate to the eldest son. Liam told me that he had invested most of his share of the inheritance in his tobacco farm. I thought at the time this didn't sound like a good idea. Gujaratis like us are born with a sense for business, so, when things started to go wrong, I told him to sell while he still could. I remember that in the first year, the rains were not good and armyworm destroyed what was left of his crop. Unfortunately, the drought lasted into the next year when tobacco crops failed again. I told him to sell, but his wife was pregnant and he said he had to make a success of the farm for her sake. But before giving birth, she died of malaria. He was now a broken man. I very well remember the day that Liam disappeared. He came to see me about a debt he had with me for machinery and supplies. I said I was prepared to accept payment by instalments, after all, I did not want the man to suffer bankruptcy as well as losing his wife. Shorty after he left here, some local people believe they saw him walking into the bush. The natives said the forest had devoured him, they are very superstitious, but the fact is, he was never seen or heard of again.

Knowing that we soon had to go back and sleep at the house, I shuddered to think of Liam and his wife perishing there. Shorty after finishing his grim story, Mr Patel followed his wife to bed and bid us goodnight. After he'd gone, I asked Raj if he thought his father would ever consider retiring to England?

Raj shook his head and said, 'Y'know, years ago, in the early nineteen-sixties, when it was still possible for Indian people to migrate to England before Tanzanian independence, my father tried to settle in London. He even started to set up a business, but in the end, he decided not to. He quickly found that there's no 'shika miguu', no respect from Londoners for Asian people, so he returned to Urambo.' Then he said rather sadly, 'I really believe that he and my mother will spend the rest of their lives here.'

***

A crisp, clear morning dawned for my first trip out to the villages. Crisp? How can seventeen degrees Celsius be crisp? Probably because I'm getting used to the unrelenting heat of this place! A long day awaited us. Since I was visiting, and in Nick's opinion, "a wiz with maps", he thought it would be a good chance for him to travel to a couple of villages he hadn't yet contacted, Sikonge and Songombele. Via his Tanzanian bwana shamba contact, Mwisaka, Nick had managed to get a message out to the Mabalozi, or village elders, that he would come and give an initial demonstration to them on how to control Dumuzi. To transport what we needed, once again, we used Nick's huge rucksack. Instead of petrol containers, this time, we packed a kihenge shoot, some information pamphlets and a small sack of permethrin, the dawa, or insecticidal powder that was recommended by the FAO to combat the little pest.

At this point, a fuller explanation of the back story is in order here. With regard to methodology around combating Dumuzi, there were two camps. In the larger camp, were Nick's fellow Dumuzi project workers in Tabora, Jane, Alexandro and Peter and in Nick's camp, well, let's just say, there was just Nick. Whilst Jane et al, were keen on getting the villagers to apply permethrin to their shelled maize to ward off Dumuzi, Nick worried about the toxicity and the health impact of people eating insecticide-treated grain. Rather than discuss these differences and come to a compromise, in common with latter-day explorers who were cut off from the outside world for months or years at a time, our band of Dumuzi hunters in Tabora had grown a simple disagreement about approach into a giant schism, which had become quite acrimonious. To the horror of the Tabora camp, rather than apply insecticide directly to grain, Nick was advocating the occasional application of permethrin to the outside of mud-brick storage structures, called vihenge.[102]

In fact, health worries aside, using an insecticide that was often in short supply had become something of a roadblock to progress with farmers only shelling their maize (which is a laborious process) if they could first obtain, or afford to buy, permethrin. Nick, on the other hand, had seen huge reductions in damage of sixty percent, or more, by just shelling the maize. Being a wood borer by trade, so to speak, Dumuzi preferred to bore into a dried maize cob at the severed stalk end so it could eat its way through the grains from the inside. Therefore, the telltale sign of infection was two neat little holes, one being an entrance and the other an exit, in what often appeared to be an undamaged cob. Inside, it was a different story. On opening up an infested cob, the whole thing would collapse into a pile of dust, pretty impressive for a one-millimetre-long bug, but not very much appreciated by farmers trying to feed their families. However, if a pile of detached, dried maize grains was presented to Mr Dumuzi, the little bug found it difficult to get a foothold on the grains, and instead, went elsewhere for his supper.

Another element of the Tabora-Urambo schism centred around Nick's avocation for the building of vihenge. The idea had originally come from Mwisaka, Nick's local bwana shamba contact. It had turned out to be a masterstroke! Like owning a Ferrari, building a kihenge had become a tangible sign of progress for any up-and-coming farmer that wanted to look "cool" to his neighbours. Apparently, it had sparked a spate of kihenge envy that drove uptake of the idea in the villages around Urambo District. Therefore, I suspected that this apparent success was also what was underlying the Tabora camp's opposition to Nick's approach. Maybe it was just "sour grapes", who knows? And who cares, so long as the job was getting done.

Suitability weighed down by the now full rucksack, it teetered alarmingly as I mounted the motorcycle behind Nick who was now togged up in his trademark military combat jacket, boots and khaki trousers. Assessing his attire at close quarters I said, 'Do you ever get

---

[102] Plural for kihenge.

worried about being mistaken for some kind of dodgy South African commando? I mean, you look pretty scary in your paramilitary garb!'

Nick shook his head.

'Nobody's ever commented on my clothes, but my mirror sunglasses get a few stares. I think some people find them quite unnerving if they haven't seen them before.' Nick then patted my knee reassuringly and said, 'Are you ready for this? It's gonna be a hard fifty, or so miles to the first village and another twenty beyond that, so there's an outside chance that we'll get benighted and have to bivouac in the bush somewhere.'

With talk of bivouacking, an obvious question sprung to mind and I asked, 'Are there any savage wild animals roaming the bush?'

Nick pondered this for a while and said, 'I haven't really given it too much thought. I've seen the odd buffalo, and then there's the pythons of course, but I've not seen anything else to worry about.'

I just smiled at the back of his head and thought, 'he's always such a bundle of laughs, and so reassuring!'

As I've already mentioned, Nick was hopeless at navigation. On the plus side, we had a map that'd been produced by the British Ordnance Survey back in the 1950s and Nick's prismatic compass. On the downside, I had doubts about my proficiency with a compass; however, Mwisaka had marked the position of the two villages on the map. So, like an ancient mariner, I noted the position of the sun in the cloudless sky and took in some of the features of Urambo as we headed towards the road out. Unfortunately, my initial confidence at being able to distinguish north from south soon evaporated. After a few miles, we entered a smothering blanket of dense miombo scrub and all thoughts of navigating by the sun evaporated. The tightly packed stems of bushes and the trunks of taller trees crowded around us reducing my view of the sky to a narrow blue strip directly above the clearing in the bush created by the track. Now I fully appreciated why Hansel and Gretel were so diligent in dropping their trail of breadcrumbs in the Grimm Brothers' creepy fairy-tale. I thought perhaps we should be doing the same.

As we travelled further from Urambo, the density of the scrub increased and the boughs of trees closed above our heads. Apart from the incessant rushing noise made by cicada beetles, there were few nature sounds, to be heard. Although the world basked in scorching sunlight above our heads, a brooding watchfulness emanated from the shadowy depths and I thought of Liam McDonald and his tragic end. Perhaps his restless spirit still roamed the forest. In Africa sometimes it felt as though anything was possible.

An hour passed and then two. On the unstable sandy surface of the bush track, we'd been travelling at a steady twenty to thirty miles per hour, so I thought we should be getting close to Sikonge. By dead reckoning, we'd taken a right where there should have been one to take, but we needed to find a left. I tapped Nick's shoulder and asked him to stop. We both got off the motorbike and Nick turned off the motor to save fuel. Silence engulfed us. Even the cicadas had fallen silent. It felt like the bush was collectively holding its breath in the expectation that something was about to happen.

We took off our helmets and I prodded the map with my forefinger at the place on the track where I thought we were. Nick nodded and said, 'Yeah, that makes sense, but it looks like we've missed a left turn that would've taken us to the village. Y'know, I often wonder how accurate the map is on the position of tracks. I mean, the position of turns are probably just approximations.'

I smiled grimly and said, 'Maybe we should backtrack; we probably missed our turn.'

As we both peered down the track the way we'd come, a man stepped out of the bush. He was maybe two hundred yards away, but I could make out that he was carrying what looked like a couple of barrels dangling from a rope around his shoulders. Looking relieved, as though people just dropped out of nowhere all the time, Nick said, 'Great! We can ask directions.'

We got back onto the bike and drove back towards the man who'd now put down what he was carrying and was standing staring at us. As we approached, I could see that the barrels were, in fact, beehives made from tree bark. I'd recently read a book in Kenya called 'Nyuki kwa Utajia', or bees for wealth, so I knew a bit about the famous Uyogo beekeepers in this part of Tanzania. My apprehensions about approaching the man were immediately reduced. Here was a bee farmer going about his business, not some mad stabber hiding out in the woods waiting to ambush us!

444

We again got off the bike and shut down the motor. Into the silence Nick said, 'Habari gani. Una wezo wa kuzungumza Kiswahili?' Looking rather alarmed, the man offered no verbal response. Nick whispered, 'He's probably Msukuma. Many Wasukuma don't know Kiswahili.' Trying again, Nick said, 'Sikonge, unaijua njia gani?' Then, perhaps trying to appear more friendly and approachable, Nick removed his sunglasses and smiled reassuringly.

The man promptly shrieked loudly and shouted, 'Yesu amekuja!'

Whereupon, he left his bee hives and ran off into the forest. Nick shook his head and said, 'Well, that went well. He thought I was Jesus! I guess it's the blue eyes and beard. Apparently, it's the fault of the Jesuit priest that used to live in Urambo. He always used to carry a painting that depicted Jesus as having blue eyes and a beard. Since then, the locals in the bush are petrified of coming across a white devil, or shetani, with blue eyes. I can appreciate why he was petrified!'

I couldn't help laughing and said, 'Yeah, exposure to the Catholic Church can be scary at times!'

Although the beekeeper had been no help regarding directions, we noticed a track nearby that he must've walked along. Taking this narrow path, we emerged onto a wide, sandy thoroughfare with a large collection of mud-brick houses with tin roofs scattered along it that we assumed must be Sikonge. Turning right, we came across a rickety wooden sign for the local primary school and the Ofici ya Kilimo, or Department of Agriculture office. Nick pointed to it and said, 'We should find someone to help us there. There's usually a bwana shamba at the office in the morning.' We were in luck! On finding the office, we were directed to a building where a meeting of the village elders was taking place where we were met by three smiling old men wearing flowing white jalabiyas. Unable to follow what was being said, I became an observer and merged into the background. We were both provided with glasses of hot, sweet chai and a plate of vitumbua was passed around the group of eight men sitting in a circle on wooden benches.

I relaxed into the relative coolness of the building and listened to the thrum of unintelligible conversation whilst Nick explained what he wanted to present to villagers in a seminar about Dumuzi. After about half an hour, everyone got up and Nick said, 'they reckon that they don't have any problem with Dumuzi. To prove it, the headman is going to take us over to his own shamba. They're pretty adamant about it, like it's an honour thing.' Together with the eight elders, we walked out of the building and back into the searing heat of the afternoon.

As we walked along a path that weaved its way past parched two- and three-acre plots, we were mobbed by an excited group of small children who were shouting 'mzungu, mzungu' at the top of their voices. After a while, I felt like the pied piper of Hamelin leading the children out of the village towards an uncertain fate!

Eventually, our greatly enlarged group stopped in a small courtyard of a farm. A group of three young women who'd been pounding maize into flour by hand stopped what they were doing, curtsied and intoned 'shika miguu' in unison to the headman.

Nick whispered, 'We're quite the celebrities today. At least we're providing everyone with some entertainment if nothing else!'

The space in the courtyard in front of the women was filled with rows of empty wooden racks where maize cobs would have been hung out to dry after harvest. The children were shooed away so we could enter a large building at one end of the courtyard. Inside, dried maize cobs had been piled up on a wooden floor that was fixed at just above head height like a straw loft. Below the loft, where the earth floor had been dug out, a little group of charcoal stoves was being used to heat large aluminium pans of water. The headman took a few cobs from the loft and handed them to Nick who shared a couple with me to inspect. Sure enough, I saw the two telltale little holes. Nick opened one of the cobs to find that the grains inside had been reduced to a milky white powder. There were gasps and tutting all around from the assembled elders. Now that he had his audience's undivided attention, Nick unleashed his party trick. He held his forefinger to his lips and cupped his ear with the palm of his hand in the universal, 'listen' sign. In the silence that followed, I could distinctly hear a chic, chic, chic sound, like some tiny creature striking a pair of even tinier stones together in unison with hundreds, or possibly thousands of his fellows, like the percussion section of a huge insect orchestra. Nick then said, 'unasikia? Hiyo ndio sauti ya kula ya Dumuzi.'[103] There were nodding heads and more gasps from the

---

[103] Do you hear? That is the sound of Dumuzi eating

446

assembled elders. According to Nick, this trick never failed to get people's rapt attention.

After the meeting was finished, we walked back to the motorbike and Nick said, 'They've all agreed that they do have a problem and are willing to have a demonstration and seminar.' Then he smiled broadly, chuckled and said, 'Another successful day in the war against Dumuzi!'

***

Besides various activities under the bedcovers, what, you may ask, does a couple of VSO volunteers do in Urambo during in the long evenings they spend when their labours are done for the day? With little food to cook and only a few cooking utensils to cook it in, mealtimes passed pretty quickly. Later in the evening, after watching yet another beautiful sunset, one was able to step outside to watch the fireflies dance around the eaves of Nick's dark and silent cooking shack that stood opposite the house. Since there was no beer to be had, or bars to go to, one might settle down to some letter-writing whilst listening to the BBC World Service on Nick's shortwave radio. If you were lucky, there might be electricity for a couple of hours in the evening, but after that, the hurricane lamp needed to be lit; if you've been lucky enough to find some kerosene that is. Finally, there's the inevitable ablutions, but without running water, it was really just a flannel wash with some soap; if you've been lucky enough to find some soap. Then bed, usually around eight or nine o'clock at the latest, followed by ten, or so, hours of fitful slumber, if you were lucky.

It was only when I'd finally had a chance to visit, that I could fully appreciate the psychological impact of Nick's isolated and spartan living conditions. As the pitchy dark crowded in around us in the lonely barn-like structure, night noises pervaded one's senses and morbid thoughts bubbled up and became mixed up with anxiety to produce a fear of the dark that I'd never experienced before. In a past life, or lives, I'd taken dark pretty much at face value. You were exhausted after a day of honest toil in the farmyard, so you pulled off your muddy boots and rank-smelling overalls so you could retire to whatever modicum of comfort you could find in the currently-available living quarters. Sleep followed naturally from physical exhaustion and the need to rise early the next morning. But at Nick's house in Urambo, as the shadows lengthened in the evening, I began to experience an intangible dread. Towards the end of my second week, I finally shared what I thought were foolish fears with Nick; however, the expected dismissal by him of such fantasies didn't happen and instead, he said, 'You feel it too? You see, a few months back, I'd have said, it's just your mind playing tricks. I may have even laughed, but then something happened. Do you remember I mentioned the robbery of cooking stuff from the house?' I nodded. Nick'd now got my full attention. 'Well,' he said, 'what I didn't tell you, I was in the house when it happened.'

I said, 'Did they wake you? Weren't you sacred?'

Nick shook his head.

'No, that's the weirdest part of it. On the night it happened, I distinctly remember lying in bed asleep. That in itself is weird because you don't really remember being asleep, you just are, right? So, I was asleep, and then I heard the splintering sound of wood followed by some scuffling and noise. I recall feeling like I should get up and check what was happening. I would have got up, but then I heard a voice. It was kind of inside my head, but I knew it originated from somebody else, y'know, not a voices-in-your-head thing?' I nodded. I was becoming alarmed about where this was going, so I held Nick's hand.

Reassured, he took a deep breath and continued, 'Well, the voice said, "that sound you can hear, it's just rats. You hate rats. You don't want to see rats, do you? So, just stay asleep and the rats will soon be gone".

'I don't remember anything else, so I guess I just went back to sleep, or proper sleep, not just dreaming about being asleep if you know what I mean. If I think about it too much, it becomes kind of metaphysical and then it messes with your head! Okay, so, the next morning, I got up and found that somebody had broken the lock on the door and taken all my cooking gear, including the jiko, kerosene lamp and thermos flask. I was stunned to say the least, but I eventually managed to get everything replaced and paid for a fundi to fit a stronger lock and put bolts on the door. The DED also had an Askari posted in the old kitchen hut as a precaution. Then something else weird happened. I started having these panic attacks when it got dark. I mean, until you arrived, I'd be like a cat on a hot tin roof at night, y'know, all jittery. I've begun having this feeling that there's something lurking in the shadows. Now, I even hop over onto the bed so as my feet don't stand in the shadow, like there's something under the bed that might grab my legs.' Nick paused at this point. His face was white as a sheet, but he composed himself and when on. 'At first, I thought it was just the effects of loneliness getting to me. But as time went on, I've started to wonder whether I'm going crazy!'

I said, 'Have you spoken to your VSO Field Officer?'

Nick shook his head.

'No! Martin and Iain would definitely think I'm going crazy! Look, I haven't yet got to the weirdest bit.'

I thought, 'oh my God, there's more? It's like a Hammer House of Horror movie already!'

Nick went on, 'Before you arrived here, these night fears were getting so bad, a couple weeks back, when my neighbour Mentewab came by with Sisi for my Kiswahili lesson, I mentioned it to her.

'Well, she took me totally seriously and said, "Mr Niki, I think these wezi had an mchawi with them.[104] [105] I think he might have spoken to you in your dreams and told you not to do anything. I also think he has left an akili shetani in your head.[106] You need to have an mchawi remove it. I know a good mchawi in a nearby village called Uliankulu. He is well known. Just ask anyone in the village and they will take you to him".

'She was totally serious. At first, I just brushed it off, but this place gets to you. You start believing anything is possible. I guess, over time, you kind of imbibe the superstitions of the local people by a kind of cultural osmosis, but now that you're feeling it as well, it seems even more real. Look, what do you say if we go over to see the mchawi? You don't need to be involved, just come along as moral support?'

I wasn't sure whether I was up for it, but I agreed to go along. It seemed crazy, fantastical even, but I couldn't deny what I felt. So, the next afternoon, after Nick had come back from the villages, we headed out to see the witch doctor.

Uliankulu was really quite close to Urambo, just five miles out along

---

[104] Thieves.
[105] Witch doctor.
[106] Mind devil.

the Tabora road, so it was easy to find. Nick had given Dumuzi seminars there, so a little welcoming party of young women and children soon gathered to find out why he was visiting. As we stood chatting, a dishevelled-looking old man in bare feet came on the scene. They seemed to know each other, and after he'd warmly shaken Nick's hand, they fell into deep conversation. After a while, the man cradled his chin with his hand like he was thinking, after which, he nodded and motioned to us to follow him.

Up until that point, I'd agreed to just wait by the motorcycle while Nick met with the witch doctor, but curiosity overcame my fear. I could never honestly say I was a devout Catholic, or that I even paid much heed to what was written in the Bible, but I did, and still do, believe that there is "someone" or "something" bigger than us out there. Yet the notion that some people might have supernatural powers was a pretty alien concept for me. In fact, at one time, I would've consigned witchcraft to the ragbag of human beliefs I might have labelled as mumbo-jumbo; but that was before I went to Africa. As is the customary habit of male friends in that region of Africa, Nick and our guide held hands as they walked off towards a group of low mud-brick buildings that was obviously at the centre of the village. Pointedly, the young women that had so enthusiastically greeted us when we'd first arrived didn't follow. In fact, I had the distinct impression they were slightly afraid of who, or what, we were going to see.

As we passed though the village centre, women, who were pounding maize, looked up and waved. There was business and life going on all around us. However, as we left the village behind and walked through a grove of papaya and banana trees, things quietened down. Then, just before the village ended and the shambas gave way to open bush, we came into a little clearing where a single, large mud-brick house was standing. Indicative that the occupant might have some wealth and status, the roof was constructed of corrugated iron rather than the usual brushwood and straw. Clearly, this was the abode of the local witch doctor or mchawi. As if to confirm this, as we got closer, I could see that two roughly hewn wooden poles had been planted into the ground on either side of the entrance doorway. Thrust into what would have been the brain case, each pole supported the skull of a goat. At that point, my reservations about what we were doing grew into fears. Apparently undeterred by these gruesome charms, our kindly guide knocked on the wooden door of the hut and we all waited. As seconds stretched into minutes, I thought, or perhaps hoped, that the door might remain closed, but after maybe ten minutes of respectful waiting, a pregnant young woman emerged. Looking neither right nor left, or engaging with us in any way, she hurried off towards the village. That was the point that my feet told me to turn around and follow her. But she'd disappeared quickly and I was worried that I might get lost if I set out after her. Not wishing to wait outside on my own, I followed Nick and our guide into the hut.

Whilst my senses got used to the dark, my eyes, craving some light, were drawn upwards to the rafters and a constellation of hundreds of little pinpricks of light presumably shining through nail holes that'd previously been made to fix the corrugated iron sheets to roof beams that'd perhaps rotted, or had been replaced over what could have been eons of time for all I knew. My eyes now accustomed to the gloom, I tore my gaze away from the roof and willed myself to contend with what was in front of me. What I saw was not in the least bit terrifying, but it was disturbing. A very old man, presumably the witch doctor, was seated cross-legged on a simple wooden chair. The crown of his head was swathed in grubby white cloth bindings. These were not bandages, but worn as a kind of headgear. Around his neck was a huge quantity of pipe clay beads of all descriptions and colours. If his other clothing could have been described as grimy or uncared for, the square-necked tunic he was wearing stood out in stark contrast from the rest of his outfit. It was dark blue and appeared to have sequins sewn onto it that, on closer inspection, looked exactly like the glass beads I'd seen in Greece that were referred to as evil eye charms, or nazars, that were worn by the islanders to ward off a curse that could be cast by a malevolent stare.

As we seated ourselves on one of the low stools that were arranged on the floor in front of him, the old man stared ahead and said nothing as if he hadn't yet seen or heard us come in. When I looked at his face to see if there was a flicker of recognition that we'd entered, I saw that his eyes had the milky-white pallor of a person with cataracts; he was probably almost totally blind.

After sitting for a while, our guide spoke to him, not in Kiswahili, but in a tribal dialect I didn't recognise. The mchawi nodded and spoke to Nick in Kiswahili, presumably to ask what he needed. After some back and forth conversation, Nick pulled out some cash and handed it to him. Apparently, like a Gypsy fortune-teller, to provide treatment, the old man required that his palm be first crossed with "gold". In return, the mchawi did something that was completely unexpected. Like a conjurer, he produced a squawking chicken from somewhere and immediately cut its throat with a small knife that miraculously appeared in his right hand. Our guide then rummaged on the floor and produced a copper bowl, which the mchawi used to catch the blood that was spurting from the severed end of the chicken's neck. Our guide then gave the bowl to the old man who expertly opened up the dead bird's breast and began to remove its intestines placing them into the bowl along with the blood. After this was done, the mchawi set the bird down on the floor and stared intently for some minutes at the bowl's gruesome contents.

Up until the point when the mchawi began to examine the chicken's entrails, everything had happened so quickly that, initially, I didn't fully comprehend what had happened. However, a feeling of revulsion now crept over me and I felt rather nauseated by this grotesque sight. Eventually, the mchawi looked up and motioned for Nick to come forward and kneel in front of him. Alarmed that something awful might happen, I moved to get up, but our guide shook his head and smiled reassuringly at me and I reluctantly sat back down. The knife now gone from his hands, the mchawi stretched out his arms and held the top of Nick's head for some minutes as he mumbled some unintelligible words. Nick knelt unmoving, as if he were in a trance-like state. Then it was suddenly over. Nick got up and returned to his stool. The mchawi now motioned to me that it was my turn. With much trepidation, I followed Nick's example and knelt in front of the old man. I vaguely recall looking into his milky eyes like I was searching for the pupils that had long-since disappeared, but that's all I can remember. After what seemed like a long time, but was probably only a few minutes, I became aware that I was staring at the largest of the witch doctor's nazars that hung from a chain around his neck. It felt like I'd returned from being somewhere else, but at that moment I knew only that I needed to get up and return to my seat. We sat for a while in silence and then the witch doctor nodded and indicated that we should now leave. Whilst I tried to avoid giving the impression of rushing, nevertheless I hastily exited the hut.

Momentarily stunned by the glare of the afternoon sun, and needing some support, I leaned with my back against the trunk of a large papaya tree that was standing in the dusty yard in front of the witch doctor's hut. It felt like I was winded, or maybe I'd been holding my breath for a long time. After regaining my composure, I joined Nick and our guide and we walked back up through the village to Nick's motorcycle that now stood glinting in glorious isolation, like it'd been forgotten about or abandoned there years ago. For a short while, as we drove back to Urambo, I again had the feeling that I was coming back from somewhere. Everything felt new and somewhat unfamiliar. My consciousness was infused with a strange euphoria. I even wondered whether we'd been drugged, but my faculties felt sharp and in focus. That night, as we sat holding hands across Nick's little wooden table and watched the shadows lengthen in the room, I experienced no impending feeling of dread or doom, just the joy of spending another night under the same roof as Nick. It seemed like the spell had been broken.

When she heard where we'd been, Mentewab had said that the mchawi had 'removed the akili shetani.' To this day, I cannot rationally explain what happened that afternoon, but all I know is, something definitely did.

***

At the end of my stay in Urambo, although my parting from Nick was painful, I knew that we'd see each other again less than four months later at Christmas when Sarah planned to visit me in Kenya with her partner Sean and their bubbly three-year-old daughter, Abigail. The Christmas of 1986–87 turned out to be one of the most wonderful on record. When you work in a country, there's little time to really experience it, but with Nick at my side, we had a whirlwind tour of what high-end tourism in Kenya was all about. There was tea at the swanky Norfolk Hotel in Nairobi, a venerable colonial-era establishment that wouldn't be out of place in depictions of that time in movies like Out of Africa or White Mischief. We travelled first class by train to Mombasa and spent time on the type of beaches you see in postcards of paradise; except you aren't in paradise and you've got to be careful not to get mugged!

During our pleasant little sojourn, there are two opposing pièce de résistance moments that stand out from Sarah's visit, one good, and the other bad. The good moment involved a slap-up Christmas dinner in the beachside restaurant of the hotel where Sarah and Sean were staying in Mombasa. At my request, Sarah had bought a smart blue and white pinstriped shirt and a natty pink bow tie for Nick to wear for the occasion in place of his usual grungy army fatigues; he looked gorgeous! And now the bad. To cut a long story short, I gave everyone, including myself, but miraculously excluding Nick, salmonella food poisoning. The plan was for us all to stay overnight at Muka Mukuu so that I could 'treat' everybody to my cooking. Unwisely, I decided to show off my backwoods cooking credentials and bought a couple of live chickens from the market. After deftly wringing their poor little necks with a broom handle (there's photographs to prove it) I cooked the meagre amount of meat I managed to wrest from their mangy bodies in a large pot along with assorted vegetables. As a tribute to the value of thorough hand-washing, or perhaps in his case, simply avoiding all contact with dead or dying chickens infested with salmonella, the next morning, Nick emerged from this culinary extravaganza totally unscathed. On the other hand, Sarah, Sean and myself spent two full days vomiting into the toilet. Thankfully, Abigail was also unscathed. You know it's true love when your beloved is kind enough to hold your hair back while you vomit. Perhaps they should include this in one of those sickly little 'Love is…' cards that I previously mentioned!

Chapter 46
A small victory

After Nick's visit at Christmas, we endured our longest period of separation since we'd landed in East Africa. Fortunately, or unfortunately depending on the way you looked at it, the time passed relatively quickly because, for the final eight months of our postings, both of us had to deal with a number of increasingly acrimonious disputes. In Nick's case this was with the Tabora expat crowd who made an official complaint to VSO about Nick's approach to his project. In my case, the hard work that had gone into the cohort of students I'd been teaching at the polytechnic was in serious danger of unravelling. Still recovering from my self-imposed bout of salmonella, I arrived back at Muka Mukuu in the middle of an epic battle between Josephine the polytechnic manageress and the group of students who'd been identified for expulsion — part of me wanted to just get on a bus and go back to Tabora!

I know teachers shouldn't have favourites, but one of the lads in the group for expulsion was Peter, one of my most promising students; I was incensed. Part of my frustration stemmed from the knowledge that the training the students were receiving was so desperately needed. I had recently visited a few of the students' family shambas, Peter's included, and it had become clear that the new approaches and ideas around keeping livestock were having a positive impact, now this all seemed to have been put in jeopardy.

I immediately knew something was amiss when Sato gave me a rather less than enthusiastic welcome when I arrived back at the house from my travels at Christmas. Rather than the usual cheery hello, he wondered into the kitchen where I was unpacking some delights I'd picked up in Nairobi and said, 'I hope you had a relaxing time down in Mombasa.' Expecting him to say something more, I turned to look in his direction, but my smile froze when I saw his glum expression. Taking a deep breath he said, 'You're not going to like what's happening up at the polytechnic... Apparently a group of the male students has been found

455

sleeping with their girlfriends in the female dormitories. It was discovered when one of the girls said she was pregnant.'

Pausing whilst I was stacking a couple of tins of Bisto gravy granules I'd picked up at Uchumi's supermarket, I said, 'Surely that's not too serious? I suppose it's just a couple of the students?'

Sato shook his head gravely.

'No, it's about twenty of them and Josephine is calling for all of them to be expelled immediately. In fact, their parents have already been told to take them away from the polytechnic.'

'So,' I said, 'the students have been tried, convicted and punished without anyone hearing their side of the story?'

Sato shook his head.

'Debbie, it's the way it's done here. There's nothing you can do about it. Mbenge the settlement manager has given Josephine his support.'

I rolled my eyes and said, 'Yes! That's because she's probably sleeping with him along with a couple of other prominent society members!'

Striking while the iron was hot, and before I had second thoughts, later that afternoon saw me once again beating a path to Döeffler's office. At the time it seemed like I'd literally worn a perceptible furrow to his door with one complaint or another and all to no avail, but this time was different. After showing me into one of his rather uncomfortable rattan chairs, a triumph style of over functionality, he fixed me with his grey eyes and said, 'I know why you have come Debbie… it's about the polytechnic students.' At this point, Döeffler patted the palms of his hands together in the fashion of a man who's trying to make up his mind.

While he prevaricated, I stole the initiative and said, 'The students need to have a fair hearing. We need to hear their side of the story. If twenty of them are expelled, it means that the current year group is unsustainable; we will probably have to finish the term early. It's a disaster!'

Whist I was lobbing various arguments in his direction, I noted whether any of them were landing, or having an effect, but Döeffler remained impassive until I'd run out of things to say. Then he said, 'You're quite right; they need to have a chance to defend themselves. It is, after all, a serious charge that is being made. I will speak to Mrs Matuku and ask her to organise a meeting with the affected students.'

Having made his decision, Döeffler went quiet and began his palm patting thing again, but this time he coupled it with a loud expulsion of air in the manner of a person who was exasperated and irritated in equal measure but was not prepared to say so out of politeness. I took the hint and left.

***

I had to wait a week before I had my day in court so to speak, so by the time the students, Josephine the polytechnic manager and a few of the society members met in one of the classrooms, I had my arguments rehearsed. In the meantime, I'd learnt via the jungle telegraph that one of the biggest "crimes" that the students had committed was to be from families who'd made an official complaint about misappropriation of society funds. Josephine and Mbenge were both among those that had been accused of embezzlement of a significant amount of money, so I wasn't surprised when I saw the settlement manager take his place beside Josephine at the front opposite the group of students who were sitting on chairs that had been arranged at the front in the manner of a courtroom.

As expected, Josephine opened the proceedings by making a little speech about the polytechnic rules regarding fraternisation of male and female students after hours. Then she read out the "defendants'" list of "crimes" after which she paused and looked pointedly over in the direction of the students to await their response. The students all looked in Peter's direction so I assumed that he'd been appointed as the spokesman. Looking apologetically in my direction, Peter stood up and said it was true that some of the boys had visited the girls' accommodation block, but this was because many of the students were related and had strong family ties, so it was only natural that they would want to see each other. Some of the women were actually betrothed in marriage, so it was again natural for them to meet after lessons. Josephine and Mbenge sat slowly shaking their heads and smirking.

I could see that nothing the students could say was going to have any impact on the outcome, so I decided to wade in. Clearing my throat loudly, I asked Josephine whether I could speak. Feigning that she hadn't heard me, she continued by reading out the students' list of crimes again. Therefore, I scraped my chair back, stood up and said, 'Mrs Matuku, I've been teaching at the polytechnic for eighteen months and I can say that neither Peter nor any of the other students that are here have ever missed a lecture. All of the students are very keen to learn and I have been to see their families and can honestly say that what they are learning is being put to practical use on their shambas. It would do no good to expel these students, singling out individuals for punishment is unfair. Staff and students must be treated equally. We all know that there have been cases where staff members have been caught meeting with female students.' Here I paused for effect. Josephine was glaring at me, I could almost feel the daggers hitting my chest, and Sato was sitting with his head in his hands, I thought, 'you're being a great help!' Since Sato clearly wasn't going to say anything useful in support, I continued and said, 'Expelling all these students will make it impossible for the year group to continue; it will be unfair on the other students. They deserve another chance.' There was a moment of stunned silence when I'd said my bit after which the students all got up from their seats and cheered! The "trial" ended with Josephine saying that she would take the matter up with the polytechnic steering committee. It was a very rare moment of triumph.

A few days after the meeting, I was summoned to Döeffler's office. This time, I wasn't alone and Josephine and the society chairman, Samuel Mbando, occupied the two other rattan chairs. Their silence and sullen faces when I entered suggested there had been a debate, probably heated, before I arrived and that a decision had been made. Döeffler rose from his chair when I walked into the room. I thought he was going shake my hand, but he stepped over towards the only other empty chair in front of his desk in a kind of blocking manoeuvre, as though he didn't wish me to sit down at all. So, rather oddly, both of us stood whilst the other two sat. Döeffler shrugged his shoulders, sighed and said, 'We've made a decision...'

In the slight pause between making this announcement and his continuing to say what the decision was, I took the opportunity to glance over to Josephine and saw that she was incandescent with rage. From this I concluded that it was Döeffler who'd made a decision and that she and

Mbando were going to have to go along with it.

After his little pause, Döeffler said, 'I'm sure everyone understands that in these situations there needs to be compromise. The success of the polytechnic is very important to the aims and the future of the cooperative society; therefore, we have decided to overlook the students' behaviour on this occasion, but Debbie, I am going to ask you to take more of a role in the pastoral care of the students to ensure that they keep to the rules in future.'

His pronouncement made, Döeffler got behind his desk, took his seat, and once again, did his palm patting routine, but this time it was accompanied by his characteristic little humming sound of satisfaction. A decision had been made and all problems had been solved; all was well with the world! Assuming, like I did, that the palm patting gesture meant that the meeting had come to an end, Josephine, Mbando and I left Döeffler to enjoy his little moment of satisfaction. While Josephine marched off to her office to sulk, I pondered the new role as student babyminder that I'd just been given and wondered how I was going to find enough time to fit everything in!

Later that same week, when I picked up my mail from the society office, in addition to the three letters from Nick, there was an unstamped envelope with "Miss Debbie" written on it. Whilst I was chastising myself for not having got a reply off to Nick's previous little group of letters (they, like buses, tended to come all at once in threes), I opened the unaddressed envelope first. It was a letter from Peter's mother. In it she thanked me *"on behalf of her family for [my] kindness and for helping Peter to stay at the polytechnic."* It went on to say that after her husband had died, she had found it very hard to find the money to educate her children and since Peter had been doing so well, she had borrowed money to pay for his education.

Thinking back, even as a volunteer, it was easy to forget that what we were doing had an impact on people's lives. In the UK we take education totally for granted. Even though student grants have been abolished, children still have access to free schooling — we really don't know how lucky we are.

Chapter 47
On safari

No account of time in Africa could be complete without a tale or three of adventures whist on safari. The term 'safari' is of course Kiswahili for journey; however, this word, like many others from our colonial, past has been absorbed in the British English language. For colonial-era British explorers, East Africa was, quite literally, the happy hunting ground and safaris were essentially hunting trips where animals were shot, or bagged. In the earliest days, explorers obfuscated this wanton slaughter under the guise of scientific discovery. An early example of this approach was recorded in a book called African Bush Adventures, by the aptly-named Scotsman, John Alexander Hunter, who, in his career as a 'big white hunter' spanning fifty years, personally offed almost one thousand members of a group of animal species that are now referred to as the 'big five': rhinoceros, lion, leopard, elephant and buffalo. In his book, during an expedition to open up game hunting in Tanzania's Ngorongoro Crater, a vast pockmark twelve miles in diameter left on the earth's crust by an exploded volcano, Hunter recounts his discovery of the first northern white rhino to be seen by a westerner. Regardless of whether this, like the unicorn, might have been the only one; he promptly bagged the animal for 'scientific' study.

Despite previously murderous connotations, at least in the English language, these days the word safari conjures up photographic tours around exotic locations where animals are protected under national and international treaties. Indeed, towards the end of his hunting career, and no doubt noticing that there were fewer and fewer animals left to bag, even Hunter became an advocate for conservation. Alas, he was too late, he and his ilk had done their work too well; most, if not all of the big five are now critically endangered.[107]

---

[107] In fact, there are only two northern white rhinos left on earth. Both are in captivity and both are female. At the time of writing, frozen sperm of the now deceased last remaining male is being used in a last-ditch attempt to avert extinction.

Back in the 1980s when Nick and I were together in East Africa at the end of our VSO postings, we were lucky and privileged enough to have an opportunity to witness the wonderful spectacle of wildlife on the great plains of the Serengeti for ourselves. However, during his last week in Urambo, when he should have been spending his time wrapping up his project and saying goodbye to his many local friends, a rather unnecessarily unpleasant incident occurred between Nick and the VSO volunteers that came to replace him that left no doubt that Jane and her gang in Tabora had spent their time disparaging Nick's work to all and sundry. Having closed down my involvement in the VSO project at Muka Mukuu, I had travelled down to Urambo to stay with Nick during the final week of his posting. Having spent the last month in Urambo, Nick knew that he would be replaced, but VSO hadn't confirmed who would be coming or when they would arrive, so it was rather a surprise when a young couple turned up one day at the front door of Nick's house. Having volunteered as a couple, Rick and Sandra were from the Netherlands. They explained that they were Nick's replacements on the Dumuzi project and that VSO in Dar es Salaam had decided that the isolation of its posting in Urambo warranted the added cost of hiring a couple rather than another single volunteer. We were happy to see them and we delayed our plans to leave whilst Nick sketched out a handover programme. However, when he tried to discuss his handover plans with them, they became rather evasive. Not wishing to press the issue further, he instead brought up the issue of all the equipment and utensils that he intended to leave behind for them to use. At this point I hold my hands up, it was I who'd encouraged him to sell the equipment to them as a job lot; after all, since the robbery, he'd paid for all the new equipment out of his own pocket. So, with some reservations, Nick brought up the subject with Rick.

The reply he got was far from what he expected and went like this, 'Oh, I see, you're expecting us to pay for the household equipment you're leaving behind? I don't see why we should pay for it since it's all VSO property anyway!' Nick then explained the situation about the robbery, but neither Rick nor Sandra believed him. Then, as often happens, a disagreement over an apparently reasonable request escalated and we learnt the real reason for their hostility.

After their flat refusal to consider paying for any of the equipment he was leaving behind, Nick took a reconciliatory approach and again offered to stay on to hand over the project. That was when Sandra dropped her bombshell and said, 'From what we've heard, we don't think you've done anything useful anyway, so if you don't mind, we'll work it out for ourselves.'

We left Urambo the next day with Nick almost in tears. So, after all the heartache and the months of work he'd put in on the project, Nick felt like he'd been cast out.

***

Despite our swift exit from Urambo, we had plenty of time to plan our safari on the three days it took us to travel up to Moshi, a pleasant town nestling in the rolling foothills of Mount Kilimanjaro. As we stood amongst the thronging crowds expectantly waiting for the Dar es Salaam train at Tabora railway station, I took a few moments to appreciate the fading grandeur and Moorish-styling of the station building. Being a keen railway enthusiast, I'd long relished the chance to travel on one of the world's great railways. Tanzania's Central Line stretches eight hundred miles from the Indian Ocean coast through the searing heat of the country's central plains, all the way to Kigoma on Lake Tanganyika near the village of Ujiji, the final resting place of the famous explorer Dr David Livingstone. Barring accidents, attacks from armed robbers and derailment, the whole journey usually took four days and three nights, but it had been known to take more than a week. It sounded like an exciting trip, but perhaps one to savour in our dotage when we'd have more time!

I'd read that construction of the Central Line began in 1905 under German colonial rule and was completed just before the outbreak of the First World War nine years later. Encountering tropical heat, sleeping sickness, malaria and ferocious wild animals, the Germans lost over one hundred navvies and had to contend with exorbitant budget overruns. Therefore, it must have been rather galling to have to hand the whole thing over to the incoming British colonials in 1918. Whilst the local Tanzanians toiled and died building the line, they were literally following in the footsteps of hundreds, and possibly, thousands of slaves that were forced to make the journey on foot from where they were enslaved in the jungles of the Belgian Congo that borders Lake Tanganyika; Africa's true 'heart of darkness' and the inspiration for Conrad's dystopian novella of the same name.[108]

With my inspection of the station, railway line and toilets (which were truly awful) completed, I foolishly asked Nick what the journey would be like. He said, 'First, we'll have to clank our way along the worn-out railway line at the painfully-slow speed of twenty miles per hour to Dodoma. Then we'll bump and swerve our way along the pothole-infested and partially washed-out tarmac of the main road up to Arusha, and finally, travel the last fifty miles to Moshi where we'll spend a couple of days with Ann and Steve Street and their three boys. The whole thing shouldn't take more than three days max... hopefully.' I nodded and thought that I rather preferred my more romanticised view of the journey. I'd rapidly learnt that if I needed the bald, unalloyed facts, I asked Nick, but if I wanted the romantic version, I'd need to stick with the little collection of books I'd brought with me to read!

In reality, the journey turned out to be all as Nick had described and more! After a night at the rather inaccurately-named New Dodoma Hotel, that was actually well past its sell-by date with toilets that were literally filled to the brim with poo, and another night at a clapped-out backpackers' hostel in the aptly named village of Mto wa Mbu near Arusha where we were eaten alive by mosquitos, I felt like I should become a correspondent for Lonely Planet guidebooks and make sure they got their facts straight in future![109] God! I'm starting to sound like an irate American tourist!

Much to my relief, Ann and Steve welcomed us with open arms when we finally arrived at their spacious villa in the expat compound outside Moshi. Nick and his cycling buddy, Nick, were locally known as the Two Nicks, which sounded rather like a circus double-act. The Nicks stayed several weeks with the Streets after they'd taken the long way to Tanzania by bicycle from Edinburgh in 1983–84 via France, Italy, the then Yugoslavia, Greece, Egypt, Sudan, Uganda and Kenya; a mammoth

---

[108] Now the Democratic Republic of Congo, or DRC.
[109] Translates as bridge of the mosquito.

journey of more than seven months of hard cycling. Characteristically, Nick had mentioned little about this little jaunt to me except for the perils of the journey that included dysentery and dehydration in the Sahara, a journey up the White Nile on a sinking boat, playing poker, and losing, to gun-toting Ugandan border guards, dodging spear-throwing Maasai boys, being stalked by packs of hyena in the Serengeti, and oh yes, let's not forget, a couple of hefty bouts of malaria.

Ann was clearly a mothering type and her boys were surprisingly well behaved, however, they were quite extraordinary in every way. Firstly, all three were bleach-blond and blue-eyed. The identical twins, Benjy and Tom, were inseparable and regularly substituted for each other at events that one or other of them preferred not to go to, including school! Then there was Andrew, who was almost indistinguishable from the twins, except that he was always the more distant 'third man' to the other two who were never more than a couple of feet from each other's side at all times. Ann was a white Kenyan by birth, her father actually farmed up near Rongai, just a stone's throw away from Barina Jerseys where we got the cows for the Muka Mukuu zero-grazing unit; small world! Steve was a Brit through and through who'd come to work as a teacher in Moshi where Ann was also working at the local mission. Their romance sounded as whirlwind as ours, so we spent a couple of pleasant evenings comparing notes. Planning our trip couldn't have been easier; with bags of local knowledge at her fingertips, Ann suggested a tour company for our safari on the Serengeti and said they could provide us with all the gear we needed for our climb up Kilimanjaro. Job done! It couldn't have been simpler! I should have remembered that we were in Africa and nothing is ever simple or easy…

***

I might have mentioned that I'd picked up, and partly read, The Snows of Kilimanjaro from a second-hand bookshop, before I'd come out to Africa. It'd been a depressing read, so I hadn't got much past the first chapter, however, a book I subsequently read based on Hemingway's diary, which included a record of his exploits on a hunting safari with the film director, John Huston, was much more interesting. Inclined towards

464

depression (well, think I knew that already!) his visit to the Serengeti had been a moment of revelation and rapture for Hemingway who wrote enthusiastically in his diary, "*I never knew of a morning in Africa when I woke up and was not happy.*" Camped as we now were in Boy Scout-style canvas tents in Tarangire National Park near Arusha, I could fully appreciate Hemingway's fascination for Africa. The environment was a virtual cornucopia of sensations that conspired to thrill the senses. Momentarily closing my eyes, I could smell dry grass and the sweet, honey fragrance of acacia trees that permeated the air and wafted over on the dry heat from the great savanna. I could hear the delicate chirring of the night sounds and feel a sting of adrenaline from being in the presence of huge beasts. This truly was the romance of Africa that I'd been looking for.

With his fluent grasp of Kiswahili, trademark jungle clobber and knowledge of the Serengeti, at least in the minds of our fellow backpackers, Nick had assumed the mystique of a swashbuckling "big white hunter". However, now that I knew something of his gentle and rather shy nature, I chuckled inwardly at this. For some reason, our guide, a beautiful Maasai man called Si, had from the start deferred to Nick's judgement on which game reserves we should visit and where we should go. Nick had scored an early hit as our newly-assembled group stood in the reception parking of Sunshine Tours in Moshi where Si had introduced himself and asked us where we'd like to go. A seemingly natural question to ask, this had nevertheless perplexed everyone since we were all assuming that our guide would have a fixed itinerary. In the stunned silence, Nick whispered to me that Maasai always seemed very polite, so perhaps this was just a cultural thing. However, after a few moments, Nick decided he should suggest something and said, 'Jambo Si! Look, it's the start of the rainy season, but it's still very dry right? That means the animals will still be keeping very close to the waterholes, so they should be easy to see if we go somewhere with plenty of all-year-round waterholes. One of the places I know like that near here is Tarangire. The great thing is that Tarangire has loads of elephant.' Everyone nodded enthusiastically and Si immediately asked Nick to join him in the passenger seat at the front of the Land Rover. It was like he'd had a job position he needed to fill for the role of big white hunter and

Nick had just passed the interview! And that's where he stayed for the duration of the safari during which it appeared that he and Si struck up quite a friendship as they chatted away in Kiswahili.

On our first evening, Nick's position as Bwana Mkubwa was further cemented when we took a pit stop at the loos of an encampment near the main entrance to Tarangire.[110] Nick had joined Si to speak to a group of young Maasai morans who he said had been living in isolation in the bush learning tribal customs, when another safari guide walked over to speak to Si. He looked agitated, so I came over to see what the problem was. This second guide, Ahmed, who spoke English, said he'd brought a group over from Kenya, but his minivan had broken down, he said, 'I cannot go any further, the axle is mbovu sana. Would you be able to take my clients? There are only three of them.' Si deferred to Nick and asked him if he was okay with this so I quickly ran over to check with the others in our party. All was good with us, so we inherited Ahmed's group of three Dutch women. Everyone shook hands and thanked Nick profusely for his generous offer of help!

As we walked back with our now newly augmented group, to help the women stow their gear on the roof of our Land Rover, I said to Nick, 'You're really enjoying your role as Bwana Mkubwa!'

He just winked and said, 'Yes immensely. One of the Dutch women is convinced she's seen me on TV and thinks I'm some kind of celebrity like David Attenborough. She just asked me for my autograph!'

Sitting outside our tent in the damp coolness of the morning, I idly watched as, in the distance, Mount Meru burped a small cloud of steam out of its mist-shrouded cauldron. I thought this is the life! We'd just eaten a surprisingly good kedgeree made from dried tilapia cooked by one of our guides who doubled as a camp chef and were now drinking a mug of chai when I felt the need to answer the inevitable call of nature. Rather inconveniently, or fortunately, depending on how you looked at it because they stank to high heaven, the long-drop loos were situated several hundred yards away from our tents on the other side of the campsite. Preparing for my solitary walk, I said jokily to Nick, 'I'm off to the loo darling. If I'm not back in half an hour, send out a search party!'

I picked up the path to the ablutions area and loos near a large termite

---

[110] The big man.

mound that must have been ten feet in height. Keeping it as a reference point, I headed off into the scrub towards two very tall acacia trees, which I knew were growing at the back of the long-drops. As I entered a large patch of scrub, I heard a branch crack near the track and I stopped mid-stride and listened intently. Assuming that it might be a creature of some kind, I tried to derive a certain measure of comfort from the deep trench and high berms of soil that formed the camp's defences against wild beasts, but I was sceptical of its effectiveness against large animals. As I stood perfectly still, stealthily, if stealth was a term you could apply to such a vast creature, a female elephant emerged out of the scrub. Towering above me, I initially stepped back from her and would have started running, but I knew it would have been futile. The elephant, an elderly matriarch, stared down at me. Was it distain? Or idle curiosity? But as she just stood there, neither moving closer nor turning to leave, our eyes met. I considered whether my gaze might be interpreted as a challenge, but seemly not as we continued our staring match for several more moments until she appeared to have got what she wanted from the encounter and her intelligent eyes broke away from mine to stare over my head. Cautiously following her gaze, I saw a baby elephant walk past me, maybe only twenty feet from where I was standing. The calf walked past the matriarch and disappeared into the bush behind her. The giant in front of me then backed slightly so as not to close the gap between us, and then ambled off in the same direction as the calf and disappeared from sight.

I was shaking. Unsure of what else to do, I turned and walked back to the camp and kept what I saw very quiet. The Askaris had rifles and might have thought it was their duty to go after the elephant, maybe even kill or injure her. It would have been another tragedy, one of many tragedies caused by illicit companies that still ran big game hunting trips despite the ban in both Tanzania and Kenya. I didn't want to give our guides an excuse for another senseless slaughter. So, until now, I've kept that treasured moment to myself, seared into my memory forever.

**

Nowadays, climbing Kilimanjaro might have almost become a touristic

467

cliché, but when we were in Tanzania over thirty years ago, it was still a big deal. Although Sarah had smuggled in a quantity of US dollars when she'd visited Kenya at Christmas, we still had to pitch in everything we had to have enough cash to pay the exorbitant park entrance fee. I wouldn't have minded if I was certain that the money would benefit the local community, but it was more than likely that most of it would disappear into the coffers of some huge Tanzanian department or other back in Dar es Salaam. We were just a group of two, but the park ranger still assigned us six porters to carry our relatively small rucksacks. I thought perhaps they needed this level of overkill so that there would be enough people to carry us as well if needs be!

Whilst we waited for our guides and porters to be assembled, I flicked through the meagre information about the climb we'd inherited from a couple of Ann's friends who'd left their guidebook behind. We were going to follow the Marangu route, apparently the main drag up the mountain. We'd been assured this was the easiest and most direct way and was basically the equivalent of walking up the huge "motorway" of a track that tourists, vintage cars and pianists carrying grand pianos had taken up Ben Nevis in Scotland or the Miners' track on Mount Snowdon in Wales that goes alongside a funicular railway. So it was going to be dead easy right? Wrong! The fly in this particular ointment was the height of Kilimanjaro. If it was just a walk at sea level, it would be easy, but we were going to be walking forty miles and going up to over nineteen thousand feet. Okay, so Mount Everest is over twenty-nine thousand feet, but hey, considering that up until that point all my climbing had been done using a car, motorcycle or an aeroplane, I thought it was a pretty ambitious start to my mountaineering career! The guidebook assured us that the start point at Machame Gate was already at almost six thousand feet and there'd be huts with bunk beds all the way up at Mandara, Kibo and Horombo, in that order. Before I'd got to the bit in the guide that spoke about altitude sickness and success rates, our guide and porters had arrived. Since they were all local Wachaga men, Nick did the 'mwanga luka/na chi cha' thing that Mushi had taught him. After that, they were all instantly thrilled to bits and his friends for life. Unfortunately, they spoke nothing but Kiswahili from then on and Nick had to translate for me for the rest of the journey!

As we started our march up the steep track and into what seemed like the perpetual drizzle and murk that sat around the foothills of the great mountain, I watched whilst Nick ingratiated himself with our gregarious group of Wachaga porters, all of whom, it turned out, were ex-Tanzanian military who'd fought against Amin's forces when Uganda tried, and failed, to invade Tanzania. I knew it to be an heroic tale. Every able-bodied man and woman were mobilised. Even children as young as fourteen were drafted into the army in a desperate effort to repel Idi's forces. Therefore, I assumed that we'd be in capable hands on a straightforward hiking trip.

The cloud forest of the lower slopes held a mysterious charm. Once we'd left the crowded and noisy gate entrance behind, we were treated to comical displays of acrobatics from groups of chattering colobus monkeys that appeared to jeer at us from high up in the trees where damp, lichenous beards hung from branches as if somebody had dressed the trees for a party. After just over three hours, we'd arrived at the triangular huts at Mandara encampment that a sign rather officiously informed us had been kindly donated to Tanzania by the Norwegian government. From the wooden veranda of the hut, we chose to sleep in, a huge vista opened up. By sheer luck, we had a clear view. The Serengeti in all its magnificence rolled on to the horizon and was dotted with acacia trees that looked like they'd been planted there. We could make out Mount Meru, which was still puffing steam, and Tarangire where we'd recently been. I was in total awe at the sheer size of it.

I said to Nick, 'I think I might take up mountaineering when we get back.' But when I saw Nick's face light up, I realised I needed to qualify my statement, so I said, 'Not rock climbing, you understand, more like hillwalking.'

Nick nodded.

'Don't worry darling, I won't be dangling you off any ropes when we get back to the UK, promise!'

The next day followed the same pattern, only this time, as we'd climbed higher, we left the cloud forest behind and passed though onto an open area of calluna scrub. We also encountered what we'd been told would be giant groundsel that, in the mist, looked like groups of punk rockers with their hair lacquered up into crazy spikes. When we arrived at Morombo hut at the relatively early hour of three o'clock, we encountered the same triangular huts as we'd seen at Mandara and the same officious notice that'd been left by the generous Norwegians. However, this time, the Norwegians had stinted on size and the huts were smaller. Shortly after arriving at camp, I left Nick sitting on the steps of our hut and went in search of the toilets. I didn't have high hopes for them, so I half wondered whether I could take advantage of the mist and nip behind a bush instead. When I returned, I found Nick hunched over his knees.

As I approached, I could see that his face was pallid and he was sweating profusely, he said, 'Deb, I really don't feel too good. It could be the altitude, we are at twelve thousand feet, but it's more likely to be malaria. I think I need to go down.'

I felt a wave of panic rising, but then remembered we were travelling with a group of six fit ex-soldiers, so I rushed over and found Solomon, our guide. I said, 'Nick isn't well, I think he needs to go down.'

Solomon nodded and surveyed the conditions, the dense mist coming in and the fact that it'd soon be dark. I could see calculations going on in his head, then he said, 'No problem, Miss. We'll get him down right now.' And off he went. I waited anxiously with Nick who'd by this time become quite moribund and unresponsive.

An hour later, and in complete darkness, our group of friendly ex-soldiers assembled in a tight little semicircle around us. They'd brought with them a stretcher, which had been fitted with a single motorbike wheel at its centre point of balance so that two carriers could guide the stretcher along but not have to bear its full weight. They half lifted Nick onto the stretcher, covered him in a thick layer of blankets and strapped him onto it. The four men, one at each corner, started off at a trot down the steep slope. They were all equipped with head torches. At the speed they were going, it was difficult to keep up with them, but I managed to catch them up at a stream, which had turned into a raging torrent since we'd walked over it just a few hours earlier. The men had just got Nick off the stretcher when he vomited, retching for some moments before he was able to continue. A couple of the porters carried Nick across the stream and he was strapped onto the stretcher once again.

At this point, I broke down in tears and wondered whether I could keep up with the men. Solomon took my elbow and said, 'Miss, your husband is very ill. We must get him down as soon as possible. My men will carry on, but I will stay with you. They will take him to the hospital in Moshi. He will be fine, I promise.' Solomon gave me a grim smile and we carried on together.

Hours and hours passed. My legs grew weak and became tired. Then I became more tired until I thought I couldn't carry on. Solomon half carried me for the final few miles down to Machame Gate where I was able to get a dala-dala to take me to the Moshi Arusha Hospital where I found Nick had already been admitted to the intensive care ward. As I was escorted by one of the nurses down one long corridor after another, I didn't know what to expect. What I saw was worse than I could have imagined. Nick, who appeared to be unconscious, was hooked up to an intravenous drip. The doctor who was with him said his name was Dr Gupta and he confirmed that he had altitude sickness. He was treating him was diuretics to reduce the blood volume and prevent high altitude pulmonary oedema. While the doctor was talking to me, I thought 'oh God, I'm going to lose him!' I sat in a chair next to Nick's bed and cried. A kindly ward sister brought me hot, sweet chai and a mandazi, 'to keep your strength,' she said. I stayed awake most of that first night. It was one of the worst of my life. I hate hospitals at the best of times, but to be in an intensive care ward in an impoverished country like Tanzania was truly awful. I wondered whether they could save him.

During the two days I spent at his side, a woman that'd been brought in with sleeping sickness died in the neighbouring bed to Nick's. On the third day, when there appeared to be little improvement, a German doctor appeared at Nick's bedside, he said, 'Mrs Gosman?'

I shook my head and heard myself say, 'No, doctor, he's my fiancé. I'm Debbie Best...'

Seeing that I couldn't say anything else, the doctor said he was called Dr Weltz. After he'd checked Nick's chart, he nodded and said, 'If it was altitude sickness, he should be getting better by now. I'm going to give him a blood test, but in the meantime, I'm going to start him on some anti-malaria treatment.'

Thank goodness he did! On the evening of the third day, Dr Welz got a message to the Streets, and Ann arrived on Nick's ward with food and drink. Unlike a European hospital, there was no kitchen, so relatives had to bring in food for the patients. Ann took me in her arms and we hugged for a long while. I said, 'I thought I was going to lose him. They started treating him for altitude sickness, but it almost killed him because he actually has malaria.'

Ann stayed with me for the next couple of days and brought food in. Dr Weltz put Nick on intravenous quinine, in a last-ditch attempt to get on top of malaria that had now entered his brain.

On the fifth night, Nick's condition remained precarious and he appeared to be only fleetingly conscious. I couldn't stand it any longer. I hurried outside and stood for a long time in the hospital garden in the pouring rain. I remember inclining my head to the heavens. All I could find to say was a single word, 'Please.'

Returning to the ward, Ann had been joined by the hospital priest and they were both knelt in prayer at Nick's bedside. Thinking he'd gone, I ran over and Ann held my hand while we prayed for Nick's life. On the morning of the sixth day, just as light began to stream through the hospital windows, Nick's head moved and he turned over so his eyes were level with mine as I sat in the chair beside the bed. He said, 'Quick, I need the bedpan!'

Unsure what to do, I ran and found a nurse who rushed over with a urine bottle and closed the curtains around his bed. When she re-emerged, she said, 'Your husband is looking much better. His fever has passed.' She crossed herself and disappeared to find a doctor.

Through it all, the nurses were fantastic. They worked tirelessly and remained unshakeably cheerful. Whilst Nick was in intensive care, three people died, one apparently, of bubonic plague. The relatives cried and there was grief, but what I learned that week was that Tanzanians believe strongly in the dictum that 'wakati kuna maisha kuna matumaini', 'while there is life, there is hope'. Solomon and four of the six Tanzanian soldiers that saved Nick's life on the mountain came to visit him in hospital. They asked for nothing in return for their help, refusing my offer of even a small gift. At the end of it all, I believed that we'd witnessed the true spirit of human kindness. Nick was treated by the Tanzanian Health Service, which was, and still is, free to all. It was humbling to discover that in a country where there was so much poverty and suffering, there was still enough common humanity, to ensure that the sick were tended, no matter what their status or background.

We had seen much suffering whilst we were in Africa, and much courage and human kindness. Despite all the grinding poverty, we experienced so much hope and a determination to strive for something better. As I recall these memories of my time in Africa, I remember Nick's emotional account of a rally he attended not long after he'd arrived in Tabora where the Tanzanian president, Julius Nyerere, gave a speech. When he asked what the president was saying, a person standing next to him said, 'We've heard the same speech many times, but we love our Mwalimu!'[111] At the end of his address, after the president had led a prayer for his country, he stood in silence, quietly raised a fist and emotionally shouted into the hush, 'mbele Tanzania, mbele!'[112] Nick, along with the assembled crowd of thousands, cheered and clapped and wept.

Our fervent hope is that Nick and I will be able to return to East Africa one day and continue our work there.

---

[111] Mwalimu, or teacher, was the honorific title bestowed upon Nyerere by his people.
[112] Forward Tanzania, forward!

The last word

I'm no longer a lost sheep. As Margaret quaintly put it, I finally recognised my husband I found him in Africa, and he was a kind shepherd who took me home. After my years of searching, I now belong somewhere and I'm with someone who cares for me. When we returned to England, Nick and I stayed with Esme who'd moved to be near to Adam after the death of her second husband John. We were married in Wensleydale at St Oswald's Church in Askrigg. Ann, Steve and their boys travelled from Tanzania to be at our wedding. I subsequently went back to college at Harper Adams and graduated with an HNC.

Colleagues, who I advocate for at work as their union representative, have supplanted the farm animals I used to care for. I've become their 'shepherd' guiding them through the problems they're having at work. I devote unstinting time to them just as I did for the animals in my care when I worked on farms. I have a keen sense of when people are not right and try and do what I can to help them. I maintain a support network of strong bonds with the women I met at WAC and the other dear friends I've met in a lifetime in agriculture along the way. Mary-Jane and Jane still live and work on their farms, whilst Pat recently retired after a career in agricultural finance.

Sadly, both Shân, and more recently my dear brother Adam, passed away from cancer. Not long after her death, Nick and I took an opportunity to pay our respects to Shân at her gravesite in the little churchyard situated near her family farm. Aptly, as it was April and lambing time in the high fells above Hay-on-Wye, we stood by her headstone, which at that time of year when the trees are free of their leaves, she has a clear view of her beloved Black Mountains. As we enjoyed the sun's warmth in the early springtime, I remembered that, before Nick and I were married, when we desperately needed money to pay for our wedding, Shân offered me some lambing work up at her parents' farm. It was there I met Victoria, a fellow traveller in farming who was destined to spend her entire life caring for the horses of numerous wealthy stable owners. I don't envy her, nor do I miss the daily grind of farm work, however, I've always had a soft spot for sheep and seeing the lambs in the fields will forever be a magical time for me. Spring is also a time when I remember the friendships forged by the hard work and comerardery that can always be found in equal measure on farms.

As for my adventures in Africa, at the time of writing, I have yet to return there. Aware of the old adage, "never go back" I'm wary that East Africa may have changed in a way that might blemish my fond memories, so, like Karen Blixen, I may never do so. Therefore, to my younger self, that lives on within these pages, to my dear brother Adam and to Shân, and to all my other friends and family that have made, and continue to make, my life so full and rich, I offer the toast that Blixen is quoted as using — it's from A. E. Housman's Shropshire Lad. So raise a glass of your favourite tipple and drink it, *"to rose-lipped maidens and light-foot lads!"*